ADVICE AND DISSENT

My Life in Public Service

Y.V. REDDY

HARPER BUSINESS

First published in hardback in India in 2017 by Harper Business
An imprint of HarperCollins *Publishers* India

First published in paperback in India in 2018 by Harper Business
An imprint of HarperCollins *Publishers* India

HarperCollins Publishers India, Cyber City, Building 10-A, Gurugram,
Haryana-122002, India
www.harpercollins.co.in

2 4 6 8 10 9 7 5 3 1

P-ISBN: 978-93-5302-021-7
E-ISBN: 978-93-5264-305-9

Typeset in 11.5/14.5 Sabon Roman at
SURYA, New Delhi

Printed and bound at
MicroPrints India, New Delhi

MIX
Paper
FSC FSC® C218906

This product is made of FSC®-certified and other controlled material.

HarperCollins Publishers, Macken House, 39/40 Mayor Street
Upper, Dublin 1, D01 C9W8, Ireland

ADVICE AND DISSENT

Dr Yaga Venugopal (Y.V.) Reddy was Governor of the Reserve Bank of India from 2003 to 2008, and its Deputy Governor from 1996 to 2002. He was Chairman of the Fourteenth Finance Commission in 2013-14. Previously, he worked in the Government of India as Secretary in the Ministry of Finance, and in the Government of Andhra Pradesh as Principal Secretary. He is also a recipient of the Padma Vibhushan, India's second highest civilian award.

Currently, he is Honorary Professor at the Centre for Economic and Social Studies in Hyderabad.

Praise for *Advice and Dissent*

'This is just the kind of book you would want from a person who has spent time in the corridors of power...The focus is on public policy choices and debates, the tale garnished with anecdotal flavouring... All of which makes this well worth a read.' – T.N. Ninan, *Business Standard*

'[One feels] a sense of marvel at the way he straddles the world of the intellect – this book offers rich pickings in that regard – and of practical management which this book describes throughout...A must-read for those who want to know more about how he managed the noisy intersections of economics and politics.' – T.C.A. Srinivasa Raghavan, *India Today*

'For a banker, Governor Reddy writes well and lucidly...He seems to have the knack to say a lot without saying too much. That does not come easily to all writers.' – Harish Khare, *The Tribune*

'For a younger generation of policymakers, IAS or technocrats, who must lead India to a future of greater prosperity, this book is essential reading.' – Dhiraj Nayyar, *The Hindu*

‘A modern classic…Lucidly written and a gripping page-turner…To the reader’s delight, the narrative is interspersed with often deeply ironic vignettes and humorous tales of encounters with the high and mighty.’ – Brijeshwar Singh, *Financial Express*

‘[A] remarkably restrained account as Reddy does not believe in gossip and hearsay, but it’s gripping because of his storytelling ability… This 480-page book, to use a cliché, is unputdownable.’ – Tamal Bandyopadhyay, *Mint*

‘In a riveting memoir, Y.V. Reddy revisits his absorbing career at the RBI, and more…[It] should be made mandatory reading for all those who work in senior capacities at both the RBI and ministry of finance, indeed for all future finance ministers.’ – N.S. Vageesh, *The Hindu Business Line*

‘*Advice and Dissent: My Life in Public Service* isn’t a kiss-and-tell book – that would be very, very un-Reddy-like – but it is a pretty frank account of his days as a bureaucrat and central banker. He doesn’t hold back on the challenges he encountered, the problems he faced and the run-ins he had.’ – Seetha, *Swarajya*

‘The book provides an insider’s account of decision making at all levels during the author’s career in public service, which began when he joined the IAS in 1964. The book appeals to the common reader and finance specialists.’ – Jatin Desai, *The Free Press Journal*

‘An insightful memoir…An insider’s account of India’s policymaking… gripping storytelling ability…Throws light on the lessons of Dr Reddy’s fascinating professional life as on the politics of his year in public service.’ – *India Business Journal*

‘An engaging look into the private life and career of a former governor of the Reserve Bank of India, and arguably one of the best central bankers of the twentieth century, Y.V. Reddy.’ – Geoffrey Wood, *Central Banking Quarterly Journal*

‘He has been an excellent civil servant, logical, intelligent, polite, even somewhat deferential, incorruptible, willing to listen, but stubborn on points of principle and prepared, if necessary, to resign (a realistic threat that stood him in good stead on a few occasions).’ – Charles Goodhart, *Financial World*

‘Very important, illuminating but also enjoyable book.’ – Lord Stern Nicholas, at London School of Economics

For my parents,
Ammannamma and Pitchi Reddy Ayya

CONTENTS

ACKNOWLEDGEMENTS

I OWE PROFOUND GRATITUDE TO THOSE WHO ASSISTED, advised and guided me during my professional work lasting over five decades. Many of them played a critical role in contributing to my thinking and actions. I tried to incorporate their individual contributions to specific policies in my narration in the first draft, but it seriously affected the readability. I then tried to acknowledge the contributions of some of them in relevant chapters, but I was told that they read like annual confidential reports on their performance. Consequently, the version in the book may give a misleading impression that mine was a solo performance. I learnt a lot from my colleagues in the workplace and some others outside of it. I had the benefit of the guidance of many elders and seniors. They do not find a mention of their benevolent influence on me for reasons of space and readers' attention. I express my helplessness and deep apologies on this account to the many who do not find adequate mention of their contribution.

My apologies are also due to some of those who do find a mention in the book. I did not take their permission to refer to them. I did not disclose to them that I was writing about them. I am sure, at that time when our interaction took place, they would not have imagined that I might draw upon our mutual experiences. I had the option of discussing my draft with them, but then felt that I may have practical and logistical difficulties in getting their permission and they may also have difficulties in raising embarrassing matters with me. Non-disclosure in advance gives them the liberty to contradict or give an alternative version of whatever has been stated in the book. Therefore, I thought that I would make a judgement on whether I was being fair in disclosing my recollections of such interactions. I stuck to substantive issues relevant to the narration rather than the emotions and passions that came up in the interaction, and to that extent I am less interesting in the dry prose here than I am in conversations.

In view of the vast canvas that I have covered, large number of subjects dealt with, and several personalities involved, I had no choice but to be selective. In the process, I must have left out important details. I seek the indulgence of those who have been involved and also the readers in general to bear with these infirmities in the book. I have, on occasion, written about the conversations that took place. That is based on many recollections. So, it may not necessarily be similar to what others involved in the exchange recall. I tried my best to stick to my recollection, though I have avoided embarrassing details.

I have been working on these memoirs for more than two years, and in the process I have consulted many people and discussed several parts of the chapters with many others. I have not been as exhaustive in listing the people who helped me as I would have liked to. I had to depend entirely on memory and publicly available information. Any factual errors, therefore, should be attributed to forgetfulness induced by age.

Some of my gurus, good friends and close relatives encouraged me to write my autobiography. A few in my extended family felt that I should desist from dragging the life I lived into the public domain. My family, in particular my father, believed in privacy and keeping a low profile. It was T.C.A. Srinivasa Raghavan's persistence that led me to start working on this book. He provided guidance in addition to encouragement, but left the matter to me the moment he felt that the work had gained sufficient momentum. Ritu Vajpeyi-Mohan then entered the picture, encouraged me apart from offering assistance and guidance in completing the book. In the end, Krishan Chopra of HarperCollins took over the responsibility for publication. Sincere thanks to all of them.

When I completed the first draft of the book, I realised that much of it was reading more like an office note than a memoir.

My daughter Kavitha took upon herself the responsibility of virtually redrafting the whole book, except the chapters dealing with central banking, to make it readable. In regard to chapters that dealt with my work in government and central banks, K. Kanagasabapathy, a dear friend of mine and a central banker himself, studied several versions of the draft. He put me on the right path whenever I digressed and helped me avoid serious indiscretions or excesses. I am beholden to both of them. My son Adithya and son-in-law Hari made suggestions when they felt that I was incoherent or inappropriate. Swetha, my daughter-in-law, made me feel that I was infallible. My wife Geetha, as usual, was fully supportive.

There were a few dear friends who went through virtually every sentence of the book and guided me personally. Foremost among them is C. Narendra Reddy, with experience of half a century in economic journalism. He went through every sentence even at the proofs stage. Others include Arigapudi Premchand, Veera Narayan Reddy and Venugopal Kasba.

Among those who have been of great help to me in select chapters are Chitra Narayanan, Durganand Swamy, Govinda Rao, Partha Ray, Rajiv Ranjan, Rammanohar Reddy, Rao C.S., and most prominently Shyamala Gopinath and Usha Thorat.

Alpana Killawala, Girija Reddy, Gunjeet Kaur, R. Krishnamurthy, Latha Venkatesh, K.B.L. Mathur, Krishnan Saranyan, Shankar P., and Sonalika Sinha were also of valuable assistance. There are a few who helped me but prefer not to be named and I am obliging them by not saying anything except thank you. I acknowledge with thanks the prompt and generous permissions given by the Bank for International Settlements, and the Reserve Bank of India for publishing some of the photographs.

I must mention my appreciation of the services rendered by Sunil Nagpal and also B. Sudhakar Reddy of my personal office in the making of this product.

Krishan Chopra, Publisher at HarperCollins India, guided me at every step, very professionally, while being pleasant, patient and to the point. I owe a deep debt of gratitude to him. Aman Arora, Siddhesh Inamdar and Smriti Khanna-Mehra have been outstanding members of his team. A word of special appreciation is due to the meticulous, timely and dedicated work put in by Rajinder Ganju in typesetting the book and carrying out corrections.

I am keeping my fingers crossed!

INTRODUCTION

This book is the story of my life – mostly of my working life. Why I wrote it is not important. There is no single reason for doing it. Why should someone read it?

Interest was expressed in the story of my life only after I became governor, Reserve Bank of India. Mainly, everyone wanted to know how I became governor. Then, after I retired, many wanted to know about my experiences in that role. But my work as governor cannot be looked at in isolation. Restricting the narrative to that time would not reveal my values, judgements and actions as governor, which result directly from influences that spanned a lifetime and were formed in a particular time in the history of our nation. While a good part of the book relates to my work as governor, it goes beyond, and looks at my life as a whole.

The story begins with my birth in 1941 and our gaining Independence in 1947. It ends with my submitting the report of the Fourteenth Finance Commission in December 2014. It shows how an individual growing up in India has been impacted by the Independence, the integration of princely states, Nehruvian socialism, the re-organisation of states, and the periodic general elections. We faced wars in 1948, 1962, 1965 and 1971. The '70s and '80s were lost decades for our economy since we refused to learn enough either from our own experience or that of others. It required a balance of payments crisis in 1991 to begin economic reforms. In a decade, by the beginning of this century, the profile of India changed. By the end of the story, we are, in many ways, proud of being Indians. The events described in this book, though related to my work life, reflect the transformation of India since Independence. I hope the readers find the nuggets on these transformations, sprinkled in the story of my work life, interesting and amusing.

The book has some unique perspectives.

Most of the autobiographies by central bankers have been written by governors. Surely, others who work with governors also have stories to tell. This book includes my perspectives as someone who assisted governors too.

Among academics and participants in the financial sector, a major area of current debate is the relationship between the government and central banks. It is hard to find the government's version of dealing with the central banks. Since I worked in the government also, and dealt with the RBI, a part of the story relates to this.

To appreciate the progress we have made on the external front to a point where we had to handle problems of plenty, one has to recall the desperation and humiliation we faced at the time of the balance of payments crisis in 1991. Why did we use gold to meet our payment obligations? What were the options? As governor my focus on securing policy independence for India through many measures, particularly the building of adequate forex reserves, cannot be appreciated without understanding the distress that provoked it.

The crisis of 1991 happened for many reasons, political and economic, as well as global and domestic. That our economic policies were unsustainable was known by the mid-'80s. This was the period of the New Economic Policy of Rajiv Gandhi – a policy that delivered modernisation and growth with borrowed money and borrowed time. A retreat to academia in the late '80s helped me study the New Economic Policy, against the background of the major shifts in theory and practice of development planning. There was a reassessment of the relative roles of the market and the state and an appreciation of the importance of incentives and institutions. It was at this stage that I evolved from an approach rooted in beliefs and ideology to a purposeful, pragmatic and eclectic approach to policy.

My work with the Andhra Pradesh government influenced the priority given by the Reserve Bank to state finances. I drew upon my experience of working with N.T. Rama Rao in my stint as Reserve Bank governor and Finance Commission chairman. NTR had the unique distinction of leading a regional party to the position of the single largest opposition party in Parliament. He initiated a new era in Union–state relations. More important, the saffron-clad leader who seldom read newspapers pioneered e-governance and popularised information technology in the state. Personalities matter in politics and politics matters in economic policy.

My experiences have been rich and varied. Interactions with political leaders at various levels of government gave me an understanding of their worldview. The lessons I learnt have stayed with me and informed my thinking throughout my career in the Reserve Bank of India. I touch upon these in the first few chapters in the book.

If I were to sum up my overarching approach to central banking, it would be this: 'Selecting what appears to be best in various doctrines, methods or styles.' In other words, it is the art of being eclectic. At the end of the day, the outcomes of my time in the RBI were a governor's dream – high growth, low inflation most of the time, stable rupee and a robust banking system; not the nightmare of high inflation, low growth, stressed banks and depreciating rupee. I am aware, however, that it would be foolish to claim credit for the achievements in the economy.

I became popular as an ex-governor more than as a governor. How and why did this happen? I have explained the reasons for our being both 'conservative' and 'innovative' in our policies. A governor has to exhibit quiet confidence – neither exuberance nor diffidence. He has to often pretend that the Reserve Bank is independent without offending the government. We are not equal to the government but have to convince others that we are not subordinate to it. My work as governor was challenging and at times fascinating. I narrate some of the important and interesting events; but I must maintain a fine balance since I have to respect sensitivities and confidences. As a result, on many occasions, I am less than forthright and frustratingly non-humorous. Making the book technical enough for public policy aficionados and finance specialists while being of interest to the common person was the most difficult part of writing. One tool that was useful in providing important detail without overloading the narrative was the use of end notes. These can be accessed by the interested reader while being safely ignored by everyone else.

In the book, I present my attempts to do what I felt was right and in the best interests of the common person. I hope to provide a sense of context and share the diversity of views and judgements surrounding memorable events. I attempt to give the reader an appreciation of the interaction between individuals, institutions and interests. I do not make any judgements nor do I engage in the game of debits and credits.

People have asked me if there is a life after having been governor. Yes, there is. One can continue in public policy or shift to the private sector. I preferred to avoid both. But, thanks to the global financial crisis, my 'wisdom' was in demand globally, which I enjoyed for a few years. I planned to end my association with finance after giving the Per Jacobsson Lecture in June 2012 titled 'Society, Economic Policies and the Financial Sector'. The title captured my approach to the role of finance in the broader context of economic policies that serve the society. After the lecture, I made another attempt at retiring. Yet, compulsions led me to chair the Fourteenth Finance Commission, which lasted for two years. In this book, I make a reference to my brief association with my work on these unforeseen but unforgettable assignments.

When I finally decided that there were no more obstacles to a totally retired life, I began the journey of writing my memoirs in January, 2015. It has been enormously challenging and great fun. Initially, I thought it would be an easy retirement hobby, but it soon became a full-time occupation. Again, all my plans for a quiet, easy retired life went awry.

Of course, I should have known. We make our plans. God laughs.

1

A WINDOW TO THE WORLD

THOUGH I WOULD SPEND MUCH OF MY LIFE TRAVELLING ALL over the world, most of my early years were spent in a small village. I was born on 17 August 1941 in Patur, a village on the banks of Cheyyeru, a tributary of Pennar River. I was born in my mother's house, where my grandfather and three maternal uncles lived as a joint family. Amma was fourteen when she married my father (who was then thirty-one) and she was eighteen when I was born. She was a strict but loving mother. My father, Ayya, travelled extensively to small towns for his work, and Amma and I lived in Patur till I was six years old. My sister Sarala, who was also called Pramila, was born when I was two, and my infant brother Madhu when I was four. Patur was good for me. Everyone was affectionate and I was a happy, pampered child.

In the village, everything was organised around caste. There was the main village where we lived. Artisans, barbers, washermen, blacksmiths and other workers were dispersed throughout, while Muslims lived in Turkapally area and peasant farmers lived in Balijapalli area. On the outskirts, there were two separate clusters. One belonged to the Brahmins (priests and teachers), who kept themselves away from the village. Everyone revered Brahmins. We called them Swamy or Ayyagaru (respected teacher). The other cluster belonged to the scheduled castes, who were kept at a distance by the rest.

Our street was Kapu Veedhi, Street of Kapus (locally known as Reddys). There were few brick and mortar houses on the street, mostly there were thatched huts. Amma's house was one of the better ones. We had a refrigerator that ran on kerosene, since the village had no electricity. There were six houses on either side of the street, with one side ending in agricultural lands and the other ending in a 'T' junction with a small Rama temple. The 'T' junction connected Kapu Veedhi to other parts of the village.

Ancient norms dictated all social interactions. When a person of higher caste or status was around, men kept their dhoti flowing down to their ankles in a formal style. They folded it up only with people of their own (or lower) socioeconomic standing. Women stayed home or, if they ventured out, they walked behind the men in their family. In Kapu Veedhi, the scheduled castes passing by walked barefoot, carrying their sandals or slippers in their hands. Once I asked an elder why. He said that was the way things were.

My maternal grandfather suffered from diabetes. He was famous for his capacity for extended inactivity. He spent hours, entire days even, sitting at the gate, watching people go by. He tried to battle his diabetes with natural cures. Every day, you would find him taking some bath or the other. He took tub baths, mud baths, and even, strangely, baths in banana leaves. His urine had to be tested daily in a mini home chemistry lab. My uncles would burn samples to precise temperatures and mix them with potions to check his sugar. As a child, I was hardly sympathetic to my grandfather's health problems. It was only years later, when I would be diagnosed with diabetes, that I would understand. Technology would make the management of my diabetes much easier as an entire home chemistry lab would be replaced by a thin sugar testing strip and all the baths would be replaced by insulin injections.

My eldest uncle was a busy man who took care of the family lands. The middle brother spent most of his time in Madras. I was under the tutelage of my youngest uncle, who was the part-time village branch postmaster. In those days, for us in villages, there was very little contact with the outside world. There was no TV, radio, or bank branch. Newspapers were hard to come by and even those were delivered sporadically.

In this vacuum, it was the local postmaster, teacher, the village karnam or official accountant, and the village munsif or the local representative of the police, who had a hold on all information and official work of the village. These people were respected and feared.[1]

My postmaster uncle thrived in this environment. He had the power to keep the villagers in the dark about their mail and, importantly, about their money orders. My uncle was also a sharp moneylender, though he always claimed he did it purely on humanitarian grounds.

The Nandalur railway station, three kilometres away, was the centre of our world. My postmaster uncle would complement my education by taking me to the railway station. There, we would wander up and down the platforms staring at the passengers from the cities and distant places. Everyone seemed sophisticated and exotic. Uncle would buy me sodas and instruct me on how to spot beautiful women on trains. On seeing a particularly beautiful one, he would sigh and say, 'Look, do you see her? She is so lovely that if you see her in the day, by night-time she will arrive in your dreams.' I often followed my uncle around the village. He would spend much of the day sitting on the stone platform of the old Rama temple. There, he would call passers-by and tell them racy stories as I listened with rapt attention.

Life in Patur was a snapshot of what much of India had been like for centuries before Independence, and in many ways, my early years in Patur and subsequent visits till my adolescence were quite an education.

I was six when we moved to Bellary. Ayya was the personal assistant (rank of deputy collector) to the collector. Shortly after we moved, India became an independent nation. It was 15 August 1947. The adults were full of jubilation.[2] There was a parade at school with drums and elephants and I felt very important as I marched in the school procession with the tricolour in my hands.

The birth of a new nation was a remarkable experiment. For the first time in history, the struggle for freedom had been based on non-violence. The country itself had been forged from many nations as British colonies, princely states and independent tribes were melded into one entity of breathtaking political, geographic and cultural diversity. Little did I know that my own story would be so closely entwined with the course of the fledgling country. Everyone around me was filled with the greatest optimism and expectations.

Ayya was a distant presence. As a public official, he was busy. However, it was also the culture in Reddy families for the father to be somewhat distant. While daughters could be pampered by the father (and so it was with my sister Sarala, who was the apple of my father's eye), it was the opposite for sons. A son could not be in the presence of his father for no reason; he had to be called for or sent by his mother. Sons and fathers rarely touched or laughed in each other's presence. By those standards, my father was unusually free in his relationship with me (to the consternation of my mother, who felt Ayya was spoiling us by not being aloof enough). Though he maintained a distance, we could ask Ayya questions and speak to him if we wanted. He, in turn, was warm and patient.

Ayya had an unusual name: Pitchi Reddy. Pitchi means mad in Telugu. His mother had lost three or four other children before him, and when Ayya was born, as per the custom, my grandparents tried to cheat death and ward off its evil eye by naming the child mad. Ayya survived, but his mother died in childbirth.

Ayya had a Bachelor of Arts from Presidency College, Madras. He and his elder brother were the first college graduates from his village, perhaps even in his taluk. Ayya was a large, portly man, with a fair-complexioned, round face upon which no frown had ever been seen. He spoke very little, and apart from tennis, he had no other hobbies. Ayya was abstemious in his habits and neither drank nor smoked. But he had one weakness that was to prove fatal for him – he was a great lover of food. Amma, who was an excellent cook, would serve him his meals. She would cut down on servings of unhealthy things such as ghee and meats. Amma was deeply worried about the heart condition which had been troubling Ayya since before I was born. But Ayya would not have it. He would sit, not looking at his plate, not eating, not saying a word, till Amma gave in and served him generous quantities of whatever he wanted but should not have had.

Ayya had a remarkably modest ego for a man of his standing. He described himself as an above average student. He often ascribed his achievements to not just work and values, but also good luck. I have friends, he would say, who are more brilliant than me and perhaps even more deserving, but I am here as a respected officer and they are there, ordinary teachers or assistant engineers. The difference he attributed to chance. These are words I have never forgotten. Whatever I have achieved, I have felt that there are others who might have been where I was, if luck, too, had been on their side.

The year 1949 proved to be an eventful one. World War II had ended a few years before, and I was now old enough to see some of the effects trickle into everyday life. Post-war shortages meant rationing. Since petrol was rationed, some buses ran on coal gas pumped from large coal-burning cylinders that were attached to the rear of the vehicle. On train trips, the police would make everyone open their luggage and rummage through their suitcases to make sure they were not smuggling controlled commodities such as sugar or rice. Wedding invitations asked the guests to bring their own rice, which would then be collected into a common pot and cooked for the wedding feast.

This was also the year my father was transferred to Madras. Due to a bureaucratic oddity, I skipped grade levels and went from third class in Bellary to sixth class in Hindu High School, Triplicane, in Madras. The result was that for the rest of my schooling, I was to be the youngest and shortest boy in the class.

Amma was expecting my youngest brother, Ramesh. In the city, there was little help for Amma. Amma woke me up early to draw water from the water pump. I helped her knead the dough for the chapatis, buy the groceries and run errands. I did not feel bad about waking up early and working hard: my expecting mother woke up even earlier and worked even harder than me.

My stint at Hindu High School was brief. We moved to Laxmipuram off Lloyd's Road in Mylapore. There, I joined Kesari High School. I did not like the school, and moved again to Ramakrishna Mission High School, T Nagar. I liked this school, particularly the composite mathematics teacher, Anna, who began his lessons with passages from Tagore, and the Telugu teacher who told us stories of Lord Shiva. My cousin, Rajanna, came to live with us and he joined the school, too.

Laxmipuram was a bustling place. There was a temple across the street and the ringing of temple bells and voices raised in chanting and song drifted into our house. Rajanna and I frequented the halls of Laxmipuram Young Men's Association (LYMA) and went into a frenzy of excitement when the reigning star of wrestling, King Kong, came to visit. We played street cricket. Rajanna, who was about four years older than me, was a leading player.

Rajanna had a toothbrush. I used the toothpowder and finger combination since a toothbrush was considered a luxury item in those days. I could not catch up with my cousin in age or cricket skills, but I was determined to have that toothbrush. For weeks, I saved money by walking some of the distance to school rather than taking the bus the whole way, and hid my savings in my clothes closet. At last, I had enough to buy the toothbrush. After school, I rushed across to Anwar Stores. I stared happily at the toothbrush and toothpaste that were in front of me. Suddenly, I wondered how I would explain the toothbrush to my mother. She would be livid that I had squandered my money. As I pictured her face, I told the clerk at Anwar Stores that I had changed my mind; now I wanted chocolates. I sat on the pavement eating the chocolates, wondering, dejectedly, if I would ever be able to own a toothbrush in my life.

One of the most vivid memories I have of my father is when we arrived at Central Station on our way back from a trip. The station was lit up and there was a festive atmosphere, as if it was Diwali. It was 26 January 1950. I asked Ayya why everything was lit up and he told me it was India's first Republic Day, the day the Constitution came into force. He must have explained about Gandhi, Sardar Patel, Ambedkar and about what it meant to be a new republic. But I did not hear most of it. I was taken by the lights in the station, the excitement all around, and the fact that my father was talking more than he ever had. Looking back, I realise that my normally quiet father must have felt deeply about this new milestone to talk so much and so animatedly. There was another time when I returned home from school or playing, I don't remember which. In the drawing room, the one radio we had was blaring. I saw Ayya at the table by the radio, his head in his hands, his shoulders shaking. I was frightened. I rushed in and asked him what had happened. Was he all right? Tears were running down his cheeks as he said, Sardar Patel is dead, Sardar Patel is dead. It was 15 December 1950. It was the first and only time I saw my father cry.

Teachers at school asked us to raise funds for the drought and famine of Rayalaseema in 1952. Patur and Kommanavaripalli, Ayya's village, were both in Rajarupet Taluk in Rayalaseema.[3] Kommanavaripalli was well-suited for horticulture. Ayya's family had orchards of orange, lime, mango and sapota trees there. But in the drought of 1952, Kommanavaripalli and most of Rayalaseema suffered greatly. All the trees in the family orchard perished. My uncle, who was managing the property, never recovered. Patur, though, fared better than other parts of Rayalaseema. It had a rivulet that had slowed the depletion of groundwater levels. It was groundwater that saved Patur from the worst of the famine and drought.[4]

The Ramakrishna Mission, the umbrella organisation for our school, received much acclaim for its efforts during the Rayalaseema famine. The mission collected funds and distributed clothes and other necessities to thousands of people. The government had set up 950 ganji kendras or gruel centres to provide emergency relief for the starving. There were works to drill wells and the army was called in to facilitate relief operations. Yet, there was great devastation and suffering. The economy of Rayalaseema collapsed. Around this time, my father was posted as the deputy commissioner of the Rayalaseema Development Board. His role was to bring some level of development and security to this region that, for a hundred years, had been famously susceptible to drought and famine. Of course, as a child, I did not know all this; I was raising funds because my teachers told me to (and the funds came from unsuspecting friends and relatives who happened to visit our house during the fund-raising time). I did not know that years later, I too would join the Rayalaseema Development Board and meet many people who had known my father.

On 1 October 1953, Andhra state was formed after the freedom fighter, Potti Sreeramulu, died following a fast-unto-death protest. My teacher prepared a speech and asked me to deliver it. It was my first foray into public speaking and I loved it. I would pursue public speaking and debating throughout my schooling.

The new state of Andhra brought changes to my family. Ayya moved to the then capital of Andhra state, Kurnool. As Kurnool had no infrastructure officers had to live in tents. Ayya had to share a tent with five other officers and there was no place for a wife and family. Amma and the younger children went back to Patur. I stayed in Madras in the Ramakrishna Mission hostel so that my studies were not disrupted.

The hostel was spartan. We slept on a mat spread on the floor with a blanket to cover ourselves, sharing the room with fifteen or twenty other students. The discipline was rigid: we woke before dawn and exercised. We had prayers twice a day. There was simple vegetarian food, and lights were out at 9 p.m. Though I was homesick,[5] I liked the teachers, especially our hostel warden, Swami Chinmatrananda. He was an engineer by training and a freedom fighter who, to our wonderment, had actual bullet wounds on his body.

It was good that I stayed; the strict discipline I learnt in the hostel became a part of my character. It would prove invaluable in my work and even more invaluable in the management of diabetes that would afflict me almost two decades later.

Intermediate, classes 12 and 13, was in Government Arts College, Anantapur. I was fourteen years old. To celebrate my admission, my eldest uncle from Patur gifted me his wristwatch. Just a while before, I had been dreaming of a toothbrush; now I had my own wristwatch. I felt I was moving up in the world.[6]

My medium of instruction was Telugu, but in intermediate, it was English. I was not very fluent in English, but the shift was not as hard as I feared since I was studying mathematics, physics and chemistry.

My father's younger brother, Chinayya, and his wife, Pinamma, were in Anantapur. Like my father, Chinayya was also in public service and was working in Anantapur as the district labour officer. For a year, I lived with Chinayya and Pinamma. In Telugu, Pinamma means 'younger mother', but my aunt, at eighteen, was only a few years older than me. Pinamma and I spent many hours of the day playing hopscotch and carrom. We became great friends.[7] I was having such a wonderful time at my uncle's house that my marks began to suffer. So, the next year, I was transferred to the hostel of the Government Arts College, Anantapur.

The college was established in 1916.[8] It had a history of strong academics and political activism. It produced stalwarts like eminent scientist U.R. Rao and Neelam Sanjeeva Reddy, the sixth President of India. Though I worked reasonably hard at academics, it was the political activism that had me in thrall. Heady new ideas were flying across the campus, with heated discussions on subjects like liberation, imperialism, exploitation, class war, the socialist revolution – and they electrified my imagination.

Anantapur was also a time of experimentation. I began to read Telugu novels and short stories. I joined any sport that I could: cricket, football, hockey, volleyball. I entered in science fairs and acted in plays.[9]

In Anantapur, I also joined the much sought-after National Cadet Corps (NCC). When I first went to apply for the NCC, I was asked to turn back because I was too young. But this refusal only made me more determined. I camped out under a tree, in a silent satyagraha, near the grounds where the others were being screened. After a few days of this, the recruiting officer agreed to let me try out.

'But I wonder how you will manage. You are smaller than the rifle you have to carry!' he said. 'Sir,' I told him, 'I will grow taller. But the rifle will stay the same.' The officer laughed and let me through. I worked hard on the entrance tests and I was elated when I qualified to join the NCC.

The NCC was a quasi-military organisation dedicated to the development of youth. It aimed to instil a sense of nation-building, discipline, duty and unity. Everything about the NCC was thrilling – the uniform, the map-reading, the gun practice, the orderliness, the parades, the public service. I loved the adventure and camaraderie of camping in the tents. Most of all, it was in the NCC that I met some of my closest friends – Sampath, Katanna and the redoubtable Veeranna.

Veeranna, born and bred in the village, prided himself on being a son of the soil. He was short and stocky and sported a luxurious moustache on his dark skin. Veeranna, or Z. Veera Reddy, smoked beedis, refused to wear anything but langot or loincloth, dhoti and kurta, and spoke with an unapologetic rural brusqueness. He called himself a peasant, and was proud of it.[10]

In those days, there were no malls or bars for college students to hang around in. Instead, we spent our time at the nearby railway station watching the trains go by and at the clock tower, which was a marketplace and a kind of public square. Eating out was reserved for special celebrations such as a top rank or a birthday. We called those occasions SKC treats: sweet, kara, coffee treats where we would order something sweet, something spicy or kara, and some coffee to go with it all.

My friends came from different backgrounds. In Anantapur I had friends who were affluent and had their personal cooks. I also had other friends who lived in ten-by-six-foot rooms that they shared with three of four others. There were no lavatories. They had a small kerosene stove in the corner on which they cooked rice and brought back limited quantities of curries sold to them at subsidised rates in the college mess.

When I think back, my education at Anantapur was unique. The children of my father's colleagues usually studied in large cities and in elite private colleges. Their interactions were with people like them. In Anantapur, my classmates were from a wide social spectrum. There were children of landlords and peasants, Brahmins and backward castes. I think it was here, in Anantapur, that I had a window into the lives of people of different background than mine. I got an inkling of how precarious their situation could be, the role of risk in their lives, their aspirations. As I shared jokes with my friends, played sports with them, and had meals in their rooms, the common man was no longer an abstract concept but was, in fact, all those young men with their stories, struggles and joys.

While the lives of these friends opened a window for me, my life must have offered a window to them too. Through our conversations, they, too, must have had an inkling of the opportunities that were possible. Years after Anantapur, Veeranna completed his master's degree. He told me that the idea to do his master's had not even crossed his mind till he saw me do mine.

'I saw you do it, so I thought I could try also,' he said.

Another time, when we both were much older, Veeranna paid a visit to my office. I had joined the Indian Administrative Service (IAS) and was working as a collector in Nalgonda. As I was sitting at my desk, Veeranna touched my shoulder. Then he touched the desk, the chair, the books on the shelves, the files.

'What are you doing, Veeranna?' I asked him.

'You are a collector. To us, in our small towns, the collectors are never seen in flesh and blood. A collector has a bungalow. An office. A car zooming by. If we are lucky, we might catch a glimpse of his wife shopping. Now, I am in a collector's office; I want to touch everything. I can go back and tell everyone in town, see, I have not only seen a real collector, but I have touched him and his desk and chair and books in his office.'

Veeranna lived his entire life in the town of Gooty, Anantapur. He was intelligent, dynamic and hard-working. But he did not want to pursue a career. Instead, he dedicated his life to social service and the communist cause. He died in his early sixties, a committed communist, though towards the end, he admitted to me that he had become disillusioned: he felt communism was still the right path, but his leaders had betrayed the cause.

In Anantapur, along with Veeranna, I too immersed myself in communist party rallies. I followed politics closely and was struck by the wit and oratory of Neelam Sanjeeva Reddy of the Congress party and Tarimella Nagi Reddy of the Communist Party of India as they sparred over competing visions for Andhra Pradesh. But the Communist Party was just one cause. There were others.[11] For a time, I was part of the movement to liberate Goa from the Portuguese. We marched at rallies and organised agitations. Once, the Goa liberators went on a protest at the railway station. We marched past the police and stormed the railway tracks. We lay down on the rails of Anantapur station. Of course, the train was stopped on the tracks before it ran us over. The press covered our protest and snapped photographs. Then, the police dragged us off the tracks. Some of the more vociferous students were picked up and dropped off outside town. I was not one of the students who were picked up. At fifteen, perhaps I was too young to be considered a threat to law and order.

Teachers in those days were more like gurus. They played a role in the aesthetic and ethical education of their students. Like the mathematics teacher in Madras who had introduced me to Tagore, in Anantapur, Y. Vishwanandham taught us chemistry (which I have forgotten long ago), interspersed with discussions on ethics and proper behaviour (some of which I remember even today). There was also Ramesh Murthy, our physics teacher, who inspired us all with his single-minded devotion to his work.[12]

My stay in Anantapur was only two years, but it was a tremendously rich life experience. At the end of it, at sixteen, I was no longer a child, protected and privileged; I was already on my way to becoming a young man intensely engaged with the world.

I got into a bachelor's degree course in economics (honours) from Vivekananda College in Chennai. It was equivalent to a master's. Economics was not my first choice.[13]

I had passed intermediate with good marks and wanted to study engineering. But I was underage. For that one year, till I was old enough, Ayya advised me to do one year of undergraduation in some field other than engineering. I had no idea what subject I should take. When the principal of Vivekananda College said that with my good marks in mathematics and English I should join economics (honours), I agreed. What did it matter? I was going to be an engineer and economics, of which I knew nothing, was to be a temporary thing, after all.

Vivekananda College was as different from Government Arts College as night from day. Many of my classmates in Vivekananda College were from urban, educated, middle class and upper-middle-class backgrounds. Their only aim was to pass the exams to become IAS officers or lecturers or lawyers or journalists. My classmates were abstemious, disciplined and focused on their futures. They were mostly city bred. In contrast, in Government Arts College everything was dynamic, raucous even. The students were from varied backgrounds and they did not know what to focus on. And though they knew that education was critical and they studied hard, they did not know what to hope for in their lives. It was a stark expression of the rural-urban divide.

When I went home for holidays that year, Ayya, in his gentle way, indicated that I should finish my studies quickly, get a job and settle down. His health was deteriorating and, as the older son, I would have to take on greater responsibilities at any moment. The engineering course that I had planned was now out of question. Amma said that in addition to his enlarged heart, Ayya had developed cysts in his bladder. I was not sure whether those cysts were cancerous. In any case, in those days, they were dangerous. They were virtually impossible to treat. Ayya had begun to bleed profusely when he urinated. I could see that everything had slowed down. His walk was slower, sitting was difficult, getting up was a strain, and other than for work and morning walk, Ayya hardly went out. He must have been in constant pain, yet, whenever we were together, Ayya was his old self, always smiling, pleasant, dignified.

I had settled in well in Vivekananda College. I made two close friends, Krishnamurthy and Bheema Bhatt. Krishnamurthy stayed a lifelong friend and retired as director general of police in Andhra Pradesh.

As a result of my previous experience in student activism in Anantapur, I quickly rose to leadership roles in the more sedate Vivekananda College. I was elected general secretary of the hostel union and the secretary of the Social Service League. I was associated with a night school in the nearby slum. Interacting with the people in the slum was a diametrically opposite experience to interacting with people in the college. I saw the deep poverty and difficult conditions in the lanes of the slum but also, I saw the hope for a better future as the students attended night school.

In the slum there was tremendous political activism. There was great support for Periyar's Dravida Kazhagam, which was then a non-political organisation that fought for self-respect among non-Brahmin backward class communities. I saw dramatic street plays and heard impassioned speeches. I witnessed street processions where idols of Aryan gods such as Lord Ganesha were carried through the streets, while people shouted angry abuse at the idols and threw slippers at them. At first, I was shocked. Ganesha and other Hindu gods were sacred in my house. To most of my classmates, the rough manners and the irreligious attitude of the Dravida Kazhagam leaders were repellant. Yet, these processions were tolerated as a part of the Dravida right for democratic free expression. In those days, the authorities never gave them any trouble.

In the college hostel, distinguished persons were invited to give lectures. The lectures were held in the prayer room, where pictures and idols of gods lined the walls. Till then, no non-Hindu had been invited. I felt I should shake things up a little. As general secretary of the Hostel Students' Union, I invited Ms Mona Hensman, the principal of Women's College, to give a speech.[14] She was likely the first Christian to enter the halls of Vivekananda College Prayer Hall. Her speech was well-received. Encouraged, I invited Syed Abdul Wahab Bukhari Sahib, founder of New Science College, to speak. Afterwards, I invited him to stay for lunch. At the mess everyone ate sitting on the floor, cross-legged. As we entered the mess, Bukhari Sahib and I waited for a few awkward moments as the warden arranged a table and chair for the guest. Bukhari Sahib opted to eat with us, on the floor. Had the warden arranged the table and chair so that the Brahmins, who were in a vast majority in Vivekananda College, could avoid having a meal with a non-Hindu? Some felt that he had. I thought not; the warden was acting out of courtesy. But, I was glad that there was, finally, some debate on these issues. Vivekananda College was a time of activity in politics, the NCC,[15] and social work.

My teachers in Vivekananda College rated me outstanding academically. But in the final exams, I scored in the lower 50 per cent. It was quite a blow to my ego.

Despite my less than stellar marks, I decided to pursue economics further. I toyed with studying for my PhD in the London School of Economics. I finally settled on Osmania University in Hyderabad. Ayya had moved there.

2

THE MAKING OF A BUREAUCRAT

For the first time, we were together as a family. My brothers Ramesh and Madhu were in the nearby Methodist High School. Sarala joined Women's College. I had applied for the PhD programme at Osmania University.

On December 1960, I was admitted into the full-time PhD programme at the university, though without scholarship or stipend. My guide was Prof. V.V. Ramanadham (VVR), commerce faculty, an expert in transport economics and the economics of public enterprises. Though I was originally interested in the study of the black market in India, VVR pointed out that it would be hard to get reliable data. Instead, I focused on monopoly and the concentration of economic power. I was one of VVR's four research scholars.

VVR gave appointments at odd times. The meeting would start at 9.05 a.m. or 8.55 a.m. and never at 9 a.m. Why? Because, he explained, in India, 9 a.m. meant about 9 a.m. which could stretch all the way to 10 a.m. But with 8.55 or 9.05, there was no mistaking the seriousness of the intention. In VVR's room, there were two cards. Both were prominently displayed; one on the wall and the other on the table. The card on the wall had a picture of a fish about to bite a hook and underneath it was the quote, 'Even a fish could avoid trouble if it kept its mouth shut.' The card on the table said: 'Your time is precious, don't waste it here.' The messages were clear – be punctual, open your mouth only when essential, and get out when the job is done. I learnt them well.

VVR was also an extremely diligent reader. All writing had to be structured and the drafting, perfect. He encouraged his students to attend seminars, present papers, and exchange ideas with others. He organised weekly seminars on applied economics, including inter-disciplinary seminars with academics and practitioners from the government and public sector enterprises. He started a journal called *Applied Economic Papers*, with eminent academics on its editorial board. As his students, we helped with the journal and spent time proof-reading.[1]

Through VVR, I met world-class economists such as Prof. Joan Robinson of the University of Cambridge, who was visiting Osmania University to deliver lectures. Professor Robinson was a trailblazer in the field of imperfect markets, which was my area of study. Once, Professor Robinson told me about a brilliant young economist. His name was Amartya Sen and she was his PhD supervisor. But he had just finished his thesis, she said, and she was looking for another student; would I be interested? I was not. I could not think of going abroad with our family situation.

At home, Ayya was to retire in a year. Financially, it would not be easy. His income was just enough to meet his family responsibilities. Ayya had not saved much. After the famine, the conditions in Kommanavaripalli were still difficult.

With all the uncertainties, Amma was worried. Whenever she needed advice or direction, she would visit a local holy man: Swami Ambadas Vithoba. Sometimes, Amma would take me along to his tiny two-room house. Swami Vithoba was a Devi bhakt who would enter trance-like states in which, it was said, the Devi would enter his body and dispense her divine advice using him as a physical vessel. When I first saw the swami, I was struck by how ordinary he looked. He could have been anyone. But then he began his puja. First, he dressed himself in a sari, put on a bottu, and tied his hair. Next, he started his incantations. Soon, there was a transformation, as if someone had taken over his body. His face began to glow. Expression, voice, mannerisms and even features seemed to morph. Swami Vithoba was a tall, well-built man, but in his trance, he seemed to shed his man's body and become entirely a woman. It was then, when the Devi was said to be within him, that my mother would ask him (or her) for guidance on the important matters in her life: how would a child do in the exams, how to stall her husband's worsening health? The advice the Swami gave was usually harmless. Mostly, he would reassure her about decisions she had already made. He was a source of strength and comfort for my mother at a time when she needed such support the most.

A few months before his retirement from the IAS, Ayya was appointed as member, Public Service Commission. This gave him five more years of service. It was a great respite for us.

In August 1961, I was appointed a temporary lecturer in Hyderabad Evening College. My term was six months and my consolidated salary, Rs 250 per month. The part-time students there were older than me and were serious about learning. For every class, I would prepare thoroughly. Teaching came naturally to me, and I loved the job. The best way of learning was by teaching. Hyderabad Evening College was a short stint. After about a month, I was transferred to the prestigious Nizam College.

The students of Nizam's were among the brightest. There were also students from the cream of society. I was nervous on my first day there. As I entered the class, I saw that it was overflowing with young men and women. They were all my age. My nervousness increased. It was the tradition for the students to ask questions after the lecturer's introduction. I expected questions on teaching style, economic concepts, or previous work experience. There was a brief pause.

'You were working in the night college before joining here,' someone spoke up finally. 'What were you doing during the day?'

I considered how best to answer the cheeky question. I said, 'In the day time, I did what others do during nights.'

There was some laughter.

The next question came quickly after that.

'Who is your favourite actress?' a student asked.

'Vyjayanthimala,' I replied.

'But isn't she too old for you?' chimed another.

Now I, too, was in the game. 'Neither of us minds it,' I replied.

There was more laughter.

'How is your love life?' someone said, getting right to the point.

I replied, 'It is too boring to talk about.'

The session broke the ice. Still, I was a demanding teacher and I took my classes seriously.

A few months into my job, the principal asked me to lead the students to an excursion to Delhi.

'Yes, sir,' I agreed, 'but only if there are no girls in the group.' The principal said he would check about the girls. Though I was their teacher, the girls in my class would often tease me since I was the same age as them. I was unused to female company. I did not know how to handle the fairer sex.

'There will be girls,' the principal said, later.

'Oh! Then I can't go.'

'But,' the principal continued, 'the girls assured me that they have self-control and that you should not worry.'

I assumed he meant they would behave themselves but retorted, 'Sir, I cannot assure you about my self-control.'

I was still only a temporary lecturer. The next year, I applied for a position as a regular lecturer. I was appointed to the University College of Arts and Commerce, or Arts College. I taught economics to undergraduate students in the commerce faculty.

Soon after, on 20 October 1962, the Sino-Indian war began. There was a surge in patriotism. Women donated their gold ornaments, young men enlisted to serve in the armed forces. But the war would give a terrible blow to our confidence. The Chinese forces entered our borders at will, while the Indian side crumbled. There was complete confusion and it was clear that we were utterly unprepared. Nehru, the non-aligned socialist, rushed to the West for support; another blow to our nationalist self-esteem. After one month the Chinese declared a unilateral ceasefire and the war ended. Their goal was to humiliate India, to demonstrate that our borders were for their taking, and they had done it easily. Suddenly, Pandit Nehru, our beloved leader, appeared weak. He even began to look old. He lost his confidence and there was bickering and a blame game. Not so long ago, we were a proud nation that had won a spectacular Independence; now we were face-to-face with this mortifying defeat. Like much of the nation's youth, I felt utterly devastated by it.

After the border war with China, the Indian government recruited young men to serve the armed forces under an Emergency Commission Scheme and decided to expand the National Cadet Corps. I signed up with enthusiasm. I was selected as a second lieutenant[2] in the NCC Rifles Division. I had to familiarise myself with the teaching manuals, conduct parades, and engage in administrative tasks as I helped raise a company.[3] Many young people came forward, wanting to serve the country in any way they could.

Back in college, VVR added two other subjects to my teaching list: 'Public Enterprises' and 'Development Planning'. I was to teach postgraduate students in the commerce department. In our university, these subjects were offered in the commerce department but not in the economics department, for no reason that I could understand. This was surprising. In economic policy those days, planning and the 'commanding heights' of public enterprises dominated. Academia began to study those subjects actively, while the study of economic history, agricultural economics and industrial economics took a backseat. Looking back, I could see no serious analysis of the economic impact of the Sino-Indian war at the time. Economic policy and research seemed to go on as they had before, unaffected by the momentous political events.

Sometime before, Amma had insisted that Ayya acquire a small plot in Shanti Nagar.[4] Ayya could not manage the construction of the house on the plot, so I busied myself with it. In those days, steel was regulated. To buy it, we needed approved construction plans and certificates and an allotment by the state controller of steel. After much back and forth, I got all the permits, but it was not enough. I had to make four visits to the steel store as the storekeeper would make some excuse or the other. It was the same story with cement. This was a result of the 'Licence-Permit Raj'; an offshoot of the socialist agenda of a planned economy where much of the commercial activity was 'ruled' by dispensing permits and licences. There were efforts to depart from this. In 1959,

C. Rajagopalachari, or Rajaji, founded the Swatantra Party. One of its goals was a more market-friendly approach; starting with a drastic trimming of the Licence Raj. But the party ideology failed to inspire the masses. Nehruvian socialism, with its promise of a more equitable society, still captured our imagination.

Ayya loved his early morning walks in the nearby public gardens. Often, I would join him. It was during those walks that we would spend time in each other's company. After the walk, I left to work at 7.30 a.m. by bus. Sometimes, if I was late, Ayya would say that he would drop me off on his way to work.

'But Ayya,' I would say, 'I should not get used to being dropped off in a car. I don't think I will be ever able to afford a car on my own.'

'More the reason to enjoy being dropped off in the car now if you think you won't have it later,' Ayya would reply. And we would ride together. It was our standard routine.

One morning, on our way to work, Ayya and I stopped for a few minutes in the hospital. We visited Ayya's friend who had had a heart attack. As we got back in the car and the driver began to pull out, my father said he felt ill. He said there was something wrong with his stomach. He asked the driver to stop. Ayya opened the car door and vomited. After a few moments, he said he felt better.

'Let's be on our way,' he said.

Something was wrong. Ayya was sweating profusely. He was terribly weak and his voice was thin. I had a bad feeling. I told Ayya to wait and ran to the hospital. I saw a doctor nearby. It turned out that the doctor was both a cardiologist and family friend. We rushed to our car and as soon as the doctor saw my father, he rushed him to the emergency room. It was a heart attack. It had been a close call, and it left Ayya much weakened.

Ayya was anxious to get Sarala married as soon as possible and asked me to look for good alliances for her. We need not have worried. A young and handsome doctor, Dr Challa Prabhakar Reddy, came to ask for Sarala's hand in marriage. He had seen her in college and was instantly taken with her. The alliance was perfectly acceptable to us and the marriage took place on 29 May

1963. It was a happy event for our family. Bava, as I called him, was a great pillar of strength for us in those difficult times. He treated my mother as his own since he had lost his mother years ago.

Ayya had plans for me also. He wanted me to join the IAS. IAS officers were expected to be men (there were only a handful of women in the service then) of integrity, intelligence, industry and independence. Getting into the IAS was hard, but there were few professions that carried greater prestige.

My father believed that my entry into the IAS was preordained: when I was born, my horoscope had been written by an astrologer, we called him Tamil Pandit. Tamil Pandit had said I would either become an engineer or that I would start my career where my father left off. Since engineering was out, it seemed that my career choice was to be public service.

But I was not enthusiastic. My work at the college was great and my salary was good. Outside of work, I was busy engaging with interesting people as I had joined, as a member, Toast Masters International, a club whose members met to improve their public speaking and leadership skills. I also frequented the YMCA, Hyderabad, a nerve centre of activity for young people interested in sports, debates, arts and social service. I was enjoying myself immensely in the college and out of it.

Yet, Ayya was keen and after some thought, I saw his point: the IAS offered stability and respectability during uncertain times. I decided to prepare for it, but I was determined to pursue my interest in academics, at least part-time.

Professor VVR was not comfortable with the IAS decision. He had wanted me to apply for a post-doctoral research fellowship at Stanford University and was reluctant to forward my application for the IAS exam. He spoke to my father. But Ayya was uncharacteristically firm.

The registrar of Osmania University was another layer in the exam application. The registrar was B.P.R. Vithal, an IAS officer himself, who was on deputation to the university. Vithal also counselled me against the IAS, but seeing that I was keen, he did not object. After his retirement decades later, Vithal would recall the incident. He said it was not unusual: I would insist on seeking his advice and not take it, though, he observed rightly, it did not detract from my respect for him nor his affection for me. Witty and wise, Vithal would become a beloved guru.

Amid my work as a lecturer, my research activities, NCC and everything else, I began preparing for the IAS. A few weeks before the exams, Ayya's condition began to deteriorate quickly. He was now bedridden and would vomit blood. Ayya told me to rent a small room so that I could prepare for and write the IAS exams without the stress of being in the house with a sick patient. I understood that, for Ayya, everything was riding on my passing the civil services exam. I rented a room with access to a mess. For weeks, I closeted myself in there. Most days, I studied from 4.00 a.m. to 11.00 p.m. I took breaks only to go to the temple and to visit Ayya.

The exams lasted for a month. The day after the last one, I returned home around 2 p.m., earlier than usual. Ayya was very ill. Immediately, we moved him to Osmania General Hospital. The doctor told us there was nothing to be done.

'Will you pass IAS?' Ayya asked me. It was now past midnight. All of us, Amma, Madhu, Sarala, Bava and Ramesh, were gathered at his bedside in the hospital room.

'I will pass the written exam, Ayya,' I told him. 'I will definitely be called for the interview.'

'Who is there for us?' he said. He meant that there was no one left to help us but God. It was to be prescient. After a while, Ayya beckoned me closer.

'Give me some vibhuti,' he said, as he opened his mouth. In Telugu tradition, it was a good omen to die with something auspicious in the mouth, usually tulsi leaves or vibhuti – holy ash – from a temple. Ayya knew I had been to the temple and was carrying vibhuti. He knew also that these were his last moments.

When Amma saw me put the vibhuti in my father's mouth, she fainted. Within a few minutes Ayya passed away. He was conscious almost till the end; he died in the early hours of 7 November.

Amma did not gain consciousness for hours. When she came

home with the body she was hardly conscious. Her eyes were blank and she was like a zombie. Hours later, I found Amma in the kitchen. She seemed cheerful and was busy cooking. As we sat down to eat, she set Ayya's plate on the table. She filled his glass with water. When we asked her what she was doing, she said she was waiting for Ayya to come and eat. The next day, she asked us to keep Ayya's shoes ready; she had already ironed his clothes. When we tried to tell her he was no more, she seemed not to hear us. In some ways, it was better since she seemed enthused and happy. We thought we could let her be, that perhaps she would understand in her own time. But she did not.

Every day, it was the same strange routine. Early in the morning, Amma got the hot water ready for Ayya's bath. At 9, she served his breakfast. At 9.30, she got his shoes ready. In the evening, she waited for him to come home so she could make his tea and dinner. We called the doctor, who said there was nothing to be done. Finally, we thought of the swami. But Amma refused to leave the house and Swami Vithoba would not do his puja anywhere other than in his room. Yet, these were desperate times and I went anyway. Swami Vithoba listened to me patiently and finally agreed to come to our house. The swami went first into the puja room and began his incantations. After some time, he asked my mother to come in and close the door. A short while later, he opened the door and walked out. Behind him was my mother. She was sobbing uncontrollably. I was both relieved and sad to see Amma crying for the first time since Ayya passed away.

Soon after, we had to battle with practicalities. We had to find a place to live: we had a few weeks to vacate our government quarters. After our house in Shanti Nagar had been constructed, we had given it on rent. The lease was still active and the tenant was living there and we wondered where we would all stay. My brother Ramesh was twelve years old, and Madhu was eighteen, and they had to finish their education. We sold our Fiat car and bought a bicycle.[5] We had a telephone in the government quarters, but no personal phone. The wait for a telephone connection was nine years. In those days, the signs of true manhood were if you could buy a scooter and get a telephone connection and a gas connection. Bava managed at least one: he bought a scooter, and that helped a great deal. But it was not our practical difficulties that hurt Amma the most.

We had thought that it was Ayya's character and Amma's hospitality, not the official position, that had gained the affection of many relatives and friends who had thronged our house and Ayya's office. But after Ayya's death, we felt that most people abandoned us overnight. Amma felt betrayed. She would rant in fury. Madhu and Sarala, too, were terribly angry. I felt my family was sinking into bitterness. I knew for certain that Ayya would not have wanted that, and for my part, I tried to be civil to our former friends. This infuriated my normally kind and easygoing brother Madhu.

'How can you not be angry?' he once asked me. 'Do you have blood in your veins or sambar?'

Of course, there were those who pulled closer to us. There were a few members of my mother's family who were as warm as they had ever been – particularly Saraswathi akka, the wife of my mother's middle brother. There were my friends from university, college, school, Sampath, Krishnamurthy, E.S. Sastry, and many others. There was Narasa Reddy, a distant relative of my mother, whom we had met only two years before. He became a great source of support for us and would be at Amma's side anytime she needed him. There was our tenant in Shantinagar, Mr Subramanian, who volunteered to vacate our house even though the lease was active and he had not found another place to stay. There was Professor Razvi, our neighbour in Shanti Nagar, who offered to take Subramanian in till he found another place, so we could move into ours. Venkatrami Reddy, Ayya's colleague in the Service Commission, helped us settle into our new reality and political leader Peddireddi Thimma Reddy was a frequent visitor and a source of moral support. It was these gestures that kept me from becoming bitter.

In January 1964, the civil services examination results came out. The news was good – I had passed the examinations and qualified for the interview. I did not know how to prepare for an interview and neither did any of my friends. Still, I asked a few friends to grill me with questions. Sometimes, I had to prompt them on the questions to ask. I scoured the newspapers and read anything that I thought might be relevant. Finally, it was time to leave for the interview. I took the train to New Delhi, and for the thirty-six-hour journey, I packed food from home – I did not want to eat anything that could cause an upset stomach. The interview went well, but not as well as I would have liked. The results came out soon afterwards. They were announced in the papers and on the radio. My rank in the IAS-IFS combined category was twelfth nationally. I thought of Ayya, who had a formidable reputation for his patience, integrity, devotion to duty and commitment to serving the rural areas. He was dignified but considerate to the poor and needy. I wished he had been alive to hear the news.

Since I had got a high rank, I would get my first choice of cadre in the IAS. Of course, I chose Andhra Pradesh. I could be with my family. Things seemed to be looking up.

When the news was out that I had made it into the IAS, scores of people came over to congratulate us; even those who had disappeared after my father passed away. Our social cold-shoulder had lasted only a few months, but it was an important lesson. There were the people who pulled away and those that came to help; it was the most intense education about human nature in the real world.

3

TRIBAL RITES

THE JOURNEY TO MUSSOORIE, WHERE THE TRAINING INSTITUTE was located, was to take over two days. I was to go to Delhi first and from there to Dehra Dun and then to Mussoorie in the Garhwal Himalayas. Bava and his friends saw me off at the Nampally railway station. After the hectic activity of the past one year, I finally had time to reflect. There were mixed emotions. I was happy that I could fulfil my father's last wish. But, then, I had to think of Amma, whom I was leaving behind. She had become emotionally dependent on me. Bava was moving to England soon (Sarala was to join him a year later) and Madhu, at nineteen, would have to take charge of the family affairs and finances. Ramesh was still in school and I hoped that he would study well. Also, I had one unfulfilled task – my PhD thesis. I wondered when I could finish it and pursue my research in economics.

I did not know what lay ahead. After Ayya's death, the family felt like a boat without an anchor. But there had been another death, an entirely unexpected one, that left the whole country feeling adrift. A few weeks before, in the early afternoon of 27 May 1964, Pandit Nehru had died of a heart attack. A nation that had been shaken by the Sino-Indian war found itself sinking into anxiety. We were uncertain as to where we were heading; Nehru had been a towering personality and his absence left a void. Lal Bahadur Shastri was appointed prime minister, and the question 'After Nehru, who?' had been answered, but not the question, 'After Nehru, what?' Ideologically, Shastri was aligned with Nehru's commitment to socialism and non-alignment. Still, there was some anxiety about how successfully the new prime minister would step into the shoes of one of the most charismatic leaders of the world.

I was looking forward to becoming a full-fledged officer. At home, also, everyone looked forward eagerly to my successfully completing my training. I recall that when the results were announced in Hyderabad, there was a surge of congratulations. My relatives congratulated me on being the second person in 'our Reddy community' to pass the IAS examination. My Cuddapah compatriots said that 'our district' was the leading producer of IAS officers (I was the fourth one). My fellow Rayalaseema natives declared that I was the 'pride of Rayalaseema'. The farming community was delighted that there would be someone in government who understood rural needs and the plight of 'us farmers'. For Telugus, 'one of us' was breaking the 'Tamil domination' of the IAS. For non-Brahmins, I was trying to 'outdo the Brahmins' in their game. It was a striking reminder of the extraordinary regard in which the IAS was held in the eyes of ordinary people (as well as an excellent illustration of the concentric circles of identity that dominate relationships in our society).

In the IAS, there was also a sense that we were embarking on something that was beyond a mere career; it was a calling. Some of my colleagues in the Andhra Pradesh cadre would later tell me that, for them, being an IAS officer was such a remarkable opportunity to serve the public that they chose to remain unmarried in order to devote their undivided and singular attention to their work. An IAS officer's allegiance was to the Constitution of India, the larger public interest, his or her own conscience, and nothing else. The IAS officer was not permanently associated with any specific function (such as police, forest, or diplomatic activities), nor with the Union or the state government exclusively; the IAS officer was to take a broader view of national interests. Importantly, the officers were expected to be beyond the influence of the political winds of the day. If there was any inquiry to take place, the government had only to announce that a senior IAS officer would be heading it to assure impartiality.

But there had been warnings, too. Before I set out, my senior colleague in the university, Ram Reddy, had warned me that the institution I was joining was a tribe. He said that the IAS officers thought like a tribe, stuck close together, and tended to be arrogant and domineering. 'Be watchful,' Reddy had told me, 'you have a mature head on young shoulders.' I was forewarned.

The training institute at Mussoorie was located in a sprawling campus. My roommate was A.K. Venkatasubramanian. It was strict alphabetical allocation, done to avoid allegations of patronage. That was an interesting principle to note on my first day at the academy: follow a rule, any rule, rather than no rule! But, I was also a victim; on the sprawling campus, our alphabetically allocated room was the farthest from the main area.

The first phase of the training, the 'foundation course', was to last four months. For these four months, I would be training with people from all the civil services: police and central, including foreign service. We were called probationers as we were under 'probation' until successful completion of training. There were four hundred of us. We were young men (in those days only about 10 per cent of the class were women), almost all of us were between twenty-two and twenty-five years of age, and we were from a variety of regions, religions, race, language and educational backgrounds. This in itself was an education.

We were taught subjects relevant for all the civil services: the Indian Constitution, public administration, basic economics and Indian economy. But, unique to IAS training, we had to learn to ride a horse since our work would take us to remote, inaccessible areas. The first time I sat on the animal, I clutched the reins and became a great believer in the Almighty. I reminded myself that there was a god in the horse, there was a god in me and, therefore, nothing untoward was likely to happen. Luckily, after the foundation course, I never rode a horse again.

A tutor once asked us to give our thoughts on our experience in the academy.

When it was my turn, I said, 'Before I joined the academy, I was wondering how I got in. Now that I have been here for a month,

I am wondering how everyone else got in.' After a slight pause, everyone started laughing. I went on to say that I had discovered that almost everybody in the academy was an ordinary person just like me. It was true; though it was also true that everyone in the academy had at least one distinctive quality: great memory, oratorical skills, academic brilliance, writing talent, or something else. And it was this unique quality that I actively looked out for in my interactions with the others.

Most of the probationers were from the north and the south. There were some from the east, particularly Calcutta, but hardly anyone from the west (any intelligent fellow from Maharashtra and Gujarat would go into business). There were two major underlying divides. There was a metro–non-metro divide and the north–south divide. The people from the metros usually went to elite colleges, mostly in Delhi. They spoke impeccable English (or so they thought), some of them wore three-piece suits (which we had only seen in magazines before), and they considered themselves a class apart (and above). The non-metros were the upstarts. Needless to say, I was in the upstarts group.

The north–south divide was pronounced for a reason. The Constitution declared Hindi in Devanagari script as the language for official purposes. English was to be used for fifteen years, up to 1965, as the associate official language. Pandit Nehru had been a protagonist of English. But now with Lal Bahadur Shastri, who was from the Hindi belt, as prime minister, the south was afraid that English would not continue beyond the fifteen years that was promised by Nehru. In Madras state, the Dravida Munnetra Kazhagam or DMK (the political antecedent of the movement I had witnessed in the processions and the street plays in the bylanes of the slums of Madras when I was in college) mounted anti-Hindi agitations. Seventy people died and for the first time, the country witnessed protest by self-immolation. To stem the unrest, Shastri assured the nation that English would continue as the associate official language until the non-Hindi states were ready for Hindi. In an accident of history, it was the Dravidian movement that ensured the continued dominance of the English language in India. Should we be grateful to the

Dravidian movement for giving us the English advantage in the era of globalisation?

My Tamilian batchmate, V. Selvaraj, was a man of foresight. He failed in the Hindi examination in the academy. He wanted a certificate to show that he failed. He said that DMK would soon come to power in Tamil Nadu, and when they did, he could claim to be a conscientious objector to Hindi. Selvaraj was right: DMK captured power in 1967, and Dravidian parties have remained in power in Tamil Nadu since then.

I enjoyed my entire time in the foundation course. We were getting paid to learn in a beautiful setting where we lived in very comfortable accommodations, wore suits for dinner and had bearers who served us at every meal. It was a carefree time without stress, or even strain.

In the second phase of the training, the civil services were separated by service. Each service had its training institute. The police went to Mount Abu, revenue went to Nagpur, audit and accounts went to Shimla.

The IAS stayed on in Mussoorie; but first we started out on the unforgettable two-month tour of India, the Bharat Darshan. We were divided into batches of twenty IAS officers. My batch had mostly south Indians. We visited the eastern and northern parts of India by train. We were given a railway compartment that was parked in the railway station and often that was where we slept. In the newly formed state of Nagaland, the chief minister, P. Shilo Ao, welcomed us to his home. We met his family and we chatted over snacks and tea. The chief minister of West Bengal, Prafulla Chandra Sen, met us at the imposing Writers' Building in Calcutta. It was one of the most impressive colonial buildings I had ever seen, with its red and white exterior and the giant statue of Minerva, the goddess of wisdom, on top. The chief minister was chatty and informal. All this was heady stuff for a young man of twenty-three. But it was also a reflection of the esteem in which the IAS was held by the leaders of the times.

For two weeks, we had an 'army attachment', where we stayed with a Gorkha battalion in the Poonch sector near the Pakistan border. The living conditions in the camp were harsh; for us it would be only temporary, but for the soldiers it was months of difficult living away from family. Yet, the soldiers maintained their cheer. During Dussehra, the Gorkhas celebrated their most important festival, Durga Puja, with us. They made a ritual sacrifice of a buffalo and after that, they revelled in boisterous dancing, heavy drinking and feasting. Army life at the border was a world in itself. The soldiers' discipline and equanimity in the face of hardship, and dedication to the nation, was an inspiration to us.

During our attachment, we found that in times of peace our soldiers had no personal enmity with their counterparts in Pakistan. While we were there, the soldiers arranged for an exchange of 'friendly fire' with the Pakistani soldiers, and the UN Peace Keeping Force at the time was informed of this.

Wherever we travelled, the dress, the food habits, the language, the entertainment all varied. In Pratapgarh district and in Bakshi ka Talab, we had to live on roti and aloo-gobi for days – and they were made the same way, every single time. In the north-east, hardly anyone knew how to make coffee, nor did they understand what a vegetarian meal was; and most of us were coffee-drinking vegetarians (here, we discovered that India had a coffee–tea divide in addition to all the others). We tried hard to find south Indian restaurants, but in Pratapgarh and in Bakshi ka Talab, there were none. In Bhubaneswar, we managed to find one, and walked two miles for our rice and sambar. It was the expansion of public enterprises, the nationalisation of banks, and recruitment of people on an all-India basis that, over the years, did more perhaps than anything else to bring about national integration.

During Bharat Darshan, we were astonished at the diversity before us. From tribal settlements to ancient cities, dense forests to towering mountains, tea gardens to lakes to barren lands – it was clear that we lived in a vast and beautiful nation. The two-month tour illustrated the great variety of challenges we would have to face in our careers.

We returned to Mussoorie for classes and seminars. On the first day, our professor in economics gave us a memorable welcome. He said: 'Ladies and Gentlemen, welcome to the IAS. You are among the best and brightest. Your Dharma is public service – serve the public. But, remember, public are those who are not in IAS.' (A couple of years later, I learnt another interpretation of the word public from a senior IAS officer who had been a district collector for several years. I asked him, 'Sir, what is the secret of your success?' I was being playful. He replied, 'I am conscious that I am a public servant. Whenever legislators or parliamentarians meet me, I make it clear that they are the public and I am the servant.' Apparently, 'public' could mean different things to different people.)

One day, I was invited to a party hosted by a few colleagues in honour of S. Rau of the famous Rau's IAS Study Circle in Delhi. Rau had coached these colleagues for the IAS examination. I thought of my friends at Government Arts College, Anantapur. Some of them were bright, hard-working young men who, if they had access to institutes like Rau's, might also pass the civil services exam and completely transform their prospects. At the party, I resolved to start a coaching centre aimed at middle-class students and those from rural areas, though it would be a few years before I could do so.

At the end of the eight months of training, there were written examinations and an assessment by the academy director. I did well in both. This boosted my overall seniority, nationally, to fourth in my batch of the IAS. I was 'Y.V. Reddy, AP, 1964 IAS', fourth in my batch. My place in the tribe was fixed forever.

4

GROUND REALITIES

I FELT LIKE I WAS IN A WHIRLWIND. IT WAS MY FIRST DAY as assistant collector. My collector, Abid Hussain, a man with a wide, almost baby-like smile, had received me in his room with effusive praise. As I enjoyed the warm welcome, his personal assistant interrupted us: Abid Saab had another engagement to go to. As Abid Saab got ready to leave, two advocates, who were working on a highly contentious irrigation dispute, were ushered into his room. Abid Saab had scheduled three appointments for the same time and as I struggled to sort out what was going on, Abid Saab introduced me to the lawyers, assured them about my intelligence and objectivity, and then assigned me to hear the irrigation dispute and write up the draft award on his behalf. I don't know who was more shocked: the advocates or me.

The next day, Abid Saab signed the draft I had written without reading it. He assured me that there was no need to read anything: it was my objectivity as a complete outsider to the dispute that was more important than knowledge of the subject or of the law. It had been a crash course on the inimitable style of Abid Saab: he had contempt for detail and a focus on long-term thinking and vision. His purpose was to be positive and helpful to everyone who approached him, even if it meant three appointments at the same time. After the orderliness of the training institute in Mussoorie, the third phase of my training had begun; and it was already proving to be eventful.

So far, I had been training in classrooms and I had very little experience with public policy implementation at the ground level. Now, as I started my year-long third phase of training, as assistant collector in the north coastal district of Visakhapatnam in Andhra Pradesh, I would be learning by experience and observation. I would immerse myself in all levels of village and district administration. All the while, my collector would assign parallel ad hoc duties and would ask me to accompany him to meetings and, in general, be a mentor to his assistant. After the third phase, I would enter the fourth phase of my training, where I would take independent charge as the chief executive of the panchayat samiti block of villages, and in the fifth phase, I would be posted as secretary, zilla parishad. The fourth and fifth phases were to be of six months each. The total time for the third, fourth, and fifth phases of my training was to be two years. In the normal course, I would finish my entire two-year district training in Visakhapatnam. A transfer during the training period was somewhat unusual, two were rare. Little did I know that, in my case, I would be transferred four times.

The transfers first happened after a year when I had successfully finished my third phase of training. I was to start my fourth phase as chief executive, panchayat samiti. The state panchayat raj had three tiers: the village, the samiti and the zilla parishad. The samiti is the elected body that oversees developmental work in a group of villages called a block. The activities were wide-ranging: agriculture, animal husbandry, primary health centres, family planning, women welfare, social welfare, loans to farmers, rural roads, and so on. I was to be a fully functioning block development officer (BDO), rather than an understudy. Looking back, it is not hard to imagine that the insertion of an inexperienced, young, officer-under-training for six months would be highly disruptive to the functioning of the offices. Yet, it was a mandatory part of the training and my collector was to identify a suitable and available block development office for me.

Abid Saab first assigned me to Pendurthi Mandal as BDO. Before I was to join, he told me that the samiti president had asked if I could be accommodated elsewhere. Abid Saab suggested Bhemunipatnam Mandal. I was fine with that. But that too was not to be: this time it was the chairman of the zilla parishad, who asked if I could be accommodated elsewhere. Would I have any objection if I was transferred to Hyderabad district? After all, Abid Saab pointed out, it was where my mother and family lived. That was typical of Abid Saab; to suggest a way that nobody could complain about. I said I was fine with that as well.

I did not know it then, but Hyderabad was to be a highly contentious posting and I would be there for six months, till I would be transferred yet again to Chittoor district as secretary, zilla parishad, to complete my training. There were times when I felt dispirited at the extraordinary number of transfers I had had before I even began my career. Other than with the transfer from Hyderabad, I am not sure of the reasons for most of the other transfers, particularly since the feedback I received from my seniors had been glowing. Perhaps there was no real reason and it was all due to a confluence of chance and unavoidable circumstances. Or, perhaps, initially, it was Abid Saab's lack of attention to the details of where to place me and his proclivity towards accommodating requests that contributed to my being placed in many posts before taking up the one in Hyderabad. In any case, being transferred so often was not a pleasant experience. Yet, looking back, I see that it was not without its advantages: working in several districts allowed me to have a wider set of experiences.

The training in the districts of Visakhapatnam, Hyderabad and Chittoor was an exceptional learning experience. I worked at almost every level and in almost every function. I would spend a few days or a week or two understanding various offices: in the municipality, the police station, the tehsildar's office, the revenue department, survey and settlement, the treasury (where I had to sign so many bills that, in sheer exhaustion, I shortened my signature from Yaga Venugopal Reddy to Y.V. Reddy). I worked with the village accountant and the village munsif. I worked on land rights, tenancy, irrigation, agriculture, heath, veterinary care, women welfare, child care. I was intimately involved in the conduct of the general election, taking care of logistics, law and order, deployment and helping in polling, counting, organising. As a magistrate under training, I would hear cases and pass judgments. I cannot think of a better education for a young person about to serve the country.

An important part of the training was to help me better understand how to work with political leaders. Any successful IAS officer would need to interact effectively with them. If the IAS was the steel frame of the government, the political leaders were the life blood of democracy. To help me learn, Abid Saab asked me to accompany him to several meetings with political leaders. Usually, I could see that Abid Saab would have his own amicable way in most interactions with ministers, but in one instance, he was outwitted.

The minister for civil supplies, A.C. Subba Reddy, was visiting Visakhapatnam along with the director of civil supplies. Visakhapatnam was one of the many districts in the country that was experiencing a deficit in foodgrain. (This was an offshoot of a policy in the Second Plan that de-emphasised agriculture as it shifted focus on heavy industries.) The minister wanted an estimate for Visakhapatnam's foodgrain allocation requirement. Abid Saab began to show the graphs and charts that I had prepared and he had brought with him. But the minister cut him short – he had no patience for presentations; he wanted only a rough figure.

When Abid Saab gave the minister his estimate, Subba Reddy snapped, 'Mr Abid Hussain, don't talk like a chairman of a zilla parishad. Indicate your requirements as a responsible collector of the district.' He meant that Abid Hussain was a collector appointed by the government rather than an elected representative of the district; while arriving at an estimate for his district, he should have taken into account the fact that other districts needed foodgrain, too.

The minister's snub stung. My collector folded his papers and said, 'The minister is not in a mood to discuss the matter. I will come later when he is.' With that, Abid Saab quietly walked out, and I quickly followed. The minister rushed after us. He was apologetic and conciliatory and brought Abid Saab back and listened patiently as the collector made an impressive presentation. Abid Saab reduced his demand marginally in light of the minister's mood. The minister thought for a while and told the director of civil supplies to allot the grain as requested. 'I hope this is all right,' he said to Abid Saab. My collector was happy, and I was impressed.

As he left the room, Subba Reddy said: 'Mr Abid Hussain, you are being transferred as director of civil supplies. I will be talking to the chief minister. In your new capacity you will handle the food requirements of all other districts. You will manage the rest of the state after honouring Visakhapatnam's requirements.' Everyone was stunned. It was now Abid Saab's turn to rush after the departing minister. My collector quickly settled for a figure for Visakhapatnam's foodgrain that was acceptable to the minister and would leave enough for the other districts. We left the meeting feeling admonished. Politicians, it appeared, were shrewd enough to distinguish between advocacy and analysis, and they had their ways of pointing it out.

There were times during my training when I had to interact with political leaders on my own. With some, it went smoothly. In Chittoor district, I was the secretary, zilla parishad, and the chairman was T.N. Nagi Reddy, an elderly member of the landed gentry. Nagi Reddy was an old-school landlord, feudal and paternalistic. Yet, with him things were above board and when it came to his interests, he was frank. Nagi Reddy was polite, almost benevolent, and brilliant. He liked to drink. But he abstained from drinking for one day of the week, and that was the day he would come in to work. Even then, he was highly efficient and in that one day, all the work would be done. Nagi Reddy created a culture geared towards problem solving and conflict resolution and I enjoyed my time in Chittoor.

There were times when things did not go so well, as was the case when I was BDO, Hyderabad district, and had my first encounter with corruption. The president of the panchayat samiti in the district was a young, dynamic and popular leader. He was a close follower of a powerful minister. He had clout with important people, including bureaucrats, as they had purchased lands in the area and were raising grape gardens. The samiti president obliged them by helping them in the process, including by laying roads to their gardens or farms as part of the government rural roads programme.

The manager at the panchayat office was instructed to collect ten per cent in cash as a precondition for issuing any cheque to the public. The amount was handed over to the samiti president. I put a stop to it. I insisted that all cheques would be handed over in my presence and there would be no more ten per cent. The reaction was swift.

The collector summoned me and asked me to call on the minister from Hyderabad district. I told the collector that, as a BDO, I could not meet the minister, but I would be happy to give any explanation through the collector, who was the head of the district. Obviously, this was conveyed. I was told that the minister wanted me transferred out of the district immediately. The chief minister agreed to transfer me, but at the end of the six-month period as BDO.

The samiti president changed tactics. The staff members were to keep him informed about everything I did or said. No order of mine was to be implemented without his approval. The samiti president filed petitions against me. He claimed that I was living in Hyderabad and was not coming in to work. One day, I had a surprise visit by an investigating officer, who came to my office at 8.30 a.m. to find me there already and busy with my work. He left, apologising profusely. I felt I was being harassed. The antagonism had gone too far. Now, neither the samiti president nor I could blink without disruption or loss of face. I took leave for a few weeks to relieve the tension and think through things. It was only a temporary reprieve: I had to eventually go back to work and wait out my term. Finally, I was transferred to Chittoor. Before I left, I wrote up a report with my findings, but I doubt it was acted upon. The collector in Hyderabad, my senior IAS colleague, was not reachable. I had thought the IAS was a tribe, but when faced with powerful political leaders, there was no guarantee that tribal affinities would prevail.

I realised years later that there were countries where ten per cent commission was the cost of doing business. Little did I know that we had our own Mr Ten Per Cent years before it became global normal practice.

My experience in Hyderabad was a run-in with an overt form of corruption. There were other cases where there was no corruption, exactly, but where the proper functioning of the system was subverted, even though procedurally there may not have been outright wrongdoing.

In my attachment with the Revenue Department, I would accompany the revenue inspector on bicycle. There was frequent travel to several villages. The travel allowance for these trips was not given to the revenue officials; instead it was used to provide food and snacks to visiting officials and dignitaries as a traditional courtesy. This meant that the revenue inspector would have no money while travelling and would have to accept local hospitality. This raised the possibility that the people who provided the hospitality might have undue influence over decisions that were important to the village economy: land rights, irrigation and identity certification. While there may not have been any overt corruption, nor even the intent, there was the possibility of unintended favouritism.

In Indian society, favouritism is usually considered to be a harmless vice. Sometimes it is even a sign of doing one's duty to one's family and community. In Chittoor, I was assigned to a collector who was an honest man. But his predecessor was known to have been not quite as strict and loved the pleasures of life. I learnt that the predecessor had liberally dispensed licences for bus routes to friends. As a young officer, I was perturbed at such blatant favouritism. It turned out, years later, that the liberal doling out of bus route licences resulted in many buses and more, better maintained roads. Chittoor became one of the most well-connected districts by road. Obviously, even not doing the procedurally correct thing could, in strange ways and on occasion, result in good outcomes.

Sometimes, it is not easy to even know what is the right thing. The Pyravikars of Hyderabad were informal agents who would, for a fee, represent poor and illiterate people in their interactions with certain government functionaries. They had been pulled up for being quacks and exploitative middlemen. During my stint as BDO, Hyderabad, I initially treated them with disdain. But over time, I saw that it was more complicated: the poor and illiterate hesitated to approach the authorities directly. The Pyravikar could do it for them at rates that were affordable. The Pyravikar was, perhaps, the equivalent of a liaison officer for the poor. Of course, the best solution would have been to have government liaisons who could guide the poor and illiterate and make them feel comfortable so there would be no need for Pyravikars. But until that happened, the role of Pyravikars would not be easy to dismiss. If anything, they would only be replaced by local political middlemen.

There are also cases when following the procedure blindly would be the wrong thing to do. Soon after I moved to Chittoor, I received a petition filed by an army soldier stationed at the border. He claimed that his sister in his village in Chittoor district was being seduced by her high-school teacher. I ordered an immediate inquiry. The detailed inquiry report had written and sworn statements from the people concerned and elders in the village. Everyone swore that the soldier's petition was baseless. As per procedure, I was required to close the file and forget about the petition. Yet, I did not. Something did not add up. Why would a brother make such a claim about his sister without being completely certain? In Indian culture, such a thing seemed almost impossible. I refused to close the matter right away and wrote a letter to the soldier, asking him if he had any evidence. A few days later, a small parcel arrived by post. The soldier had sent me a bundle of love letters written by the teacher to his sister. That was enough to suspend the teacher. In my career, I have not relied on official inquiry reports only, but have tried to look beyond and behind them. If I had followed protocol, I would not have contacted the soldier to unearth the truth.

Training in the districts also brought me in close contact with humanitarian issues. As a magistrate and magistrate-in-training, I saw court cases where the poor could not afford to plead their cases adequately while cases against the rich were not even filed. Sometimes, I would plead the case for the poor, even while hearing cases as a magistrate. I saw a woman testify against her brother and uncles who had murdered her lover because he was from a different caste. I saw the daughter of a freedom fighter who did not have money even to buy food after her famous father passed away. I saw a brave doctor who had performed an autopsy on a murder victim testify against a powerful landlord and his followers as she refused to kowtow to pressure. It was a powerful kaleidoscope of the workings of human nature and society.

During my one-year stint in Visakhapatnam, I visited Burmese refugees of Indian descent in a refugee camp. They had come to the large, prosperous port city of Visakhapatnam after they fled from Burma following a wave of anti-Indian sentiment. In the refugee camp, I saw the tiny living quarters for entire families, and the lack of access to good sanitation or jobs. The living conditions of the refugees were harsh, but even more so was the fear and uncertainty about the future. I would visit them and hear their stories of hardship, but it was all I could do – there were no resources to help make their lives better. It was, perhaps, one of my most difficult assignments as I was helpless to make any difference.

In that same year, the Indo-Pak war began. As a large port city, Visakhapatnam was a possible target. People became watchful and wary. One evening, in my neighborhood, a group of people saw a man up on a nearby hill. Immediately, they took him to be a Pakistani spy. They trudged up the hill and accosted him – but he was only a local person taking an evening walk. A sense of paranoia and fear had pervaded Visakhapatnam.

There was a large Pakistani cargo ship that had docked and was scheduled to sail out soon. When the fighting began, the ship was seized and all the crew members were ordered to stay on board. I was one of the officers assigned to speak with the Pakistani crew and assure them of their safety. The crew members were terrified. They were certain they would be tortured and killed. We tried to reassure the Pakistanis, we told them no harm would come to them, that they were our guests. But they remained hostile, frantic and petrified.

The training in the districts was extraordinary. I had thought I would learn about policy, but I ended up learning about reality. Decisions that we would make as public servants, that I would make in my later career, were not just government orders or numbers and statistics – they had the potential to make a difference in the lives of people. I had started out armed with theory and certainty about 'the right thing to do' and 'the rules'. I believed completely in institutions. I had thought that with determination and hard work, I could solve all problems. But I learned that the world was much more complicated than that, and rules could be arbitrary or even wrong, institutions were as strong as the people who worked in them, and there were problems that, despite everything, would be almost impossible to solve.

My training did not end in Chittoor. I thought I would be posted in the district as sub-collector, Madanapally. But three months after I arrived in Chittoor, I was posted in Rajahmundry. There, I worked with the then sub-collector, K.R. Venugopal (who would later become secretary to the prime minister). Venugopal was meticulous, diligent, and honest. He took the task of guiding me as understudy very seriously. A day before I was to take charge as sub-collector, there was a surprise. A wireless message was received from the state government that I should not take charge till further orders. Such a change in the posting of an understudy was unprecedented. I was posted to Ongole subdivision. I was to start on Ugadi, the Telugu New Year's Day. That day, I travelled by car so I could get to Ongole as soon as possible: I was taking no chances of being transferred before joining. Perhaps that was the final lesson of my training – take no chances!

My unique tenure as assistant collector under training began in June 1964 and came to an end in April 1967. And though there were some bumps on the road, the time spent had been invaluable. It gave me an opportunity to experience the country in its entirety and as it was. I would witness the interface between the government and the people and the dynamics of society in many of its manifestations. From tehsildars' offices to voting booths, from development to administration to legal disputes, from interacting with the poor in their village huts, refugees in their camps to leaders in their mansions, there was much that I had learnt from these ground realities. I internalised them; I absorbed them in my system. Throughout my career in public service, I would draw on them.

5

WORK, STUDY AND WEDDINGS

The tehsildar came to me, distressed. I was sub-collector and sub-divisional magistrate, Ongole. The tehsildar was the sub-collector's plenipotentiary and general functionary. In the rice-rich village of Karamchedu, the famously wealthy landlords, who owned much of the lush paddy fields of the area, had refused to comply with government rules. They were to give up a prescribed portion of their paddy at far less than market price for government food procurement programmes. It was, in a way, a tax on farmers. The landlords were used to dictating terms – they would give the portion of paddy they wanted to give, and nothing more. When the tehsildar had gone to negotiate with them, they surrounded him and refused to let him move any further. It was a show of power and an attempt to make the tehsildar, an important local official, lose face.

The compulsory food procurement programme was an important part of public policy. It was now even more essential as the country was facing a second year of monsoon failure and serious food shortage. Food from areas with a surplus was shipped to other places in the country where there was a shortage. But procurement was a policy despised by all farmers, though only the powerful could resist. The farmers' sentiments were understandable in a time of food shortage and, for us in the administration, it was not a pleasant policy to implement. Yet, it was critical that it was done; and we could not be soft on anyone. The gherao of the tehsildar was a message that I could not ignore.

'We will take action,' I told my tehsildar. The situation was a tinderbox and I quickly decided on my strategy. The landlords were powerful and any challenge to their authority would mean that the whole programme of rice procurement from Karamchedu could be derailed: the landlords not only grew the paddy, they owned the surrounding rice mills and controlled the lorries that would transport the rice. But it was no longer just a matter of rice, it was also a question of who represented the legitimate rule of law: the landlords who had wielded almost absolute authority since medieval times or the democratically elected government that had authorised us to implement programmes in the interests of the people. I felt this was an important issue and since my collector was out of station, I was to handle it on my own.

All this while, I had a wedding card from a friend, B.V.L. Narayana. He was a doctor at Ongole, an ex-MLA, and a communist leader. He ran a people's clinic that provided free medical services to the poor. We had got to know each other well. BVL and his nephew, D. Rama Naidu,[1] had invited me to a wedding in their family. The marriage was to be in Karamchedu. Many of BVL's relatives were the powerful landlords who were involved in the incident with the tehsildar, and they would be at the wedding. With everything that was going on, my tehsildar was unhappy that I was planning on attending the wedding, but I reassured him. The ceremony was to take place in the morning, and later in the day, my tehsildar would be making his visits to the houses of some of the most powerful men in the district.

As I walked into the wedding hall, I was uncertain about what to expect. I tried to avoid weddings, but on this occasion, I did not want to refuse my friend. Besides, I also wanted to signal to the landlords that my official actions were nothing personal; I was only doing my duty. BVL was happy to see me. The landlords seemed a little tense. But everyone was gracious. Perhaps, my reception was courteous because we were all governed by the same rules of old-world hospitality, or perhaps they, too, wanted to signal that their actions were not personal.

After the wedding, I spoke to the deputy superintendent of police, who was my old college friend, Krishnamurthy. I requested for a police convoy to accompany the tehsildar. It was only to accompany him; the police were not to dismount from their vehicles or take any action until the tehsildar requested it. The police would wait, a symbol of government authority, as the tehsildar did his duty.

Later that day, the tehsildar went to the village as ordered by me. The police accompanied him. He went from house to house and no one obstructed him. To the landlords, who prided themselves on *paruvu*, which means reputation or honour, having the police enter their houses would have been shameful and I did not want to go to such lengths unless absolutely necessary. I was relieved to learn that the landlords agreed to the demands of the tehsildar. The police had to do nothing, except wait in their vans.

While an ugly confrontation was avoided, it was hardly the only difficult issue I was dealing with in Ongole. Locally, while Karamchedu had plenty of water from irrigation facilities, there were areas of Ongole that were reeling under drought. Nationally, also, the country was going through difficult times. Prime Minister Lal Bahadur Shastri had passed away almost a year before. During his brief leadership of just two years, he had continued with the Nehruvian commitment to socialism, but had also differed in that he had focused on agriculture while Nehru had focused on heavy industries. During the Indo-Pak war, Shastri's rousing cry of 'Jai Jawan, Jai Kisan', extolling the soldier (jawan) and the farmer (kisan), had become popular. But he died before he could fully realise his vision and in his place Nehru's daughter, Indira Gandhi, became prime minister. Thinking that she would get massive support from international financial institutions, Mrs Gandhi devalued the rupee by over 50 per cent (though the support we finally got hardly matched her expectations).

In addition, the food situation in India had become so dire that in some places, the main source of nourishment was from the food supplied under the US Public Law 480 plan where the US shipped agricultural products to developing countries. For many people, that was all they had to eat; to our great humiliation, the country was living a 'ship-to-mouth' existence. The US was providing assistance, but it was felt that they were also using the food as leverage to dictate policy. The rupee devaluation made the price of imports go up, and that caused a further stress on the economy. Our budgetary crisis meant that at a time when resources for drought relief (such as food and drinking water distribution, fodder for animals, public works to create employment) were badly needed, they were not there. It was in this environment that I visited the drought-ridden villages of Ongole.

Floods were a dramatic calamity. The waters swooped, submerged and subsided. With drought, the process was a slow depletion. In the drought areas of Ongole, that was what one saw – a depletion. Fields that were meant to be green with growing crops were now parched and broken. Women walked for miles to find water, carrying back as many pots as they could for their families. Dead animals lay on the ground and flies rested on their carcasses. People were emaciated; the most difficult was seeing hungry, thirsty children. I was overseeing drought-relief works for transporting water and food and for digging wells. But anything and everything we did was hardly enough.[2] The situation was critical and the resources were entirely inadequate. On my visits, people would ask me where I had been for so long. They said that they were in great difficulties; please help us, they would say. Some were bitter, and some pleaded with me. My visits would raise people's hopes; their expectations from me, or rather from me as their sub-collector, were high, but I was powerless to help them as they hoped. We, as a nation, were just not up to it.

My posting in Ongole was cut short by some unexpected news. I had been troubled by all my previous transfers and had wanted to get away to study. I had, on impulse, applied for a diploma course in planning at the Institute of Social Studies in the Netherlands. I now found out that I had been accepted. Eight months after I was posted in Ongole, I was to fly to the Netherlands. I was excited as I was going abroad for the first time and I would be studying economics, a subject that I loved. I was to fly out of Delhi. Getting the visa involved excruciating formalities and that meant that I had no time to visit Amma and Ramesh, but Madhu met me at Kazipet junction, where my train from Ongole to Delhi stopped for some time. He had brought me the suitcase of clothes that Amma had packed for me in Hyderabad.

The Institute of Social Studies (ISS) in The Hague was in Palace Noordeinde. It was a smart, elegant building with an open courtyard surrounded by symmetrical buildings with large, rectangular windows and tall arches. Lectures were in spacious classrooms that overlooked elegant gardens with ponds and fountains. We had waitresses serving us at government-sponsored teas and dinners for which everyone came well-dressed. We course mates were mostly from the developing world and we mixed with the local Dutch, who would attend the parties to interact with the diverse student body from Argentina, Ireland, Ethiopia and Brazil.

It was beautiful and elegant, but in the initial one month, I was shy, homesick and unhappy. After the hullaballoo of India, everything seemed strange and cold. On one occasion, I was in the dining room. I had picked up a chicken piece with my fingers. A diner next to me noticed.

'You're eating with your fingers,' he said. He sounded disapproving.

'Yes, I am,' I told him. 'Can you eat with your fingers?'

'Well, no,' he said.

'No? But I can eat with a fork and knife. And I can eat with my fingers. I can do both.'

The idea had not struck him before, and the awkward moment passed innocuously.

Soon, I began to settle in. The professors were excellent. The Nobel Prize in economics[3] was started in 1969, and one of its two first recipients, Jan Tinbergen, gave us a few lectures on econometric modelling. He placed great importance on common sense. He told us that economic modelling was important, but if the model was contrary to common sense, we should check the model again to make sure it was robust.

For the first time, any research data that I wanted was freely available, and recently released books were available as soon as we wanted them. In India, students would not get them for a year as it took six months for them to be shipped to the library and they were first borrowed by the professors, then the lecturers and then the rest of us.

It was 1968, and momentous events were unfolding the world over. In Cuba, the beloved revolutionary, Che Guevara, had been killed. In Paris, students held massive protests against capitalistic institutions and traditional values. They occupied universities and plunged France into a crisis, forcing President de Gaulle to secretly flee the country for a few hours. Communist Czechoslovakia had been moving towards a Prague Spring, and the Soviets and other nations of the Warsaw Pact invaded it to quell the threat to the communist order. Just as it was de-colonising, Africa became the playground of a bipolar world. Students in the US were protesting against the Vietnam war. The American government was perceived as an imperialistic, neo-colonial power, which used the CIA to assassinate leaders who stood in the way of its economic agenda. That was the ideological mood of the time; if you were an active intellectual, these were the ideas you debated. And, unlike today, these conversations were virtually the only way for us to understand the happenings in other nations, particularly developing nations, which were hardly covered in the media. It was at the ISS that I began to engage with the events and ideas that were sweeping the world.

The ISS was also an eye-opener to differing ideas of gender relations. In 1960s Andhra Pradesh, women were considered different, an 'other'. Women were to be respected, but a distance was always to be maintained. In the Netherlands, women were treated, and expected to be treated, the same as men. They mixed with us freely, many of them shared drinks with us, they stayed in the same dorms, and they danced, debated, studied and laughed with us. It was an entirely new approach to gender and I was quite amazed by it. For the first time in my life, I put aside my inhibitions and danced. Soon I was partying till late (and woke up early to study, getting by with four to five hours of sleep) and I began to understand the difference between friendly girls and girlfriends.

The ISS was an exciting time of intense learning and, for the first time, an exposure to the larger world. When I started the course, I hardly knew econometrics, but at the end of it, I stood first in my class in input-output analysis. In all the other subjects, too, I did very well. Once again I saw that the scope and opportunity in economics were enormous. I also learnt a great deal socially and, importantly, I gained confidence. But I had been away for six months and I was eager to get back. There was work to be done and family responsibilities to be taken care of.

When I returned to India, I was posted as sub-collector, Gudur. And it was in Gudur that I would get married.

Gudur was an easier posting than Ongole. My boss, who was the collector and district magistrate, was S.R. Sankaran. A small, wiry man, Sankaran was one of the IAS officers of Andhra Pradesh cadre who had decided to stay unmarried so he could devote all his life and his almost indefatigable energies to his efforts for the poor, especially the scheduled castes. Sankaran was an ardent leftist and knew his Marx inside out. Towards the end of his career, he would be one of the government officers who would be kidnapped by the revolutionary Marxist organisation, the People's War Group (ironically, he had been an intermediary in the negotiations between the government and the group). He would be held for twelve days before being released. He spent hours debating Marxists teachings with his captors, and he knew his Marx even better than they did. Dynamic, idealistic and fearless, Sankaran was the opposite of the paper-pushing bureaucratic babu that government officers are sometimes associated with. His life in service and in retirement was simple, almost austere. Sankaran politely refused a Padma award the government presented to him, but after he passed away many years later, the government gave him a state funeral in recognition of his extraordinary work and life.

In Gudur, Sankaran was an inspiration. While I did not share his instinctive distrust of all landlords and politicians, I was taken by his zeal for working for the downtrodden. My leanings were pro-poor, but working with Sankaran made me more actively reach out to the poor since they were often afraid to voice their true concerns to people in power. Like Sankaran, I too was known to be strict in my work, always wary of even the slightest perception of cronyism. This meant I could not take the hospitality of the local landlords in any way (something that I had learned in my training days with the revenue inspector). When on official tours, I would pack, in the left pocket of my jacket, two boiled eggs. In the right pocket there would be two pieces of toast. That way, I was not obliged to anybody for my lunch. In those days, many of us were that punctilious.

While I was in Gudur, I told my close friend Seethayya that I was thinking of getting married. He said he had a cousin who was a simple and well-educated girl. Seethayya took me to the house of the prospective bride. Her name was Geetha. We met each other briefly. It was a casual occasion and both of us were dressed ordinarily. Geetha was a delicate-looking, pretty girl of nineteen. The marriage was fixed soon afterwards and I made all the arrangements on my side: printing the cards, getting my clothes stitched, inviting friends and relatives. The ceremony took place on 24 April 1969. Geetha had lived a sheltered and privileged life as the daughter of a well-to-do landlord family, and it would be difficult for her, initially, to adjust to my basic lifestyle.

The posting in Gudur was short; soon I applied for leave so that Geetha and I could spend some time with Amma and my brothers. After my leave, I was promoted to district revenue officer (DRO) and collector, Guntur district. It was in Guntur that I intensified my drive for land rights for the poor.

Starting from the British times, land rights for common citizens were documented on 'pattas', or occupation certificates. With the increase in population, many were left without land. The landless were the most vulnerable in the community as land was virtually the only asset or security available to many people. Without any other recourse, poor farmers sometimes occupied community lands for which they had no pattas. Getting a land patta was far from easy. In addition to bureaucratic delays, there were many conflicting interests. There was the genuine concern to keep communal lands for people's use, but village officers also had an incentive to keep the farmers on tenterhooks and at their mercy. Besides, it was not just the poor who occupied lands, the well-off did it too. Handing out of pattas was not an easy matter, it had to be evaluated on a case-by-case basis after resolving all these interests. While the collector's office was already issuing pattas, I wanted to take it to the next level. I wanted to tilt the balance to favour the poor.

Instead of waiting for individual farmers to come to us, I organised the official apparatus to go from village to village, calling the farmers to petition their claims on the lands they had been cultivating. These farmers were given temporary pattas that could be later made permanent. It was an intensive drive that was implemented across the district. What I was trying to spread was an increased sensitivity to the issue of land rights and I wanted to show our willingness to favour the poor farmers.

But it was not enough. I also wanted to send out a strong signal that land rights were of enormous importance. At that time, President V.V. Giri was travelling through Guntur district by train. I requested him to hand out pattas to poor farmers at the station. President Giri, who had once been a trade union leader, readily agreed. It was a short, ten-minute ceremony. Several farmers assembled at the station and received their pattas from the president. People were astonished. It was highly unconventional. After all, the act of handing out pattas to a few poor farmers was hardly a matter worthy of a president. But I wanted to show that while it was a small matter to everyone else, to the farmer who was getting the patta, it was everything.

Of course, there were people like Sankaran and others who were devoted to the ideals with which India had gained its independence. But times were changing. It was 2 October 1969, the centenary year of Mahatma Gandhi. I took personal interest to make it a special celebration and devoted myself to logistics, budget, invitations and the rest. Amidst the celebrations, orders were issued that Andhra Pradesh, which had till then prohibited intoxicating drinks, would now allow liquor to be bought and sold freely. The order was to take effect on Gandhi's centenary. I was torn. I had started having my evening drink in Hyderabad, where there was no prohibition, so I enjoyed my peg and I could hardly complain about being able to buy my whisky freely. Yet, Gandhi had been a passionate advocate of prohibition. Abstinence was an essential part of his life and philosophy. To rescind the prohibition on his centenary seemed pointedly disrespectful. It was a first hint that the country was moving away from the Gandhian ideals from which it had been fashioned.

In Guntur, I was working as DRO and collector and I was busier than usual. Geetha had grown up in a joint family, in a household bustling with people and activity. She was now living in the collector's big bungalow and must have been lonely as I was working from early in the morning till after midnight every day. Geetha was afraid to be alone, and while she was in Guntur, she would come into my home office (officially called 'camp' office) and sleep on a straw mat on the floor while I worked till very late in the night.

6

THE ART OF GETTING THINGS DONE

MOST IAS OFFICERS WILL TELL YOU LATER IN THEIR CAREERS about the special mentoring they received from this senior or that boss. In my case, my mentor was Baru Pandu Ranga Vithal. Vithal had, as registrar, Osmania University, advised me to not join the IAS, but once I was in it, he took me under his wing.

One of the first things I learnt from Vithal was the real reason I was packed off from Guntur in just three months. In Guntur, the chief minister, K. Brahmananda Reddy, had praised me to the skies in a public meeting during the Gandhi centenary celebrations. He praised my integrity, capabilities, intelligence, and anything else he possibly could in public. Naturally, I was immensely pleased. Later, my colleague, the seasoned superintendent of police, Hanumantha Naidu, pulled me aside. Be careful, he warned. Such high praise by such a senior political leader usually meant that there was a hidden agenda.

I had been warned. Sure enough, on the eve of his departure from Guntur, the chief minister suggested that I move to Hyderabad so I could be close to my family. Though I indicated my preference to be in Guntur, I received my transfer orders through police wireless. I was not unhappy with the transfer, but I was intrigued by the alacrity with which I was ordered to be united with my family.

Vithal later clarified things about the transfer. Some time earlier, M.T. Raju, chief secretary, had asked Vithal for advice on 'this officer named Venugopal Reddy'.

'I do not know what to do with him and where to post him,' Raju had told Vithal. 'He is a very good officer. But he is very difficult also.' Here, the word 'difficult' meant inconvenient to politicians and bureaucrats alike.

Vithal said he would be happy to take me as a deputy secretary in Planning. For many reasons, I was happy too. In my new role, I could be in Hyderabad with my mother and brothers. I was also keen to relieve Madhu, who had taken on a great deal of responsibility. He was studying for his master's degree at law, preparing for the IAS and also applying for jobs in the private sector alongside. He was looking after some agricultural lands in Nandyal that Amma had recently inherited and was taking care of the finances and other household responsibilities. Emotionally, Madhu was the glue in our family. He made Geetha feel comfortable in our house. Sarala had left her son, Prashant, with us as she and Bava tried to make a life in London, and Madhu cared for the young boy as well. After Ayya passed away, it was Madhu who was brother and father to Ramesh. Madhu was the one who cared for us all.

In addition to personal reasons, I was also looking forward to working in the field of applied economics, something I had been wanting to do ever since my course in the Netherlands. Also, I would be working with, and learning from, Vithal, a man highly respected for his knowledge, wisdom and humour.

When Vithal disagreed with me on any matter on a file, he would call me for discussions. He liked to hear my views and presented his own. It was only if we were unable to convince each other that he would overrule me. He was careful to explain that he did it not because he was necessarily right and I was wrong. We were all equally capable of logic and were endowed with integrity, but as a senior in office, he had to take his stand as a matter of convenience for doing business. This respect for people without reference to hierarchy was a guiding principle for me.

Vithal had a lighter side, too. When I said that I hoped that he would become chief secretary as it would benefit the state, he laughed. He asked me if I remembered a certain officer that we both knew.

'Venu,' he said, 'that officer was chief secretary. He was half-mad. Still, no damage was done to the state. If a half-mad officer could not damage the state, can even a genius officer improve it?'

Along with my duties as deputy secretary, Planning, I was also made secretary of the Rayalaseema Board. Initially, that was the most important part of my work. When I took charge, the state of Andhra Pradesh was going through a turbulence that was rooted in the history of the three distinct regions of Andhra Pradesh: Coastal Andhra, Rayalaseema and Telangana.

The three regions had a common language, Telugu, but different socio-political and economic challenges. Coastal Andhra was under British governance from the second half of the eighteenth century. It had a developed railway line and irrigation facilities. It had a long coastline, rich natural resources and quality educational institutions.

At the start of the nineteenth century, Rayalaseema districts were ceded by the Nizam of Hyderabad to the British. Rayalaseema lagged coastal Andhra in social development and was prone to factionalism and drought. For long, there was a move to carve out the Telugu-speaking areas of the old Madras Presidency to form an Andhra state, but the people of Rayalaseema feared cultural and economic domination by the coastal areas. They negotiated the 'Sribagh Pact'[1] to protect their interests. In 1953, Andhra state was formed after the fast-unto-death of freedom fighter Potti Sreeramulu.

The former Hyderabad state's Telangana region, which was mainly a Telugu-speaking area, was backward compared to coastal Andhra and Rayalaseema. In 1955, the State Reorganisation Commission (SRC)[2] proposed that in deference to Telangana's fears of domination by the Andhra and Rayalaseema areas, the Telangana region should form a separate state for around five years and after that, the SRC opined, an integration of Telangana and Andhra could be considered. Yet, the Government of India was keen to form a united Andhra Pradesh without any delay. Telangana's immediate fears were addressed through a 'gentleman's agreement'.[3] Importantly, the agreement assured the revenue-surplus Telangana that its revenues would be spent within it, and it assured the natives of Telangana, who were called Mulkis, of government jobs in the Telangana region. The leaders of all three regions then agreed to a united Andhra Pradesh, which formally came into existence as part of the reorganisation of states in 1956.

But over time, many in Telangana felt aggrieved that the 'gentlemen's agreement' was not, in practice, being honoured. By the late 1960s, an agitation for a separate Telangana was launched and in the ensuing protests, over three hundred people died and hundreds were arrested. The Telangana Praja Samithi (TPS) fought elections on the platform of separation and won ten out of eleven Lok Sabha seats. However, Prime Minister Indira Gandhi persuaded the TPS to merge with the Congress. The protests subsided. The Union government again gave assurances to Telangana that financial packages would be available to the region and the Mulki rules for government jobs would be honoured. In addition, a Telangana local, P.V. Narasimha Rao, was made chief minister of Andhra Pradesh. A case was filed in court questioning the legality of the Mulki rules, but the unrest had dwindled into an uneasy quiet by then.

To counter the Telangana agitations and pre-empt similar ones in Rayalaseema, the government constituted the Planning and Development Board for Rayalaseema in 1969. It had a precedent of sorts in the Rayalaseema Board of Madras Presidency which was set up during the 1952 famine and was disbanded when Andhra state was formed in 1953. This was the Rayalaseema Development Board in which Ayya had worked a decade before. One of the reasons, perhaps, that I was appointed on the board was that I had the trust of the Rayalaseema political leadership as I was a 'son of the soil'.

As the first secretary of the Rayalaseema Board, I had the opportunity to devise the approaches to planning and the work procedures of the board. The board, whose chairman[4] was of minister of state rank, was in many ways an innovation among institutions for planning and development of regions. The government set aside funds for development, to be allocated on the recommendations of the board. It was an exciting opportunity, but it required long hours to manage my duties as deputy secretary, Planning, and my work in the Rayalaseema Board.

I was again working very late in the office. Most days, I was not home in time for dinner. My brother, Madhu, would pack my food and bring it to the office. Though he was younger than me, he was protective of me. Madhu would keep me company as I ate my dinner at my desk, and it was only after I was finished eating that he would go home to have his own dinner.

In April 1970, my daughter, Kavitha, was born. Geetha had gone to her parents' house for the delivery. Madhu and I went to see the mother and child in Nellore. I was afraid to pick up the baby, but Madhu was not. He cradled her briefly. As he put the baby down, he told Geetha he was going away, but would be back very soon. But fate had it that it was not to be.

It was a workday, just like any other. It was around 10 a.m. and I had an important presentation to make. Just as I was entering the meeting hall, my personal assistant stopped me. There was a phone call. Madhu had been driving from Amma's lands in Nandyal to Hyderabad, where he had to give a job interview in a private company. On the way he met with an accident. I was to rush to Kurnool, though I was told that there was nothing to worry about. But I had my misgivings. I knew it was serious. I knew that if Madhu had been conscious, he would never have allowed them to telephone me: he hated to have me worry, even a little. By the time I arranged for a car and picked up Amma, it was close to noon. The roads were bad and we seemed to crawl along. The car got two punctures. The obstacles seemed endless. I felt frustrated and anxious – we had no way of knowing how Madhu was doing. It was early evening when we arrived at Kurnool General Hospital. We were directed to the mortuary.

There had been a head-on collision between Madhu's car and a lorry. Some said that the lorry driver had been drunk. A bus passing by had picked my brother up from the road and had driven him to the hospital. Somewhere along the way he had died. We had not reached in time to see him alive.

Madhu's death was a blow that would never heal. For Ramesh, too, it was a great loss. He had hardly known Ayya, and I had been away or busy at work for much of his life. It was Madhu who had been there for him. Geetha always maintained that Madhu was the finest of all of us in the family.

But work would not wait and I threw myself into it. The intense lifestyle and the four to five hours of sleep was not good for my health. Perhaps it was the lifestyle or perhaps it was the stress of Madhu's death, but my health worsened and when I went in for a medical examination, I was diagnosed with diabetes. It was April 1972. My son, Adithya, was just born and Geetha was at her parents' place in Nellore. Geetha received the news of my diabetes with acceptance and stoicism. Over the years, that would be her approach to any problems that arose and she would never make me feel diffident about my health.

Like my grandfather in Patur who attempted to battle his diabetes through natural cures, I made my attempts, too: kakarkai (bittergourd) juice, water soaked overnight in a red wooden cup, menthullu (fenugreek seeds). I started yoga and pranayama with Ramananda Yogi, who had become famous for his ability to temporarily stop his heartbeat (I remember also that he had cut his tongue in half so that when he stuck it out, he could keep it together or split it like a snake). Again, as with my grandfather, none of the cures seemed to make much difference, and yoga was taking too much time. I stopped everything. I learnt to manage my diabetes through a diet that was disciplined (though not as disciplined as it could have been), a regimen of insulin injections, rigorous morning walks, and an active social life. Of course, I would still insist on my whisky every evening. I tried to maintain that fine balance between good health and bad habits.

I put my heart and soul into my work with Rayalaseema. It was an emotional commitment. Besides, I was keen to show my Rayalaseema compatriots that I was committed, though I was not entirely sure how much of a difference I could make. In fact, during the first meeting of the Rayalaseema Board months before, everyone warmly welcomed me and expressed the hope that under my leadership, the development of Rayalaseema would be achieved. I told them that my father was in the Rayalaseema Development Board after Independence and he had worked hard at it. I was in charge now and I too would work hard at it. At this rate, I expected my son to work hard at it also. I was not entirely joking.

There were two important considerations to keep in mind: the political and the technical. For the elected representatives, politics and programmes for development were inseparable; the plan was intensely political. For the planners, the development programmes were meant to flow from rationality. But creating a plan that took only technical considerations into account would mean the plan would risk becoming irrelevant as the political leadership on the board would not be interested in approving it. Yet, without a strong technical and rational basis, the plan would be less than effective. Therefore, at the outset, I reached out to the political leadership of the Rayalaseema Board. We agreed on a set of objective technical criteria, based on which the recommendations would be made. For example, electricity would be provided first to villages that were already within a certain distance to an existing electrical line or where there were a certain number of wells so that there would be demand for and revenue from electricity.

Once the leaders agreed on a set of objective criteria, proposals were considered only if these were met. The leaders had the discretion to choose among the proposals. Thus, the final outcomes would not be entirely outside of the band of technical and rational considerations. With this mechanism, the analytical framework, the participation of people's representatives, and the interaction with the operating department were worked out in a smooth manner. Of course, the process of reconciling planning and politics was facilitated by the enlightened chairmen, B.V. Subba Reddy[5] and Nivarthi Venkatasubbaiah, both freedom fighters. If the political leadership was impervious to any rational considerations, the outcome would likely have been very different.

The technical aspects of preparing the plan, comprising a long-term plan, a medium-term plan and annual plans, were also exciting. I studied regional planning techniques and spatial analysis in Italy and Brazil and other countries. We organised seminars and collaborated with the National Institute of Rural Development.[6]

We interacted with the Bureau of Economics and Statistics, Directorate Town Planning, and the Agricultural University, and the departments of agriculture, mining and industry. We used cartographic techniques to depict and analyse the developments in the past, with the village as a primary unit. These exercises, unprecedented at the state level at that time, attracted the attention of the Planning Commission, including two of its members: the internationally distinguished economists Sukhamoy Chakravarty[7] and B.S. Minhas.[8] We then received additional funds from the Planning Commission and this generated even more interest from various departments and leaders who were keen to work with us. Finally, 'A Perspective Plan for Rayalaseema' was formulated and published. The United Nations Development Programme found our work pioneering and made a case study of it.[9]

My work in planning was not restricted to the Rayalaseema Board. I was also working on the five-year plan in the Planning Department.

Planning in India was going through a period of revival. In the background of the tumultuous events of the past few years – the 1965 war, the drought, the political changes and the drastic devaluation – the country did not have either the resources or the confidence for a five-year plan for the states; there were only annual plans. The lack of a five-year plan was euphemistically called a 'plan holiday',[10] but now, planning was coming back into the public discourse. We in the Andhra Pradesh State Planning Department were full of hope and confidence.

We thought we were making a difference. With the medium-term plan, we thought we would improve the welfare of the people and accelerate the development of the state. However, Minhas had the last word on the subject.

'Planning in Andhra Pradesh is excellent,' he told us, 'but growth in Punjab is the best, with no planning.'

A five-year plan is put into operation through the annual plan. The annual plan is the most relevant because it is the one that gets into the budget. At the Planning Department, we were to identify important sectors for development (such as irrigation, power and welfare of scheduled castes) and then make proposals for projects based on the sectoral allocations identified. This was meant to be an important exercise, keeping in mind technical considerations and the directions indicated by the five-year plan and Planning Commission guidelines. For my first annual plan exercise, Vithal called me to his office. He had had extensive discussions with the chief minister and the result was a document in two neatly typed pages. When I read the document, I was quite surprised to see that it had a list of important projects to be given priority and allocations to be made to select sectors; in short, it was a large part of the annual plan that we were supposed to have arrived at after extensive technical exercises.

'Venu,' Vithal said to me, 'this is your annual plan. Now you go and write it.'[11] The eventual plan, based on that two-page note, would be 150 pages – a test of writing ability.

In our draft of the annual plan proposal to be sent to the Planning Commission, I had to use my creative and analytical skills to justify the allocations indicated in the document I was given. And it was only for the rest that I could actually do the planning exercises and apply all the knowledge and wisdom that emanated out of our perspective plans, five-year plans, and guidelines of the Planning Commission. The politics and the technicalities of planning both had their place.

As IAS officers, our lives were directly, and sometimes, profoundly, affected by the events in the state. In 1972, the Supreme Court judgment upheld the legality of the Mulki rules allowing government jobs in the capital city of Hyderabad to be assigned to Telangana natives. This time, it was the coastal and Rayalaseema areas that erupted in protest. It was a deeply emotional issue as the coastal and Rayalaseema people felt that they were being treated as aliens in their own state, their own capital. They felt that there were already vast quantities of funds being invested in a capital in which they had an unequal stake. Students felt that their future was in jeopardy as many government jobs, the most sought-after forms of employment for most people in those days, would be denied to them. Almost all the ministers from the coastal and Rayalaseema region resigned and joined the agitation.[12] The protests took a violent turn. The army was called in.[13] My friend K.R. Venugopal, who was then collector, Vijayawada, was widely praised for his resolve and courage. My close friends and colleagues, G.P. Rao (who was endowed with special magisterial powers), S. Narayanan and T.R. Prasad, also braved danger and played crucial roles.

The first reports of violence were from Ongole, where Prasad was collector. An angry mob stormed the collector's bungalow. Prasad went out to pacify the crowd, while his wife fled to safety in a neighbour's house. The mob would not relent; they burnt down the bungalow.

While the agitation was in full force, in the first week of January 1973, I was appointed liaison officer between the state government and the army. The appointment took me by surprise, but I made arrangements to leave for Vijayawada.

Within a week of my joining as liaison officer, Chief Minister P.V. Narasimha Rao had to resign on 10 January 1973 and President's Rule was imposed.[14]

On one day, there were fourteen police firings in Vijayawada, which fast became the epicentre of the unrest. As the police shot at the crowds, young men danced in front of the police, shouting, 'Shoot me first, shoot me first!' Women gheraoed the All India Radio offices and stopped the broadcasts for two hours while the special police waited for orders on whether to fire on them or not. Other than at the highest levels of the government – such as collector, the superintendent of police, some paramilitary forces – many of the government officials joined the agitation. People associated with the authorities were treated with hostility and anyone else known to be with the government would not be able to buy even sodas or peanuts as shopkeepers refused to sell anything to them. My colleagues on the ground described it as a civil war. An estimated four hundred people lost their lives.

As liaison officer I had with me one plainclothes policeman for company and protection. I eschewed all other security as I preferred to travel incognito since I would drive though troubled areas. My job was to liaise between the intelligence reports on the extent of the unrest, the requests of the district administration for army assistance, and the views of the army on whether they were really needed in that situation. If the collector got a call that there was trouble in his area, he and the superintendent of police would not want to take any risks; they would want to call the army. But the army was reluctant to intervene unless absolutely necessary; they were loath to use force against their own people.[15] In addition, I was a trusted resource for my colleagues in the administration who would ask me for advice and information about what was happening in the rest of the state since there was a virtual blackout of news. Being a liaison officer was a unique experience as I could see the perspectives and working of the army, the intelligence agencies, the police force, the magistracy, and political activists.

I also got an insight into the working of the media in the good old days when there were hardly any active civil society organisations, and all that was available for information were the government-controlled All India Radio and Doordarshan bulletins.

One morning, H.C. Sarin, one of the advisors to the governor of the state,[16] convened a meeting in Vijayawada. He had to fly in. It was a secret visit, and the Vijayawada Air Traffic Control (ATC) did not have prior notice; ATC officials were taken from their homes to the airport for last-minute clearance to the flight. Secrecy was maintained all through, beginning with his drive from the airport to the meeting and to his departure. The next morning, I opened the newspaper. The news was flashed all over that Sarin had come to Vijayawada. Astonishingly, the newspapers reported that Sarin was welcomed warmly by political leaders and went on to describe how happy the people of Vijayawada were to receive him. The government had 'managed' the only free media into reporting what they had wanted reported and the newspaper correspondents stretched the morning news into official fiction.

On another visit, Sarin flew to Cuddapah where there had been a police firing and reports of excessive force and other irregularities. I joined Sarin in meetings with the local police and other officials. In addition to the discussions on the police firing, there were other concerns. Sarin asked the collector of Cuddapah about the vast quantities of country-made bombs that were reported to be in the district. Cuddapah was famous for its factional violence and family feuds. Both were sustained by a steady stream of illegal firearms and country-made bombs which, Sarin said, had the potential to aggravate the agitation. The collector of Cuddapah was unfazed by Sarin's questions.

He said, 'Sir, in Cuddapah, country-made bombs are as ubiquitous as vegetables. In fact, they are named after vegetables. We have small vankaya (eggplant) bombs, big tenkaya bombs (coconut). Bombs here are like vegetables. We don't take them seriously.'

Sarin also discussed the case of a Central Reserve Police constable who was paraded on a donkey with his head shaven when he tried to molest a woman. The incident had become quite famous, but when Sarin asked the superintendent of police about it, he vehemently denied it. Afterwards, I spoke to the superintendent privately. How could he deny it, I asked him. There were many witnesses.

'Sir,' the police officer told me, 'you know, when big people ask, you should never tell the truth.' This astonishing statement from a senior official made me wonder if this was a reason for the unrealistic assessments of ground realities by the higher echelons of the government.[17]

The Jai Andhra agitation ended when the Government of India announced a six-point formula.[18] The army was withdrawn. Things settled down. The state had been united, but at gunpoint. I returned to Hyderabad and resumed my duties. An after-effect of the Jai Andhra agitation was that the Coastal Andhra Board and the Telangana Board were formed to help the case for a united Andhra Pradesh. Based on my work in the Rayalaseema Board, I was also, briefly, the secretary of the Telangana Board and the Coastal Andhra Board. But as long as I was in the Planning Department, I was secretary of the Rayalaseema Board. After all, I was considered 'the Son of the Soil'.

Around this time, there were two important events in my life. With one, I began to rekindle some old beliefs, and with the other I fulfilled an old dream.

For a few months, from September 1973 to April 1974,

I was posted as collector and district magistrate, Nalgonda. President's Rule in the state was lifted on 10 December 1973 and Vengal Rao became the chief minister. True to tradition, he visited Yadagirigutta temple, a famous cave temple dedicated to Narasimha Swamy, the god who was half-lion and half-man. Protocol required that I was to be with the chief minister and to accompany him into the temple. At the entrance of the main temple, I told him that I could not enter as I did not believe in God. The chief minister was surprised, but did not object. He went in without me. I waited outside in the guest house close to the temple. After Madhu's death, I had stopped believing in God and stopped doing puja or going to temples, but now I felt torn. As the chief minister was having his darshan, I began to pace the floor. How could I be so sure that God did not exist? In any case, how could I be so against God when I did not know anything with certainty about Him? I decided that I would not be averse to God, or puja, or temples when I was so unsure of everything. That day, I did not visit Yadagirigutta, but I would visit it many times over the years.

In March 1975, I qualified as doctor of philosophy from Osmania University. I had thought I would need only to update the research work and submit the thesis since before joining the IAS I had already completed my attendance requirements and had done significant work on my thesis on monopoly and concentration of economic power in India. But I was wrong. My guide, Prof. V.V. Ramanadham, had left Osmania University to join the United Nations and my new guides were willing to work with me only if I changed my thesis to one they were familiar with: multi-level planning in India. With the new subject and the strict requirements of the university, I had to make a concentrated effort. I took leave from work for short periods, and once for a few months. I went 'underground' at the house of our old friend, Narsanna. There I would work undisturbed. Finally, almost fifteen years after I was admitted to the programme, I got my PhD. After joining the IAS, I had fulfilled Ayya's dream for me; after I got my PhD, I felt I had fulfilled my own.

My academic interests led me to participate in several seminars and conferences where my practical, on-the-ground experience was of special relevance. Prof. Sukhamoy Chakravarty inducted me as member of the task force on multi-level planning. With that, I attended and presented papers at many more seminars and conferences. I wrote articles in journals, the most prominent among them being the *Indian Journal of Regional Science*.[19]

I also gained academic exposure at the international level. I was invited to participate as a panelist in a United Nations correspondence seminar on comprehensive development at local and intermediate levels.[20] I was appointed by the Planning Commission to join a team of experts, as regional planner, to prepare an integrated rural development plan for Singida region in Tanzania on a three-month assignment.

With my active academic work, presentations, seminars and papers, some thought there were two Y.V. Reddys – one who was in the IAS and one who was an economist.

In Telugu literature, there is a famous poet, Vemana, who lived, perhaps, in the seventeenth century. In one of his verses, he says:

In a shell, the raindrop fell, and became a pearl,
In the water, the raindrop fell, and dissolved,
So it is that destiny determines the fruit of the action.[21]

The events of those years seemed to embody the idea that not everything is in our hands. The state and the country were going through calamitous times and sometimes major events seemed to erupt out of nowhere. In my life, also, there were ups and downs. The birth of my children, the satisfaction and recognition I got with my work, my PhD, my academic work; all these were signs of a life going well. Yet, my diabetes meant that for the rest of my life, my health would work against me rather than for me. And, of course, there was Madhu's death. It is a gap that nothing will lessen. I try not to think of his death, but if I ever do, I make it a point to instantly erase the memory.

7

A STATE OF EMERGENCY

IN 1969 THE CONGRESS HAD SPLIT AND THE COUNTRY WAS MOVING in entirely new directions with a new approach to governance. As administrators, we were in the thick of things. Our work, the way we worked, the way we thought about our work, all were in doubt. As professional civil servants, we were going through a period when we were confronted with unforeseen predicaments.

It was a question of ends versus means. The ends seemed to be in the right direction, but the means were arbitrary. Institutions and processes were being systematically undermined. There was a policy of 'committed bureaucracy' and 'committed judiciary' where the bureaucracy and judiciary were meant to align themselves with the commitments and causes of the ruling leadership. Slowly the civil services began to be politicised as the leadership played favourites and rewarded loyalists. Traditionally, the hallmarks of the IAS were 'Objectivity, Neutrality, and Anonymity'; with the introduction of a 'committed bureaucracy' all these were undermined. There was something of an identity crisis within the ranks. We did not know it then, but it was a turning point in the direction in which our country was headed.

In my (Andhra Pradesh) cadre of the IAS, the reactions varied. Many of the officers were indifferent; they did their job regardless of political leadership. Many others felt palpable discomfort. However, for a few pro-poor, left sympathisers, Indira Gandhi seemed to be a messiah with her slogan of 'Garibi Hatao'. She welcomed communist leaders into her party. The communists joined Indira Gandhi's Congress in pursuit of their policy of 'infiltration' into left-of-centre organisations. Their goal was to move policy leftward. Under her regime, most of the largest commercial banks were nationalised in a bid to provide banking for the poor. Coal mining too was nationalised and that was popular with the workers. The Monopoly and Restrictive Trade Practices Act (MRTP) was drafted.[1] Leaders, such as Mohan Kumaramangalam and K.V. Raghunatha Reddy, with intellectual backgrounds and 'progressive' views, became prominent. Many in the progressive camp were excited and enthusiastic. But behind the eagerness with which many of us greeted the new determination to alleviate poverty, we were distressed with some of the methods adopted in the name of enlightened policies.

If the changes in governance after the Congress split had presented predicaments before us in the IAS, we were about to be struck by a bolt from the blue that posed a far more serious dilemma.

On 25 June 1975, it was announced that Indira Gandhi had imposed a state of Emergency. That day, I was to give a lecture to trainees at the accountant general's office. I started my presentation, which was meant to be a purely technical one on planning, but I could not contain myself – I burst out in a tirade against the Emergency. I saw it as the death of democracy and I could not believe it was happening.

In one stroke, the Emergency called into question everything we were taught to value as administrators and everything we had cherished about our nation since the idealistic days of Independence. In some ways, it empowered the 'committed' civil servant and enfeebled the citizen. The Emergency bestowed power without responsibility.

Within the IAS, again, attitudes to the Emergency varied. A surprisingly large number were for it. They saw that government services were being delivered with unprecedented efficiency. Officers worked longer hours, bribes decreased, and, famously, the trains ran on time. Any decision that came from the top was executed with the full force of the official machinery and some in the IAS were excited to see a government working effectively towards defined goals.

A few officers were indifferent; they saw themselves as mere implementers of leadership policies and they felt that nothing had changed except the leadership and that would change again.

But there were a few of us who were greatly disturbed. We were overcome with moral and intellectual abhorrence as newspapers were gagged, political leaders detained or arrested or tortured, protesters vanished, banks were forced to fund pet government programmes. We heard of intelligence officers using drivers to spy on their employers and magistrates who signed blank arrest warrants. I learnt that my phone was tapped and I was advised against being vocal in my comments against the Emergency. The democratic rights which we had thought were solid and inalienable had been taken away so easily, so completely, and with so little struggle that their very validity seemed to have been nothing but a mirage.

After the split in the Congress, an enthusiastic embrace of the directives of the leadership had implied promotions and a fast-track career, while a distancing from those directives had meant that brakes would be applied to career progression. But, now, after the Emergency was announced, everything went to an entirely different level. Any criticism or thought of defying official (and unofficial) directives meant that we had to worry about our safety, both physical and professional. Following some official dictates was abhorrent, but in the final analysis, as IAS officers, we were a part of the government and our job was to implement its orders. We had to make difficult ethical and professional choices and each of us had to find our way to balance duty and conscience. Yet, it must be said that it was easier for some of us than it was for others as the way the Emergency was implemented varied across regions.

In some regions, the Emergency was embraced wholeheartedly. Where oversight and accountability disappeared, there were widespread abuses of power by local authorities. During the Emergency, though the means were disturbing, the goals behind some of the measures were good. After all, who could argue with the desirability of greater efficiency in government services, or with reduction in growth of population, or with trains running on time? In Andhra Pradesh, we had the benefit of the enlightened leadership of Vengal Rao and others and we were buffered from excesses. And that meant that we were able to implement Emergency policies, some of which had a positive, progressive thrust, with our conscience reasonably intact.

In 1976 I was informed that I was to be the collector of Hyderabad district. I called on Vengal Rao.

'Sir,' I told Vengal Rao, 'as you are aware, I am not very happy to be a collector.'

'*Telusu*,' the chief minister said in Telugu, 'I know.' It was well known that I was disinclined to be a collector in any district.

'But I want you to take charge of Hyderabad district,' Vengal Rao continued. 'You are needed here.'

I pointed out that I had worked in Hyderabad district before and that I had faced political pressures. I did not oblige the politicians then and would not do so now. Wouldn't it be best to avoid such unpleasantness?

Vengal Rao looked at me, stoic and unflappable behind his large, thick-rimmed glasses.

'Don't worry,' he said, 'that is why I wanted you. You will not succumb to pressures. I will support you.' This was true. Vengal Rao operated by finding the right person for the job and empowering him by extending full support. It was said that if Vengal Rao was with you, he was completely with you.

'But, sir, what if the ministers put pressure on me?' I asked.

'You need not oblige them. All you need to do is to listen to them. Listen, and then do what is fair.'

That sounded reasonable. But I was not finished.

'Sir, suppose you make a request? What should I do then?'

He replied, 'If I recommend something, you do it if it is the right thing. If it is not the right thing, tell me. You need not do anything that you do not think is fair or correct.'

I was reassured and joined as collector, Hyderabad district.[2]

Most of my tenure in the position coincided with the Emergency period. During that time, there was a tremendous push to implement family planning, particularly through vasectomy. We had district-level family planning targets and there was pressure from ministers on officials such as government doctors. But the patients on whom the vasectomies were performed were not always willing or fully informed and the methods employed were questionable. As a collector, I took special interest to cushion the administration in Hyderabad district from these pressures. That meant I would completely miss some of the targets, and I was happy to do so.

I had thought that the Hyderabad district administration was immune to family planning programme targets. I was mistaken. Late one evening, my son, Adithya, had a sudden problem requiring a minor surgery. I rushed him to Osmania General Hospital. The doctor on night duty had questions to ask me before examining my son. Had the father of the patient undergone a vasectomy? he wanted to know. Obviously, I had not cushioned the administration against family planning targets well enough, and after the incident, I redoubled my efforts.

During the time I was collector, Sanjay Gandhi, the son of the prime minister, visited Hyderabad. The Protocol Department of the government informed me that I was to receive him at the airport. It was to be on an informal basis as Sanjay Gandhi had no official position.

I called on Vengal Rao. I told him that it would be inappropriate for me as collector to receive someone who had no official standing, and as I wanted to avoid causing any embarrassment to the chief minister, I requested him to transfer me. He said that he would not transfer me, but that I could proceed on leave if I wanted to. I said I would take leave.

'I wish I could also go on leave,' Vengal Rao said, just as I was leaving the room.

During the Emergency, political leaders opposing the ruling party were sometimes detained. It was, obviously, a practice that I wanted no part in, but it was also very difficult to openly canvass against it. I had to find a more strategic alternative. As collector, I had to approve detentions in my district. I made it very clear to my colleagues in the Police Department that I would be extremely reluctant to approve any detention. In a way, I was alerting them to my attitudes in advance so everyone could avoid the embarrassment of having potential requests rejected. But it appeared that I had not got my intentions across fully. My brother Ramesh called me to say that his close friend and an activist leader, Venkaiah Naidu, had been targeted by the Hyderabad district police for detention. Ramesh had wanted to keep me posted. Immediately, I called the police and inquired whether that was, indeed, true. The police claimed that they had not put him in preventive detention. I had to reiterate my intentions and I tried to be more vigilant, but in situations like these, the reality of ground-level practice is hard to gauge.

One of my duties as collector and district magistrate was to send a report on the prevalence of bonded labour in my district and actions being taken if it was there.

In rural areas, power structures were entirely unequal and access to economic and social opportunities was restricted to a privileged few. Unable to approach banks or tap any other sources of capital, people had no option but to take loans from landlords when crops failed, during drought or famine, for health expenses, or for ceremonies such as marriages and funerals. The terms of the loans were often extortionary and the borrower would have highly unequal bargaining power. The borrower often worked for food, a pair of chappals and clothes, and a *gongilli* or shawl while the wages were set off against the interest due on the debt. If the borrower was unable to pay the interest, he or she would pledge his labour to the landlord, and in case of death or injury, his son's labour would be pledged, and then that of his son's son and so on. Sometimes, these terms would be recorded in formal written contracts that were signed and witnessed.

I doubted that bonded labour existed in Hyderabad district. Hyderabad was a metropolitan city with many opportunities and it seemed inconceivable that bonded labour existed in the surrounding areas. My officers reported that according to their inquiries, no one had heard of any case of bonded labour in the district. I sent in the report and thought that was the end of the matter.

But it was not. Once, on an official visit to a village in the district, I was making my rounds. It was my habit to informally talk with passers-by in their local dialect of Telugu to make them feel at ease. When I stopped and began to chat to an agricultural labourer, he told me about the hardships in his life. He mentioned that he owed some debt to his landlord.

'How do you repay the debt?' I asked him.

He said he had pledged his labour to the landlord to service the debt. Here was, essentially, a case of bonded labour where none was supposed to exist. It then dawned on me that there was a fundamental disconnect: the villagers thought the pledging of their labour for the servicing of debt was not bonded labour; it was just an age-old way to honour their debt contracts. When the villagers had told my officers there was no bonded labour in their village, we had not thought to inquire more deeply.

I realised that it would not do to just ask outright whether there was bonded labour. To locate cases of bonded labour, first one needed to identify indebtedness. When we began our inquiries, we were shocked to learn that not only did bonded labour exist, in some villages, it was common and there were written contracts which were enforced by caste panchayats or village elders who used pressure tactics, including ostracisation, to ensure compliance. I was determined to accord it the highest priority.

The district administration was mobilised to conduct 'a drive' to identify bonded labour and to release them from their bonds. A team of officials visited each village for a survey of indebtedness. An on-the-spot note for each village was prepared on the state of indebtedness, including the details of the terms and conditions of the debt for individual cases. If a case of bonded labour was found, the bonds were destroyed and the creditors had to undertake a pledge to not indulge in bonded labour in the future. The bonded labour drive was, naturally, not popular with the landlords since we were changing power equations.

Technically, it was possible to prosecute every person who had employed bonded labour, but I desisted. It would have been extremely problematic, operationally, to launch criminal proceedings on such a massive scale and obtaining timely convictions in a court of law would be very difficult. As a policy, we wanted to resort to prosecution only if there was serious resistance, partly because of the burden on the administration that prosecution imposes. Our goal was to change the social balance in the village, not to create acrimony. All the while, we made it very clear which side of the bargain the administration was on.

The drive to do away with bonded labour was most successful in Vikarabad division, where the revenue divisional officer, Rajaiah, worked with considerable enthusiasm and commitment. But in other places, too, the drive had an impact. The attitudes of the landlords, the labour and the administration in the district underwent a significant shift and many people were freed from their bonds. I had made an error in my initial understanding of the case. I stood corrected, and I was immensely grateful for it.

As collector, Hyderabad, I was to also monitor the implementation of the Land Ceiling Act. In a village economy, land was everything. In those days, being landless meant that you had no independent means of livelihood and therefore were entirely dependent on the landed for daily wage labour. Conversely, when most of the land in the village was in the hands of the few, power equations were firmly in favour of the powerful landowners. The Land Ceiling Act aimed to decrease inequity in landholdings by capping the number of acres a farmer could own, and anything in excess was taken away and distributed to landless farmers.

I wanted to send strong signals that I was serious about the implementation of land ceiling, even if it meant that it would, necessarily, invite the ire of the powerful and well-connected landowners in the area. I reasoned that if the Act was implemented with some farmers while the ones with large holdings and the well-connected got away, the measure would be flawed and meaningless. To signal my seriousness and to empower the officials who were implementing the Act, I asked for the files of the 'big cases'. These were the cases that most officials were afraid to touch as they pertained to former or current legislators and their immediate relatives. When I began to monitor the application of the land ceiling to them, my efforts caused discord.

I was accused, perhaps not unfairly, of discriminating against large and powerful landowners. But this was an eternal problem of administration: do you treat unequals equally? In the eyes of the law, everyone is equal, but in the real world of rural India, the inequality is staggering and the administrator cannot ignore it. Also, there was nothing personal in my actions, I was acting in the interest of efficiency: a great portion of the land in the villages was concentrated among the most powerful and applying the Act to them first meant a quick, and not unfair, way to achieve maximum results.

There were a few instances of improper declaration of assets by senior leaders. Since I was monitoring the important cases in the Land Ceiling Act, these cases came to my notice. I felt it was our duty to file the cases in court. However, doing so could have political repercussions. Therefore, I brought the situation to the notice of the government informally. If I was to continue as collector, I explained, I would have no choice but to file the case. I was hoping they would transfer me, but for unknown reasons, I was asked to continue as collector. Now I had no choice. I asked the officials to file the cases. Of course, I was less than cognisant of the political implications than, perhaps, I should have been.

Soon after, late in the evening, I got a phone call from Vengal Rao. Prime Minister Indira Gandhi had inquired about some cases in which there were allegations of political vendetta. Vengal Rao asked me to prepare a note for his use.

The Land Ceiling Act affected many large landowners. Some of the landed gentry in the Telangana area were from the Reddy community. They had thought that, as a fellow Reddy, I would be sympathetic to their concerns. I understood their mindset: it was their landholdings that was the basis for their social and economic standing, as well as the way of life that they had been used to for centuries. But, as IAS officers, we had our duties to perform. The vigour with which I approached my work with bonded labour and the Land Ceiling Act must have rankled. It was one thing to have someone act against your interests, but when that someone was one of your own, it would cut even deeper. A powerful landlord-politician was reported to have questioned in somewhat abusive terms whether I was, actually, a Reddy.

My efforts at eliminating bonded labour had yielded results, but with the Land Ceiling Act, I was less than successful. In April 1977, I was relieved of my responsibilities as collector, Hyderabad, to work with the Government of India as deputy secretary in the Department of Economic Affairs (DEA), Ministry of Finance. My Hyderabad posting had lasted a little over one year.

The transfer to Delhi was unexpected and unusual. I was to be on the International Monetary Fund and World Bank desk in the DEA. It was a prestigious posting and people vied to get it. In my case, I had been unaware of the proposal till my senior colleague had sought my informal consent. I did not give it as I did not want to leave Hyderabad.[3] Yet, to my surprise, I was picked up by Delhi and sent to the capital by the state government.[4]

The years in Hyderabad had been busy. In addition to my official work in Hyderabad, I had along with a few friends started a study centre. Years before, as an IAS probationer under training, I had attended a party for Mr Rau of the famous and highly successful Rau's IAS Study Circle in Delhi. At that time, as mentioned earlier, I thought of a study circle in Hyderabad for people, particularly from villages and towns, who had no access to coaching or study material. Along with some friends, I started an affordable, not-for-profit coaching centre for rural people writing the civil services examination. My friend and colleague from the police services, Anjaneyya Reddy, persuaded Mr Rau to give lectures and we got some of the best lecturers in Hyderabad to teach part-time at our centre. Many rural candidates from the study circle passed the civil services exams. In time, we had students from other states and our teachers began study circles of their own (though these were for profit) and Andhra became a model for channelling the rural population into the civil services.

I also assisted some friends in the start-up of a Telugu newspaper. There were numerous English-language newspapers of excellent quality in India. But there was a lack of high-quality local-language newspapers in those days. To fill the void, we encouraged the launch of a Telugu newspaper.[5] The logo and the format were finalised by the scholarly Abburi Ramakrishna Rao garu, the designated editor. The first edition was to be brought out from Kurnool and extended to Hyderabad. Preliminary assessments indicated that the circulation would be immense, but in the initial stages the company would not be able to raise adequate revenue through advertisements. The company decided against seeking the support of rich and influential people since that would have compromised the independence of the newspaper. Regrettably, it was decided to wind up the effort and sell the machinery, which was already installed in Kurnool, and settle the loans we had taken.

The registered name of the newspaper was 'Inadu'.

Subsequently, a newspaper with the same title, spelled the same way in Telugu, and with almost the same logo was started from Visakhapatnam. A Hyderabad edition followed, and it became extremely popular. It was an idea with great potential, but we could not execute it though others did.

We were living in interesting times. The Emergency had ended. Parliamentary elections had been held. Indira Gandhi had been confident that she would win. She thought she had been successful: public services were being delivered efficiently, inflation was down, growth had been revived, exports were up and imports were moderate. Many populist measures had been implemented, and, of course, to the continued amazement of the public, trains were still running on time. But Mrs Gandhi was handed a humiliating defeat in the elections. She was stunned by the result. She lost in every state, except Andhra Pradesh. One reason could have been that Andhra had been buffered from the worst of the Emergency excesses. In any case, the nation was elated that the Emergency was over.

It was heartening to see how soundly the people had rejected the subversion of democratic forces. People wondered why Indira Gandhi had been defeated in spite of making government offices more efficient and trains run on time. She was defeated, it was said, because she took away our right to complain. Whether for rich or for poor, in India, the right to complain was something very dear to us, indeed.

8

A GLOBAL PERSPECTIVE

IN THE STATE, PEOPLE KNEW ME AND LIKED ME, BUT HERE, AT the Centre, I was one of the many scores of officers. I became a cog in the wheel. Our office in the Secretariat, the North Block, had a massive central dome, neat manicured lawns and a striking cream-and-red sandstone exterior; it was impressive and the rooms were spacious. But everything in it – the people, the offices, the work – was overwhelming. (And I am compelled to note, the toilets too.) For Geetha, also, who was accustomed to spacious houses, the adjustment to our one-bedroom flat in Delhi was tough. But soon we began to make friends and settled down.

I was assigned to the World Bank desk in the Fund-Bank division, one of the most prestigious assignments.[1] This desk handled the Government of India's relations with the World Bank.[2] The subjects were entirely new to me. To compound matters, my colleagues in the department viewed me with wariness. Only Dr Manmohan Singh, who had pushed for me to be given this posting, greeted me with great warmth (and, perhaps, this added to my colleagues' wariness).

Given the atmosphere, I decided on 'a hundred-day low-profile strategy'. My old professor from Osmania University had an adage on his desk that read, 'Even a fish could avoid trouble if it kept its mouth shut.' That is what I did. I kept my mouth shut and my eyes, ears and mind open as I began to read, listen and learn. After a hundred days, I was confident that I knew almost as much as anyone else and I began to delve into my role.

Manmohan Singh was secretary, Economic Affairs. Scholarly and soft-spoken, Dr Singh would sometimes walk across the corridor to my room and ask me to examine files that did not concern my desk. My job was, no doubt, intense but it also made for great learning. In time, I was glad that he had brought me to Delhi.

In a short period of fifteen months, I got a sense of the range of issues relating to policies, programmes and projects of our country. In addition, since several projects involved state governments, I could appreciate the variety of conditions and multiple challenges in several states. It was impossible to get deep insights, but I was exposed to several perspectives on national policies, sectoral issues and complexities of project design and implementation. Above all, I was exposed to the intricacies of international competitive bidding and negotiations and discovered that I had an aptitude for negotiations.

The World Bank gave loans to creditworthy borrowers for the long-term economic development of the borrowing country. Borrowing countries, who also contribute capital and are shareholders, typically want to borrow from the World Bank as they can get the loans at a little lower than market rates and for longer duration. While it was in the interest of both the Government of India and the World Bank to negotiate and agree on projects, their approaches did not necessarily converge. India is one of the bank's biggest shareholders and also a large borrower. The Planning Commission and the Ministry of Finance preferred to obtain funds for projects which were strictly in conformity with their priorities and practices. The World Bank, on the other hand, had to demonstrate that they were not merely transferring money but creating a developmental impact, and they attempted this through sectoral or project conditionalities. The conditions prescribed by the World Bank often reflected an ideology or way of thinking which did not necessarily coincide with that of the Planning Commission, finance ministry or some other ministry in the government.[3] Further, the World Bank line was to make a minimum contribution and insist on maximum funding contribution by our government. From the Indian point of view, it was necessary to ensure that developmental conditionalities were not inconsistent with our own approaches.[4]

The World Bank team were systematic negotiators. They normally had several internal meetings in which any differences in perspective were worked out, and they came to the negotiating table with well-worked-out strategies. On the other hand, the Indian team did not have systems to evolve a coordinated negotiating position in advance. During the negotiations, ensuring a cohesive approach within the Indian team was an even greater challenge for us than negotiating with the World Bank team.[5] The World Bank had many negotiating advantages, but we had our advantages, too.

The World Bank needed a good borrower, and India, then, was a large and sought-after borrower. It was considered a better utiliser of World Bank funds than most other countries. Further, different sectoral divisions in the bank competed to have their projects picked up by India. We had levers as a large borrower and we could signal them to extract maximum benefit. These strategies had to be worked out in a careful manner, and in such a way that each member of the negotiating team knew only what he or she needed to know.

The negotiations in Washington, D.C. normally lasted five working days and, therefore, were very intense. After a couple of negotiations in which I was the coordinator, I developed what I thought was an efficient approach. Prior to the formal negotiations, I would have discussions at an informal level with my counterpart in the India Division at the World Bank. At the informal discussions, we would categorise the issues into three types: those that were mutually acceptable, those that were non-negotiable, and those that needed negotiation to be acceptable. The acceptable elements were carried forward to the formal negotiations, where they would be the initial focus so that formal negotiations could start out on a positive note. What was not negotiable would be clearly identified, and there was no point discussing them at that point; they were to be resolved before the formal negotiations began. It was the third area, the negotiable items, that we could work with. The negotiations on these aspects would normally be the objectives, the path to meet them, the pace of achieving the objectives and the rigour of conditionalities that should accompany the project or programme. It was these negotiable aspects which required careful deliberations.

Ultimately, negotiating was about people. Each participant had to satisfy his or her boss and, therefore, had a role to play. The purpose of the negotiation was not to convince the participant, but to convince the participant with the logic that she would need to then convince her boss. In doing so, we had to appreciate the logic and the flexibility of the mandate given by the bosses to each of the negotiators, and this had to be done at a semi-personal or informal level, in total confidence, and required a fair degree of mutual trust.

A senior official in the World Bank once asked me what was the secret of my negotiating success. I replied: I am a Hindu. If we commit a sin, we can do *prayaschit* or prescribed atonement, so we believe everything is negotiable. And, if we cannot complete a task in this lifetime, we can do it in our next life, so we can wait for a long, long time. Flexibility and time, it is a winning combination!

A little over a year after I moved to Delhi, I learnt that the job of technical assistant to the executive director of the World Bank was vacant. They were looking for candidates and, though I did not want to approach anyone or ask for any favours to get the job, I was gratified when Dr Singh proposed my name.[6]

When I received the orders to join the World Bank, I thanked Dr Singh.

He said, with his usual, quick smile, 'You don't have to thank anybody. You deserve it. In fact, it just got delayed a bit. That's all.'

It had been an eventful year and a half in Delhi. When I joined the World Bank desk in Delhi, Morarji Desai had come to power with a disparate set of political allies bound by righteous indignation and high moral ground. But there was a lack of cohesiveness. Fortunately, the finance ministry was headed by the distinguished civil servant H.M. Patel and we were shielded from the worst of it. That year, the government was preoccupied with their anti-Indira Gandhi sentiments, with the happy result that we had been left to ourselves to do our work.[7]

At this time, I had worked on my first book, *Multilateral Planning in India*, and it was released not long after I moved to Washington, D.C. It was a gratifying achievement for me because I was now an author of an academic publication in economics, my field of interest. In addition, Geetha and I had some old friends in Delhi and we could spend time with them. There was Narendra Reddy (whom I had first met as a research scholar with Osmania University) and his wife Kulsum, who were more than friends and became family. We also got to know the brilliant Dr Srinath Reddy and his wife Dr Sunanda. My batchmate and friend, P.L. Sanjeeva Reddy, and his wife Rama, became closer during our stay in Delhi. We were fortunate in that we also made so many lifelong friends: Jitender and Sunita Sibal, Valluri Narayan and Rajani, S. Vardhachary and Laxmi, and R. Swaminathan.

Geetha and I had not been keen to move to Delhi, but at the end of it, we felt our time there had been happy and eventful. I tell my children that it is better to wish not for what you want, but for what is good for you. In many ways, this stint in Delhi had been good for me, and I was now looking forward to going to Washington, D.C.

The Indian executive director of the World Bank, M. Narasimham, poured me a glass of Scotch. From the windows of his spacious living room in the stately Irene apartment building, we looked out over the night lights of the plush suburb of Chevy Chase in Washington, D.C. As India's executive director, Narasimham was a member of the World Bank board, which governs and supervises the operations of the bank. I had recently joined as his technical advisor. Our relationship had already become informal and we often joked in our native language, Telugu.

'Venu,' he confessed that day in his apartment, 'you know that you were not my first choice.'

'Yes, sir.' I knew that I was also not his second choice.

'I hope this will not stand in the way of our relationship.'

'Sir, you will get my loyalty as long as you deserve it.'

Narasimham laughed, 'Let us make a toast to that!'

I had moved to Washington, D.C. in September 1978. Initially, Geetha had had a hard time adjusting to the move. She was lonely in our rented house in the quiet suburb, where she saw no people, only cars zooming by.

'Venu,' Narasimham said as we sipped our Scotch, 'don't rent a house. You should buy a house.' There were, he pointed out, capital gains advantages to buying a house for the three years I was to be in Washington.

'No, sir,' I said. 'I want to have the freedom to quarrel with my boss, pack up and go without any hassles.'

He toasted again and said, 'That would make for an excellent relationship.'

On the World Bank board, the Indian executive director represented not just India, but Sri Lanka and Bangladesh[8] as well. It was customary for me, as his advisor, to be present in all board meetings and to occupy the chair of the executive director in my capacity as temporary alternate executive director when called upon by him. This meant that I was exposed to deliberations on global finance at the highest intellectual and professional levels. But, importantly, I was exposed to global finance at political levels, too. After all, as a creation of governments which are essentially political, it would be impossible for the World Bank to be apolitical.

In India, too, unforeseen events were again under way. In 1980, Indira Gandhi, who had been so resoundingly defeated three years ago, won the elections. I lost a bottle of whisky. I had made a bet with my senior and mentor, Rajamani, that Indira Gandhi would never come back to power. Along with her, Sanjay Gandhi again began to gain prominence and was a recognised extra-constitutional centre of power. On 23 June 1980, however, Sanjay Gandhi died in a plane crash and Rajiv Gandhi was inducted into politics.

During the initial period in the World Bank, I had to learn global finance. I was lucky to have been assigned to work under Narasimham. He initiated me into the basics of global finance. He was an able teacher and within a year, I became familiar with its complexities. Narasimham was a former governor of the Reserve Bank and had a razor-sharp mind, inexhaustible energy and enthusiasm and ready wit.[9] He was a diminutive man, but he could handle two or three cocktail parties followed by dinner and a nightcap, with just the two of us meeting over a bottle of wine after midnight. By the next morning, he walked into the office, fresh as a daisy.

In our work, Narasimham and I had a clear division of labour. He concentrated his energies on matters relating to the board and I on matters relating to India, especially operational issues and projects. While I was dealing almost independently with all issues relating to World Bank projects in India, Narasimham as executive director had to intervene with some boldness in one instance.

The World Bank was providing assistance to a fertiliser factory in India. The assistance was subject to the condition that the consultant company associated with the technology of the project be acceptable to the World Bank. An expert committee in India selected a global consultant company for this purpose. However, with a change in the government in 1980, a decision was taken by the government to change the consultant company in favour of a Danish firm owned by an Italian company. The World Bank felt that there was no reason to change the consultant company; the initial one had been selected after due process. In addition, the World Bank had doubts about the technology viability and cost efficiency.

The Indian government was confident that the World Bank would not dare cancel a prestigious loan given to an important borrower. But we in the executive director's office thought differently. China had just entered the World Bank, providing another more important potential borrower to the bank. Also, we sensed that the World Bank's discomfort with the technology was considerable. Therefore, Narasimham wrote a letter to the government that cancellation of the loan was imminent if we did not revert to our consultant company. He added that a loan cancellation would be unprecedented in the case of India, and the government should seriously consider the repercussions of such a decision.

But the government did not relent. The World Bank then decided to allow the loan agreement to lapse and was to send a letter to India to this effect. There was an informal suggestion from India that the letter not be dispatched while Parliament was in session. I put forward the suggestion and the World Bank obliged us on the timing of the communication.

R.N. Malhotra, who was at that time finance secretary, made out a case in support of the decision taken by the government, as was his duty. But he did not succeed with the bank. The decision was to remain unchanged.

A loan to India was cancelled for the first time in history. The government preferred to forego the World Bank loan of $250 million and went ahead with the implementation process with its own funds after hiring the consultancy company of its choice.

In contrast, months later, there was another incident where Malhotra could assert himself. Malhotra had again come to Washington, D.C. for discussions with the World Bank. I was assisting him in a meeting with David Hopper, the vice president of the bank. The World Bank was considering a loan of $200 million for a project in India. They were insisting on several conditionalities and Malhotra explained, in considerable detail, that India would find it extremely difficult to agree to them.

Vice President Hopper said, 'Mr Secretary, I hope you realize that two hundred million dollars is at stake for you. It's a lot of money.'

There was a long pause. Malhotra finally said, 'Mr Vice President, please keep your money with you.' Later, David Hopper called me. He requested me to pacify the secretary and hammer out a compromise, which we did. To me, it was striking that we could be assertive in this instance. It was because we were on strong ground.

After about one year of my joining the World Bank, Narasimham left the bank to join as Indian director in the International Monetary Fund located across the street.[10] We continued our friendship through the years and he bought a house in Hyderabad near mine so we could be close by after his retirement.

Narasimham was succeeded by H.N. Ray. An officer of the Indian Civil Service, Ray was a thorough gentleman and was known for his integrity. He was punctilious about details, precedent and legality, but less adept at handling US-style negotiations and functioning. This put me in an awkward position of having to advise the government on matters where the advice was contrary to Ray's views. Though he treated me as a son, I am ashamed to say that I was not mature enough and was, perhaps, arrogant. Once, during a disagreement, Ray protested at my style of arguing.

'Dr Reddy, I joined the Indian civil services before you were born. Learn to show some respect.'

'Sir,' I said, 'I will certainly come to your house and show my highest respect. However, in the office, if I feel you are wrong, I have to say you are wrong.' Of course, I should have been more polite. In spite of my attitude, Ray requested for my services to be extended from the original three years to five years.

By now, I had worked with Dr Manmohan Singh, M. Narasimham, and R.N. Malhotra. Dr Singh and Malhotra would go on to be governors of the Reserve Bank of India, while Narasimham had already been one. All three governors had a few things in common. They were all workaholics. Whatever the stress, they kept their cool. They encouraged others to brief them and valued those briefings (or at least, they acted like they did). And, however late they slept or hard they partied, by morning, they turned up at work fresh.

During my time in Washington, D.C., I did not participate in the negotiations with the Government of India since I was technically an employee of the World Bank. But I would guide the Indian delegation. The World Bank was also comfortable with my help in the resolution of any occasional issues related to negotiations. Often I would be invited, informally, to parties which were meant strictly for the Indian delegates and the World Bank negotiators.

But negotiating across cultures posed unique issues.

A negotiator from the World Bank team once said to me that they were having difficulty in understanding the Indian team.

'The English spoken by some of the officials from India is difficult to understand,' he said. 'It is a problem.'

'That's good!' I replied. 'I am glad you have a problem understanding Indian English. The Indian team has a problem understanding your English. So, now both teams share a similar disadvantage and there is no problem at all for negotiation on an equal footing.'

In another instance, the World Bank was insisting on a particular conditionality that the Indian team was not authorised to concede. The Indian team asked me to intervene. They felt the loan was essential and they wanted me to advise the government to agree to the conditionality. But I disagreed. I felt that the government was justified in not agreeing to the conditionality, even though the World Bank loan was essential for us. I told the Indian team that my advice was that they should break the negotiations and change their ticket and depart to India the next morning. As expected, the World Bank authorities contacted me. They began to explain their position. I informed them that the negotiations were off and that the Indian team had already booked their tickets for India the next day. The World Bank team said that they would get back to me soon. After hurried consultations, they informed us that they had changed their mind. They would not insist on the conditionality.[11]

In July or August 1983, I received a call from Hyderabad. The chief minister of Andhra Pradesh, N.T. Rama Rao, wanted to invite me back to the state. According to the rules, I was supposed to go back to India, but there were some who had quit the government and stayed behind. I, too, had gainful opportunities in the US and staying back would have meant a very comfortable life for the family. Also, Geetha had settled down very well and loved the US with its financial and personal freedom. We had made many close friends, Murali and Hema, V.N. Rajagopalan and Bhavani. She was reluctant to leave the US.

Professionally, too, Washington, D.C. had been a great experience. I had gained exposure to developments in the global economy, the theories and practices of macro-economic management, the economies of individual countries, the dynamics of power politics in a multilateral institution, the relationships between the World Bank and other multilateral institutions like the International Monetary Fund and the Asian Development Bank, and the conduct of economic diplomacy. There was an in-depth exposure to the relationship between a member country and the World Bank. The World Bank's assessment of the country's economy, the sectoral policies and the individual projects that were funded was a source of learning. I also took classes from Georgetown University and gained exposure to the academic atmosphere in the US. It was an immense broadening of perspectives from the state level to a global level.

Leaving the US meant a change in lifestyle for the whole family.[12] But I was clear. Our future was in our country and I did not want to work anywhere else but in the government. It was in the government that I could best serve the country and I was confident I would reach the top of my profession in public service.

When asked why I was leaving, I replied that in the US, I would exist in luxury, but in India I could live in comfort.

Before we left the US, Geetha and I called on Mr and Mrs Ray and they greeted us with their usual warmth.

'Venu, you are going back,' Mr Ray said. 'You could have easily got important and senior positions in the World Bank or International Monetary Fund. Still you are going back. I do not know why. But, I am sure you will come back one day as executive director.' My respect for him grew even more, as did my regret for the manner in which I had interacted with him.

The executive director from Bangladesh at the time, Ghulam Kibria, gave me parting advice.

He said, 'Venu, you are talented and a true professional. You are successful here in America because they value merit. When you go back to India, it is not only your merit that matters. They will categorise you by religion, caste, language and other things. This is how it is in South Asia. You have to be very careful when you go back home, and don't assume that only merit counts.'

I told the chief of the India Division, my good friend Ann Hamilton, about my departure to Andhra Pradesh. Ann knew a lot about Indian politics. She knew that the Andhra chief minister had once been a wildly popular, top-rated movie star, known for his roles as Krishna and Rama.

'Venu,' Ann said, 'how do you feel about working with a hero? I hear your state has elected a movie star to be a chief minister.'

'Ann,' I said, 'your country has elected Ronald Reagan as the president. In America you elected a B-class hero of B-class movies. In Andhra Pradesh, we have elected an A-class hero of A-class movies.'

Ann laughed and wished me best of luck. But she had a point, it would be an entirely new and fascinating experience working with a movie star.

9

MY DAYS WITH NTR

'VENUGOPAL REDDY GARU, AM I NOT A GREAT MAN?' NANDAMURI Taraka Rama Rao asked me one day. The chief minister of Andhra Pradesh sat on a sofa in one corner of his office as his kurta and dhoti, both a startling saffron, billowed around his enormous frame. NTR was a man with vision, flair, imagination and great instincts; he was dynamic, disciplined and had iron resolve. He was known to value honesty and he was hardworking.[1] NTR felt he was a great man, but of what use was that if others did not know it?

'Why, sir?' I asked him; I was in a mood to be playful and did not want to acknowledge his greatness too quickly. I was secretary, Planning, and mostly reported directly to him as he had kept the planning portfolio. In our one-to-one meetings, digressions like these were not uncommon.

NTR said, 'I was a very successful actor and a hero in many films. I was making crores of rupees. I sacrificed everything and joined public life, only to serve the people. Have I not sacrificed a lot?'

'Sir,' I replied, 'during the Independence movement also, many people had sacrificed everything for the country.'

'But I started a party on my own. In a year, I built a party and captured power. Is there a precedent in history?' he said. When NTR had started the Telugu Desam Party (TDP), his popularity as a god of Telugu cinema galvanised the imagination of the people. He founded his party on the cause of Telugu pride. Telugu people, he felt, were being disrespected[2] by the Centre and he won the elections as a strong and proud alternative to what he felt was the autocratic central regime of Indira Gandhi. He started his party in March 1982 and came to power in January 1983: his ascent was, indeed, historic.[3]

'Sir, I don't know if there is a precedent. Perhaps, not,' I said. Just watching NTR was a treat. He punctuated his sentences with grandiose eye expressions and dramatic, upraised gestures. He often came to the office in his saffron clothes, for a time in a Vivekananda-style dress with dangling headgear, and for a time in something that resembled a sari. I was never sure whether NTR was acting or not, and, I suspected, neither was he. But he was a charismatic man and he posed a real threat to the Congress leaders at the Centre.

NTR said, 'The Centre has been trying to destroy me. It has been using the Income Tax Department to harass me. They are influencing the courts, even the courts, to give me trouble! Yet, I am surviving. I am the chief minister and the people love me. Am I not a great man?' When he was confronted with cases filed by the tax department, he dramatised the situation by appearing before the court even though he didn't have to.

'Sir, since you have a lot of achievements and successes in all battles,' I said, 'perhaps, you are indeed a great man.'

NTR was not very happy with this guarded response.

'To get rid of me, the Government of India used the governor of the state, encouraged my legislators to defect, they even replaced me, but they failed. I fought back. I made a comeback.' On 15 August 1984, the governor, Ram Lal, dismissed the NTR government and installed Nadella Bhaskar Rao at the helm. NTR, who had just returned from the US after a triple bypass, flew to Delhi with the 161 legislators who were supporting him (out of the 295 in the Vidhan Sabha, clearly a majority). He sat in his wheelchair as he paraded his ministers before President Giani Zail Singh. The state was up in revolt, the media was sympathetic to NTR and everyone realised that if it could happen in AP, it could happen anywhere. On 16 September, NTR was reinstated as chief minister.

NTR continued, 'I fought back, I made a comeback. Even the *rakshasi* had to relent and reinstate me. Such a thing has never happened. *Na Bhuto, Na Bhavishyati,* it has never happened in the past, it will never happen in the future. Am I not a great man?' By rakshasi, or demoness, he meant Indira Gandhi.

At this stage, I relented, 'Sir, now I am convinced that you are a great man.'

N.T. Rama Rao and I had a unique relationship. I was not sure why he had called me back from Washington. Perhaps Dr Y. Nayudamma, an eminent scientist who had heard good things about me from Robert McNamara of the World Bank, had advised the chief minister to take me; NTR trusted Nayudamma's judgement. Also, since I had left the state years before, I was not, in NTR's view, 'polluted' by any close association with the Congress. For whatever reason, I had been called back to Andhra by NTR and so I was 'his man'. I would work very closely with him and would be privy to his many confidences.

Luckily for me, U.B. Raghavender Rao, the secretary to the chief minister, was my best friend. I told him that I was glad I was not secretary to the chief minister, but I was happy that my best friend was. That way, I could have access to the chief minister, without the responsibility of taking care of his interests.

Nandamuri Taraka Rama Rao, popularly known as N.T. Rama Rao or NTR, was immensely popular as a film actor from 1949 onwards, apart from being scriptwriter and directing and producing films. He was identified with Lord Krishna. On 29 March 1982, he founded the Telugu Desam Party to rid Andhra Pradesh of what he termed as the corrupt and inept rule of the Congress. He swept the elections in 1983 – thanks to his image, his 'sacrifice' in leaving the rich and glamorous life of an actor, his oratory, and his innovative electioneering style. He addressed roadshows criss-crossing all the districts, 75,000 kilometres in a campaign vehicle called 'Chaitanya Ratham'. He was sworn in as chief minister on 9 January 1983. By the time I joined the government, he had been in office for about nine months, but was still in the process of settling down. His term was interrupted by President's Rule for a month (16 August to 16 September 1984).

He was instrumental in forming the National Front, a coalition of political parties opposed to the Congress, the front that eventually captured power in 1989.

NTR came to power questioning Indira Gandhi at a time when people were declaring 'India is Indira and Indira is India'. NTR courageously went against the tide; though, of course, it was a key foundation stone in his ascent to power. NTR famously declared that the central government was a conceptual myth. The state government was a reality. The Centre, he felt, was only a Union of states. Technically, he was right; there was no mention of the central government in the Constitution. By asserting the primacy of the state government, NTR had become a leader amongst those opposed to the Congress party at the Centre. This made my job as secretary, Planning more complex than usual.[4] As a representative of an almost hostile state, I had to navigate the Government of India and the Planning Commission to ensure that the state government did not suffer in financial resources. While coming to agreements with them, I had to assure the leadership of the state that we had retained the mandated policy autonomy.

During the discussions for the Annual Plan of 1984-85, the officials of the Planning Commission pointed out that ongoing schemes should be fully funded before new schemes were financed. I was quite sure NTR was aware of the advantages of this. But ongoing schemes often reflected the priorities of the previous government, while new schemes reflected the priorities and poll promises of the NTR cabinet. As planning secretary for the state,[5] my mandate was to promote the new schemes, which meant some moderation in allocation for ongoing schemes. I had to justify the large number of new schemes at great length. But the Planning Commission insisted, and there was some back and forth.

'Let me be frank,' I said, finally, 'off the record. If the people of Andhra Pradesh wanted to give priority to ongoing schemes, they would have elected an ongoing government. I am sure that there will be similar change of priorities from time to time in the Government of India also. So, we should take a balanced view.'

The Planning Commission pointed out that funding a large plan would be difficult. I explained that we were confident that we could raise resources and could prune the plan. They persisted.

I said, 'Where does the Planning Commission get its inputs to decide on the availability of resources for us? From the state. Also, the Planning Commission has no more expertise or better information than the state in this regard. Perhaps the Planning Commission should respect the assurance of the state government about the resources that it can generate?' This position was accepted with some reservations and we reached an agreement. We all wanted to avoid an escalation of political differences.[6]

While the process of planning in Andhra Pradesh was already a contentious matter,[7] things were made even more interesting with NTR's dramatic manoeuvrings.

The National Development Council (NDC) meeting was scheduled for 12 July 1984. The NDC is the highest body to guide and promote development. It is presided over by the prime minister and consists of all chief ministers, select members of the Union cabinet, and the deputy chairman, Planning Commission. It is a forum for the states to put forward their concerns. Usually, the prime minister and the deputy chairman, Planning Commission, spoke first, followed by a speech by each chief minister. As planning secretary, I was to draft the speech to be delivered by my chief minister. We spent hours with him, preparing a speech that reflected his priorities and ideologies.

As per normal practice, copies of the final, approved speech were sent to the Planning Commission in advance. Rao Sahib, the cabinet secretary, called and asked me whether this was the authentic copy of the speech to be delivered later in the day. I was surprised; such an inquiry was highly unusual. But I had seen NTR rehearsing the speech just early that morning and confirmed that this was, indeed, the speech that NTR would be delivering at the NDC meeting.

At the NDC meeting, the chief secretary and I sat behind the chief minister. The speeches were to be made in alphabetical order, and Andhra Pradesh was to go first among the other chief ministers. The folder with our speech was lying on the desk in front of NTR as he rose.

From behind, I could see NTR's hand reach into his pocket and pull out a folded paper. The speech we had so carefully prepared, which focused on planning and economic considerations, lay unopened. We were mute with shock as NTR unfolded the paper and launched into a highly charged political oration. He protested the dismissal of the Farooq Abdullah government in Jammu and Kashmir. He denounced it as going against the spirit of the Constitution. He attacked the Union government for its high-handedness and manipulation.

As NTR began reading out a statement on behalf of himself and three other chief ministers – Jyoti Basu (West Bengal), Ramakrishna Hegde (Karnataka) and Nripen Chakraborty (Tripura) – he was interrupted by chairperson Indira Gandhi. The NDC was not a political forum, and was convened to discuss the Seventh Five-Year Plan, she said, but the three other chief ministers insisted that he be allowed to complete his statement.

At the end of the impassioned speech, he announced that he was walking out of the NDC meeting. The three other chief ministers also followed him. As he walked out, he signalled that we were to stay seated. We were not sure why; perhaps it was to brief him about the ensuing proceedings.

On the dais, the prime minister and the deputy chairman, Planning Commission, engaged in hushed consultation. Soon an announcement was made that all officials of the chief ministers who had walked out were to withdraw from the meeting. Embarrassed and still reeling from surprise, we picked up our papers and left.

I was furious at being so deceived. I felt indignant since it was I who had assured the cabinet secretary that NTR was going to deliver our prepared speech. Later, it was explained that the decision to walk out was taken the night before, but it had been kept a closely guarded secret. NTR worried that if any whiff of his intentions came to be known to the Centre, the order of speaking would be changed. The dramatic effect of making the first speech and disrupting the meeting at the start would have been lost.

We were assured that we were kept in the dark so that we would not be put in the uncomfortable situation of having to prevaricate on any questions about the speech. I did see the point. Had I known beforehand, I would indeed have been in an unenviable situation while answering the Planning Commission's unusual query. Though I was somewhat mollified, I was not convinced about whether we were kept in the dark for the reasons explained to us or whether we were simply not trusted. With this, I wondered whether NTR distrusted me as a person, a professional civil servant, or an intellectual. Or was it because I was an IAS officer? Many chief ministers at that time were not sure whether an IAS officer was loyal to the state or to the Centre. NTR treated me as an intellectual. His attitude towards intellectuals was very respectful, but was it only an outward respect? I was never sure.

It was said that NTR viewed intellectuals as his harem. Whenever he found an intellectual whom he fancied, NTR liked to court him, but once the intellectual settled down in the harem, he would lose interest and pursue other intellectuals. Others said he treated intellectuals as a movie star would treat his heroines. It was a well-known formula: to keep the audience interest alive, the hero had to change his heroines periodically.[8]

In his dealings with civil servants, things were equally uncertain. NTR's impression of the bureaucracy was based on his brief experience decades ago. He told me that he had once worked as a clerk in the sub-registrar's office.

'In those days,' NTR said, 'we used to wear a coat. We hung the coats on our chairs in the morning. At the end of the day, the peon used to put some money in the coat pockets. At first, I did not know what the money was for. Then someone told me that it was my share of the money taken as bribes in the office for that day. All we had to do was just wear the coats with the money stuffed in them and go home. I simply could not stomach it. In three weeks I quit the job.' His early experience and, perhaps, his subsequent transactions convinced him that the bureaucracy was almost universally corrupt.

It was a surprise to all of us that UB, who had been the principal secretary to the Congress chief minister, T. Anjaiah, was taken by NTR to be his secretary. Though UB had, in NTR's eyes, been 'polluted' by his work with a Congress government, NTR trusted him completely.

UB was a tiny man of startlingly fair complexion. He was brought up by his uncle, who ran an Udupi hotel in Vijayawada. UB was more than a friend; he was a brother. We had shared our quarters years before, when I was assistant collector in Chittoor. We had called each other Sac and Jac. I was Sac (senior assistant collector) and he was Jac (junior assistant collector). He was close to Amma because he had lost his mother and we were often in each other's house. UB won the trust of NTR because he was a man of outstanding moral and intellectual calibre, and remarkable courage. He was a civilising influence over NTR, often protecting NTR from himself. UB was more than a secretary; he was a protector of the state's interests. He was perhaps the only person in the establishment whom NTR could not overrule.

Though UB had NTR's trust, that was not the case with most others in the establishment. NTR felt that he did not belong to the establishment. To strengthen his position in power, therefore, NTR had to try to change the systems. He created an authority, the Dharma Maha Matra, to act against corruption amongst government officials, but disciplinary action against some of the senior officers was uneven. His obvious distrust and erratic enforcement of disciplinary actions increased the distance between NTR and the senior bureaucracy, and this discord was strengthened by a hostile Union government.[9]

In interactions with civil servants, NTR's approach to problems was essentially through some instinct which went beyond normal analytics – and that was his strength, and also a weakness. This instinctual approach was sometimes unreasonable and deflecting his arguments required some ingenuity.

In one meeting, the chief minister wanted to have a very large annual plan. It was patently unrealistic. Vithal, who was deputy chairman, Planning Board, explained that additional taxes would have to be raised to fund such a plan and proposed a few ideas on taxation schemes and fees. NTR dismissed them all.

'Our government,' NTR said, 'is not a kirana shop, counting pennies. We are dedicated to the welfare of the poor. For rapid development we should think big, invest in the future. We cannot burden people with fees and taxes.' NTR wanted more ideas. But all the ideas that Vithal advanced were unacceptable to the chief minister.

'Vithal garu, you are a brilliant man,' said NTR. 'You are an eminent intellectual; you are a wise man; you are an internationally recognised expert. That is why I am asking you for ideas. But you are not giving me any new ideas.'

'Sir,' Vithal said, 'I am sorry. I have no more ideas. But let me suggest somebody who does. He, and he alone, is capable of showing you the path towards painless resource mobilisation.'

NTR said, 'Tell me. Tell me, who is that?'

Vithal said, 'Please look behind you.'

Behind NTR was a framed picture of Lord Venkateswara. With that, the meeting closed.[10]

In spite of his eccentricities (and sometimes because of them), NTR's regime had deep and considerable impact. He brought about institutional changes that would fundamentally alter existing economic and social structures. There were two major ones that I was actively involved in: the creation of mandals, and the abolition of the village officer system. Was NTR's motivation in replacing the new structures genuine social change or was it to politically capture the new structures? It was not entirely clear. Yet, whatever his motivations, the changes had the potential to disrupt feudal dominance; and working on them was an exciting opportunity for me.

While taluks as basic units of revenue administration had been inherited from the British days, blocks and their headquarters were brought into existence in the 1950s and 1960s as developmental units. Often, in the rural areas, they were co-terminus. But blocks and taluks had become outdated as the population had exploded over time and the nature of services demanded by the people had changed. NTR wanted to split each taluk or block into three or four units to bring the administration nearer to the people. I had worked on a technical paper years before which tried to apply centre-place theories for the location of public services. The exercise resulted in the identification of different tiers for a hierarchy of growth centres and a hinterland (in terms of area and population) to be served by each centre.[11] I was surprised when NTR called my attention to the technical paper and requested me to use the area approach for the reorganisation of taluks and blocks into revenue mandals and developmental mandals – the latter being co-terminus with rural self-government.

I explained to NTR that such a reorganisation could ensure smaller units with changed boundaries, but that it would not necessarily serve his political intention that his party be able to capture the reorganised locally elected bodies. For the measures to hold up in a court of law, the redrawing of boundaries had to be based on clear-cut criteria and detailed analysis and therefore it might or might not serve political ends. NTR explained that he was willing to take the risk.

He said, 'Reddy garu, I can face the consequences of my decisions. I am like Lord Shiva. I can swallow poison and hold it in my throat.'

The task before us now was to identify the headquarters and the hinterland for the new administrative units. We used detailed data, maps and computer analysis. We had state- and district-level consultations. The plan was finalised at the cabinet level.[12] As expected, the orders redrawing the boundaries were questioned in court as having a male fide motive. The case went from the high court to the Supreme Court. But in the end, since the reorganisation was based on rational and defensible criteria, the government won the case. With the disturbance of old structures, political alignments were redrawn and this provided an opportunity in which new political alignments, favourable to NTR, could gain a foothold. I was indifferent to the political consequences. I believed that the implementation of the mandal system would be a positive change as it would make the administration more accessible to the people.

A second major institutional change was the abolition of the age-old village officer system. Each village had a set of local persons appointed to maintain its revenue accounts (patwari or karnam) and village munsif or, in some areas, patel, sometimes split into mali patel and police patel. Mali patel was in charge of revenue collection, while police patel was in charge of reporting crimes and related matters to the police authorities. In some parts of the state, the village munsif performed the functions of both mali patel and police patel. Traditionally, they represented the administration at the village level and they were part-time employees. They were village residents and the post holders were, more or less, though informally, hereditary appointees. During training, I had seen the munsif and karnam at work. I saw how the karnam and munsif had the potential to work together to capture power and information in the village. Therefore, I realised very early on the social impact the abolition of village officers would have on existing hierarchies.

NTR wanted to abolish village officers and replace them with full-time government employees. The traditional system perpetuated feudalism, so in a way, the change implied erosion of authority of the entrenched powerful local families, giving way to opportunities for the less powerful. But, there was a downside. The local village officers were effective and had deep local knowledge and a trusted working relationship with the villagers; with the change, all these would be lost. In addition, as people argued, full-time government employees recruited through open competition could be amenable to corruption. Yet, I believed that the new system, however corrupt, would allow anybody to access the services of the government, which under the old system would have been impossible without the consent of the village officers.

The change had not only economic but social and caste implications, generally adverse to Reddys and Brahmins, who were traditionally munsif and karnam. To bring about these changes, NTR trusted Mr Kasipandian, revenue secretary, who did not belong to any of these castes. It was not a function assigned to the planning secretary, but the chief minister desired that I assist Mr Kasipandian. We had consultations and we went to meet eminent lawyer Nani Palkhivala in Mumbai. Despite considerable political opposition and bureaucratic resistance, NTR pushed the change through. It would disrupt the status quo and it would introduce a new balance that was more monetised and less feudal.

Many of NTR's changes were often opposed by MPs and MLAs. Some of NTR's policies (as well as his erratic ways) were not popular even within his own party. Yet, NTR had brought about, or tried to bring about, positive changes. It must also be recognised that he inducted a large number of well-educated and well-qualified people to the legislature. At meetings, Telugu Desam Party MLAs and MPs were given lectures on various subjects by experts, including on matters relating to budgets. But for all the attempts at empowerment and knowledge dissemination, NTR did not tolerate anyone questioning his leadership or authority.

Once, I was with NTR when he met with some TDP legislators about their concerns. There were a dozen or so legislators in NTR's room. The legislators, one by one, expressed their concerns. They, too, were democratically elected representatives, they pointed out. They wanted to have more say in the functioning of the government.

NTR was gracious. He agreed with everything they said. He extolled the virtues of democratic values in eloquent terms and superb Telugu. He assured the legislators that he was a defender of democracy. Gratified, the legislators turned to leave.

As they walked to the door, NTR looked towards me. He said in a voice loud enough for the departing legislators to hear, 'Venugopal Reddy garu, you see those fellows? Those are the fellows who won their election by parading my photograph on the streets. If you put one rupee on their heads and auction them in the bazaar, they will be sold for half a rupee. And they say they represent the people! Those are the fellows who are trying to teach me how to run the government.' The hapless politicians could do nothing but continue on their way out.

It is not widely known that it was NTR's pioneering efforts that made Andhra Pradesh the leader in computer education and the use of technology in the government.

NTR was very excited about the National Informatics Corporation (NIC) establishing its regional centre in Hyderabad. The NIC would provide free computing facilities for the government at the state and district levels. I worked with T.L. Sankar, principal secretary, Finance and Planning, on this.

Sankar and I felt that the NIC's programme did not preclude the state government's own efforts at computerisation, which would ensure greater autonomy. There were many advantages. A computer, we felt, was like a fountain pen. It was to be used by each person and everyone was to feel a sense of ownership about it. State government offices were to be computerised in a decentralised manner and at some stage, they were to be connected. We also argued for the early installation of computers at district offices by the Planning Department, which was accustomed to managing data, and for immediate installation in individual departments where it would be a natural fit, such as in commercial taxes. Technology could also reduce the exorbitant overtime payments that were typically incurred for the preparation of budgets by the government's printing press.

NTR lived in a curious dual reality. In one he was a lead player in a celluloid mythological drama, taking place in a bygone era. In the other reality, he was a proponent of change and champion of modern technology. It was unlikely that he understood computers, but he instinctively equated computerisation with modernisation and became excited, in a way that was almost childlike, at the thought of computers being used in his state. It was no surprise that the chief minister readily agreed to the proposal, and A.P. Technology Services Limited was established for computerisation of the state government. It had (if I recall correctly) a modest capital of Rs 25 lakh.

The opposition was vocal in its criticism. They called it a wasteful expenditure by the state government.[13] Again, NTR pushed it through. Ironically, the foundation for modern e-governance, for which Andhra Pradesh became a leader in the country, could be attributed to this initiative, led by a man who dressed in saffron robes and talked like he was Lord Krishna fighting against the ancient evils of the world.[14]

There were ideas which were, at first, promising and even successful. But then they went awry. One of these was the Crucial Balancing Scheme. I made a proposal to the chief minister that a fund should be kept at the disposal of the collector and district magistrate to invest small amounts in incomplete projects, the ones that had reached the 'last mile' of implementation but had stalled.[15] This scheme was called the Crucial Balancing Investment

Scheme, and the fund was allocated to each district. There were detailed guidelines on the use of funds which restricted their use only to last-mile investments. The chief minister liked this innovative scheme despite the advice from his trusted aides that it would go against the principles of appropriate planning and budget procedures. When it was initially adopted, the scheme worked very well and was considered extraordinarily productive, popular and useful.

However, in some districts, the legislators started demanding explanations from the collector, who was in charge of disbursements, as to how the amounts were being distributed in different areas within the district, especially in relation to their respective constituencies.[16] Soon, the scheme in Andhra Pradesh deteriorated to one of automatic funding of schemes suggested by the legislator in the constituency.

Over the years, the impact of the scheme went far beyond the state. The Government of India adopted a similar scheme kept at the disposal of a member of Parliament with significant discretion within very broad guidelines. What was intended as a crucial balancing investment meant for last-mile investments became a source of patronage by elected representatives. I cannot but take some blame for this initiative in Andhra Pradesh which resulted, perhaps, in a not-so-healthy practice at an all-India level, and in several other states.

NTR also introduced many popular schemes, and one of the most important was the Rs 2 a kg rice scheme. The scheme would provide rice through the Public Distribution System at Rs 2 per kg for a large section of the poor. Despite considerable criticism from the central government in those days, NTR was totally committed to this programme.

Instead of subsidised food distribution, I argued for an employment-guaranteed scheme for many reasons. First, the data at the time seemed to indicate that the poorest of poor did not have enough money to buy a kg of rice even at Rs 2.[17] In addition, I felt that employment guarantee would help empower women and the landless.[18] NTR was not prepared to consider the employment-guaranteed scheme as an alternative, or even as a concurrent scheme with the Rs 2 per kg scheme. He made an interesting observation.

He said, 'As it is, farmers in the villages are finding it difficult to get labour for their farm operations. If we give the employment guarantee, it will make life difficult for farmers in the villages.' In evaluating the interests of the farmers and the landless labourers, NTR clearly weighed in with the farmers.

Consistent with NTR's priority to farmers' interests, he was keen to take up new irrigation projects. In this regard, the idea of betterment levy, a tax or fee on land, was advocated by NTR to partly fund new irrigation projects.[19] I argued that before considering the betterment levy, the government should ensure that the water rates in the existing irrigation systems should be able to pay for their maintenance and upkeep. I pointed out that farmers in Telangana and Rayalaseema would resent the levy: farmers in coastal Andhra did not even pay for the maintenance of the existing irrigation works, while Telangana and Rayalaseema farmers, who did not have the benefit of canal irrigation in the past, would be forced to pay for the irrigation works now. NTR was from coastal Andhra. He brushed aside my objections.

He said: 'Krishna and Godavari delta is a gift of Sir Arthur Cotton. It was a gift given to these farmers. We cannot now levy all sorts of charges on them.' I argued that farmers in Telangana and Rayalaseema regions, who were dependent on well irrigation, were forced to invest in digging wells and also pay for electricity. I felt strongly about the issue. I reminded him that I was from Rayalaseema and that betterment levy was highly iniquitous if even the cost of operations was not collected from canal-irrigated lands. After considerable discussion, there was a stalemate. To my knowledge, nothing much happened in this regard.[20]

In May 1988, tragedy struck. UB had taken leave to travel by bus to Vijayawada, to visit the Kanaka Durga temple. Early morning, he was on his way to the temple on his friend's scooter when he was hit by a lorry. He died instantly. It was a huge loss to me, to NTR and to Andhra Pradesh. I did not go to the funeral, as it would have been too painful for me. I was told that NTR did not display distress on UB's death, though he did visit UB's wife and made some provision for her future. But with UB's death, NTR was left unprotected. There were no shields between him and vested interests and slowly, the balance tilted in favour of those interests.

After about two years of working in planning and with NTR, I developed a fatigue with both. More important, I was disillusioned with the relevance of the planning work that I was doing. I was missing the intellectual challenges that I had become accustomed to in the World Bank and wanted to take some time from work to pursue academic interests. NTR agreed.

'How can I say no to what you want to do?' he said. 'But I hope you will guide me whenever I want.'

I said, 'It will be a pleasure and honour for me, sir.'

In the next few years, I would alternate between academic pursuits and work in the state government. But my interactions with NTR became less frequent and less close. I missed my friend UB dearly.

On 31 October 1984, NTR's bête noire, Indira Gandhi, was assassinated by two of her bodyguards. Her son, Rajiv Gandhi became prime minister. Elections were coming up in 1989, and NTR was certain he would defeat the relatively inexperienced Rajiv Gandhi. In December 1989, the Telugu Desam Party lost the election to the Congress. The voters, for whom NTR had been a darling, had rejected his policies, eccentricities and style of governing. NTR's entire persona as both a hero and a leader was built on the idea that he was loved by the masses and their unexpected rejection was a severe blow.

With the new government, I sensed that I was unwanted. The chief minister's office hinted that I was not welcome to make the routine courtesy call on the new chief minister, Dr Marri Chenna Reddy. When the finance secretary, Government of India, Gopi Arora, proposed that I move to the finance ministry in Delhi to help with Fund-Bank work, I gave my consent. But by the time the formalities were completed, the position I was allotted became joint secretary in charge of currency and coins, since my predecessor was given an extension. It was a far cry from Fund-Bank.

My senior colleague, B.V. Rama Rao, said, 'Venu, there is a curse on officers who work as joint secretary, currency and coins. They are never empanelled to become secretaries to the Government of India.' That prospect did not deter me from accepting the job. Did I have a choice?

Working with a hero turned out to be quite an unforgettable experience. I had heard of the dark side to NTR's personality, though I was not exposed to it. Many people detested him, and he was said to have been as autocratic and ruthless as his long-time opponent, Mrs Gandhi. In the media, he was compared to Hitler. (Of course, this left NTR unfazed and he used it to his advantage. What was wrong with that, he wondered. NTR said there was no better *Desa Bhakta,* a person devoted to his country, than Hitler and like Hitler, NTR too was devoted to his country.) With me, NTR was almost always respectful and warm.

NTR was a study in contrasts. He was erratic one minute and resolutely determined the next; outwardly he was a master of melodrama while internally he was coldly unsentimental. He could be both cutting and extraordinarily considerate. I had once mentioned to him that, as a diabetic, I liked to have my lunch around 1 p.m. In almost all meetings, he remembered this and either completed the meeting in time or postponed it. He also shared with me his firm views on diabetes.

'Don't waste your hard-earned blood by giving it for blood test,' he said. 'I am a diabetic. Every morning, I try to smell my breath by blowing air into my palms. If it smells bad, it means my sugar is high.' To help me manage my diabetes, he offered to send diabetic meals to my home.

There are many memories I have of NTR.[21]

I remember one day when we sat in his office at one of our one-to-one meetings.

'Venugopal Reddy garu,' NTR said, 'how is my handwriting?'

'It is very good, sir,' I said.

He pulled out a piece of paper and showed me his writing. The words, in red ink, were in both English and Telugu.

'Are the words not like a string of pearls?' he asked, as he looked eagerly at me.

Here was a man, larger than life. NTR had power, glamour, riches. He had millions who adored him. He felt he was Shiva, Vishnu, a sanyasi, a reformer, a hero. And yet, here he was, looking at me, his expression almost childlike, for the smallest hint of praise.

'Yes, sir,' I said. 'They are, indeed, very good.'

10

RELEARNING POLICY AND PRACTICE

THE PERIOD BETWEEN SEPTEMBER 1985 AND APRIL 1990 WAS a time of intellectual and professional churning. In 1985, I was planning secretary in the N.T. Rama Rao government and in 1990, I left Andhra Pradesh to work in the ministry of finance in New Delhi; during that time, I oscillated between academia and government work. It was a time for relearning, and to some extent, unlearning.

I went on academic deputation and study leave not because I was unhappy with my work. I had been closely involved in planning and finalisation of the seventh five-year plan. The exercise had been challenging and I felt that we had done a good job of planning in Andhra Pradesh.[1] Yet, in India, we had not been performing well in terms of many fundamental socio-economic indicators such as poverty levels, life expectancy, literacy, etc. We were missing something.

The world over, there were significant new developments that needed to be studied. In advanced economies like the US and the UK, there was an effort to increase the role of the market and reduce the role of the state in economic activities. This was led by President Reagan and Mrs Thatcher. In the UK, privatisation of public sector enterprises was widely practised. In developing countries also, there was increasing trend towards greater role for the markets. East Asian economies which adopted market orientation or business-friendly philosophy experienced rapid economic growth, developed very fast and were called miracle economies. China, which was a communist country, not only joined the World Bank and adopted many of its policies, but became a very enthusiastic borrower from the bank. There was impressive growth in China also and its market orientation was described as socialism with Chinese characteristics. In contrast, our performance was not very impressive as a planned mixed economy.

Personally, I was disillusioned with communism after my experiences during a visit to Leningrad (St Petersburg) in 1982. One day at lunch in Leningrad, I was given a standard menu. There was soup on the menu. When my waiter bought the soup, I told him that I did not want it. He said it was his job to serve the soup so I had to have it served. It was another waiter's job to clear the soup and after my soup was served, I had to wait for the other waiter to clear it. Another day, to make a telephone call to India from my hotel, I had to spend four hours going from one desk to another. Once, I was out walking and saw a long queue before a small storefront. I asked what the queue was for. It was for a broomstick. Everyone was waiting for hours for one broomstick each. Though we had heard of these queues and inefficiencies, experiencing them through these small incidents was an eye-opener. Life in a totalitarian state was unbearable. It was absurd. It was painfully evident that the USSR's model of development was failing. Yet, it was the USSR that had been the beacon for leftist thinking and its failure would leave us intellectually adrift.

At home, too, communism was on the wane. It was no longer as attractive to the youth in our country. The split in the Communist Party of India and the infiltration of some communist leaders into the Congress diluted the movement further. Some of the excesses during the Emergency in the name of the poor added to the disappointment with 'progressive' ideas.

I knew also that much work had been done that questioned the assumptions made about functioning of the market and functioning of the state, and their interrelationships. I wanted to understand and explore these theoretical contributions, particularly their relevance to the Indian context.[1]

In short, I wanted to explore the developments in theory,

policy, and practice. I look a leave of absence from my job to pursue academic opportunities full-time. I was deputed to Osmania University for six months (and at the same time, as requested by the chief minister, I was honorary consultant to the Planning Department, Government of Andhra Pradesh).[2] Later, I moved to Administrative Staff College of India for one year, followed by a stint to London School of Economics and Political Science as a visiting fellow for over three months.

The stint away from work proved invaluable. During that time, I re-examined fundamental ideas that would change my way of thinking intellectually as well as professionally.

Some of the ideas that I engaged with looked at the relative and dynamic roles of state and market. There were failures with both state and market. While the failures of markets were well known (externalities, information asymmetry, etc.), failures of the state, such as public choice theory in relation to government and regulation, etc., were being examined at the time. There were other factors too common to both state and market inefficiencies such as the principal-agent problem. Further, it was evident that markets could not exist without the legal and institution framework determined and enforced by the state. Therefore, the discussion was not state or market but state and market. Considering this, it was not constructive to view policy from an ideological standpoint (pro-state or pro-market). Instead, an assessment of the relative strengths and failures of each was important since these could be constantly changing, particularly in the light of technological developments.

In addition to the roles of state and market, what was of great importance was the evolving interface between the two. One of the original justifications for public enterprises was that they were natural monopolies. But the idea that natural monopolies could be unbundled (aided in large part by technological advances) and that the resulting components could be amenable to competition was a significant development. It was clear that with technology not only could monopolies be unbundled, but the state could provide services more transparently and regulate more effectively. All this would lead to new and innovative functioning of the state. Markets could also be more connected and immense gains in efficiency were possible. This made a tremendous difference to the relative efficiency of the state and the market.

Today, many of these ideas seem self-evident, but in the mid-1980s in India – both in the government and in the academia – it was not that clear to most of us. Perhaps these ideas took time to percolate down to us. Perhaps we were wedded to our old ways of thinking. Whatever the reason, my time in academia helped me explore the changing developments and thinking around the world.

With this background, I examined the situation in our country. The state–market discussion was further complicated by the societal and cultural structures that India inherited. Much of the country lived in medieval conditions. Endemic discrimination (caste, gender, rural–urban, language, etc.), weak trust among people outside immediate social circles, the lack of validity given to contract and transaction-based interactions were some of the many unique issues we faced.

In my work at the time, I had made some observations on the political economy aspects of our country. Firstly, in India, the burning issue was not state versus market, but it was state and market versus the people. Secondly, Gunnar Myrdal had described India as a soft state (where rules and regulations are seldom enforced) while I described it as a hard-soft state: hard on 90 per cent of the people and soft on the other, highly privileged, 10 per cent. Thirdly, I had observed that this 10 per cent consisted of organised labour (both in public and private sectors), select industrial houses and a rentier class encouraged by the political system and that this 10 per cent not only determined policy, they also cornered the benefits of state action (such as subsidies) and prevented essential reforms that would endanger their self-interest. I called it the 'Tyranny of the ten per cent'.

It was the resistance to fundamental changes by this 10 per cent that was a major impediment to the reforms that were attempted in Rajiv Gandhi's New Economic Policy in the 1980s. The New Economic Policy tried to strengthen markets, but could not bring about the fundamental shifts needed for the reforms to succeed. I also concluded that attempts to change the role of the state in a piecemeal fashion or a technocratic response was inadequate to meet the challenges unless there was a change in the belief that the government always does good for the people and market should always be viewed with suspicion. For example, the New Economic Policy wanted physical controls to be replaced by financial controls but was not prepared to accept that controls themselves might not be necessary. In another example, the New Economic Policy undertook reforms in the working of public enterprises through memoranda of understanding, but the rationale for continuing state ownership was not addressed. These reflected an inability of the state to move forward with effective reforms. I called this 'stalemate in state action'. It resulted in a stalemate in state–market interface.

In short, in addition to inefficiencies inherent in markets, public institutions and conditions that markets needed to function effectively were weak or even non-existent in our country. We had a deeply entrenched privileged class that was resistant to a market-enabling ecosystem. The world changed, theory changed, but we didn't change fast enough. These observations on the Indian context formed an important part of my academic work at the time.[3]

My understanding of the roles of the state and market as well as the state–market interface was deepened with practical experience. In the 1980s, privatisation was not mentioned in India, while that was ruling the roost in the UK under Mrs Thatcher's leadership. Soon after my academic leave, I was given charge of public enterprises and for some time was the chief executive of a development finance institution, the Andhra Pradesh Industrial Development Corporation. In those capacities, I was working on the state and market from various vantage points.

In 1989, I enabled the privatisation of a public enterprise, Allwyn Nissan Ltd. It was, perhaps, the earliest case of privatisation in India. It was an exercise in the retreat of the state. At the same time, I worked on establishing a venture capital company with the assistance of the World Bank – a case of advance of state. There was an attempt to privatise another public enterprise,

A.P. Scooters, but unfortunately it could not be liquidated. This was a case of a failed state unit with no exit option.

Between my academic and professional experience, the insights gathered on macro-economic policies were helpful in the Ministry of Finance, Government of India, dealing with the balance of payment crisis and reforms in 1990-93. This experience also helped greatly when I was a member-secretary of the Committee on Disinvestments of shares and public enterprises (chaired by Dr C. Rangarajan), where we submitted, in 1993, the first policy document on the subject in the Government of India. All these helped me significantly in my functioning as deputy governor and governor. Finally, in the Finance Commission, we could work on the issue of fiscal implications of ownership and functioning of public enterprises keeping in view the dynamics and practicalities of the state–market interface.

More importantly, I realised that a set of beliefs or ideology may not be relevant for all times and in all societies. The distinction between socialism and capitalism and advanced and developing countries was useful for analysis but for the conduct of policy and programmes there were common concerns. It was therefore necessary to be constantly aware of evolving theories, policies and practices, applying them to the specific circumstances of a country or a society. This idea of drawing from various beliefs and ideologies and arriving at what appears to be a appropriate solution to the context became the guiding principle for me. The fundamental concerns and moral compulsions that guide a society were as important as they always had been; the question was: would the state serve these compulsions better or would it be the market? Depending on the country and the circumstances, the answer could be the state or the market, but more likely, it was both together.

11

THE POWER OF GOLD[1]

I WAS IN NEW YORK CITY. IT WAS SEPTEMBER 1990. JUST A few months before, I had joined as joint secretary, in charge of Balance of Payments (BoP), Department of Economic Affairs (DEA), Ministry of Finance.[2] Papers and files were on the table in the hotel suite of Dr Chakravarthi Rangarajan, deputy governor, RBI. Rangarajan, a thin man whose professorial air reflected his scholarship, was already a seasoned and respected policy maker in India. At that time, I was just getting to know him. Rangarajan and I were in the hotel room, preparing for an important meeting with Standard and Poor's (S&P) on a credit rating for India.

S&P was one of two important global credit rating agencies and its rating was an assessment of the sovereign's likelihood of discharging its financial obligations. A good rating was critical for maintaining credibility and continued interest from lenders and investors. A good rating, for us, was thus crucial in preserving the ability of Indian borrowing entities (private or public) to raise money.

Rangarajan and I had to make the case that India deserved a rating higher than the one the agencies were intending to give us. I was new to this, while Rangarajan was a veteran. One of the main concerns of the rating agency was the uncertainity surrounding the Vishwanath Pratap Singh government. V.P. Singh, a composed, neatly dressed man from a royal family, became the prime minister during a period of enormous turmoil. He was at the helm for less than a year, but in that time, there was a threat of war from Pakistan, a public tussle with powerful business houses, the kidnaping of a minister's child that led to a controversial release of convicted terrorists, the Ram Janmabhoomi movement and, as the recommendations of the Mandal Commission report (which expanded reservations to backward classes in government employment and educational institutions) were being implemented, there were violent agitations, bandhs, protests and cases of self-immolation by youth. The V.P. Singh government faced political uncertainties, it was true, but I wanted to argue that, despite any uncertainties, India had continuity of political systems. Whatever the turmoil, our political transitions took place smoothly. On these grounds, I felt that a strong case could be made for a higher rating. Rangarajan cautioned me.

'Venu,' he said, 'we should be sure of the facts. We should analyse the situation. We can give a positive twist, but we cannot afford to be overenthusiastic and excessively optimistic in our presentation. Remember, our own professional and personal credibility could be at stake. We may have to deal with these agencies in the future.' This was wise counsel: never compromise long-term professional credibility while pursuing advocacy that the compulsions of immediate circumstances demand. In the end, we were not unhappy with the rating that was finally confirmed: BBB / Stable on the long-term scale and A2 on the short-term scale.

The rating was short-lived. Within a few months, Standard and Poor's downgraded our rating. Rangarajan proved to be right to be cautious; we landed in a balance of payments crisis less than six months after the presentation. It was a crisis where both the government and the RBI, in sheer desperation, resorted to using our stock of gold to raise foreign currency to discharge our immediate international obligations.

It was not as if the crisis landed from nowhere; there were already stresses. What were the origins of stress on our balance of payments that led to the crisis? The root cause can be traced to unsustainable fiscal policies in the early 1980s. The finance minister, Pranab Mukherjee, presented three budgets from 1982 to '84, that increased plan allocations to all ministries to spur growth. India was already in an internal debt trap by 1986. The banking system was forced to invest more than half of its deposits in government securities. The RBI had to prescribe high levels of statutory liquidity ratio (SLR), making it obligatory for the banks to make such investments.

Prior to becoming the prime minister, V.P. Singh was the finance minister in Rajiv Gandhi's government from 1984 to '87. His budgets of 1985 and 1986 reduced taxes and liberalised imports. Rajiv Gandhi kept with the trend when he took over the finance portfolio in 1987. Sustainability of high fiscal deficits was already in question and there was a spillover of the fiscal stress to balance of payments. The RBI sent out warnings, but the deterioration in fiscal conditions and external situation continued. While imports were liberalised, exports did not increase correspondingly. This was mainly because the exchange rate was favourable to imports and unfavourable to exports. The exchange rate policy did not allow the necessary adjustments in import–export balance. Overall, the current account deficit increased. As a result, large capital inflows were needed to finance the deficit.

The government decided to obtain financing through external commercial borrowings and specifically to encourage public enterprises requiring foreign exchange (as well as those who did not) to take recourse to external commercial borrowings. In addition to ECB, large-scale recourse was taken to foreign currency deposits from non-resident Indian deposits by a variety of means, including provision of exchange guarantee by the Reserve Bank. In view of the scarcity of foreign exchange to finance import of oil, the banks, in particular SBI, raised short-term loans. Since the problem of availability of foreign exchange was not entirely short term, the banks were asked to roll over the short-term loans repeatedly, with the result that the short-term loan outstanding of India began to climb steadily to huge proportions.

It also became necessary to draw down foreign exchange from the IMF under the compensation and contingency financing facility available for meeting unforeseen contingencies in BoP, such as drop in export earnings or steep increase in oil prices. The government also decided to draw down the foreign exchange reserves that were built over a period. There were also some foreign currency balances available with overseas branches of Indian banks. The RBI had issued instructions to banks to repatriate all surplus balances back to India so that they could come under the reserve pool. All these details were known only to select senior officials in the RBI and in the Ministry of Finance, the secretary, the chief economic advisor, the senior economic advisor and myself as joint secretary.[3]

Extensive recourse was taken to finance current account deficit through short-term borrowings at high cost, with built-in vulnerability. In addition, the extent of resources drawn down from forex reserves was understated, the true level of reserves overstated and huge exposure of banking system to short-term forex liabilities not recognised. The acute stress in balance of payments and needed policy responses were known in policy circles and were pointed out to them at that time by the RBI. However, the policy responses were not forthcoming and recourse to short-term palliatives aggravated the stress.

In brief, political expediency to spur growth at any cost from 1982 led to an unsustainable situation by 1987. Warnings by the IMF, World Bank, and in particular by the RBI about the difficult conditions were ignored. From 1989, domestic political uncertainties and leadership changes made the necessary bold policy action difficult, if not impossible. In the meantime, developments in the erstwhile USSR and the First Gulf War in 1990 affected our economy adversely at a time when our political leadership was not well placed. Though there was not yet a full-fledged crisis, these were some of the stresses that the country was facing that portended serious troubles ahead.

How did the stress on balance of payments turn into a crisis? Our domestic economy was highly vulnerable in view of unsustainable twin deficits for several years, that is, fiscal deficit requiring large amounts of borrowings by the government domestically and current account deficits requiring dependence on borrowed capital from external sources. Global developments impacted India adversely, particularly on account of the steep increase in oil prices and disruption of trade with the USSR, which was undergoing turmoil that eventually lead to its collapse. These coincided with political uncertainties in our country, affecting the capacity to take timely corrective actions. The frequent changes in the government did not inspire confidence that they would be in a position to successfully manage the severe challenges. This resulted in a liquidity crisis, that is, minimal foreign exchange was not available to keep the economy going.

The vulnerabilities of our economy were well known, and that remedial actions were overdue was recognised from as far back as 1987. Approaching the IMF was not ruled out, though not favoured. But the political leadership was not willing to act with timely responses. In August 1988, a National Front was formed with V.P. Singh as convener. Prime Minister Rajiv Gandhi was hesitant to take measures that could be unpopular and hence deferred approaching the IMF and other actions. The hesitation to approach the IMF continued when V.P. Singh formed a government in 1989. The budget speech of Prof. Madhu Dandavate noted the stress and articulated the inevitability of hard choices, but fell short both in approaching the IMF and in taking remedial measures. The agitations associated with the implementation of the Mandal Commission report diverted the attention of the government to non-economic issues.

From September 1990, there was a sharp rise in the import bill of oil due to the Gulf War. It rose from an average of $287 million per month in June–August 1990 to $671 million in the next six months.

The Gulf war that broke out in August 1990 reached its peak in 'Operation Desert Storm' (17 January to 28 February 1991). This transformed the stress on our balance of payments into a full-blown crisis. A disruption in oil supplies and higher oil prices due to the Iraq war weakened the external position of the country. In addition, there was disruption in exports to West Asia and workers' remittances from overseas, especially from the Gulf region. The deposits made by non-resident Indians dried up and there were large-scale withdrawals. This led to a reluctance by global creditors to open letters of credit in the banking system for cross-border trade. The officially stated level of foreign exchange reserves available with the RBI included the reserves which were invested by it in the overseas branches of the SBI. This meant that some of the foreign exchange declared as reserves was not readily available for use by the RBI when needed, since the SBI itself suffered serious constraints in raising liquidity in the overseas markets. In fact, the SBI was finding it difficult to roll over commitments in excess of $2 billion it had run up to finance our oil imports.

By November 1990, Chandrashekhar, a serious, dynamic man from an agricultural background, who had founded a socialist group within the Congress party, became prime minister. He had been waiting for long for the position. He replaced V.P. Singh with outside support from Rajiv Gandhi, but within a few months, the support was withdrawn.

As the stress on India's balance of payments intensified, the global economic environment deteriorated rapidly.

All the facilities readily available for us from the IMF were used up in July 1990, in September 1990, and in January 1991.

The foreign exchange reserves declined from $3.1 billion at the end of August 1990 to $896 million by mid-January 1991. In 1990-91, the trade deficit increased by 26.5 per cent over the prior year, and net invisibles declined mainly on account of workers' remittances. The current account deficit was 3 per cent of GDP, but financing it became a problem due to lack of confidence in our creditworthiness. The short-term credit which was available to our canalising agencies (public sector agencies such as MMTC and STC that had a monopoly over import of key bulk commodities) became expensive. The rate which was at 0.25 per cent over LIBOR (London Interbank Offered Rate, the rate at which the world's banks charge each other for short-term loan), went up to over 2.0 per cent. The volume of external commercial borrowings approved dried up, and non-resident Indians were withdrawing their deposits even at the cost of loss of interest.

By the end of March 1991, gross official reserves stood at $5.8 billion (little more than a month's imports). But the point is, this level was after economising on the use of forex and obtaining $1.8 billion from the IMF in January.[4] As all sources of extraordinary financing were being exhausted, the balance of payments crisis turned into a crisis of confidence in our ability to manage the situation.

In brief, imbalances in our economy were evident from the mid-1980s. Disruption in trade with the erstwhile USSR due to its breakup added to our vulnerability in the external sector. Timely corrective measures such as improving the fiscal position and reducing the dependence on external capital could not be taken due to uncertainties in the political arena in the late '80s. This exacerbated the stress and made us vulnerable to crisis by 1990. The crisis was triggered by the sharp increase in oil prices following the Gulf War. We had to desperately respond to this grave situation in a period of political transitions and turmoil.

What did the crisis mean for us? It meant that we did not have enough foreign exchange to continue to import even essential commodities like oil and fertiliser, nor had we enough foreign exchange to continue to pay interest on the loans or repay principal instalments for the debt that the government, banks and corporates had incurred. Potential lenders were not willing to lend and those who had lent before were not willing to renew their lines of credit. Foreign banks were not willing to open trade letters of credit in favour of Indian banks unless another foreign bank stood guarantee. The world lost confidence in India's capacity to honour its external obligations or obligations to non-residents in foreign currency.

Since I was heading the Balance of Payments Division at the time, I was continuously associated with the design and implementation of measures intrinsic to these historic events – events that saw our country move from despondency in 1990 to hope by 1993.[5] In these three years, there were three different prime ministers, three finance ministers, three RBI governors, three finance secretaries, and three chief economic advisors.[6] This did not make things easy, though of course I had the advantage of having worked with many of the functionaries previously.[7] Regardless of the churn, the crisis had to be managed and we explored our options. What options did we consider and act upon?

The use of gold for managing the crisis was certainly not the first or preferred option. Its use was one part of our response to the crisis. There were many other important options.

The options included default in honouring obligations, either by design or because it was forced upon us; promoting exports and compressing imports; obtaining short-term credits; seeking support from bilateral and multilateral sources, including the IMF; confidence-boosting actions; loans from private sources; and use of gold. These options had to be considered for managing the crisis, keeping in view the need to get back to normalcy. Credible assurance of medium-term measures had to be spelt out. These included reforms accompanied by assistance from the IMF and the World Bank. In this background, each option had to be assessed.

There was a strong consensus that default on any payment obligation was unthinkable in the long-term interest of the country. Some of us in the government resisted even attempts to analyse the path and consequences of default. I am aware that such an analysis was done in the RBI. Both S. Venkitaramanan and Deputy Governor C. Rangarajan were firmly of the view that under no circumstance would a default be allowed to occur. But the governor ordered that technical work on disaster management be undertaken by the RBI in secret, so that we were not unprepared if matters went out of control.

At one stage, my opinion was asked about freezing outstanding NRI deposits with banks in India. This meant that NRIs would not be able to temporarily cash their foreign currency deposits. I suggested that such an option should not even be brought up in any discussion or any background document. Once the nation lost the confidence of the Indian diaspora spread over various countries, its self-respect and pride would stand seriously undermined.

One of the steps taken was to make all imports other than essentials expensive by insisting on huge cash margin (so as to impound rupee cash resources, which would have the impact of dampening the demand for foreign exchange). A number of items which were freely importable under open general licence were transferred to licensing category while others (imports essential for purpose of exports) were exempt from these restrictions. Import of capital goods was restricted and confined to financing made available by development financial institutions. Fiscal measures such as surcharge on fuel to discourage consumption were also taken. As already mentioned, all the facilities readily available from the IMF were used up.

Export promotion was difficult in the short run and, in fact, the export sector had to be protected from adverse consequences of the crisis to avoid interruption. Severe import compression measures became inevitable. However, they were applicable to all commodities except essential ones. The restrictions could also be withdrawn at short notice.

I had the unpleasant task of executing severe import compression. The chief controller of imports and exports had to get clearance from our division for every import of more than Rs 1 crore. At one stage, I had to sit on sixty files. Canalising agencies had to get our approval for imports of more than Rs 20 crore. We were monitoring the availability of reserves on a daily basis, to implement import compression. The more stringent the import compression measures, the greater were the distress signals to the world at large about our situation. I pointed out the limits to administrative measures in alleviating the stress. We had to look at ways of getting short-term credit, which was increasingly proving difficult.

There were several suggestions that the STC or the MMTC, which were canalising agencies, should be asked to seek short-term credit facilities directly from overseas suppliers. I had consistently advised against this because I believed that this would not yield any positive response. Even if we got some small amount of credit and a brief respite, these existing suppliers would view this as a reflection of deeper distress. The risks of seeking short-term credit from suppliers would be disproportionate to the relief. Unfortunately, the media reported that an unsuccessful approach was made by a canalising agency.

In one particular case, there was an offer made by a French bank to give a short-term credit facility to the Industrial Development

Bank of India. As it was being processed and cleared in the government, the proposal was withdrawn by the offering bank for undisclosed reasons. Strictly speaking, it was not illegal, but it was a violation of the commercial practices in international markets. The finance secretary, Bimal Jalan, was furious and ordered that the bank be blacklisted for future dealings with India, brushing aside my repeated advice to the contrary. I approached the additional secretary, S. Kanungo, and pleaded with him to convey to Jalan that we cannot afford to get into an open adversarial relationship with anybody in difficult circumstances. An open admonition of a foreign bank by the government would get wide publicity in financial circles, prompting the markets to probe into the reasons behind it, thus bringing into the open our creditworthiness issue. Kanungo conveyed my strong feelings to Jalan, and convinced him to revise his orders.

There were also suggestions to boost the foreign exchange reserves by securitising future export receivables. It meant that identified future export earnings would be mortgaged to one or more specific lenders, who would front-end the payment from them (after deducting the agreed charges and fees). In the process, such export earnings would not be part of the general pool of forex flows into the country. This option was not pursued since any such securitisation would undermine the comfort of unsecured foreign lenders and the international banks that were opening letters of credit on behalf of commercial banks in India for normal trade transactions.

The leeway available in commercial agreements entered into by the government with other governments and agencies was also explored. The intention was to delay such payments, without technically incurring default. Large payment obligations were looked at to explore the scope for temporary relief. One such agreement that involved large payout was identified as the arms purchase contract signed with the Swedish firm Bofors. My hope was that when the order was placed with this firm, as is often the case, it was linked to some offset arrangement, such as mandatory export of commodities from India. I, therefore, sought access to the relevant papers and found that all instalments for the Bofors arms supply had to be paid promptly without any reference to the timing of fulfilment of any offset export of commodities from India to Sweden. Our exercise proved to be futile since all such agreements were watertight in terms of discharging our obligations to pay for imports.

Prior to the onset of the foreign exchange crisis, there were many global banks and financial institutions offering us loans and short-term credits. Japanese investors were among those who were very keen to lend even towards the end of 1990. However, as the crisis unfolded, all these 'friendly' bankers disappeared. Many times, my calls were not returned. That was a bitter experience.

Bilateral support from Germany ($60 million) and Japan ($300 million) was also availed. We approached the IMF for balance of payments support, which involved some conditionalities.

Even as we were negotiating with the IMF, a new crop of unrecognisable institutions surfaced with offers of 'millions of dollars' to India. All of them were looking for the government or the RBI or SBI to acknowledge the offer and agree to consider the loan or deposits. It was common knowledge that these offers were not genuine. Issue of such mandates or authorisations to raise money could be misused to bring funds from questionable sources, or commit other forms of fraud. Yet, there was considerable political pressure on us to examine such offers and engage them in discussions. As the pressure mounted, a communication was sent to all the banks reiterating that they should not even acknowledge any such offer from anybody or any institution.

Typically, my response to people meeting me at the behest of ministers or influential persons to bring in funds as a deposit was that they should do so under the standard NRI deposit scheme rather than seek any specific letter or communication from a public sector bank or the government. There were cases where I was advised by the office of the state minister for finance or the Finance Minister's Office to meet individuals who claimed to be able to give billions of dollars to India if only we authorised them to do it. I used to meet such intermediaries, but never gave anything in writing. Often, I insisted on getting more and more details about the sources, till the other party was exhausted. In one case referred by a minister of state, I asked for the contact details of the person or institution offering the loan. I got it after some reluctance from him, and when I tried to reach the party offering the loan, I found that it was the telephone number of a Holiday Inn in New Jersey.

In one instance, there was pressure on me to meet an individual who was offering a few million dollars of loan. I suggested that we meet the next morning because I was busy at work, but the person insisted on meeting me the same evening as he had booked a train ticket to Ahmedabad that night. Clearly, he could afford to lend us millions of dollars but not change a railway ticket. In another case, one of the persons who offered such money and with whom I had to deal repeatedly turned out to be a tailor regularly engaged by a political leader.

Venkitaramanan, as RBI governor, called me and said that there was a large loan offer and that we might have to consider it seriously as an exception. He mentioned that Prime Minister Chandrashekhar wanted this offer to be examined carefully. After considerable discussion, we agreed that we should not give any written authorisation or acknowledgement to the party. We could depute an officer of the SBI to meet the banker representing the counterparty, at the premises of the counterparty's bank. An officer from the SBI visited the designated overseas branch which was in a tax haven located in the Caribbean. The SBI officer came back with the report that he visited the designated branch, that the party did not turn up and that the bank informed him that a bank account opened by the said party at one point of time was quickly closed.

Jalan's successor was S.P. Shukla, a senior IAS officer, who would handle the most acute phase of the crisis. Shukla called me and said that I should be prepared to travel to Brunei that night to secretly obtain funds. I explained to him that it was not possible to bring significant amounts of money and still keep the source of money a secret. Shukla was sympathetic to my view, but explained that he was under instructions from the finance minister, Dr Manmohan Singh. I suggested that R. Krishnamurthy, officer on special duty in the Ministry of Finance, who was on deputation from the SBI, would be in a better position to represent the government and handle such a large value transaction, as he could represent himself as a banker and negotiate, instead of doing so on behalf of the government. After a while, the finance secretary called me, presumably after consulting the minister, and said that I should be ready to go to Brunei personally, the same night. He also clarified that I should not even inform my family about my trip and that I should be prepared to travel by a special private plane which was in readiness at the airport. He said that I need not worry about a visa. However, I was advised to be ready with a packed suitcase (which I did, telling Geetha that I was going to Mumbai on an urgent mission), and wait in the office for final approval. Finally, a little before midnight, the finance minister's office sent a message that I could go home since the proposal had been called off.

Despite such pressure to get into dubious deals, we thankfully retained the sanity to evaluate genuine cases and take quick decisions. One example relates to the purchase of aircraft by Air India. Air India was awaiting delivery of planes ordered earlier, before the crisis. The funding arrangements proposed for the purchase were disrupted because of the prevailing crisis. So, the management of Air India suggested an innovative package: the planes would be leased by Air India from a special purpose vehicle in Japan created for the purpose. The proposal was promptly cleared. There was no disruption in accepting the delivery of planes and hence no adverse impact on our reputation.

All these illustrate how desperate our balance of payments position was, and how we could have become gullible victims of fraud or faced reputational risks in our position.

Forex reserves consist of foreign currency reserves and gold held by the RBI as part of reserves. Our law stipulated the rate at which gold has to be valued at a fixed rate. At the time of the crisis, this happened to be one-fortieth of the market rate. An ordinance was issued in October 1990 that facilitated realistic valuation of gold. Thus, the stock of gold valued at $521 million in September 1990 was correctly valued at $3,678 million in October 1990. Correspondingly, our forex reserves went up from $3,514 million to $6,212 million, though foreign currency assets dropped from $2,515 million to $2,102 million. This step was aimed at boosting confidence in our capacity and in our determination to honour all our payment obligations.

We reached the low level and maintained at that level only because of severe compression of imports and recourse to short-term borrowings. The low level of foreign currency reserves, however, does not fully represent the distressed situation.

The presentation of the interim budget for 1991-92 instead of a regular budget meant that the government could not initiate credible policies to boost confidence in the economy. We had to manage the situation with ad hoc measures till the current, relatively weak, government was replaced by one with a mandate that was up to the challenges.

Among the measures considered was one for the sale of government properties outside the country, particularly the Indian embassy building in Tokyo. There was no agreement within the government about pursuing this. This was the penultimate option considered before the use of gold.

Gold is no longer used as money or as a fixed unit of account for financial transactions, but it has not lost its uniqueness as a store of value universally. Gold is the ultimate globally accepted currency in times of turbulence. It is not easy for a democratically elected government to decide on the eve of elections to utilise its stock of gold holdings. Yet, we had to consider it.[8]

The proposal for using gold was based on the recommendations of the governor, RBI. He suggested that the government hand over gold to the SBI on lease to raise forex currency and add to reserves for utilisation by the RBI. The proposal was accepted and we had to work out the details and implement the decision. The government had to first hand over the physical metal to the State Bank, but lease or sale of gold by the government required the approval of the cabinet. Any agreement would need the vetting of the draft by the Legal Department. We did not want the file to make the rounds in the various ministries, both to maintain utmost secrecy and to avoid any risk of delay in processing. We circumvented this procedure of involving other wings of the government by inserting a clause in the agreement that the SBI would abide by any changes in the agreement that might be made subsequently. We went ahead with implementing the agreement and handing over gold to the SBI, in anticipation of formal approvals as required by the rules of business. Technically, the SBI could not sell gold that it had only leased, and hence we felt that leased gold could be used as collateral, but through a sale with a repurchase option.

This transaction of the SBI with the Union Bank of Switzerland in April 1991 fetched us $200 million. We reckoned that any sale and repurchase of gold would amount to temporary use of gold by the SBI, and hence the lease arrangement could be defended in public discourse if necessary. Further, this procedure reinforced our contention that we were facing a temporary liquidity crisis and the leased or pledged gold would be recouped. After all, in true Indian tradition, we pledged or leased gold to get over the crisis but did not sell gold in the ultimate analysis. The SBI returned the redeemed gold in a globally acceptable form to the government. The government sold most of it to the RBI to add to its gold holding. This became part of unencumbered foreign exchange reserves held by the RBI.

In addition to using the gold belonging to the government, we had to supplement with the use of gold with the RBI. The RBI had to ship 47 tonnes of gold to the Bank of England to raise $405 million. Broadly speaking, foreign exchange reserves consist of gold held with the RBI and foreign currency reserves available with it. A forex reserve means that it is readily available for use by authorities and acceptable in international markets. Hence, conversion of gold into foreign currency and using such currency would not have been out of order. We could have sold the gold, but pledging the gold was considered appropriate for two reasons: one, the sentiment attached to gold in our society and two, to signal that our problem was temporary.

One view during internal discussions was that the use of RBI's gold itself would have been a sign of desperation. On the other hand, it was argued that gold available in the forex reserve was meant to be used when necessary. If a policy decision was taken that it would never be used, the financial markets in their assessments might not include gold as part of forex reserves. The decision to use the gold through a pledging arrangement for purposes of raising foreign currency resources demonstrated our willingness to use it when needed, and our confidence that there would be enough money soon.

There are some twists to all tales and the one about the RBI's transportation of its pledged gold was no exception. The van that was transporting gold from the vaults of RBI to the airport in Mumbai in a night-time operation punctured a tyre. While the sound of the tyre burst drew attention, more noticeably still, as the van came to a stop, armed guards escorting the truck jumped out and took position all around it instantly. This invited curiosity among a few bystanders (mercifully there were no mobile cameras at that time to record the scene!). As the gold reached the airport and was loaded on a chartered plane, someone took a photograph. Fortunately the plane landed safely at its destination with all the gold intact.

The use of gold by the government and the RBI happened in a short period of four months, April to July 1991, and it was retrieved in a few months thereafter.[9]

When we were working on the balance of payments crisis, our work became more than just a full-time job. For those of us dealing with the situation, crisis management was almost literally a 24/7 obsession.

At one stage, Jalan was so frustrated with some of his interactions in the cabinet that he said to me: 'Venu, you don't seem to understand. My relations with the cabinet are more complex than India-Pakistan relations.'

Shukla told me, 'Venu, I am not able to sleep properly. For the first time, I am taking sleeping tablets.'

In the middle of this, my daughter's wedding was fixed for the end of May 1991. I took leave for the wedding preparations, but Shukla asked if I could shift the venue from Hyderabad to Delhi. Of course, this request was not a serious one, but that is how tense the situation was.

Once the crisis was behind us, I went on a pilgrimage to Tirupati and offered prayers at the Balaji temple there. Kulkarni, my colleague at the RBI, did one better. He offered to get his head tonsured as a traditional token of gratitude to Sri Venkateswara Swamy.

It was appropriate: Sri Venkateswara Swamy, the Lord of the Seven Hills, had a stock of 200 tonnes of gold. Outside of central banks, He was, perhaps, the holder of the largest stock of gold in the world.

12

ALL THE FM's MEN

On 21 May 1991, Rajiv Gandhi was assassinated. He was a leading prime ministerial candidate.[1] A few weeks before, the Chandrashekhar government had resigned. That meant, we had a caretaker government at the Centre while elections were under way. The acute phase of the balance of payments crisis in 1991 coincided with these traumatic developments in the political arena.

The crisis had to be managed in a political vacuum till a new government was formed. On 21 June 1991, Congress veteran P.V. Narasimha Rao was sworn in as the prime minister. Rao had been a grass-root political leader with decades of experience in ministerial positions in the Union government and in Andhra Pradesh, where he had also served as chief minister. He was a surprise choice, but proved to be more than equal to the challenges. The tasks ahead of the new leadership included managing the exit from the crisis and initiating reforms. Rao, who acquired the reputation of being modern India's Chanakya after becoming the prime minister, proved that it is not charisma but statecraft that matters.

India was fortunate that Dr Manmohan Singh became finance minister in 1991 since he was closely involved with the policies in the past, good and bad. He was best equipped to appreciate what had been done in managing to survive the crisis. He had the knowledge and experience to carry forward on the path already set to restore confidence, provide appropriate credibility to what was done and, above all, bring about a paradigm shift in the public discourse on developmental policies. He was required to evolve a new framework that should govern our policies. For this, he built a team that he could trust.[2] Balance of payments and external debt continued to be under my supervision, but now the focus was shifting from crisis management to exit from the crisis and a reform path.

The prime minister's tasks at this stage were to manage political processes to implement the remaining fire-fighting measures and the envisaged reforms. As an interesting aside, when Rao was sworn in as PM, I asked my guru, B.P.R. Vithal, who was his friend, about what he thought of our new prime minister.

Vithal said, 'PV is generally an outstanding number two but a disastrous number one.' Then we recalled that President's Rule was imposed when he was chief minister even though the Congress party was in power in Delhi. Further, he was home minister in the central government when the Sikh massacre took place after the assassination of Indira Gandhi. After a few months into the office as prime minister, it was very evident to all of us that he was on track to be an exceptionally successful PM. I asked Vithal if he had changed his views. He replied, 'PV is still number two, he gets his directions from Washington, D.C. – IMF and World Bank!' As always, Vithal was unusually perceptive: the fact remains that the IMF and World Bank not only provided financial support but also contributed to the evolution of our policy through research, advice and conditionalities. However, what was needed was political sagacity that would solve the problems which had accumulated over a decade due to the absence of political courage. Rao understood the complexities of Indian society well enough to be able to influence the course of history at a critical time.

The budget speech of Dr Manmohan Singh on 24 July 1991 was forthright in admitting the reasons for the crisis, and the criticality of balance of payments to restore normalcy.

'There is no time to lose,' he said. 'Neither the government nor the economy can live beyond its means year after year. The room for manoeuvre, to live on borrowed money or time, does not exist any more. Any further postponement of macroeconomic adjustment, long overdue, would mean that the balance of payments situation, now exceedingly difficult, would become unmanageable and inflation, already high, would exceed the limits of tolerance.' The agenda for reform included fiscal consolidation and changes in industrial and financial sector policies. Manmohan Singh had already made a statement in Parliament on 18 July 1991 explaining the gold transactions by the SBI and the RBI, thus obtaining endorsement of whatever was done to manage the acute phase of the crisis. The most significant step for exit from the crisis was behind and not ahead of the budget speech, namely, depreciation of the rupee.

The Balance of Payments Division turned its attention to managing a smooth exit from the crisis. During a crisis, there is a premium that is charged by financial intermediaries, including banks, on all forex transactions in view of the risks involved. As the crisis is managed and risk moderated, the financial markets and the bankers have an interest in maintaining high premia relative to the risks. Leading financial market players have an incentive to delay recognition of exit from the crisis and restoration of normalcy to preserve premia. Availability of reserves which we could draw upon as an alternative was used as leverage in negotiations with the bankers and other providers of short-term credit. This is best illustrated by the management of oil companies' access to foreign exchange.

The large and lumpy demand for foreign exchange from the oil companies could be met either through the forex markets or through short-term credit when available. It was possible for us to ease immediate pressure on the spot market by recourse to short-term borrowings by the SBI to make available the forex for the import of oil by Indian Oil. This mechanism was used extensively prior to the crisis, which in a way landed us in trouble. It was decided to use the same mechanism, but only for tactical purposes, purely as an ad hoc measure. It was used for its impact on the evolving cost of credit for us, but not as a source of funding imports. The ministry ensured close coordination between the RBI, the SBI and Indian Oil. In fact, the terms and conditions offered to the SBI and approved by the government gave a progressive indication of restoration of normalcy and improving perceptions of financial markets about the creditworthiness of India and our prudent use of forex reserves. The margin over LIBOR reflects the risk premium. A margin of 0.25 per cent over LIBOR for short-term facility (six months) to the SBI indicated, in our view, the restoration of normalcy in balance of payments situation. This was the margin prevalent till November 1990. It went up to 0.65 in March 1991, to 1.25 by May and availability of credit dried up almost entirely at the height of the crisis. By the end of 1992 the premium went back to 0.25 per cent, reflecting the restoration of normalcy.

To the extent that the analysis and assessment of balance of payments was relevant for the negotiations with the IMF, I had to be closely involved in the discussions. In our balance of payments projections to the IMF, we had proposed that we would be able to mobilise foreign currency resources from non-resident Indians through the issue of bonds. The IMF team was sceptical about this possibility since during the crisis, the NRIs had withdrawn considerable amounts from the Indian banks. I explained to them that the NRI bonds proposed during the crisis were different from the routine NRI bank deposits. Now that we had honoured our obligations, to the extent of selling gold, the NRIs had confidence that India would never default in honouring its external obligations. Unlike the formal credit rating that guided financial markets, NRIs could make their own assessment about the creditworthiness of India. The IMF team remained sceptical.

'So, Dr Reddy,' Hubert Neiss, director of the IMF, Asia Department, said, 'you think you will be able to get a lot of money in suitcases from the NRIs?'

'Yes,' I said, 'we are confident.'

As anticipated, foreign exchange was, indeed, mobilised from the NRIs.[3]

The crisis highlighted the need for reforms to ensure that growth was maintained in an environment of sustainable external account. The parameters for such reform were fairly well known in the country during the 1980s. These had been worked out in

India's policy circles and included fiscal, monetary, trade, and external sector policies and key structural aspects such as industrial licensing. The IMF was aware of this thinking and the associated policy recommendations. The IMF was also convinced that the indigenously designed framework of reform was appropriate for our conditions. Hence, the conditionalities of the IMF in the context of its programme were expected to be virtually an endorsement of the reform path designed indigenously.

The overall package of reforms formally posed to the IMF for obtaining not only resources but also endorsement of our policies to restore confidence in our economy were finalised under the leadership of Yashwant Sinha, duly advised and assisted by S.P. Shukla and Deepak Nayyar. However, the package was subject to the final view of the government that would be in position after the elections in May/June 1991. Therefore, it was left to his successor Dr Singh to work out the full details of the reform, set out the path, indicate sequencing, and operationalise the measures. I was closely involved in this phase of reforms in so far as the external sector was concerned.

I was a member secretary of the high-level committee on balance of payments constituted in November 1991, under the chairmanship of Rangarajan, at that time member, Planning Commission. One of the important reform measures recommended was the introduction of Liberalised Exchange Rate Management System (LERMS), a term coined by A. Seshan, advisor in the RBI, which was an important landmark in the transition from officially determined exchange rate to a market-based exchange rate system. Basically, it introduced a system of surrender of 40 per cent of the export earnings for financing critical imports at an official (lower) exchange rate. The remaining 60 per cent would be free to be sold by the exporters in the market at a market-driven (higher) rate. This was essentially a dual exchange rate system like the dual prices for food grains or sugar – one under the Public Distribution System (PDS) and the other in the open market. Under LERMS, the open price subsidised the official imports market. The design of this dual exchange rate system required an assessment of both supply of foreign exchange and the demand for foreign exchange from different sources. It also required disaggregation of the different components of supply and demand into what could go into the market and what proportion of supply should be pre-empted for imports at controlled rates. We had to work on what may be described as critical imports such as oil, which had to be financed at the official exchange rate as part of the foreign exchange budget and the rest to be financed by the unsurrendered part of the export earnings at the market rate. We had to arrive at the percentage that should be surrendered by the earners of foreign exchange in order to comfortably finance our requirement of it for import of critical items. The analytical work for this scheme was done by me with the assistance of K.B.L. Mathur and R. Krishnamurthy. We had enormous support from professionals in the RBI. Technical parameters regarding partial convertibility of the rupee were worked out by Dr Arvind Virmani. The entire work was done under the overall policy framework and guidance given by Rangarajan.

The rupee had to be allowed to depreciate during the period of stress but that was simply not adequate to restore normalcy. A dramatic adjustment was made in the exchange rate on two days, 1 and 3 July 1991. This dramatic adjustment ordered by Narasimha Rao and Manmohan Singh, and executed by Venkitaramanan and Rangarajan, was meant to make imports costlier and exports more profitable to gradually bring down the imbalance in the trade account. The magnitude of adjustment was large because the imbalance was large. It had to be swift since continuing expectations of further adjustments in the exchange rate would worsen the situation because of anticipatory actions by market participants.

The report of the high-level committee on balance of payments had some unique features. An interim report was given in the strictest confidence by the chairman in February 1992 and policy actions were taken for introduction of LERMS. The system was meant to facilitate the transition from the officially determined exchange rate to a market-based exchange rate and finally, to the accepted goal of full convertibility on the current account. The final report was given in February 1993, on which policy actions were taken. The report itself, which contained comprehensive proposals for the management of current account, capital account, exchange rate and data needs, along with appendix, prepared by Virmani, was formally signed and submitted in April 1993. Usually, the reports of committees are seldom acted upon promptly. Here, the committee's recommendations were implemented before the report was made public in view of their market-sensitivity and a critical part of the suggestions was implemented through a confidential interim report. When the committee on balance of payments was appointed, Rangarajan was member, Planning Commission. Rangarajan moved over as governor, RBI, by the time it was submitted.

The dual exchange rate operationalised through the LERMS scheme was successful beyond expectations. It was possible to assess the implications of moving to a unified exchange rate earlier than expected. At the same time, it was necessary to take an integrated view of the current and capital account in managing balance of payments. I had to do substantial analytical work leading to full convertibility in current account. In particular, recommendations related to management of capital account served the country very well, and were path-breaking. The recommendations included a stipulation that no short-term credit should be permitted except for trade purposes. Ceilings in overall recourse of external commercial borrowings were proposed. Safeguards were put in place to avoid misuse of current account convertibility for capital account transactions.

There was some unpleasantness for me in processing the proposal for unifying the exchange rate. After discussions with Montek Singh Ahluwalia and Rangarajan, and in the light of the material available on the implementation of LERMS and experience gained, I floated a formal note on the proposed unified exchange rate. It was a brief, two-page note. The note was submitted to Montek, who was secretary, Economic Affairs. He forwarded it to the finance secretary, Geethakrishnan. The finance secretary called me to his room.

He said, 'This is an important proposal. This note is very cursory. This is not the type of note we expect from a joint secretary.' He expressed his worry as to where the exchange rate would go if unified exchange rate was announced.

I explained that the exchange parity with the US dollar for official transactions was at that time in the range of Rs 27-28, and the open market rate was Rs 31-33. Hence, I expected the unified exchange rate to settle somewhere between these two rates. He, however, said that according to his information, it was likely to hit Rs 40 if not Rs 50 per dollar. Montek also conveyed to me similar reservations expressed by Vaghul of ICICI and Nadkarni of IDBI. I mentioned to him that logically, the integrated or single rate should settle between the lower and the higher of the dual rate. I explained that my proposal was based on significant work that was already done, and the global experience of other countries moving into market-determined exchange parity for the first time. It also reflected my informed judgement on the matter. It was obvious that the finance secretary was not convinced when he said, 'I do not know whom you are trying to please.' I was offended, especially given my regard for him; he was brilliant, sharp-witted, and had impeccable integrity.

When I conveyed my resentment to Montek, Rangarajan contacted me immediately and explained to me that I should not worry about these things. The finance minister had been apprised of the matter and the proposal would be approved by him. I felt mollified and after a few days of leave, came back to office. During the period of my leave I continued to work on implementing the proposal for unified exchange rate from my home in Chanakyapuri as well as from the office of the RBI in Parliament Street. In retrospect, perhaps, this was a rather impetuous response on my part. In any case, I was relieved that my judgement about where the exchange rate would settle proved to be correct.

An operational challenge for implementing the unified exchange rate was for the RBI to announce a reference rate on the first day of the unified exchange rate at which all official transactions had to take place. Kulkarni and I worked at my home on a rate that was realistic enough to be a guide to the evolution of the market rate at that transition (from dual to single). The announced exchange rate on the opening day also reflected the official view of where the market rate would be that day. After the first day, the official rate was fixed at noon every day by the RBI, after obtaining the market rates from select authorised dealers (banks) in foreign exchange.

I had a very pleasant experience in regard to preliminary discussions on related policy initiatives like current account convertibility, which was formally announced in 1994. My proposal was that there should be no requirement of approval for release of foreign exchange for all goods, including capital goods. However, Venkitaramanan, governor, felt that import of capital goods through a current account transaction might involve significant foreign exchange. Such lumpy demand would induce volatility in the forex market, which was shallow in the initial stages. He suggested that there should be a prior approval mechanism for import of capital goods above a particular value to ensure adequate supply of forex in the market. He was also concerned that there could be a surge of imports in general due to liberalisation and, therefore, we should be cautious in allowing imports involving large foreign exchange without some prior approval. I had taken the view that the liberalisation of imports might increase them, but it would also discourage the build-up of inventories due to ending of uncertainties of supplies. On capital goods, I said that it should be possible to monitor the import of large volumes through the banking system without insisting on prior approval. In fact, any liberalisation or deregulation should be accompanied by strengthening monitoring mechanisms so that we were not caught by surprise. Any prior approval, even with a ceiling, might invite artificial slicing, uncertainty and discretion. That should be avoided.

After considerable discussion, Ashok Desai, an eminent economist and chief consultant in the Ministry of Finance, commented, 'Venu must have done his homework. I think we can go along and get rid of approval for release of foreign exchange for import of all capital goods, irrespective of the value.' This was consistent with full convertibility on current account.

While managing the crisis, we realised that neither policy

makers nor public opinion had credible data on the total external debt of the country. In the 1980s, external debt by non-governmental entities through the banking system increased without a strict reporting and monitoring mechanism in place. So, I suggested establishing a working group to study and recommend measures for collecting statistics on the external debt of India and put these in the public domain.

I did not find much enthusiasm for this proposal in the ministry. However, Venkitaramanan fully supported the proposal, and at my request, he constituted a working group of external debt data with Seshan of the RBI and myself as members. We were assisted by a technical group drawn from the offices of the RBI and the Ministry of Finance. This group made some path-breaking recommendations which were adopted in full.

Dr Singh approved the idea to put the external debt data in the public domain. I had proposed that the External Debt Monitoring Unit (EDMU) should ideally be in the RBI since it had the expertise as well as access to information from financial intermediaries, in particular, banks. The RBI could be provided with data on government debt from the Ministry of Finance. However, the finance ministry felt that such a unit should be located within the ministry, though as the division in-charge of external commercial borrowings, I was willing to cede this work to the RBI. Dr Singh discussed it with me and struck a compromise. He suggested that the EDMU should be established in the Ministry of Finance, but expertise should be drawn from the RBI to man the unit. It was also decided that the external debt statistics would be released every six months, alternatively by the Ministry of Finance and the RBI. Much of the work done by this working group was used later by World Bank, and in particular, by the Commonwealth Secretariat, in providing a framework for such compilation by other developing countries.

We had some problems in the data relating to the balance of payments. There were difficulties in incorporating the transactions under the rupee trade agreement with Russia. There were large and increasing discrepancies between the data in imports from the Customs Department and payments made for imports through the banking system. Some of the discrepancies related to defence, some to oil import and export, and some due to leads and lags. Work was done on mechanisms for reducing these discrepancies and improving the quality of data relating to balance of payments. The disclosures relating to forex reserves were also increased and rationalised. This work was done under the guidance of Rangarajan.

Manmohan Singh, as finance minister, once asked me to send him a note explaining the course of events that led to the crisis and the people involved. I prepared the note by examining all the relevant files in my division and surmised the following.

The RBI had warned the government on several occasions about the emerging stress in the balance of payments and the risks associated with the continuance of the fiscal and trade policies leading to large and persistent current account deficits. The RBI expressed concerns about the recourse to short-term measures to finance the import requirements. The Economic Division in the DEA, in particular, Shankar Acharya and Bimal Jalan, expressed their concerns in no uncertain terms. However, the finance secretaries, Venkitaramanan and Gopi Arora, had felt that the growth momentum would have been seriously compromised if corrective actions had been taken at that stage. They recorded on the file that the adjustments in policy and reforms were necessary, but that they had to be addressed in the future, implying that this was not the time to do it.

In the note that I presented to the finance minister on what led to the crisis I mentioned that on the basis of the files I had examined, it was clear that the government had considered all aspects relating to the problem of balance of payments and the possible solutions in full and in detail. The note summarised that there was virtually no relevant factor that had not been considered and none that had not been analysed. In these circumstances, the fact that the government had not taken the corrective steps was obviously a matter of judgement and a matter of weighing of the risks involved, rather than lack of information, analysis, or advice. While it was true that balance of payments was increasingly and progressively under stress, the stress may or may not have become a full-fledged crisis if not for the Gulf crisis, which was impossible to anticipate. I, therefore, concluded that there were no serious shortcomings in the considerations of various policy measures during the relevant period by the functionaries concerned.

Obviously, there had been serious hesitation on the part of the political leadership both in taking the painful steps that were required to relieve the stress as well as reconciling themselves to the possibility of recourse to IMF support. Equally obviously, the leaders were not confident that they could muster political support for the needed policy reform, with or without endorsement from the IMF. The unwillingness or incapacity to act when needed had exacerbated the situation while the Gulf war had triggered a serious crisis.

One might argue that the finance secretaries had failed in their duty by not firmly supporting the views of the RBI and Economic Division. It is true that there was no evidence on file that the finance secretaries made their recommendations for timely actions, and, therefore, they could not have been formally turned down by the ministers or the prime ministers, but I was well aware of how the interactions between ministers and secretaries took place in politically sensitive matters. After going through the files to prepare the note, I surmised that the secretaries would have certainly briefed the ministers about the seriousness of the situation, though the crisis was ultimately triggered by the Gulf crisis. Therefore, the crisis could have been attributed to the political economy: there had been a lack of political will to do what should have been done over a decade.

As per protocol, I sent my note to Dr Singh through Montek. Montek called me to his room.

'Venu,' he told me, 'I don't think the finance minister will like this note.'

'Montek, I considered all aspects. Let it go to the minister. Let's see later if we need to do more work.'

Montek laughed. The note was sent. The finance minister returned it without any comment.

I was given additional charge of the Capital Markets Division towards the end of my tenure as joint secretary in the Ministry of Finance. My duties included interacting with Securities and Exchange Board of India (SEBI), the regulator for the securities market in India. SEBI, which was established in 1988, was given statutory powers in 1992 and G.V. Ramakrishna was the chairman. As a statutory body, SEBI had to issue several regulations and notifications which required the concurrence of the government. There was little progress in the issue of notifications, which were required to effectively commence the work of SEBI. I had worked with Ramakrishna before in Andhra Pradesh and we had a good equation. It was possible for us to help resolve many of the differences between the ministry and SEBI, and issue several regulations in a very short time to lay the foundations for work of a statutorily constituted SEBI.

I had to perform a dual role – as a member of the board of SEBI from the ministry, and that of processing the cases from SEBI in the ministry. I was a member of the board of SEBI from 17 November 1992 till 5 March 1993. In the formal meetings of the board, my participation was consistent with my conviction that as a representative of the ministry I should focus on policy and not on operational issues.

There were several issues relating to the coordination between the RBI and the SEBI. Venkitaramanan and his senior in the IAS, chairman Ramakrishna, were not interacting with each other to the extent desired by the ministry. I had, therefore, suggested that there could be an informal group on capital markets consisting of the RBI governor, SEBI chairman, and Economic Affairs secretary, with me as joint secretary as convener. We used to meet in Delhi in the RBI building. The meetings were informal, but the minutes were recorded by me as joint secretary. Subsequently, this has been formalised through an administrative order.

As joint secretary, I had courted the wrath of many secretaries to the government and the Prime Minister's Office, because I consistently refused to agree to any exception or concession in regard to the rigid implementation of serious curbs on imports. Many cases were referred by the ministries and the

Prime Minister's Office and some of them were very genuine. My problem was that under such difficult circumstances, any concession or special dispensation to any individual request, however genuine, would be opening the flood gates. Further, granting exemptions without a publicly available transparent framework would be not only inefficient but would undermine the efforts and the credibility of the government. Most importantly, I held the view that vigorous implementation of a strict regime negatively affecting the powerful and interested parties would force them to support the systemic reform that would bring relief to all, including them.

At the end of the day, a key to realising reform is to make the powerful feel the pain of the status quo.

Since I was in charge of the ECB, I had three difficult and memorable issues that I dealt with. In one instance, it was suggested that we allow external commercial borrowings for a project to be executed by BHEL in Iran. I objected. We were finding it difficult to obtain enough foreign exchange for funding power projects within the country. If we allowed commercial borrowings for executing a project in an offshore location for the benefit of another country, that would still fall within the aggregate limits of external commercial borrowings of our country. I was told that this project had to be implemented in view of the assurance of the prime minister during his visit to Iran.

I insisted on studying the minutes of the meeting to understand the nature of the commitment. Of course, even if there was a commitment, it was the duty of the finance ministry to explain the implications and bring its discomfort to the notice of the prime minister. I was given access to the minutes of the meeting, which involved an assurance to consider, but not a commitment. The proposal was then dropped.

In another important instance, I consistently opposed the package involving the counter guarantee for the Dabhol Power Company (Enron power project). In 1993, the project was being processed in the ministry for according 'unique' guarantees. My involvement was in the context of external commercial borrowings, not other issues.

There was a view that a case-by-case approach would lead to policy change in Indian conditions and hence fast-track cases like Enron should be supported. There was also a view that no one would invest in the power sector if the payment of dues by power utilities was not guaranteed by the government. I disagreed. It was my position that it was a large amount at extremely favourable terms not available to others. I felt that if guarantees were to be given, all power-generating companies, including NTPC, should get such a benefit. In this background, Montek wanted me to accompany him to a meeting in the Prime Minister's Office, chaired by Amarnath Verma, principal secretary to the PM. Montek requested that I explain in detail the reasons for my opposition, particularly to guarantees by the Union and state governments. I was overruled in the meeting because these decisions were taken as part of a policy mandate.

Eventually, the project got into a serious controversy, resulting in a huge financial burden on our economy.

When I look back, I cannot comment on the political dynamics of crisis and reform since I was relatively junior to know these factors first-hand. However, I had the privilege to be of assistance to very senior policy makers in managing the crisis and initiating the process of reform in the external sector. In my view, if there is one person who showed extraordinary leadership in managing the balance of payments crisis, it was Venkitaramanan, as governor, RBI. It was the country's good fortune that Rangarajan with his long experience in central banking was available both for crisis management and reform. During this period, he was deputy governor, a member of the Planning Commission and later governor. He provided guidance to us, whatever formal official position he held.

Yashwant Sinha as finance minister proved the right man to manage the crisis at its height and initiate reforms. S.P. Shukla and Deepak Nayyar assisted the minister in steering the economy during a historic crisis, to save it from default and disgrace, under unprecedented domestic political turbulence. The origin of the BoP crisis was essentially political in nature, and Prime

Minister Narasimha Rao provided political solutions to it and enabled his finance minister to do the rest. Dr Singh has rightly been acknowledged as the most distinguished reformer of the Indian economy. It is also acknowledged that he built an enviable team to assist him in the process. Most of the post-crisis reforms were implemented under his leadership. Montek and Shankar Acharya made an excellent combination in the design and smooth implementation of reforms. In many ways, the team we were in, described as 'All the FM's men' by Shankar, groomed me to transition from civil servant to economic administrator.[4]

In retrospect, the framework for external sector management that was put in place under the leadership of Dr Singh and Rangarajan, more than twenty years ago, has stood the test of time and defied ideological onslaughts. The pillars of the framework are: full convertibility on current account coupled with effective management of capital flows directed to ensure a realistic exchange rate and a current account deficit that can be financed by normal capital flows. This framework was a pioneer in indicating the importance of vulnerability due to short-term liabilities in the external sector. This was also a pioneer in suggesting a hierarchy among different types of capital flows in terms of stability. To illustrate, in view of the larger share of external debt in our external liabilities, the framework was in favour of non-debt flows. This framework was the basis for both Tarapore Committee I and II on capital account convertibility and subsequently for the design of the foreign exchange management Act. The global crisis has further reinforced the relevance of the policy framework.

Manmohan Singh was not the first economist to be appointed finance minister. In fact, Pandit Nehru had Prof. Shanmugam Chetty (economist and at one time member of the Justice Party), John Mathai (part-time professor of economics in Madras University), C.D. Deshmukh (central banker), and T.T. Krishnamachari (visiting professor of economics in Madras University) as finance ministers. The only exception made by Pandit Nehru was in the case of Morarji Desai after 1958. Most of the non-economists as finance ministers in India since Independence had little or no political following. The exceptions were V.P. Singh and Charan Singh, apart from Morarji Desai.

It is interesting that over the years since Independence, prime ministers have generally chosen as finance ministers either technocrats or politicians with negligible political following. In a way, the finance minister's remit was less political and more economic management. In brief, whether the finance minister has a team of his choice depends on the equation with the prime minister and the manner in which the finance minister chooses the members of the team. In any case, the experience and expertise of the senior functionaries is important; their functioning as a team is useful; and a diversity in their views is helpful.

An interesting question for me, after being one of the 'FM's Men', is, how important is it for the finance minister to have his or her own team of economists, bureaucrats and central bankers. The evidence from the crisis management that I have discussed is that individuals do not matter and the system responds well to challenges. The experience with the reform, on the other hand, brings out the advantages of teamwork. The contrast may be attributed to the nature of decision making at the time of the reform being different from the time of crisis. My experience in the ministry convinces me that in all circumstances, a diversity of views is critical for optimal decision making, but in the absence of trust and mutual respect among them, there could be issues. The team that the finance minister has by and large depends on the extent to which the prime minister allows the finance minister to have his say in building the team.

During these three critical years, 1990 to '93, I was working in North Block. The stately colonial building was where Lord Mountbatten sat during the Second World War. While working in the North Block, I faced many challenges and had to overcome difficult hurdles and often, we had to work late in the evening.

When we were ready to go home, we had to take precautions. Late in the evening, monkeys would rule the corridors of the North Block. If we attempted to leave our office alone, the monkeys would become ferocious; snarling and pouncing on us, especially if we had leftover food. To walk to the parking lot, we had to call the guards and watchman. They would come with six-foot sticks. They matched the ferociousness of the monkeys by waving their sticks and snarling back at the simians. It was through this battleground, tense with drama, that we were escorted safely to our cars.

13

THE WORLD IS NOT FAIR

IN THE FIRST WEEK OF MAY 1993, I GOT A PIECE OF GOOD NEWS and bad news. The good news was that I was being promoted to the rank of additional secretary, and the bad news was that I was being posted in the Ministry of Commerce, though there was a clear vacancy in the finance ministry. It is inconceivable that this would have happened without the knowledge of the finance minister. I asked the additional secretary (budget), Janaki Kathpalia, the senior-most functionary in the ministry available in New Delhi, to relieve me immediately as joint secretary. She was reluctant. Relieving a senior officer without the minister's approval was not ordinarily done. I insisted on getting relieved the same day. She obliged out of personal affection and professional regard for me.

After Manmohan Singh returned from his foreign tour, I called on him as additional secretary in the commerce ministry. He was unhappy that I had been relieved from my post in his absence. He said he had wanted to retain me as additional secretary in the Department of Economic Affairs. He said that he would take up the matter with the prime minister. While thanking him, I suggested that he should not take the trouble.

The commerce minister at the time was Pranab Mukherjee. The subjects allotted to me in the Ministry of Commerce were relatively light in terms of workload or importance. The work on the subjects allotted took no more than a couple of hours a day.[1] Yet, time was not wasted. I spent many hours studying the Indian economy.

On one occasion, I joked to my dear friend, Shankar Acharya, who was the chief economic advisor at the time:

'Shankar,' I said, 'I know more about the Indian economy than the chief economic advisor to the Government of India! You must do your work while understanding the Indian economy. I have all the time and resources and I can study the Indian economy on a virtually full-time basis.'

On a serious note, there were three areas of work that were noteworthy: two of them for the satisfaction I derived and one for the helplessness I felt. In retrospect, I made some contribution in establishing the Anti-dumping Authority and initiated a change in approach to overseas investments by Indian corporates, but was helpless in being a party to a farce in dealing with export-oriented units.

I did enjoy being the 'Anti-dumping Authority'. I was the first person in India to occupy the position. I used to joke that I was dumped into the position of Anti-dumping Authority.

Basically, dumping occurs when some units in foreign countries export goods to our country at a price that does not generate a profit, but is meant to capture our market. We in India lowered tariffs under the obligations accepted by us in the WTO and so we had to protect ourselves from dumping by exporters from other countries. Such protection was obtained under WTO commitments by the exercise of levying anti-dumping duties. Anti-dumping duties can be levied in respect of import of a commodity from a specified country, but after a due judicial process that establishes dumping; interim levies pending detailed inquiry are permissible. For initiating the work, I had to devise the procedures, conduct hearings and finally pass orders levying anti-dumping duties as appropriate. This was a new experience, and so attention had to be paid to install the systems, regulations and procedures. Orders in consonance with WTO obligations and our legal provisions were passed, creating precedents. The Anti-Dumping Authority requires hearing the parties through advocates and experts, and passing interim and final orders. It has survived till this day.

I chaired a committee for the approval of overseas investments by Indian corporates. Any unit in India that sought to invest in a business abroad required approval by the government and the RBI, based on recommendations of the committee chaired by me. Till I joined, the assumption in the deliberations of the committee was that our corporates were ill-informed or wanted to siphon off foreign exchange. Our experience with investments by our corporates overseas was not good in the past. However, I felt that with the opening up of the Indian economy, capital flows could not be only one way. I felt that we should be prepared to allow our enterprises to also invest in other countries, especially if they were not capital intensive. Such investments would help our industry to acquire domain expertise, which they were lacking since they tended to concentrate on the domestic economy. Indian enterprises also did not have enough size and, therefore, overseas investments or acquisitions could produce synergies. I was in favour of encouraging investments in sectors where we had significant dependence on imports, such as oil and fertilisers, thus giving us an opportunity to understand the sector in the global context. Hence, I was in favour of a liberalised environment for overseas direct investment by our corporates. This was in contrast to the prevailing belief that we should not allow outflow of valuable foreign exchange at a time when we were seeking inflows.

In addition to a liberalised approach, I suggested that the RBI should be the appropriate authority to approve overseas investments by Indian corporates. There were no fiscal implications since the government was only permitting the use of foreign exchange to invest, but not extending fiscal concessions. Commercial risk was being borne by the Indian enterprise concerned. Since the use of foreign exchange was involved and the RBI was administering the Foreign Exchange Regulation Act, I felt that the RBI should attend to this work. This proposal was accepted in due course and finally implemented well after I left the Ministry of Commerce. I was pleased to read the order transferring the work to the RBI and liberalising the regime after I joined as deputy governor. The preamble to the order incorporated the note written by me as additional secretary in the commerce ministry a couple of years earlier.

As if to balance the satisfaction, I had to preside, as I mentioned, over a farce. As chairman, for approval of export-oriented units I was party to an impractical stipulation in the procedures. One of the stipulations was that there should be a firm commitment from the customer (in the importing country) for imports from the proposed unit. It is difficult to visualise a situation where a customer in a foreign country would give a firm order committing to import commodities from an export unit which was yet to be established. Apparently, all the documentation required for submitting an application for EOU addressed to the Ministry of Commerce was handled by a group of consultants in Delhi. They made the arrangements to produce all the necessary documentation. They were able to virtually forge documents of a foreign firm's commitment to import from the proposed EOU. There was no point in trying to make an inquiry into the genuineness of these documents, because the stipulation itself was unrealistic. It was not worthwhile to seek dispensing with such requirements because information provided by the party was the only relevant information for approval or disapproval of a unit as per rules. And, at that stage of our policy regime, prior approval was the norm. The futility of issuing a licence or prior approval entirely based on documentation produced by the party, without any means of advance verification by the authorities, dawned on me.

Chidambaram, who replaced Mukherjee as minister in the latter part of my tenure in the commerce ministry, took considerable interest in overseas investments, export-oriented units and work related to anti-dumping. My interaction with the minister, therefore, increased after Chidambaram took over.

One of my first interactions with Chidambaram was a meeting I had with him regarding a matter in which I had made an error on a file.

He brought out the file. Chidambaram, a towering figure clad in a traditional south Indian snow-white dhoti and shirt, had the reputation of being an overbearing, brilliant man. He was known to be a master of detail, an unforgiving boss, and a man of impeccable logic.

'This is a mistake,' he pointed out as he looked at the file.

'Yes, sir. It is a mistake.'

After a slight pause, he looked at me and said again, 'It is a mistake.'

'Yes, sir, it is a mistake.'

He repeated, 'It is a mistake.'

'I'm sorry, sir. It was, indeed, a mistake.'

Soon after this meeting, I had another interaction with Chidambaram, which was an even more memorable one.

There was a proposal to utilise rupee balances that were with us and were available for Russia. Normally the balances could be used only for the import of goods from India. The proposal was to use them as an investment in an Indian company. I felt that this amounted to a 'double swap' from rupee to a convertible currency and debt to equity; the whole deal would, therefore, be totally non-transparent.[2]

Chidambaram called me to his room. He did not agree with my views on the proposal. He asked me to explain why I did not concur with his views. I went through my logic and clarified my analysis. It was clear that his stance was wrong. I pointed that out in no uncertain terms.

'Oh,' he said, 'it was a mistake.'

'It was,' I said, 'a mistake.'

He understood immediately. 'Yes, it was a mistake.'

I repeated, 'It was a mistake.'

He looked at me for a few seconds and said, 'Yes, it was. I am sorry.'

He smiled. I smiled. And we both began to laugh. The ice was broken.

I could not get over the fact that I was moved out of the Ministry of Finance in 1993. I felt the move was unfair. Further, I was not given substantive work during my entire tenure in the commerce ministry. Hence, I was seeking opportunities for employment outside with a scope for deputation from or lien in government. I sought many avenues, but most of them did not pan out.[3] However, I joined a World Bank mission to China and IMF missions to Tanzania, Ethiopia and Bahrain.

In these assignments, I had the opportunity to work on fiscal management, with a focus on expenditure management in these countries. The most educative experience was in China. The mission had to consider both federal and provincial government budgets. At the time, the detailed budget in China was still a secret document. They were in the process of introducing a budget system compatible with a market economy. They were trying to rework the fiscal relations between the federal government and the provincial governments. They were also working on a clear distinction between taxation and payment of dividends in regard to public enterprises to replace the prevailing system of contracts with individual enterprises.

The working style of the officials of the Ministry of Finance in China, both in the central government and the provincial government of Mongolia, was impressive. First, almost everyone was keen to find out and understand the budget practices in other countries, especially the US, and about India from me. Second, they were forthcoming in giving information, strictly warranted by the terms of reference of our mission. Third, they made it very clear that their objective was to beat the US by 2020 in every aspect of the economy. Fourth, the officials were absolutely punctual for all meetings. Fifth, officials came fully prepared for meetings. If any questions were asked without prior notice, they preferred to answer the next day. In other words, adequate preparation and internal consultations were insisted upon before interaction with World Bank/IMF missions. China had the basic work culture of a developed economy and, therefore, it was clear that it would grow rapidly. This is the learning part of my posting in the Ministry of Commerce from May 1993 to August 1995.

In August 1995, I was posted as secretary, Department of Banking, in the Ministry of Finance. I was happy to be back in the finance ministry.[4] I was given charge of work which had been, for the most part, handled by additional secretaries or special secretaries in the past. Yet I joined as secretary, Banking, on 2 August 1995 without a murmur. A couple of days later, Montek explained to me that my posting order would be changed to clarify that though I would be the secretary to the government,

I would be heading the Banking Division and not the Banking Department. I would still be reporting directly to the minister as the secretaries normally do, but should send cabinet notes and other important files to the minister through him, the secretary, Department of Economic Affairs.

The Banking Division in the Department of Economic Affairs dealt basically with administrative matters. Policy issues were considered and finalised in other divisions in the department.[5] Much of the work in the Banking Division was not exciting for me; I was interested in policy. Still, I decided to wait it out for some time, though I felt the signals were not good.

One of the functions of the Banking Division was to process the appointment of non-official directors to the boards of the vast empires of the public sector financial institutions. The directors were expected to represent the owner – the government. They were also to serve the public interest while ensuring good governance of the enterprise to which they were appointed. In public sector banks, the appointment of directors was an opportunity for political patronage. The finance minister, Dr Manmohan Singh, was keen to have well-qualified persons with integrity to fill the various vacancies. Non-official directors were to be drawn from specified areas, such as small industry, agriculture, accountancy, economics, and so on. On the basis of suggestions received from various quarters and after soliciting some suggestions, I prepared a comprehensive list of possible candidates and had detailed discussions on them with the minister. I then submitted the file with specific proposals to him. The file did not come back for several months.

Manmohan Singh called me later. He expressed his annoyance at the Prime Minister's Office, at how the file was being processed. He said that whenever a name was proposed by the finance minister, he was informed that he or she was against the ruling party. Basically, the process was made to come to a grinding halt till such time that the finance minister accepted candidates informally proposed by the ruling party.

Soon after this meeting, we started getting names from the PMO to fill up vacancies. They sent résumés. They indicated the specific banks to which their choices should be appointed. We had to formally propose the names given by the PMO to the Appointments Committee of the Cabinet (ACC) for approval. (The ACC was responsible for these appointments and was headed by the prime minister.) After some time, even that formality was done away with; the ACC approved the appointments of the candidates without waiting for any proposal from our department.

I was reminded of my senior colleague C.R. Krishnaswamy Rao's complaint about the government when he was cabinet secretary in the Union government.

He used to say often, 'The wretched government.'

Once I asked him, 'Sir, how can you say that? You are in it, with it and of it.'

He replied, 'So what? The government is wretched; we are part of it. That is most frustrating.'

Influence peddling was also not uncommon in the appointment of chairmen and managing directors (CMDs) of the banks and development financial institutions. These appointments were normally based on the recommendations of a selection committee. The RBI governor was the chairman of the selection committee; the RBI deputy governor, secretary (Economic Affairs), and the secretary (Banking), were members. Eligibility was restricted to senior bankers in the public sector. The eligible candidates were generally called for an interaction with the selection committee or a sub-committee of the selection committee, consisting of the deputy governor and the secretary (Banking). The deputy governor concerned, Talwar, was a pivot, since he had knowledge about the various candidates in the banking sector, being from the commercial banking sector himself. In the absence of domain knowledge and familiarity with the candidates, I would go along with the chairman and other members while sharing my assessment of the performance of the candidates in the interviews. In most cases, the process was smooth and non-controversial.[6] On paper, the process appeared reasonable. Yet, there were cases where the process was manipulated. The classic case was of that of the Indian Bank chairman, who had been reappointed before I joined as banking secretary. During my tenure as banking secretary, I had to recommend his suspension, just before his retirement, and I also had to process permission for his prosecution.

Making public sector financial institutions accountable to Parliament was one of the major responsibilities of the Banking Division. Accountability to Parliament in operational terms meant placing the required documentation before Parliament, such as annual reports of the public sector banks, annual reports of the RBI and reports of CAG. This involved considerable work and attention to detail. It also meant I would have to appear before parliamentary committees. I appeared before several of them and often officers from commercial banks were also invited. There were two problems which we faced in interacting with the committees. Some of the members deflected productive discussion by asking unrelated questions, questions that were not on the agenda and that were asked only to put the bank officials on the defensive. Sometimes, individual cases were canvassed by some MPs with the bank officials on the sidelines of the meetings. In fact, the bank officials were sworn to secrecy regarding the proceedings and were debarred from disclosing any matters discussed. It is only the final report that was put in the public domain. Despite these limitations, on the rare occasions when substantive policy or legislative issues were discussed seriously in the committees, it was enlightening since some very new perspectives were brought to the table. Also, the proceedings were conducted by all the chairmen with impressive dignity.

One morning in February 1996, I was asked to attend a meeting in Finance Minister Manmohan Singh's room where Rangarajan, RBI governor, Montek Singh, finance secretary, and Shankar Acharya, chief economic advisor, were present. There was pressure on the forex market which was causing depreciation of the rupee. They were discussing measures that could moderate the pressure. On a request from the finance minister the previous day, I had prepared a note on this subject, though it had nothing to do with the work of the Banking Division. The pressure on the rupee was a result of the effort to build forex reserves by crediting inflows on account of aid, including from World Bank, to the reserves, while insisting that all outflows should be funded from the open market. It was a way of building reserves without direct intervention in the forex markets. In a way, the supply of foreign currency into the markets was taken out while the demand for foreign exchange on account of aid was injected into the market. Partly due to the knee-jerk reactions of the market participants, the net effect on the supply-and-demand position in the market was more than originally expected, resulting in excessive depreciating pressure.

After the discussions, Dr Singh, said: 'Montek, Venu will be working on this issue for now. He will assist the governor.' As we were all going out, Dr Singh called me in and said: 'You be with the governor and hold his hand till the market stabilises. He will appreciate it.' My involvement had obviously been decided through prior consultations between the finance minister and the governor. Soon after the meeting, I proceeded to assist the governor. A series of administrative measures were taken and announced to influence the leads and lags in conversion of currency for meeting current account transactions. In Bombay, we tried to temporarily remove the demand for foreign exchange in the forex markets on account of import by oil companies. A mechanism for short-term credit facilities to finance imports by Indian oil companies was worked out. This was done by encouraging the State Bank of India to borrow short-term credit in overseas branches and pay for the imports. This measure moderated the demand in the forex markets. The market stabilised in about two weeks.

One day in July, I received a telephone call from Surendra Singh, cabinet secretary. I went to meet him at his office in Rashtrapati Bhavan.

He said, 'Venu, you are senior and you have long service left. So, we are thinking of posting you to an important ministry I have in mind – Ministry of Defence. I just wanted to mention it to you personally.'

I responded by saying, 'Sir, please do not bother about giving me a posting. I have decided to quit. I want to retire from the service. Thank you very much, sir.'

He asked me to think about it.

My reaction was spontaneous, though not entirely thoughtless.

Vacancies had arisen in the positions of revenue secretary and expenditure secretary in the past, but I was not considered for either of them.

I was reluctant to move to the Ministry of Defence. It was an important position, no doubt, but it was not in my area of interest or expertise. I reasoned that if my work was satisfactory, I would have to continue there till my retirement. If my work was not satisfactory, I would be reverted to the state government. I felt it was better to retire from the service.

Later, I met Chidambaram and told him about my decision to leave the government. He took up the matter with the cabinet secretary. Consequently, I was sounded for textiles or public enterprises or heavy industries. But I was determined to leave the service.

Around this time, S.S. Tarapore, deputy governor, RBI, met me. He said that I should seriously consider succeeding him in the RBI since he was retiring in a couple of months. I said I would think about it. Tarapore took up the matter with Rangarajan. Rangarajan told him that he had asked me to join the RBI during my days in the Ministry of Commerce and that I had not agreed.

'Call him now,' Tarapore said. 'This is the time he might agree.' Tarapore was right.

Later, when my candidature was formally proposed by Rangarajan, Chidambaram called me. He asked me whether I really wanted to go.

I told him that Rangarajan wanted me.

'I know that the governor wants you,' he said. 'But do you want to go?'

'Yes,' I said. 'I want to go.'

I flew to Bombay on 13 September 1996. On the flight, I started reminiscing about my life, family and career. I never dreamt that I would work in Bombay or in central banking. I was sad that I was leaving the government that I had served for over three decades. I could not become a full secretary to the Union government and head a department in the finance ministry, but merely headed a division.

I was full of emotions. Strange were the ways that fate treated people. I felt the world had not been fair to me.

Suddenly I realised something. I had been offered the defence ministry, one of the most prestigious positions. I was given a choice of other ministries – textiles or public enterprises or heavy industries. The government had given me good choices, just not my choice. How could I complain?

I felt ashamed. Of course the world was not fair. There were millions in our country who were deprived of basic education and access to opportunities. Amongst them, there would have been many better than me, and yet their options in life were incomparably poorer than mine. I thought of my father who would point out that he had friends who were brighter and more deserving than him, yet he had succeeded where they did not – the reason, he told me, was destiny.

In the larger picture, destiny had treated me unfairly; it had treated me unfairly well.

14

A CHANGE OF PROFILE

MUCH TO MY SURPRISE AND EVERYONE ELSE'S, I BECAME A central banker.

Even when I was banking secretary, the thought of a career in the Reserve Bank had not occurred to me. Family and friends were not exactly enthused with my decision. A senior position in the government meant prestige, whereas the RBI was not an institution that they had heard much about. Geetha was happy in Delhi with her many friends, and was not keen to move to Bombay, where the RBI headquarters was located. The press was divided: they worried about whether the 'IAS lobby' had captured the RBI while others extolled the appointment of a 'desi economist'. In bureaucratic circles my departure went almost unnoticed. As for me, I was looking forward to my new position since I would be working on economic policy.

I joined as deputy governor, RBI, on 14 September 1996. My term lasted till August 2002. During these six years, my contributions were essentially through interactions with the governor. These interactions are explored in the latter parts of the book. During this period, there were important developments in the Indian economy overall and the RBI went through major transformations as an institution, which I have tried to put in context in this chapter. In addition, there are a few contributions that I initiated, which this chapter describes. Personally, from being an economic administrator, I became a central banker, and it is in this chapter that this transformation is explored.

I was certain that being a central banker would be a different experience. I was familiar with the culture in the IAS and the government, but was a stranger to the RBI. In addition, there would be a change in visibility. A secretary in the government exercised considerable influence and authority, but was away from the public gaze. A deputy governor had a duty to communicate and often had to speak out, especially if the governor encouraged him. Though there was much to learn in my new role, my experience in the government was not without its advantages.

I was a bridge between the government and the RBI. Since I had worked in the government, I was aware of their concerns and processes. Since I had worked in or was on the board of banks, development financial institutions, financial regulators, mutual funds, and re-financing institutions such as SEBI, UTI, SBI, APIDC,[1] among others, I got a sense of their point of view and their issues in their interactions with the RBI. The RBI had to interact with the state governments, and as I had worked in the state government for many years, the states viewed me as someone who understood their perspectives. My exposure to development planning and socioeconomic realities was useful to the RBI in appreciating the broad concerns of society in matters relating to money and finance. My work in the finance ministry, while handling the balance of payments crisis and reform, was also very valuable when I put forward my views on gold policy in the public domain. Therefore, due to my background, I could understand the bigger picture, the ground realities, the legal implications, the institutional dimensions, and the behavioural equations in the various institutions and systems.

Though my previous experience was useful, the RBI culture was unique, and I had to spend some time in understanding it. The Reserve Bank, like other central banks, has traditions that have evolved over time. Most central banks are governor-centric, and the RBI was no exception. The officers and staff were very respectful to the governor and protective of the governor's reputation. They believed that their strength as an institution depended on the personality of the governor and his capacity to manage the government, the markets, financial institutions and his own public image. Deputy governors were also given special treatment, but their importance depended on the trust and confidence that the governor reposed in them. Protocol was observed very strictly and the seniority of deputy governors was based on the date of joining.[2]

Interestingly, the RBI as an institution was, perhaps, even more hierarchical than the government, but functionaries were more independent in expressing opinions on file unless, of course, the governor desired otherwise. The RBI generally operated in a highly compartmentalised fashion, given the work requirement and the culture. In the RBI, there were a large number of well-trained, top-class economists, statisticians, and other professionals.[3] Most of all, the RBI had the reputation for enviable personal and professional integrity. The many things I found while working in the RBI – the professionalism, the focus on research, the interactions with bright young officers – fitted in very well with my preferences and personality. In fact, the first book that I published as deputy governor was dedicated to the talent and commitment of the professionals in the RBI.[4]

I was one of four deputy governors in the RBI. Mostly, I was handling the economic policy research department, monetary policy,[5] public debt management, external sector management, and to some extent coordination amongst various departments. Each of the other three deputy governors handled (mainly, though there was some overlap and additional responsibilities) regulation and supervision, developmental finance, and currency and other housekeeping functions.[6] The camaraderie and coordination among the deputy governors was impressive. In particular, my predecessor, Mr Tarapore, was respected for his knowledge, admired for his integrity, and feared for his forthrightness. I felt that his qualities shone like gold. Tarapore and I overlapped for a few weeks, but he remained my friend, philosopher and guide for almost two decades after, till his death.

When I joined, the public profile of the RBI as an institution was not as prominent as it would be in later years. But even then, the RBI was of primary importance to both the economy as well as the people. The RBI is concerned with price stability and the value of money, and these affect our everyday lives. It influences interest rates, which matter to depositors and borrowers and are important in financing growth and employment. Financial transactions involve banks and clearance of cheques, or more broadly, payment systems. The RBI is a banker to the Union government and state governments. All payments to the government by citizens, such as taxes, and receipts, such as salaries or pensions, are made through the banking system. Actually, the RBI authorises banks as its agents to carry out the government business and compensates them. As a banker to the government, the RBI serves people in their financial transactions with the government. The exchange rate is of concern to many, especially the millions of students and non-resident Indian workers. Above all, the RBI's functioning is relevant to anyone who deals with banks and uses currency that it produces and makes available, and the coins that it distributes on behalf of the government.[7] The RBI has an essential role to play in the functioning of the economy and in the lives of people, though at that time, not many were fully aware of its role. This changed over the years. The most dramatic change in the RBI's profile, however, happened during the six years when I was deputy governor and I was fortunate to have been a part of this transformation.

The reasons for the change were systemic, encompassing structural and policy elements. Prior to the reforms in 1991, the Indian economy was a planned economy. Therefore, money and finance – and by implication, the RBI – were subordinated to the objectives of the government; they too were an instrument of planning. After the reforms of 1991, there was greater dependence on market forces, and as money and finance gained importance in the allocation of resources, the prominence of the RBI increased.

The RBI culture during the earlier years was different from that in the later years. Overall, officials in the RBI viewed the government and the financial markets with a sense of discomfort, and they preferred to keep a safe distance from both the government and the institutions that they regulated. By and large, officials in the RBI were inward looking, and had minimal interactions with the financial markets and banking institutions.

The general complaint was that the RBI was too conservative and too slow to change. The challenge before us was to make the cultural transition in a manner consistent with the market-oriented monetary and financial sector reforms in progress. I had the privilege and pleasure of being one of the people involved in bringing about this change.

The major challenges for us in transforming the way we worked to meet new challenges were twofold: ensuring better internal coordination among departments, and facilitating interaction with the world outside the RBI. We started constituting interdepartmental working groups on various subjects with a working group on monetary policy and extended the approach to other subjects soon. The working groups had representatives from related departments. We worked closely with other deputy governors in constituting the working groups and getting the approval of the governor. The idea was to ensure that the group got an awareness of the big picture, explored theory, studied global best practices, and appreciated the Indian context. This system worked very well in evolving an institutional approach rather than a departmental approach to the subjects. After a few months, the governor, Rangarajan, felt that we were overdoing the idea of working groups and committees, and said so. Yet, both Rangarajan and his successor, Bimal Jalan, approved every one of the groups we proposed.

The second challenge was to encourage the RBI professionals to be interactive with other stakeholders. Till then they considered it inappropriate to interact closely with the regulated institutions or financial market participants. In a way, that was good in the earlier years of the command and control system. We recognised that under the changing circumstances we might have to learn from other institutions and market participants, including foreign banks, when we were attempting market-oriented financial sector reforms. Moreover, the financial sector reform required us to understand the concerns of the market players and to ensure their cooperation in an informal and interactive fashion. Therefore, we constituted two advisory committees, one for money markets and one for the government securities market. The membership was drawn from both the public and private sectors, and also academics and practitioners. The advisory groups helped us to get to know people in the private sector well enough to be in continuous touch. The success of the arrangement depended on the selection of members for the advisory committees and that itself warranted assessment by us of individuals and the institutions they were associated with.

As a central banker, I had greater freedom than in the government to state my positions on broader policy issues.[8] I took the earliest possible opportunity to do so. My speech in the conference organised by the World Gold Council in Delhi on 28 November 1996 was given soon after I took over as deputy governor. It was titled, 'Gold in the Indian Economic System'. I concluded it with the words: 'Finally, how should policy towards gold be integrated with financial sector reform and in the final analysis what would be its link with the currency convertibility on capital account?'

Foreign exchange management demanded that we recognise the huge demand for gold in India, which is met almost wholly by imports. Till 1997, a critical part of the foreign exchange earned by our country was used up for the import of gold. The planning era was dominated by two beliefs: namely, savings by households in the form of gold was an unproductive use and hence should be discouraged; and valuable foreign exchange should not be wasted by importing gold. So, public policy imposed severe controls on domestic trade and import of gold was prohibited, except for re-export as jewellery. Simultaneously, several policy measures were taken to wean away people from investing their savings in gold. Yet, people continued to use savings to buy gold. Why?

For most women, gold is the only wealth they possess. They do not have much by way of other property rights. Generally, gold is inherited by women from women in the family. Therefore, its importance in the fabric of family relations cannot be ignored. Further, gold is both an investment good, and a consumption good that is held mostly in the form of jewellery. It also helps in providing liquidity since it can be pledged readily as collateral for borrowings in times of necessity. For many women, it is also the asset of last resort in the sense that in a time of acute distress, it can be converted into cash. It is the ultimate insurance available for middle- and lower-middle-class people in a society where there are very few insurance schemes.

The policy was coloured by the belief that gold is used as an unproductive investment and as a store for black money. But gold used for those purposes is usually in the form of bars and not jewellery. Gold bars form a small part of the gold used in the economy, and, significantly, the number of people who have them are very few as compared to the number who have gold as jewellery. Whenever someone from a lower-income or middle-income group is able to save, one of the first things they do is to buy some jewellery. Therefore, with increased population and economic growth occurring, the demand for gold would naturally increase. For the reasons discussed above, this is inevitable.

The conclusion was that it would be extremely difficult to contain or manipulate demand in the short-to-medium term. The only way in which the demand for gold (and therefore its import) could be moderated would be when higher incomes, change in cultural attitudes, and greater confidence in financial assets took hold in the longer run.

It was the disconnect between the policy and the reality that resulted in gold smuggling. In India, after oil, the largest amount of foreign exchange (official and unofficial) is utilised for import of gold. To some extent, the unrealistic gold policy was within the prevalent ideological framework. Before the 1991 reforms, the attitude was one of severe restrictions on non-essential imports across the board. As a part of the reforms, this changed and imports and consumables like luxury cars could be imported freely, though they were depreciating assets. In what could be a gender bias among us policy makers, the liberalisation was not extended to gold initially, even though it was a non-depreciating asset.

In the speech, I suggested that since gold imports were inevitable, it was better if they were through legal channels and within the ambit of forex markets. I said this in my speech and a few months later, the Committee on Capital Account Convertibility recommended the policy. The chairman of the committee was Tarapore. He was generous enough to acknowledge the contribution made by my speech. He described it as a watershed in gold policy.[9] The government took a decision to liberalise gold imports and levy a nominal duty. But the question was, who should be allowed to import the gold? One view was that there should be an open general licence, so that anyone who wanted to could import it. My advice to the government was that this was not desirable. I said that only authorised banks should be allowed to import gold. This surprised my colleagues in the government, since I was a champion of gold liberalisation. I explained that gold had the characteristics of an international currency and therefore it should be closely monitored, while being freely imported in normal circumstances. Finally, the licences were restricted mostly to select banks and a few canalising agencies.[10]

Another instance where I took the initiative was redefining the relationship between the RBI and the states. The RBI has several areas of interaction with state governments, in addition to its developmental role through the banking system. Since I had worked in the state governments, I was aware that the RBI was virtually operating as an agent of the Union government, though it is debt manager to the states through agreements. The states had no say in the manner in which limits to ways and means advances were decided by the RBI. The RBI was yet to play the role of fiscal advisor to state governments. At the same time, the RBI was the only institution that compiled and consolidated data on state finances. These efforts were instrumental in transforming the bank from being identified with the Union government to being a national public institution.

There were many instances where I assisted the governor in important polices and because of my previous experience in the government, the governor often assigned me the role of a negotiator with the government. In this task, I was representing the RBI but I was also a trusted former colleague of the officials in the government; I was generally viewed as someone who protected the interests of both the government and the RBI. During my period as deputy governor, there were five finance/

economic secretaries in the finance ministry. Though this lack of continuity might have made coordination difficult, I was fortunate enough to know them all personally, and to have had continuous association with the developments during this time.[11]

Among the earliest tasks given to me was that of preparing a draft agreement between the government and the RBI for introducing a new system of ways and means (akin to limited overdraft facility from a bank) to replace the system of automatic monetisation (provide money to the government as needed) that was prevalent then. The proposed system meant that the flexibility in budget and cash management to the ministry was curtailed. The bureaucracy was naturally averse to it, but since a policy decision was taken, they were willing to go along, provided the constraints were not too severe and they did not face the prospect of the Union government's cheques bouncing for lack of funds with the government. My friends in the ministry trusted me as a colleague who understood the political and bureaucratic dynamics in the system. This is a case of a mutual agreement that worked so well it was codified in law.[12]

Of all the policies that I worked on as deputy governor, perhaps the one that affects people and businesses the most was the Foreign Exchange Regulation Act (FERA). FERA was a draconian law that governed all transactions in foreign exchange. Reforms were carried out by recourse to diluting or liberalising the regulations and providing an array of exceptions to the rules. The government decided to replace the existing law with a new one that would be fundamentally different. The relative roles of the government and the RBI had to be redefined so that the market-oriented approach was replaced by a control-oriented approach. R.V. Gupta, my fellow deputy governor, and I worked to draft the legislation for the government to process it.[13]

While working on the fiscal responsibility legislation proposed by then Finance Minister Yashwant Sinha, I became a sort of bridge between expertise in the RBI and the authority of the Ministry of Finance. The RBI had, by then, done significant analytical work on statutory ceilings on debt, consolidated sinking fund, and debt sustainability. Perhaps there was no institution which could claim such expertise in India. We in the RBI worked on the subject and assisted a committee chaired by secretary (Economic Affairs) E.A.S. Sarma. I led the team in the RBI to make the proposals for a legislation consistent with what was desirable and feasible.[14]

Governor Jalan once said that if he were to point to my most valuable contribution as deputy governor, it would be my work on the RBI balance sheet. This was a complex matter that required the resolution of legacy problems and managing the transition to restoring the integrity of the balance sheet, and involved close consultations with the auditors and the government. The most sensitive element of the task related to the payment of dividends to the government. The RBI is owned by the Government of India and, thus, the government has a claim over the surpluses generated by its operations, after transfer to reserves to meet its capital needs. A bone of contention between the RBI and the government is the amount that should go to reserves before transferring surpluses to the government, which as per law should be determined by the board of the RBI. The critical factor in these matters was obtaining the consent of the government. To its credit, our proposals were approved in toto by the government, and then by the board. The policy package[15] had a logic, a goal, and an agreed path to reach the goal; something that we in the RBI and the government could be proud of.

We could be proud of the manner in which we could obtain special financing to meet the anticipated shortfalls in capital flows as a consequence of the sanctions that had been imposed by the US after our nuclear tests in May 1998. The government, in consultation with the RBI, decided to raise foreign exchange through issue of bonds to non-resident Indians to make up for the loss of capital inflows caused by the US sanctions. Bonds had to be issued by the SBI. The SBI argued that it was not commercially viable for it to assume foreign exchange risks involved in bonds. The RBI had decided, as a matter of policy, that it would not bear forex risks, as a prudent central bank. It had done so during the stress on balance of payments a few years earlier and it did not want to commit the same mistake again. The government felt that assuming foreign exchange risk whenever enterprises borrowed externally to serve public interest would create a bad precedent. The issue boiled down to having an arrangement for sharing of risk between the SBI and the government, with the RBI providing enabling conditions. Having been on the board of the SBI and worked in the government, discharging relevant responsibilities in the RBI, I was able to work on bringing out an innovative and burden-sharing formula that was fair and acceptable to all stakeholders.[16]

There were certain developments during this period that moved India and the RBI further into the global economic scene. In this environment I, too, was extremely lucky in that I could progress as a professional and gain invaluable exposure to international practices and policies. One of the most important was the G-20. In response to the global repercussions of the 1997 Asian Crisis, the G-20, a group of finance ministers and central bank governors representing twenty countries was created in 1999.

I was a deputy from India representing our central bank and this gave me an excellent opportunity to meet and interact with almost all the leading central bankers in the world. Another important development was in 1999, when the Financial Stability Forum was established by the G-7 countries (Canada, France, Germany, Great Britain, Italy, Japan, and the United States) to facilitate international financial stability. India and China were kept out of it, but were associated with its work in some of their working groups, mainly those dealing with evolving international standards and codes that should ideally govern the financial sector.

I was a member of one of the working groups which dealt with the evolution of standards in the forum. When the issue of compliance of individuals came up for discussion, we in the RBI and Government of India decided that we would make our own assessment of our compliance with international financial standards and codes. As a result, we developed invaluable expertise in these areas and established our credentials globally. I was also fortunate when the RBI became a member of the Bank for International Settlements (BIS) soon after I became a deputy governor; the timing was serendipitous. The mission of the BIS is to serve central banks in their pursuit of monetary stability. In a way, it acts as a bank for central banks. The BIS is an important source of information and research in central banking and a forum for exchanging knowledge and experience among central bankers. It facilitates global coordination at an informal level. For me, the BIS proved to be an invaluable resource for learning.

To sum up, there were many important events in the global space and fundamental changes within our economy and the RBI. During this period, the RBI acquired a prominent role in the economy and hence a higher profile. This was on account of both structural changes in the economy and a policy reorientation by the RBI. The bank ceased to automatically make available funds to the government without limits – hence, there was no more unlimited printing of money for the government. Capital inflows and outflows had an impact on money supply in our economy. Financial markets started playing a greater role than in the past. Monetary policy became more important and, therefore, the RBI initiated a more active role than before in the management of the economy. It became critical for the design and implementation of reforms of financial and external sectors. The skills of the Reserve Bank in managing externally induced shocks and in preempting the transmission of serious global uncertainties came into prominence. India escaped almost unscathed from the Asian Crisis, the impact of US sanctions after the nuclear tests, war in the Kargil region, the effects of problems in Russia and Mexico, Y2K (that is, onset of the new millennium), and 9/11.

The international standards of regulation and supervision of banks, then known as Basel II, were formally adopted and gradually implemented. Rapid strides were made in the application of technology. Development and regulation of financial markets consistent with policy reforms in related areas became a priority. Strides were made in technology application and a vision statement was evolved for the payments system. The work culture of the RBI changed from being inward looking to that of an institution interacting with financial institutions and financial markets. A distinct shift from 'control' to regulation and from command to service commenced.

It was also a period of immense satisfaction for me. The RBI had the stature to urge and obtain advice from several distinguished experts, financial market participants, and leaders of the corporate world, through several channels. For me, the members of the two committees on capital account convertibility, both chaired by Tarapore, and various advisory groups on international financial standards and codes and advisory committees on government securities and money markets were of great educative value. My speech on gold was not the only one I gave during this period. I also gave a speech on the adequacy of reserves in May 2002 and described it as a personal journey, from agony to comfort. While in 1991 I was agonised by the shortage of foreign exchange, by 2002, when I was leaving the RBI, we were managing a level of reserves that some felt was excessive. My speech in Goa on the exchange rate became a landmark one in respect of its impact on forex markets. In fact, the speeches I gave as deputy governor were a source of greatest satisfaction for me.

At a professional level, my six-year tenure was a period when momentous and rapid changes were happening in the RBI, and to be part of it was both an education and a delight.

15

THE RANGARAJAN ERA

Dr C. Rangarajan had a formidable reputation as a central banker. He had been governor for close to four years. He was deputy governor for almost a decade. Rangarajan had provided a vision and an intellectual framework for reforms in India in many areas. When I joined the RBI, it was to be his last year as a central banker and my first year as one. Here is the story of how a veteran and a fresher worked together. The areas that were close to Rangarajan's heart were: monetary policy framework; redefining the relationship between the government and the RBI; and his approach to external sector management.

Rangarajan was the principal author of the report of the Chakravarty Committee to assess the functioning of the Indian monetary system in 1985. The foundation for a new monetary policy framework was laid by this report. It asserted that price stability was essential for promoting growth and achieving other social objectives. Over a period, Rangarajan refined his thoughts and began a process of fundamental changes in the monetary policy framework in 1991 with support from Manmohan Singh and, later, P. Chidambaram. The new framework was meant to increase the role of market forces and of monetary policy. In early 1997, political uncertainties cropped up, potentially making it difficult to proceed with reforms. But in the Annual Policy of 1997, described as a big bang policy, a political vacuum was used as an opportunity to accelerate the reforms. How and why it was done is a story worth telling.

Rangarajan had redefined the relationship between the Union government and the RBI, beginning with his famous Kutty memorial lecture on putting an end to automatic monetisation (that is, the RBI printing money whenever the government was in need). Rangarajan signed an agreement to end this practice in phases. The next step was to operationalise it with a ways and means advance system acceptable to both the RBI and the government. To achieve this, the finance ministers were won over by Rangarajan, but the bureaucracy had to be brought on board and my involvement was helpful. That is an interesting story of designing a supplementary agreement on financing of temporary mismatches in government revenues and expenditures of the Union government.

The ending of automatic monetisation and of financing of budget deficit at below market rates (that is, the RBI giving loans to the government at concessional rates) had a positive impact on the bank's balance sheet. This and other related changes as part of reform brought to the fore the issue of sharing of surplus of receipts over expenditures of the RBI between its reserves and transfer to the government. This was a complex, unexplored area, encompassing macro factors, fiscal, monetary and external management and autonomy of the RBI. There was little or no awareness in India of the features and quality of a central bank balance sheet in a market-oriented economy. Though somewhat technical, the designing of a modern balance sheet for the RBI was a fascinating experience.

I sought to extend Rangarajan's initiative in redefining the relationship between the Union government and the central bank to state governments. Without annoying the Union government, we had to institutionalise a forum for state finance secretaries which was basically owned and driven by them, with a facilitator role being played by the RBI. How my close association with the state governments enabled successful innovation merits narration.

Rangarajan as chairman of the high-level committee laid the framework for external sector management. A sound legal backing for the new policy framework replacing the Foreign Exchange Regulation Act was desired by the government. Rangarajan wanted to design a law that incorporated the legitimate role of the government and the RBI as envisaged in the new framework, but provided adequate flexibility to adapt to evolving circumstances. We initiated the work under Rangarajan's guidance but completed it in Jalan's time.

This period saw innovation of what is at times referred to as open-mouth operations influencing the financial markets, by the governor or deputy governors speaking out on a subject in forex markets. I was, in some ways, a messenger, but ended up taking the credit or blame. There is an element of comedy in the episode that I will be describing later in the chapter.

I expect the reader to be interested in how we worked together on matters dear to Rangarajan, to which I made a brief reference earlier. The timing of the big bang policy of 1997 was fortuitous. Rangarajan fixed 5 May 1997 for announcement of the Annual Credit Policy Statement. Banks were informed of the date and the news was put in the public domain. In the meantime, the Congress party withdrew support to the government of the day, and there were uncertainties about the future of the government. The governor was initially inclined to postpone the date of the policy announcement so that full-fledged consultations with the government could take place and its backing assured for the policy. I urged the governor not to consider postponement of the date of announcement.

My argument was that by not changing the date of the monetary policy, the RBI would be in a position to give a signal that we were apolitical, and that we could act independently during periods of political uncertainty. I also explained that the government might not approve some of our proposals when formally consulted, but it would not be in a position to disapprove them once measures were already taken. I added that the state of political vacuum provided a window for us to push through some proposals as long as we were convinced about their importance and the likelihood of their not being reversed by the government. Further, we already had the advantage of preliminary discussions with the ministry at a technical level and, therefore, we had an inkling of the thinking of the professionals in the ministry.

'Sir,' I added, to liven up the atmosphere, 'autonomy is seldom granted. It has to be grabbed.'

Rangarajan, who appeared to be in two minds before our discussion, opted for going ahead with the statement of policy.

The big bang policy was announced on 15 April 1997, but it was a result of significant background work done in the RBI, and a small window of opportunity provided by a political vacuum.[1] The mechanisms of working groups within the RBI helped inter-departmental coordination, without the drudgery of formal processing of files. The process of consultations enabled inputs from academics, market participants, and industry associations. The expertise, long years of experience, and the stature of Rangarajan made the big bang possible.

The nature of relationships among different institutions in the economy was changed by the big bang policy. The policy changed the relationship between the RBI and banks from micro regulation to macro management. It changed the relationship between banks and borrowers by giving greater choice to borrowers among banks and among the modes of financing their requirements. To the extent the process of integration of financial markets had started, it changed the relationship between different market participants, especially banks. The relationship between the RBI and market participants was also changed by expanding and reinforcing the consultative process.

The big bang policy sought greater market orientation in the financial sector by empowering banks with more operational flexibility. The RBI started to move out of micro regulation. Banks acquired freedom on consortium arrangements and the methodology of assessing working capital requirements. At the same time, prudential guidelines continued to be prescribed by the RBI. Borrowers were also empowered to reinforce market orientation. Borrowers could choose to go through a single bank or multiple banks or take the syndication route. Access to commercial paper was made relatively free.

The bank rate was to emerge over a period as a signal of the stance of monetary policy and determine the rate at which funds would be available to the system from the RBI. The RBI refinance rates and the rates at which it provided liquidity support to primary dealers were all linked to the bank rate. Lendable resources to the banks were sought to be enhanced through a commitment to reduce, as per preannounced time frame, the statutory liquidity (SLR) and cash reserve ratios (CRR).

'If countries could make their way to prosperity by printing money, no country would be poor' is a comment Manmohan Singh made in a meeting of select members of Parliament. But the government was addicted to making the RBI print money at its command. The process of de-addiction started with Rangarajan's famous Kutty memorial lecture. He pleaded for putting an end to the system of automatic monetisation through recourse to ad hoc treasury bills.[2] But that could be done only if the government agreed to do it. It was not difficult for him to prevail upon Finance Minister Manmohan Singh to enter into an agreement with the RBI on the subject. An agreement signed on 9 September 1994 provided for limits to such monetisation and a gradual reduction in it between 1994-95 and 1996-97. The next step, the period from 1997 to 1999, was to bring the Union government into the discipline of ways and means advances (the overdraft facilities available) similar to that of the state governments. The discipline provides a limit on ways and means advances, and specifies the number of days beyond which the expenditure cannot be incurred, if the excess over limits persists continuously.

The challenge was to work out the operational details of the application of ways and means advance system to the government that was acceptable to all parties. Rangarajan assigned this task to me not only because I was dealing with the subject in the RBI, but also because of my professional association with the Ministry of Finance and personal contacts with them. There was reluctance at the official level in the Ministry of Finance to accept such an arrangement. Their argument was that in the case of state governments, the RBI could stop payments if the overdraft exceeded a particular period. It was inconceivable that the RBI could do that in the case of the Government of India because it would undermine the image of the sovereign. The challenge for me, therefore, was to devise a mechanism which would avoid such a contingency. I proposed that the RBI could use its hat as the debt manager of the government and ensure that debt was raised by the government through issuance of bonds well before the overdraft limitations came into effect. I suggested that the RBI would, under the proposed agreement, be obligated to issue bonds the moment the level of ways and means advance reached 75 per cent of the ceiling. The ceiling itself was to be mutually agreed upon between the Union government and the RBI every year, but at two levels during the year – broadly, one for the first half and the other for the second half, on the basis of the liquidity requirement of the government. As regards the interest rate also, I suggested that we could move gradually from the prevailing low but fixed interest rate towards a rate consistent with policy as the ultimate objective.

The officials in the Ministry of Finance were sceptical about the implications, especially regarding losing the freedom to access funds whenever they wanted, and also having to incur the additional burden of paying out larger amounts as interest. I pointed out that such limits would actually strengthen the hands of the ministry in resisting pressure from various departments on spending. I also explained that what the government would pay to the RBI as higher interest on ways and means and overdraft would be given back by it to the government in the form of higher surplus or dividend, which would accrue to the government's budget. It was, thus, possible to convince the officials to moderate their opposition to the agreement. The bold decision to adopt the new system was taken by Chidambaram, who had become finance minister by then.

It was a memorable experience for me to design operational details of a transition from an anachronistic practice to a well-defined framework of monetary–fiscal relationship and to work closely with my colleagues and friends in the finance ministry. This agreement was a precursor to the subsequent provisions made in the fiscal responsibility legislation that enabled operational autonomy in the conduct of monetary policy by the RBI.

In 1955, the spending authority, namely, the Government of India, acquired total control over the authority for creating money, namely, the RBI, thus undermining the spirit of institutional arrangements for conduct of monetary policy. It took about forty years to change it, and it needed a governor like Rangarajan and a minister like Dr Singh to do it in 1994. I had the privilege of facilitating replacement of the system of ad hocs with ways and means in 1997.

I believe that the states play a critical role in economic activity, especially in providing essential public services. In the state governments, the RBI was considered essentially an institution belonging to the Union government, though it had a relationship with the states similar to the Union. The RBI as a debt manager and banker to state governments also had the potential to be a fiscal advisor to the states as it had always been to the Union government. In regard to the dispensation of credit, in particular, mobilisation of institutional finance and priority sector lending, the RBI interacted with state governments. In addition to the development role, the RBI had to coordinate with state governments in regard to some regulatory aspects where there were shared responsibilities, such as regulation of urban cooperative banks and, to some extent, rural cooperatives. But in practice it turned out in a way that the RBI was distant from state governments and was identified closely with the Union government. Soon after joining the RBI, I was convinced that it had not realised its potential for influence on the state governments. It could enable interaction between the state governments on matters of relevance to the RBI. It could even play a positive role in resolving procedural and operational issues that might arise between the Union and the states from time to time.

We invited representatives of the Comptroller and Auditor General, Comptroller General of Accounts, Department of Economic Affairs, Expenditure Department and Planning Commission to attend the meetings with state finance secretaries, so that the Union government did not get the impression of being bypassed.

Rangarajan supported the idea of an annual conference of state finance secretaries and, in fact, gave the inaugural address for the very first conference. The agenda for the meeting was finalised after consultations with the state finance secretaries. Working groups of state finance secretaries were constituted at the time of the meeting for specific purposes for in-depth examination and submission of reports to the annual meetings. The ownership was entirely with the group of finance secretaries. The RBI provided only secretarial and technical support. In fact, fiscal responsibility legislations in the form of ceilings on debts and guarantees were actually taken up by the state governments with the guidance of the RBI as a result of these deliberations.

This initiative dramatically changed the relationship between the RBI and the state governments, particularly at a time when the political equations between the Union government and the state governments were complex. Since the commencement of the conference, the RBI is perceived as a national or federal institution and not merely an institution of the Union government.

Once, when he was finance minister, Manmohan Singh told me, 'The excess profit of a central bank is a reflection of profligacy of the government.' If the government borrows directly or indirectly from the Reserve Bank, the interest accrues to the bank and adds to its income. An end to automatic monetisation meant that the government had to borrow at market-related interest rates. The changed relationships between the Government of India, the RBI and financial markets had an impact on the RBI's balance sheet.[3] These developments have implications on the surpluses generated by the RBI over which the government has legitimate claim as the owner of the bank after making necessary provision for reserves needed by the RBI for its operations. The issue was the basis on which the surpluses had to be distributed between reserves of the RBI and transfers to the government, on which there was lack of clarity at that time.

In 1994-95, the statutory auditors of the RBI had suggested that transfers to reserves must have a relation to the total size of the balance sheet, as also to the size of the profits for the year. They also expressed the view that a distribution policy of the profits of the bank should be supported by an express resolution of the central board of the RBI. Hence, during the period 1996-97, an informal group was set up within the RBI to study and recommend suitable guidelines for creation of internal reserves and allocation of profits. The group studied international practices, our legal provisions and our circumstances. It identified three risks as having an impact on the RBI's balance sheet, namely, risks arising out of monetary and exchange-rate policy compulsions requiring intervention by the RBI in the securities, money and forex markets; risks arising out of revaluation of foreign assets and gold; systemic risks and requirements relating to the central bank's developmental role, internal frauds, unforeseen losses, etc.

The group recommended that an indicative target of reserves at 12 per cent of the size of the bank's assets would be appropriate. The prevailing level of reserves was well below the recommended 12 per cent. Our proposal was to gradually increase the share of transfer to reserves. The objective was to reach 12 per cent over the medium term and maintain it at that level thereafter. I sent a formal proposal to the Ministry of Finance for acceptance, before the matter was taken to the central board of directors, since this affected the availability of funds to the budget from year to year from the RBI. Montek Singh Ahluwalia, finance secretary, wanted to have a detailed discussion on the subject in regard to both monetary and fiscal implications. I tried to explain it to him in detail.

Montek then asked me only one question: 'This is too complicated. If you were in the Ministry of Finance in my position, would you agree to this proposal?'

I told him: 'Yes, definitely.'

He gave me a go-ahead. That was the mutual trust and level of respect for professionalism we had in each other.

The central board of the RBI approved the recommendations of the group and agreed that an indicative target for CR at a level of 12 per cent of the size of the bank's assets would be reached by the year 2005. Thus, the issue of provision for reserve and transfer of balance to the government as profits had been resolved by making it somewhat formula based. It could be said to the credit of the government that they accepted the proposal 'out of trust', confident that it took care of the interests of both the government and the RBI.

Yet another challenge related to the large stock of special government securities on the balance sheet of the RBI. They were accumulated over a period of time with no fixed maturity and a fixed rate of interest which was far lower than the market rate of interest. Sound accounting practices demanded that they must be marked to market, but such an exercise would be virtually impossible due to underdeveloped markets and, in any case, huge losses would have to be shown in the balance sheet, eroding the capital and reserves of the Reserve Bank. The auditors were keen that there should be a policy.

The auditors were told that we needed time to fix this legacy problem. The issue was taken up with the government and a mechanism worked out. The RBI entered into an agreement to convert non-marketable assets into marketable assets from time to time as per the needs of the open market operations, that is, whenever the RBI needed to absorb liquidity from the market, it could sell the government bonds. But conversion meant additional cost to the government, so the RBI agreed to compensate the government for interest rate differential when it converted special securities into marketable securities. The RBI benefitted by not incurring any capital loss on these securities. The practice of exchange guarantee was given up. This whole process required intensive interactions with the auditors and the audit committee of the central bank, which called for attention to detail, approvals of the Union government, and above all, perceptions of the financial markets about the RBI's balance sheet. With these arrangements, the RBI acquired some discretion to determine the acquisition of domestic assets and also foreign currency assets, and thus have a framework for exercising operational autonomy.

One of the prized possessions of the RBI archives is a letter in June 1961 from Indira Gandhi, seeking release of foreign exchange for expenses. Rajiv Gandhi's training in Cambridge had to be funded and justification was to be given for accessing valuable foreign exchange, even if the application was from the daughter of the prime minister.[4] There was liberalisation since 1991, but the law remained. The government in consultation with the governor decided to replace the Foreign Exchange Regulation Act with a new legislation more in tune with global thinking and Indian realities. The new legislation was meant to put a liberalised environment for foreign-exchange transactions on a firm footing. After considerable discussions with what was then known as the Exchange Control Department, a framework was prepared that should govern the new legislation. In the first week of July 1997, I made a presentation to Montek Ahluwalia (secretary, Economic Affairs), Governor Rangarajan and other deputy governors on the eve of the meeting of the board of directors in Chennai.

The proposed legislation, I suggested, should emphasise external sector management based on broad principles rather than regulation and control of transactions. FERA made it obligatory on citizens to declare the stock of external assets, in particular foreign currency, to the RBI. The proposed legislation, on the other hand, should only be tracking transactions, and not the stock. All current account transactions that had been legally authorised should not require any further approvals by the RBI. However, what constituted a genuine current account transaction could be defined by the RBI, and no restrictions or approval process be prescribed. Any restriction on current account transactions would, therefore, be exceptional and could be authorised only by the government.

The presentation proposed that all capital account transactions ought to be in the regulatory jurisdiction of the RBI. The RBI could stipulate those transactions that could be undertaken without specific approval and those that might require some sort of approval. In other words, while there was a negative list of prohibited transactions in current account, there were only positive lists for undertaking capital account transactions. An authority to compound offences was proposed, since many violations of the legal provisions could take place by oversight or merely for procedural reasons, often due to business contingencies. However, the compounding authority could also refuse to compound, in which case the matter could be referred to the Enforcement Directorate. Thus, violation was not necessarily construed as a criminal act. A provision was needed to regularise several pending cases with the Enforcement Directorate and the RBI so that legacy problems did not persist. The draft legislation based on the framework agreed between Rangarajan and Dr Singh was discussed in detail with Jalan and Chidambaram, and finally enacted when Yashwant Sinha was finance minister.

Legal and structural changes do take time and effort, but immediate challenges demand quick action. By early August 1997, we in the RBI felt that the rupee was overvalued in forex markets. The overvaluation appeared to be persistent and at an uncomfortable level. The RBI could find it difficult to manage overshooting of the correction if there was an attack on the rupee by speculators. It was felt that timely correction in the exchange rate should be induced at a time of our choosing. We felt that before attempting to undertake intervention in the market, which involved open market operations – buying US dollars – an attempt should be made to influence market sentiment by expressing our concerns.

It was, therefore, decided by the RBI governor that I would take the opportunity to speak on exchange rate management in Goa on 15 August 1997 at the conference of the Foreign Exchange Dealers' Association of India. The speech was carefully drafted and reviewed by the governor. It tried to explain our concerns and nudge the rate in a desired direction without creating knock-on effects in the market. The Goa speech was my maiden performance in 'central bank speaks', or 'open-mouth operation'.[5]

The speech had the intended effect on all accounts. But something more happened. I received a call from the governor. He mentioned that as per a news item, I.K. Gujral, the prime minister, had given an interview to the *Economic Times* wherein he expressed his intention to change the exchange rate policy to a formal band of exchange rates within which the market could operate. That was not our policy and Rangarajan was seriously concerned about a possible panic reaction in the market. Apparently, immediately after seeing the news item, Rangarajan called Chidambaram. He was also taken by surprise and confirmed that the prime minister had had no official briefing. However, the PM's interview with the journalist was tape-recorded. Therefore, it was not possible for the prime minister or the government to deny it, but the government did not have objection to the RBI clarifying the position. How were we to do that? We could not deny a statement when somebody else gave the interview.

We in the RBI were clear that somebody had to deny, to correct the impression, and so we did it. The press release titled 'RBI Clarification on Exchange Rate' dated 20 August 1997 read as follows: 'The *Economic Times* issue of 20 August 1997 in a front-page article attributes to the prime minister the view that the government would shortly fix a band to signal the exchange rate of the rupee in relation to the US dollar. This report is misleading. It is clarified that while the Committee on Capital Account Convertibility had recommended a band in relation to a neutral real effective exchange rate, no decision in this regard has been taken by the government and the RBI. While the exchange rate will continue to be determined by market forces, it is recognised that the exchange rate management will have to balance the needs of the exporters to have a favourable exchange rate and the need to prevent monetary expansion from going beyond what is considered appropriate for maintaining price stability.'

Here is an unusual case of the RBI denying something that the prime minister had said about the exchange rate policy. These developments added to the confusion prevailing in the markets about both the exchange rate policy and the comfort of the RBI with the prevailing exchange rate. However, the desired rapid correction started taking place.

There was a twist to the tale. The government was unhappy with the rapid depreciation, and in a way, I was blamed, though the need for depreciation was conceded by the government in internal discussions before I delivered the speech. Rangarajan clarified that he had cleared the speech since there was a broad agreement with the government on this. The finance minister felt that the ongoing depreciation was too rapid for comfort. We were, therefore, advised by the minister to intervene in the currency market to moderate the pace of depreciation. I was strongly of the opinion that the depreciation should be behind us and not ahead of us. Hence, we should not try to moderate the pace of desired depreciation but allow it freely as long as there was no serious panic, and in the process, we should be prepared for an initial marginal overshooting over the desired level of depreciation.

Governor Rangarajan, Secretary Ahluwalia and the chief economic advisor, Shankar Acharya, took me along to a meeting in Delhi with Chidambaram at his residence one evening to discuss this matter. The minister urged intervention by the RBI to moderate the pace of depreciation that was triggered at our initiative, but I was against it since the markets would be confused if my speech favouring depreciation was followed with intervention in forex markets to moderate depreciation. The governor and the finance secretary were inclined to support me, but left it to me to argue my case strongly. I did that faithfully and vehemently.

Chidambaram, referring to the Goa speech, pointedly said, 'You will never be forgiven for what you have done.' I persisted with my arguments in favour of allowing depreciation of the rupee even if it were to overshoot. Finally he took me aside.

'Venu,' he said, 'this is a complex matter. We cannot take a purely technical view. We want to avoid possible disruptions in some markets. Depreciation should not be too fast.' At that point, it was clear that the disorderly correction in markets was a matter of judgement. The minister's judgement was different from ours. We, therefore, decided to intervene to some extent, to smoothen the pace of depreciation.

The Goa speech succeeded in its original intent of inducing exchange rate depreciation at an appropriate time. In contrast, the currencies of the countries affected by the Asian Crisis, such as Thailand, Indonesia and Korea, had to incur the cost of steep depreciation of their currencies brought about by market forces. The role of the induced exchange rate depreciation in moderating the impact of the Asian financial crisis on India was appreciated. It is in this context that Tarapore, my predecessor, wrote that when the definitive monetary history of the recent period is written up, Dr Reddy will come out as the saviour of Indian exchange rate policy.[6] To this day, there is a debate whether I was a sinner or a saviour, but in reality I was a messenger who happened to concur with the message.

Life is not only about successes. Failures are almost as common as successes. Our notable failure involved an issue that combined currency, public debt, forex reserves and bilateral trade matters. I was closely associated with a failed move to make one-time settlement of our rupee debt to Russia. The assignment was taken up towards the end of the Rangarajan era and closed in the early months of the Jalan era. Chidambaram took personal interest in this settlement and I was enthusiastic.

In 1997, it became clear to us that Russia was in desperate need of foreign convertible currency, that is, US dollars. On an alert from Ronen Sen, our ambassador in Moscow, it was decided in the Reserve Bank that we could arrange for a one-time payment of the whole of rupee debt owed to Russia by paying in dollars.[7]

In other words, it involved a discount for making a non-convertible rupee debt into convertible currency debt and also discounting of the future debt obligations by an appropriate interest rate for arriving at a one-time settlement amount. I was to work out a negotiating strategy and details of the scheme for one-time payment. Accordingly, and on the basis of authorisation by the Ministry of Finance, in particular, Chidambaram, and as approved by Rangarajan, I worked on a scheme for the purpose.

I went to London along with my executive assistant, Ananthakrishnan Prasad, to hold discussions with the finance secretary of the Russian government, in total confidence and on a one-to-one basis, in a mutually agreed/neutral location (a hotel). On return, the matter was pursued. A second round of discussion, again on a one-to-one basis, took place in the RBI building on an early morning over breakfast to clinch the deal. It was possible to agree on terms which were of great benefit to both the governments.

In order to reduce the fiscal impact on our government, arrangements were made to provide a loan from the Reserve Bank to the Government of India to enable it to buy the foreign exchange from RBI and repay the whole of rupee-denominated debt in US dollars at a discount of little less than half the total amount. Soon after my breakfast with Mikhail Kasyanov, deputy minister of finance (who later rose to become the first prime minister of Russia), I went to North Block and met Chidambaram, who was guiding the process, at 8.45 a.m. one day. He was fully supportive of the package. The deal was to be finalised the same day with a visiting ministerial-level delegation from Russia. Chidambaram gave me a surprise at the formal lunch with the Russian delegation that day. He said that the proposal was not approved. He did not give any reason. I did not ask.

My understanding was that the deal had been acceptable to us till a few hours before and that it was to be clinched in Delhi. All the discussions were held in strictest confidence in both countries because of the fear of what was known as 'Russian debt mafia in India and Indian debt mafia in Russia'. I felt saddened that a deal which could have had a huge positive impact on our external debt liabilities and been a source of considerable cleaning up of vested interests had failed, despite Chidambaram's best efforts. I kept Rangarajan, during whose tenure the negotiations commenced, and Jalan, in the picture.

The appointment of the successor to Rangarajan, Bimal Jalan, and appointment of Rangarajan as governor, Andhra Pradesh, happened simultaneously. On 22 November, Jalan took over as RBI governor from Rangarajan. As per tradition, the incoming governor is received at the RBI by the secretary to the board and escorted to the eighteenth floor, where the governor's office is located. The outgoing governor is seen off from the RBI by the secretary to the board. However, Jalan insisted on escorting Rangarajan to the car and seeing him off. In addition, he insisted on seeing off his predecessor at the airport when he was boarding the flight. These courtesies were unprecedented. They reflected the temperament and the character of Jalan – informal, affectionate, pleasant, and cheerful.

Later in the day, Jalan walked into my room on his way out of the office. It is not often that the governor walks into a deputy governor's room in the RBI. Jalan said, 'Venu, is Geetha here? If so, are you free this evening? Meenu and I want to come over in the evening for tea.'

'Of course, we are free. Please come over, and we would be delighted.' They came over to our flat and we chatted about old times.

Jalan said, 'I look forward to working with you again.'

I responded, 'Let me think it over, sir.' I had worked with Jalan, and we worked well together. Yet, I had been brought in by Rangarajan. I was not sure if Jalan would want me, or would prefer to have his own team.

Jalan, with his typical disarming style, said, 'Man, you cannot do this to your friend. You better stay put. We will have fun. Let us work together.'

I was, of course, happy that I was wanted by the incoming governor. I stayed on to learn new things from a new governor.

16

JALAN TAKES ON A CRISIS

C. RANGARAJAN'S TERM CAME TO AN END ABOUT A YEAR AFTER I joined. I had become close to his successor, Bimal Jalan, since my days in the World Bank, when he was chief economic advisor. Jalan had a distinguished, intellectual look, with a large forehead and oversized glasses. He was a perpetually cheerful man who usually kept his cheer even in times of turbulence. Rangarajan, too, had a distinguished look, though he had a more formal style. Both Jalan and Rangarajan had similar backgrounds in that they were economists. Both were very warm-hearted people.

Rangarajan, a product of Madras University, spent half of his career in academia. He was a teacher, a research guide, and a prolific writer on academic and policy issues. He taught at prestigious universities in the US and in the Indian Institute of Management, Ahmedabad. He had a long and distinguished tenure as deputy governor, RBI. He was briefly a member of the Planning Commission and the Finance Commission before he took over as governor. Almost his entire career was in India.

Jalan had studied at Presidency College, Kolkata, and Oxford and Cambridge universities. He had a career devoted to working in public institutions, mostly in the government, but also in the Commonwealth Secretariat, World Bank and IMF in several stints. He was chief economic advisor for several years and was also secretary to the government. Jalan dealt with monetary policy issues for several years in his capacity as chief economic advisor, executive director in IMF and finance secretary. He was associated with the Planning Commission briefly as member secretary, before moving to the RBI as governor.

The differences and similarities in their backgrounds were reflected in their styles of functioning. Rangarajan believed that there was no practice without theory. He viewed all issues in the light of a deep understanding of theory and a careful analysis of relevant facts and factors. Jalan believed that theory was merely a tool for understanding the reality and so familiarity with the contours of theory as needed was adequate. He was essentially a strategist, with a quick and instinctive grasp of complex realities. Rangarajan believed in deep understanding of systems and liked to drive changes. Jalan addressed the issues on hand and brought about better outcomes as the situations warranted and evolved. Rangarajan's main focus was on improvement of the system and getting over the problems as they arose, while Jalan's focus was on solutions to problems on hand as well as emerging ones, thus inducing systemic improvements.

Jalan had an informal personal style, but was known for adroitly managing political and bureaucratic elements. Rangarajan, on the other hand, tended to be formal in official dealings and also professorial in discussions. Despite apparent informality, Jalan kept thoughts and plans close to his chest, and shared information only on a need-to-know basis. Rangarajan invariably shared all information, including interactions with the government functionaries and other central bankers. Rangarajan believed in articulation and communication of his ideas, while Jalan encouraged others to do the communication, and kept his options open. However, where he thought necessary, Jalan was quick to react and was firm in his stand. He was equally at ease with politicians, academics, bureaucrats, and businessmen.

The contexts in which they became governors were very different. For Rangarajan, it was continuity in central banking with a brief interlude in the Planning Commission. For Jalan, it was virtually a culmination of his long career as an economist in the government. When Rangarajan became governor, he was continuing with the reform agenda and the systems improvement that he envisaged for a decade and a half. Except for a brief interlude in the Planning Commission, he was a quintessential central banker with a strong academic background. Jalan was, for most of his career, associated with the government, and a central bank's perspective was something which he had to absorb after being inducted into the organisation. They had known each other and interacted professionally for over a decade, but from different perspectives. They had good personal equation and mutual respect.

I worked with Rangarajan basically representing the government when he was in the central bank, though I assisted him in some specific tasks when he was in the Planning Commission. At a personal level, I had known Jalan for a longer period and worked directly with him as joint secretary when he was finance secretary. We worked alongside on several occasions earlier when I was in the World Bank and he was chief economic advisor. My role as deputy governor in assisting Jalan was, therefore, different from my role in assisting Rangarajan.

The Jalan era commenced in November 1997. It was virtually at the height of the Asian Crisis when there was capital flight out of several fast-growing East Asian economies resulting in a contagion effect in India. Our markets were in turmoil. Our efforts to moderate the turbulence in the forex markets were still continuing, with no clear sign of abating, when a change at the helm of the RBI took place. Jalan demitted office in September 2003, after managing several challenges, leaving behind a robust economy and a confident Reserve Bank.

It was baptism by fire for Jalan. He had to face many critical challenges as governor. The Asian Crisis was where he established his credentials as a successful governor.

The impact of the Asian Crisis was at its peak. There was already a severe downward pressure on the exchange rate of the rupee. Rangarajan had, in response to the challenges, adopted conventional measures to arrest the pressure – open market operations, that is, selling foreign currency available in our forex reserves, and issue of statements aimed at moral suasion and calming the nerves. When the change of guard took place, Jalan dramatically altered the strategy. He decided to take all measures aggressively on all fronts to counter the pressure on the rupee. The new strategy was not confined to intervention in forex markets, but encompassed many measures – policy rate, liquidity, and administrative measures, including imposition of controls. Several administrative measures, which may be described as control and command types, were used to manage the exchange rate volatility, for instance not allowing rebooking of cancelled contracts, restrictive use of balances, and expecting earners of foreign currency to repatriate the earnings.

At that time, conventional wisdom frowned upon such administrative measures. Taking strong and unconventional measures demonstrated boldness. Notwithstanding the danger of an element of overkill, Jalan felt that the risk was worth taking. He did not want to take any chances, and was adept at anticipating speculative activities or contagion and taking strong preemptive measures. I presume that he was worried about the possibility of financial markets taking advantage of a change of guard in RBI to mount speculative attacks.

Jalan used to discuss many of the steps that he was contemplating to meet the pressures in forex markets. My views were based on the predominant influence of Rangarajan's thinking, discussions with professionals in the RBI, and assessment of the situation. I was not uncomfortable with the wide and broad thrust of the range of monetary policy measures, including bank rate and liquidity measures suggested by Jalan, though a little disconcerted with the recourse to administrative measures (which were some form of control). Many of these were meant to influence exporters to repatriate their foreign currency earnings expeditiously and importers to avoid advancing their dollar payments. In other words, the objective of the measures was to reduce the scope for leads and lags influencing the spot market in foreign exchange.

Some of the measures suggested by Jalan amounted to a reversal of the progress in the reform measures along the path already envisaged. Jalan was clear that these should be undertaken irrespective of their immediate impact on the envisaged path of reform, but he was willing to revert to the reforms in due course. Hence, in each of the measures that were undertaken, it was made clear that these were temporary in order to meet the extraordinary situation, and that they would be reviewed or withdrawn later. On some occasions, the period for which the extraordinary measures operated was also indicated. Jalan felt that short-term measures could be undertaken even if they ran counter to the reform path in the longer term; a wedge between short-term measures and medium- to long-term policies could be driven when necessary. In other words, while moving in the direction of a desired long-term goal, a temporary retreat could be an effective tactic, provided credible commitment to the goal was maintained. This perspective was new to me. The outcomes proved that Jalan was right.

It was not as though Jalan had a prepared strategy to start with. But he was agile enough to respond to developments; he was prepared to discuss options and evolve tactics to tackle what he felt at that time to be the natural tendency of markets, namely, to profit from excess volatility. He was uninhibited and bold in fighting his battles but with a smile on his face.

After the induced correction in exchange rate through my speech on 15 August 1997, and forex intervention to smoothen correction in August and September, there was relative calm during October 1997. In November 1997, however, there was significant volatility in the forex markets due to the worsening situation in East Asia. It warranted intervention again in the foreign exchange markets by the RBI. This was followed up with some assuring statements that we were vigilant. When these did not have the desired effect, a statement from Rangarajan indicating the comfort of the Reserve Bank with the then prevailing exchange rate was issued. As it happened, there was no evidence that this statement had the desired effect either.

Jalan focused on fighting volatility but did not say a word about the exchange rate. He took a decision to aggressively intervene on several fronts to counter speculative attack, and a massive intervention in forex markets was a major component. As part of the new strategy, Jalan desired that there should be what may be called indirect intervention in the forex markets. Direct intervention, which had been the normal practice, involved the

RBI directly buying or selling the forex at the market's two-way quote. It was transparent. It showed the intention of the central bank and, thus, influenced expectations. Indirect intervention was an unknown practice and not transparent, but an innovation by Jalan.

Jalan noticed that whatever effect intervention had had lasted only as long as the RBI was in the market. Thereafter the market quickly reverted to the original levels. He felt that we might have better impact if we used the State Bank of India and a few public sector banks which were, in any case, active in the market, to sell at opportune times. The market would then not be quite sure whether we were in the market or the bank concerned was in the market. He also took large and lumpy payments out of the market by selling directly to the banks handling oil and defence payments at the ongoing market rate. Consequently, the demand for foreign exchange to finance such imports was taken out of the market.

I was opposed to indirect intervention on two grounds. First, that the whole operation was non-transparent, and as such, it should not be favoured by public policy. The second objection was that the banks concerned were operating in the forex markets on their own account. While operating on our behalf at our behest, the concerned banks were exclusively privy to the policies of the central bank and, thus, might be tempted to profit by misusing the information available to them on a real-time basis.

The objections were overruled by Jalan on the ground that the extent of indirect intervention was reported after a lag of one month and, as such, withholding information was only for a short period. As regards the possibility of misusing the information, he felt that the banks concerned might fall in line with our intentions once they became aware of them. In any case, the RBI could actually intervene through the banks without formally acknowledging that it was intervening. According to him, since only a few banks were used, the gains of indirect intervention or what could be described as surreptitious intervention by the RBI were more than the costs involved in select banks being privy to such intervention. Finally, the anchoring principle set out by Jalan was that such intervention was consistent with the philosophy of reducing volatility without being committed to holding a particular exchange rate. In other words, the strategy was to keep the option of intervening in the forex markets in a real-time, non-transparent manner without giving a signal of defending a particular level. Jalan felt that the very short term was what mattered to speculators in forex markets. The extent of indirect intervention would, in any case, be reflected in the level of reserves, on a net basis, after a lag.

The strategy designed and tested by the governor worked very well. Before long, I was convinced that my initial stance was wrong. The overall approach to management of foreign exchange to contain volatility designed by Jalan guided me during my entire tenure as governor.

Close on the heels of the Asian Crisis, Jalan faced a predicament. Prime Minister Vajpayee of the Bharatiya Janata Party had been sworn in on 19 March 1998. Around that time, a political leader from the ruling party expressed a commitment for a strong rupee. Immediately, Jalan took up the matter with the government. He made a presentation to the prime minister and several minsiters on the state of the economy. Pointedly, he urged political leaders to abstain from commenting on the exchange rate. He commanded the trust and confidence to get his point across.

This was followed by another, even more potentially serious issue. On 11 and 13 May 1998, India conducted five underground nuclear tests in the Pokhran desert. This was counter to the US efforts to prevent nuclear proliferation.

The day the second round of nuclear tests was conducted, the board of the RBI was in Kashmir for our periodic board meeting to be held the next day. At around 6 p.m., Sandip Ghose, executive assistant to the governor, came to my hotel room. Ghose handed me one sheet of paper. It was folded and there were a few lines in Jalan's handwriting.

Ghose said, 'Sir, governor wanted me to show this draft press release. It is in the strictest confidence. It is to be issued tomorrow morning.'

This was out of the blue and I went through the note carefully.

From the statement, it was evident that the US was to impose sanctions on India after our nuclear tests. Jalan's statement was to assure the financial markets.

I said, 'The draft is fine, but my advice is to not issue any statement. Please inform the governor.'

Ghose took the note back.

Later, at a cocktails and dinner reception hosted by the chief minister of Jammu and Kashmir, Farooq Abdullah, Jalan drew me aside. Jalan said that he had received information from the Prime Minister's Office that President Clinton would be announcing the US sanctions on India during the night, our time.

Jalan wanted to issue the statement that he had sent to my room. He wanted to assure the markets that the RBI did not expect any serious disruptions and that we were in readiness to intervene in the markets, if needed. This was meant to preempt possible panic in the markets. I disagreed. The US sanctions was an extraordinary event. I felt that it would be inappropriate to guide the markets without first assessing the possible reactions to such an event. In fact, I felt that the issuing of any statement by the governor might itself trigger panic in the financial markets. In times of such uncertainty, the risks of issuing a statement outweigh those of not issuing.

Jalan pointed out that that not issuing a statement on such an important development could amount to negligence, especially when we were notified. His instinct was to act on information rather than not act, which would leave the RBI open to criticism for not having acted. As we sipped our drinks, we both were left to our own thoughts, trying to decide what would be the right course of action.

Dinner was served. We laughed and made conversation with the host and other dignitaries. All the while, we were under great pressure, but we could not afford to show it.

Again, Jalan took me aside. 'I have already told the principal secretary to PM that we would be issuing a statement.'

'Sir, no problem,' I told him. 'You may like to tell the principal secretary that we thought about it and decided to observe and act as needed and that we are not issuing a statement in advance of reactions.' Jalan looked pensive and we both went back to our dinner. We were served the traditional Kashmiri feast: wazwan. But Jalan and I were hardly in a mood to enjoy our meal.

During dessert, Jalan took me aside again. He said, 'I told Alpana to be in readiness in the morning in the office. Talwar also should be there. How can we call it off?'

'Sir,' I repeated my argument, 'my only point is no statement and no comments till we observe the reactions.' I felt that we should give a statement or decide on any course of action depending on the evolving situation. In other words: don't stick your neck out when there are so many imponderables and uncertainties.

He said, 'I say, Venu, would you be personally responsible if we don't give a statement and the markets tumble?'

'Boss, who would be responsible if you give a statement and then markets tumble?'

We were both asserting our stand, without being sure about ourselves. The tension between us was palpable.

The party ended late at night. We stepped out. It was a clear night, with a slight nip. Jalan was leaving. I accompanied him for a final word. Only Ghose, his executive assistant, was with us. I wondered if I had spoken out of line with Jalan earlier. I wondered how he would react.

Jalan said, 'Sandip, no statement need be issued.'

He looked at me with his usual disarming smile and said, 'Okay, goodnight, Venu.' It was to his great credit that he took my words in the right spirit. I do not know many people who would have.

Around 10 a.m. the next day, Jalan rang me up and said, 'Venu, you must congratulate me for accepting your advice. We did not issue any statement, and the markets are reasonably normal.'

The imposition of sanctions by the US resulted in a significant reduction in the flow of foreign savings, particularly through the debt route. As a consequence, our assessment of the balance of payments situation had to be revised and it was necessary to organise a special source of capital flows, if financing of our imports and the exchange rate were not to be seriously affected. In other words, a judgement was made that there would be a disruption of the flows of foreign exchange, which would have to be bridged through special mobilisation of funds with the aid of public policy. Therefore, on a suggestion by the RBI, the government decided to take advantage of the positive sentiments of the non-resident Indians as a result of the nuclear tests.

We studied a precedent when NRIs helped the flow of forex resources soon after the crisis in 1991 through a scheme known as India Development Bonds 1991. These funds were mobilised by the State Bank of India, and surrendered in return for rupee equivalent to the RBI to add to the reserves, and used as needed. The funds were again made available by the RBI to the SBI at the time of repayment by exchanging rupees into foreign exchange. The SBI thus borrowed in foreign currency, swapped it into rupees with the RBI, used the rupees for lending, and at the time of repayment, reversed the process. The foreign exchange risk was borne entirely by the RBI. These bonds, which were in the nature of interest-earning deposits, were open only to non-resident Indians. At that time, immunity was also granted to the funds thus mobilised from NRIs, which implied that such funds could be repatriated to India without any fear of questions regarding their source or legality. It was assumed that, with reform and hope of a resurgent India, Indians would have the incentive to repatriate funds stashed abroad and cease taking recourse to illegal outflows in future. The precedent was useful in some ways, but the context in which the bonds had to be raised was different in view of sanctions imposed by the US and liberalised rules of monetary and financial management in India.

In view of its success, there was preference to adopt exactly the same pattern as the India Development Bonds. I was averse to such an approach. First, immunity was not necessary for the success of the bond, considering the fundamental economic strengths and the bright future of India. Second, the idea of a central bank bearing the foreign exchange risk was already discarded as part of reform. The risk should, therefore, be borne by the financial intermediary, namely, the SBI, to the extent commercially viable and prudent, and excessive risk, if at all, should be borne by the government at whose instance the SBI was raising the bonds. Third, it would be most appropriate to encourage the participation of US-based banks in this bond issue, signalling in a way the ineffectiveness of the economic sanctions. After considerable deliberations, my suggestion was accepted, and no immunity was granted.

In regard to foreign exchange risk, I was authorised to negotiate a scheme for the purpose between the SBI and the government. The former's stance was that the government should bear the entire forex risk as the bond was at its instance. On the other hand, the government insisted that there was no precedent for it to bear forex risks of borrowings by another entity. We devised a unique mechanism which was acceptable to the government, the RBI and the SBI, whereby SBI took upon itself a bearable modest extent of gains as well as losses (0.5 per cent per year, as I recall) and anything beyond that on either side was with the government. The SBI could price the loans factoring in measurable risk. As it turned out, there was no foreign exchange impact on the government since the rupee did not depreciate significantly.

I had to visit New York to convince US-based banks to cooperate with us despite the sanctions. They assured me of their support, mostly through their operations from outside the US. In a way, their support was sought to moderate the impact of US sanctions by assuring them significant share of the bond issue. We did not allow overseas branches of Indian banks to grant loans for subscription to bonds.

Jalan lent his unqualified support to this unprecedented initiative to meet an extraordinary situation. The SBI was taken into confidence. The chairman and both MDs were convinced that we had the interests of SBI also at heart. The additional secretary (Expenditure) came over to the RBI office in Delhi with the relevant file. We discussed in detail, and presented an agreed proposal to the finance minister for approval.

In 2001, there was a follow-up of issue of non-resident bonds which was somewhat similar to the Resurgent India Bonds of 1998. These were called the India Millennium Bonds. The purpose was to raise resources essentially to add to forex reserves, rather than bridge unanticipated deficit in balance of payments.

I had reservations about this scheme, though it was modelled on the Resurgent India Bonds. There were no special circumstances warranting recourse to special arrangements to finance our external payment obligations. Extraordinary arrangement for borrowing merely for adding to the reserves above a minimum required level was expensive since the return on the forex reserves was low relative to the cost of servicing the debt. This would create a bad precedent of recourse to extraordinary financing in normal times.

The governor disagreed with me, but felt that it was appropriate to bring the reservations to the notice of the finance minister, Yashwant Sinha. Finally, the scheme was implemented. There was no difficulty in garnering the amounts planned through the issue of the bonds. It is true that financial sector regulators in other countries had concerns regarding the sources of funds that were used for financing such bonds. But it is also true that foreign exchange reserves were boosted.

Jalan instinctively sensed dangers that might be encountered due to political economy factors in India. There were two examples, namely, establishment of an independent debt office and issue of sovereign bonds, where he exhibited his sound judgement.

I thought that a step in the right direction to develop financial markets would be to separate debt management from monetary management functions. A working group was set up in November 1997 to study global practices and propose an institutional mechanism for this purpose. The group recommended establishing an independent corporate entity under company law owned by the Union government, but operated by the expertise available with the RBI. The working group appointed for the purpose in its report in December 1997 favoured an independent office.

Jalan agreed that the proposal for an independent public debt office was sound, and should be done at some stage, but he was not willing to support it. His argument was that such a separation would be premature and inadvisable till such time the public debt was brought down, the fiscal deficit was sustainable and the financial repression was eliminated. My argument was that such a programme of fiscal consolidation had already been agreed to by the government. The governor's view was that there were serious risks to the financial system in case fiscal adjustment did not take place, as envisaged. He, therefore, favoured that fiscal consolidation should precede establishment of an independent debt office. I was convinced of his argument and I assisted my boss in overruling my own recommendation once I recognised the importance of assessing risks.

In the annual monetary policy statement in April 2001, we revisited the subject and referred to the report of the working group of 1997. It was clearly stated that once the legislative actions with regard to fiscal responsibility and amendments with regard to RBI Act were accomplished, it was proposed to take up with the government the feasibility of and further steps for separation of the government debt management function from the RBI. These events illustrate the farsightedness of Jalan.

Jalan had an array of tactics to retreat from any hasty policy initiatives. I recall two such instances. In December 1997, Jalan constituted a working group (Khan Committee) to examine the harmonisation of the role and operations of development finance institutions and banks. I sent a one-page note explaining how this would not be appropriate, and that the matter had to be viewed in the context of the Narasimham Committee recommendations and the importance of keeping intact traditional banking operations in banks. Jalan called me to his room and tore up the note in my presence.

He simply said, 'What is all this? You should walk in and discuss with me if you have any problems. Let the report come, we will work on it.' Some time after this, I sent him a speech by Eddie George, governor of the Bank of England, highlighting the importance of traditional banking in the financial system, both for growth and stability.

Jalan called me and said, 'I say, Venu, this is a very important perspective.' On receipt of the report, Jalan appointed a consultant to prepare a note on the subject. The note was used for preparing a discussion paper by the RBI. The discussion paper was then put in public domain. A final decision was taken, which nullified the intent of establishing the Khan Committee, but the process took a long time. The process provided an opportunity to suggest a path for development financial institutions to become banks. Jalan had his unique style of steering his way out of complex situations.

Jalan adopted a different tactic in another instance. To encourage exports, Jalan announced special refinancing for incremental exports. It was impractical since it was difficult to define what was incremental in exports at a micro level. The scheme did not work. I suggested a way out in a circuitous manner – modifying that scheme to make it appear to be an improvement, but virtually closing the scheme. Jalan decided to simply announce withdrawal, admitting that the scheme did not work. A press release was issued accordingly.

One of my most memorable interactions with Jalan relates to the exposure of banks to equity markets. That was a matter relating to regulation, but Jalan took me into confidence. He asked me to comment on a proposal to increase the regulatory limit of exposure of banks to equity markets from 5 per cent of incremental deposits to 5 per cent of the total outstanding advances. The intention behind the proposal was to increase avenues for investment in equity markets for banks, bringing them closer to universal banking from traditional commercial banking and, at the same time, provide a boost to equity markets, which were yet in an infant stage.

I opposed the proposal on several grounds. First, banks accept deposits and should appropriately invest most of their funds in fixed income assets corresponding to their fixed expenditure liabilities, for discharging their liabilities. Second, investments in equity also implied excessive risk-taking with the funds of depositors. Banks should be encouraged to focus on financing working capital. Third, the banks in India did not have adequate expertise while equity markets were not as transparent and efficient as they should be. Fourth, if a limit were to be imposed on the exposure of a bank, it should be related to the net worth of the bank concerned, which reflects its capacity to absorb risk, rather than as a proportion of total advances. Finally, and above all, a regime shift from 5 per cent of incremental to 5 per cent of total advances would provide a sudden and huge window of exposure to equity in one go; besides this could be exploited if a bank were to collude with a broker.

The counter arguments advanced by Talwar and Jalan were that at some stage we had to encourage participation of banks in equity markets. They explained that safeguards had been put in place. Banks were permitted to use the mutual fund route in case they did not have expertise in investing in equities. The proposal would be of benefit to both banks and equity markets while adding to the movement towards liberalisation of the financial sector. All aspects were examined in detail by a technical committee consisting of RBI and SEBI officials. The committee made comprehensive proposals which were submitted in August. The report was put in public domain, and the RBI discussed the matter in the light of comments received with the chief executives of major banks. The draft guidelines were also circulated for feedback. Therefore, Jalan and Talwar felt that I was not bringing to the table any new factor that had not been considered before, and that I was only expressing my fears. A decision was taken to issue the guidelines with appropriate safeguards by way of a review soon.

This is the only instance when Jalan underestimated the risks involved in relaxing restraints imposed on the banks in their non-traditional activities. The liberalisation measures were exploited by unscrupulous stock-market speculators in collusion with a few banks, culminating in what has been described as the Ketan Parekh Scam.

The scam came to light when there was a crash in the Sensex on 1 March 2001. Panic ensued. The president of the Bombay Stock Exchange had to resign due to allegations of use of privileged information. In the month of March, eight people were reported to have committed suicide, and hundreds of investors were driven to the brink of bankruptcy. Media reports said that a private sector bank had exceeded its prudential limits set by the RBI on exposure to capital markets, which added to the volatility in the markets in March 2001.

One day (in the first week of April 2001), we received a request for liquidity support for a large amount from Global Trust Bank. I recall it was about Rs 430 crore. There was reportedly wholesale withdrawal of deposits of about Rs 500 crore. Global Trust was not in a position to roll over its borrowings in call money market from other banks since other banks had lost confidence in it. The bank assured that it had adequate safe assets in the form of bonds issued by public sector enterprises and other securities against which liquidity could be provided by the RBI. Since the matter related to liquidity support to the bank to discharge its overnight obligations, the RBI had to take a decision on the same day, and within a few hours.

The RBI as a central bank performs functions of lender of last resort. There were precedents, but this request was of a far higher magnitude, the largest in our history, and in a complex situation. There are no prescribed guidelines for provision of such a facility. Central banks believe that they should never concede that they will give support in desperate situations but should be ready to do so, at their discretion, whenever circumstances demand. This is called a policy of constructive ambiguity – ambiguity for a good cause. There are, however, a set of principles that should govern our approach to such requests. As a lender of last resort, we had to assure ourselves that the bank had exhausted all other options; and in this case it was clear that the banking community had lost its confidence in GTB to lend. However, the central bank had to assess whether GTB had a solvency problem or a liquidity problem. If it was not solvent, the central bank would ordinarily desist from lending, but often it is a matter of judgement. In the case of GTB, it was solvent strictly on the basis of latest accounts submitted to the RBI. But the RBI had suspicions about the veracity of their classification into performing and non-performing assets. There were reports of huge exposure of GTB to stock markets in the recent past, after the latest accounts. Valuation of assets at times of market turbulence was, in any case, difficult. We had to contend with a questionable solvency, but the bank had its strengths in terms of technology and skilled manpower. Above all, the bank's exposure to other banks posed systemic consequences if we did not provide liquidity to GTB at that time.

Even when giving support as a lender of last resort, one should be assured of adequate collateral. GTB offered public sector bonds as collateral; and we accepted that offer after consulting the Legal Department. We had to make sure that the margins were appropriate (that is, difference between the value of bonds and our liquidity support). The interest rate charged had to be steep, as per standard principles, and we naturally priced the support at penal rate.

As a final step, we assessed the reputational risk for the RBI in providing the liquidity support. The media was full of reports that the bank had violated the prudential limits set by the RBI. Other banks had lost confidence in GTB. That the operations of the bank were closely related to a scam that was being unravelled was in public domain. By this time, the Reserve Bank had on record considerable discomfort about the functioning of the CMD. If we decided to lend, could we afford to be a lender of last resort to an institution that was a suspect in criminal conspiracy? If we decided not to lend, could we face the threat of systemic impact if Global Trust defaulted in its obligations? As the deputy governor in charge of monetary policy and financial stability, it was my responsibility to take a call and advise the governor for a final decision.

Considering all the information available in the RBI from different departments, I proposed to the governor that (a) we should provide liquidity support against the collateral for the amount requested, before the end of the day; and (b) that this should be done only on the resignation of the CMD, about whom we already had discomfort in the RBI. It was necessary to make a distinction between bailout of the bank and bailout of the management of the bank. The image of the RBI might be adversely affected if we appeared to be supporting a bank's management that was instrumental in driving the bank to distress. Jalan broadly concurred with my approach, and left it to Talwar and me to work out the details. It was already past 5 p.m.

Talwar conveyed that in response to our message, the CMD assured over phone that he would send in his resignation the following day, and that it could be so recorded on file. I wanted the resignation letter on our file before providing liquidity as our capacity to enforce our conditions might be diminished the moment we bailed out the bank.

Talwar recommended that we record his response on file and release the liquidity because non-release of liquidity would have serious systemic implications. I countered that the CMD should be told that if he was not willing to send in his resignation letter forthwith, he would be removed from the position by withdrawing approvals granted for his appointment as CEO, before we released liquidity.

Talwar later confirmed receipt of the CMD's resignation over fax, with effect from the following day. We released liquidity support immediately; it was about 6.30 p.m. or so. We briefed the governor about the outcome.

Jalan called me to his room as soon as he came to the office the next day. He explained to me in detail his apprehensions about the reactions of financial markets and the banking community to the simultaneous actions of RBI involving removal of the CMD on one hand, and giving liquidity support on the other. Contradiction or confusion could be perceived in such action. However, he added, on balance, he went along with my recommendations.

In summary, the first half of Jalan's six-year tenure as governor was characterised predominately by successful preemptive and unconventional measures to prevent shocks transforming into crises. From the first day in office, Jalan had to intensify the fight to counter the spillover effects of the East Asia Crisis that was causing havoc in our forex markets. In March 1998, a new government was sworn in and the statements of some leaders injected uncertainties in forex markets. The sanctions imposed by the US consequent upon the nuclear tests in May 1998 posed further challenges to managing balance of payments. Between May and August 1998, the currency and debt crisis erupted in Russia which could potentially impact us. There were disturbing developments in currency markets in some of the Latin American countries, especially Brazil, which called for a vigil to minimise adverse effects on our economy.

In May 1999, the Kargil war broke out. War is a tragedy in

and of itself, but as policy makers in the RBI, we had to view its potentially disastrous effects on our financial markets, especially on the value of the rupee. Then came the Y2K problem. Much of the critical software at that time had been designed to work smoothly till 1 January 2000; the world was terrified about what would happen the second after. In the RBI, we worked overtime to prepare for the Y2K, and, like everywhere in the world, the new millennium came in without any glitches. The dotcom bubble burst in 2000. Its fallout was severe in advanced economies, but we could not afford to be indifferent to it. It goes to Jalan's credit that he provided extraordinary qualities of leadership and conceived innovations in policy responses to meet these unprecedented challenges.

It is said that people are seldom aware of crises that have been averted. These go not only unappreciated and unnoticed, but also unanalysed. Jalan was at his best not only in managing crises, but also in taking actions to prevent shocks from becoming crises.

17

TEAMWORK ON A CLEAN NOTE

It is not often that an RBI governor and a finance minister work together for long periods of time. Jalan worked with Finance Minister Yashwant Sinha for a little over four years, starting 1998. Jalan was lucky to have Sinha as finance minister for most of his tenure, and Sinha was lucky to have Jalan as governor for most of his.

I had worked with Sinha before; he was my minister when I was in the Ministry of Finance during the balance of payments crisis of 1990-91. Sinha and I had mutual trust and respect, and since he had been an IAS officer, four years my senior, he understood both technical and political realities. Sinha was a dignified man, measured in his speech and deliberate in his actions. He was always decisive, firm, but pleasant.

While I was deputy governor, my working relationship with Sinha was more indirect. I was in a different city and in a different institution which was expected to be independent of his ministry. Yet, the relationship between the RBI and the finance ministry is always a crucial one for the economy. The Sinha–Jalan team was responsible for directing our economic policy and the RBI in new directions. I had the privilege of assisting the team in several instances since I was closely associated with several measures that Sinha and Governor Jalan undertook.

Jalan's reputation as a crisis manager overshadowed his leadership in giving new direction to central banking in India. He gave a central place and credit to the government, even when he personally steered policies in the Reserve Bank on his own initiative. With regard to structural measures, Jalan was particular that we mention in all our policy statements that we would take up the matter with the government, or would consult the government, or that we were acting upon the budget speech, and so on. He was also particular that we mention in the policy statements that we had consulted experts and market participants. Often, he assured a review of policy measures on the basis of feedback or experience. Jalan's approach, coupled with Sinha's personality, meant that there was no clash of egos. Since I had the trust of both, I was closely associated with some of the important initiatives. Among the most memorable ones for me were a reduction in the government's shareholding in public sector banks, fiscal responsibility legislation, administered interest rates, and the appointment of directors on the board of the RBI.

Jalan's discussions with the finance minister used to be invariably on a one-to-one basis. There were very few occasions where he took the deputy governor along. Similarly, the finance minister rarely had finance secretaries or chief economic advisors assist him in the meetings with the governor. The deputy governors were expected to deal with the secretaries. This arrangement was equally applicable in Jalan's meetings with the prime minister. There were, however, a few occasions when Jalan took me along for meetings with the finance minister.

On one such occasion, while finalising the budget speech for 2000-01, Sinha said that he had agreed with the governor's suggestions about reducing the government's share in public sector banks from a minimum of 51 per cent to minimum 26 per cent while maintaining the public sector characteristic. I was curious. I asked him, why 26 per cent? I was not dealing with the subject in the RBI and was not aware of the intricacies of the proposal.

The reasoning was that the government would be able to retain strategic control with 26 per cent ownership, in consonance with the provisions of the Company Law.

'But,' I pointed out, 'the Company Law does not apply to public sector banks.' Public sector banks were nationalised under different statutes. Therefore, there was no sanctity for a special resolution of 26 per cent. 'Are you opposed to reduction in share of ownership of the government?' Jalan asked.

'No,' I said, 'I am only saying that we will not be able to give a justification for retaining 26 per cent.'

'Okay. So, what do you suggest?' Jalan asked.

'Why not accept the Narasimham Committee recommendations? They recommend 33 per cent.'

'Well, what is the basis for 33 per cent?'

'Sir,' I said, 'I too had that same question. So, I asked Mr Narasimham. He said that some people in his committee wanted 51 per cent to retain management control and others wanted 26 per cent to maintain strategic control. Apparently, Mr Narasimham as chairman decided to arrive at a compromise figure. That was the basis for 33 per cent. So, all I am saying is, it is better to accept the recommendation of the Narasimham Committee and avoid the embarrassment of giving a justification for a particular percentage.' That was the basis for 33 per cent.

Sinha and Jalan directed me to prepare a paragraph for the budget speech on the subject. The draft paragraph proposed by me was substantively incorporated in the budget speech of the minister. It was a last-minute input, though I am not sure whether it mattered since no action has been taken on the budget announcement till now.

Jalan was acutely conscious of the importance of fiscal policy, and he was a real driving force behind the fiscal responsibility legislation proposed by the finance minister in the budget speech of 2000. Jalan wanted me to prepare a draft legislation. I said that it would not be appropriate for me, as a central banker, to work on a draft of legislation on fiscal matters.

Jalan said, 'I do not see any problem. I discussed with the finance minister. We agreed that it will be good if you do it.'

My initial reaction was that we were better off passing a legislation imposing a ceiling on public debt as envisaged in our own Constitution, rather than 'ape' the newfound wisdom from the West. Jalan felt that it was wise to go along with what the government wanted as long as the purpose was served.

Being a central banker, I was prepared to assist the government with technical inputs, but was not willing to formally take on the responsibility of working on a fiscal legislation. Ideally, the government should have a committee to work on such a legislation chaired by the secretary (Economic Affairs). I was willing to be a member of such a committee. I also suggested that a working group in the RBI could work on fiscal legislation, since it had expertise. This is the origin of the Sarma Committee Report (named after E.A.S. Sarma, who succeeded Vijay Kelkar as secretary in the Ministry of Finance) which formed the basis for the legislation. K. Kanagasabapathy, R. Pattnaik and N.V. Deshapande made valuable contributions while A. Premchand, fiscal expert from the IMF, gave informal advice.

Transparency in budget and sound accounting practices were a pre-condition for fiscal responsibility. Other countries had followed such a sequence. I discussed with Jalan and it was agreed that the legislation would incorporate appropriate obligations on transparency. In this background, the words 'budget management' were added to the proposed legislation as the Fiscal Responsibility and Budget Management (FRBM) Bill.

I made a suggestion that this opportunity should be utilised to put legal restrictions on the government borrowing from the RBI, including through participation in primary auctions of government securities. This would, besides formalising the supplemental agreement between the government and the RBI, put an end to the automatic monetisation through the issuance of ad hoc treasury bills. It would also prevent the RBI from participating in primary issues. No doubt, in most countries restrictions in such funding of the government by the central bank are put in a legislation governing a central bank, but I felt that the fiscal legislation was a good opportunity that we could take advantage of to provide legal sanctity to what was agreed and was working well.

Jalan agreed with this view, but wanted a provision whereby in extraordinary circumstances, such as threat to national security or unanticipated severe shocks, there should be an opening for the government to borrow directly from the RBI in the law under contemplation. This was a wise suggestion which was accepted. We from the RBI continued to give inputs to the government as the legislation was introduced in 2000 and finally passed in 2003.

Among many steps taken by the Sinha–Jalan combination, a significant one relates to administered interest rates. Administered interest rates had been posing serious problems for the transmission of monetary policy and had been resulting in fiscal costs. The stakes for state governments in small savings scheme with administered interest rates made any change in the system complex. Sinha in his budget speech of 2001 announced a proposal to set up an expert committee to provide recommendations on a better system for the determination of the administered interest rates. The Government of India notified the committee with me as chairman and membership drawn from the Union government, selected state governments, and financial sector experts.

We did a comprehensive and in-depth analysis of a host of administered interest rates. We built on recommendations made by several committees, relevant to the subject, in the past. We recommended a set of policy and institutional measures to establish a system for encouraging long-term contractual savings that would be fair to savers, related to market rates, reduce the burden on government, and finance long-term investment means for development. The recommendations formed the basis for several steps in the direction of reduction in administered interest rates. The significance of the report is not only that it was a joint effort of the government and the RBI but that it established the principle that the interest rate environment should be driven by monetary conditions managed by the RBI.

The Reserve Bank's affairs are governed by a central board of directors which is responsible for general superintendence and direction of the bank's affairs.[1] The board is appointed by the Government of India. As a courtesy, it consults the governor. At the time the reconstitution was being considered, Jalan asked me for suggestions in the field of economists and civil servants. I suggested Mihir Rakshit.

Jalan asked, 'Do you know Rakshit? He is a Keynesian. Do you understand what that means? He is not going to be positive towards our monetary measures.'

I said, 'Yes, I know. I believe that we should have on our board somebody who is generally opposed to our thinking. It helps us to know the other point of view clearly. It will help us to be well prepared in our policies if we know the likely criticism before taking decisions.' Rakshit was appointed.

I had brief glory as a teacher to the distinguished members of the board. An eminent scientist who contributed enormously to the space programme of India was A.P.J. Abdul Kalam. Kalam was a self-effacing and soft-spoken man who would later become the president of India. Kalam mentioned in the very first meeting of the board that he had been formally briefed about the RBI. He had received the material. However, he wanted a presentation as a primer to the subjects to be deliberated by the board, and basic issues that needed to be understood and addressed. Jalan suggested that there would be an informal meeting of the directors on the next occasion they met. He added that I should make the presentation to the board members. Many directors including, in particular, Kalam and N.R. Narayana Murthy, attended the presentation, which lasted a couple of hours. They were very attentive and took down notes. The preparation for the presentation itself clarified my thoughts on some issues. More important, the keenness to learn, determination to contribute, and devotion to duty of these distinguished and busy people was not lost on all senior officers and staff.

The lessons I learnt from Jalan in dealing with ministers came in handy when I stuck my neck out in a speech in October 2001 about the independence of central banks. I mentioned that the central banks might gain independence from the government, but still be forced to recognise the influence of large corporates in the financial markets. Soon after, Jalan called me and said that the minister of state for finance had called him up and wanted to know the basis for my speech. Jalan explained that it was from an academic point of view. However, the minister wanted me to meet him and explain the position, and the governor suggested that I do so. I agreed to meet the minister. I rang up his private secretary and said that I would meet the minister in one of my forthcoming visits to Delhi, and that the minister should be informed. Whenever I visited Delhi, I informally checked up whether the minister was in town or out of town. Whenever he was out of town, I left a message with his office that I was trying to meet him. Thus, I managed not to meet him for a few months but kept officially trying to meet him. After some time, I decided to call on him when he was in the ministry. I entered the room and paid my courtesies. Then I asked him whether there was anything that he wanted to discuss with me. He said that he did not recollect any particular subject. Obviously, he had forgotten or changed his mind. We exchanged pleasantries. Time does help in giving a healing touch.

A comprehensive account of the new directions that Jalan scripted and implemented can be found in his Annual Monetary and Credit Policy Statement of 19 April 2001. It also contained some indication for the future. I called it a landmark policy.

There is an interesting background to the unusual and important statement. On 1 March 2001, equity markets tumbled and it involved a stockbroker, Ketan Parekh, a new private sector bank, and a clutch of urban cooperative banks in Gujarat, mainly Madhavpura Cooperative Bank. Jalan called me to his office. I had had serious reservations in the matter and had expressed these to him.[2]

He said, 'Actually, there has been very little increase in aggregate exposure of banks to equity markets. Still, this scam took place. It was just fraud. Tell me, Venu, how did you, and why did you, suspect that something like this might happen?'

I told him, 'Whenever I assess a policy proposal, I think of only one thing. How could the players in the finance business make money? If I am on the other side, I can think of only making money out of every change in policy. That would be the market's reaction. So, I keep asking, what would that attitude of markets mean to my policy?'

Jalan smiled. He said: 'I am glad that you are not on the other side.' We sat down to discuss immediate tasks, mainly relating to cooperative banks. I used a pre-arranged media appearance in some other context, as advised by Jalan, to assure RBI support to provide liquidity to banks as needed. The unintended consequence was a landmark policy statement. How did that happen?

Jalan wanted the statement scheduled for 19 April 2001 to give in detail the RBI's view of the unfortunate developments in equity markets and select banks, in particular, cooperative banks. He wanted to recognise the new challenges to the regulatory system and the conduct of monetary policy in the context of urban banks. He wanted a detailed account of the events, and a list of actions to be taken to ensure that such risks to the system did not arise in future. His proposal had two components, namely, prudential, including governance, and an institutional set-up for regulation and supervision of urban cooperative banks. I had no problem with the former, but had doubts about the feasibility of a new supervisory structure for urban cooperative banks (UCBs). He strongly felt that the Reserve Bank was taking the blame and was becoming a scapegoat for the mess in the urban cooperative banking system caused by the Union and state governments, who exercised significant regulatory powers on them. He wanted a new apex supervisory body and the Reserve Bank could provide manpower and other assistance to the new body, as necessary. I could appreciate his unhappiness.[3]

I expressed reservations on two counts. A new apex supervisory body would not be acceptable to the government, just as our earlier proposals for reforms in policy relating to urban cooperative banks were not. Jalan's response was that it might be acceptable to both the Centre and states since his proposal for a new apex body gave exclusive authority to the government. In any case, he was determined to go public to say that we had had enough of undeserved blame for the urban banks' problems.

The second count related to the articulation of the issue of market turbulence, role of banks, and proposed actions and the new institutional set-up with regard to urban cooperative banks. Jalan wanted to explain the position in detail. I felt that the policy statement would sound 'very defensive' if it focused on issues central to the scam. I felt that only a brief account would be better. But Jalan was very clear that his anguish should be expressed and his proposal put in the public domain.

To balance the defensive and negative sentiments that would be conveyed in the policy statement by focusing on the scam and related matters, I made a suggestion. We could expand the coverage of the statement to explain fundamental structural reforms that were underway and indicate the future course of reforms. That, in brief, is the origin of the landmark policy statement of Jalan which, perhaps, contains a more comprehensive account of reforms than any other periodic policy statement by any governor.[4]

In terms of its significance, this landmark policy of 2001, Jalan's masterpiece, was akin to the Big Bang Policy of Rangarajan in 1997. The provocations, however, were different. In the case of the big bang policy, the provocation was a political vacuum,[5] while this landmark policy was in response to the reputational risks faced by the RBI on account of the Ketan Parekh scam.

Jalan's lasting contribution to the common person was his 'clean note policy'. At that time, we were ashamed of the dirty and soiled notes in circulation. The notes were in continued circulation mainly because of the outdated processes in the RBI, including industrial relations. Jalan brought about the changes by skilful political management and by mobilising internal expertise. For instance, he told the chief minister of West Bengal that people in the states that did not cooperate with the clean note policy might have to continue to face the prospect of dirty notes circulating in their states. Under his leadership, a dynamic sampling model was developed.[6]

There was one battle which I lost and which I can never forget since I was right, law was on my side, and public interest was involved. But the manner in which the battle was fought and lost reveals some aspects of our system.[7] In the context of the Harshad Mehta scam, there was a dispute between ANZ Grindlays Bank and the National Housing Bank about crediting a large amount to an account other than the one to which a crossed cheque was issued. ANZ Grindlays held that it was market practice. The obvious legal position was that a crossed cheque meant that the amount had, necessarily, to be credited to the account payee.

Yet, the NHB, fully owned by the Reserve Bank, was advised to agree for arbitration, ostensibly due to diplomatic pressures at the highest level.

While I was banking secretary in 1995, I was given, for some time, additional charge of the position of chairman of NHB. I noticed then that we were spending huge amounts and much time on arbitrators, though arbitration was meant to save time and money. At that time, there was nothing that could be done as the process was already in arbitration.

By the time I joined as deputy governor, the arbitrations went in favour of ANZ Grindlays. The process itself had taken five years, and the amount spent was reported to be Rs 15 crore.

The award was questionable and it involved a payment of hundreds of crores by the NHB. The NHB approached its owner, the RBI, for financial support to implement the order.

I was aghast. The award was patently inconsistent with the law. I insisted that we go on appeal. Obviously, most people would have considered it futile to argue the legality of the award by top-rank judicial brains. The arbitrators consisted of two former judges of the Supreme Court and a former chief justice of a high court. Yet, I persisted, and Jalan consented to my proposal to go on appeal to court.

We went on appeal. The special court of Justice S.N. Variava upheld our contention and set aside the Rs 912-crore arbitration award. Delivering the verdict, Justice Variava said there were 'errors of law apparent' in the award. He added, 'They are all based on applying wrong principles of law. The award, in my view, must be set aside.' ANZ Grindlays then approached the Supreme Court.

The judge of the Supreme Court who heard the appeal advised that the NHB should compromise with the foreign bank instead of indulging in litigation. Wide publicity was given, castigating us for dragging on the case! My contention was that we should have clarity on the legal position. If there was a loophole in the existing law, the law should be amended.

We had a strong legal case. We insisted on a ruling. The honourable judges, however, found fault with us, again, for litigating. They said that the judgement could go either way. They said that the NHB was, through this litigation, gambling with public money and that the government should take note of this. The case was again adjourned. The judge's comments were given wide and repeated publicity. The government felt strengthened to encourage us to enter into a compromise settlement with the foreign bank. Finally, in December 2001, an out-of-court settlement was reached. The disputed amount was Rs 506 crore in 1992. The settlement with interest turned out to be Rs 1,645 crore. NHB was getting Rs 1,025 crore and the rest, Rs 620 crore, went to ANZ Grindlays.

We fought the battle for a right cause. The law was on our side. We went up to the highest court, yet we lost the battle. The reasons were unknown.

In one case, I irritated Jalan. ICICI had made a proposal for merger of ICICI, broadly in consonance with the guidelines finalised by the Reserve Bank on the subject. Under the guidelines, the path for such migration had to be specific to the institution. In this case, ICICI wanted regulatory forbearance in terms of statutory liquidity ratio. I argued that the statutory requirements, namely, CRR and SLR, should be maintained on par, as with any other bank, from the moment the merger takes place. However, I was willing for forbearance in regard to priority sector lending. My argument was that a bank would command the trust of the people only when it satisfied all the prudential requirements from day one.

ICICI argued that they would manage to satisfy the CRR requirements on the due date. However, they felt that they could not satisfy the SLR requirement since it would require large-scale purchases of government securities. Such huge purchases were likely to artificially boost the prices of government securities and, thus, distort the markets, making the securities too expensive for purchase. However, I would not relent: I said that there was no half-pregnancy in banking; a bank was a bank from day one, or it was not a bank.

Jalan called me and said that the finance secretary, Ajit Kumar, wanted me to have a meeting with the managing director of ICICI and the deputy governor to sort out the issue. I told Jalan that I was not willing. The matter related entirely to the regulatory regime of the Reserve Bank.

Jalan was annoyed.

'I say, tell me frankly, Venu,' he told me. 'Are you against the merger or are you for the merger? Let me understand clearly what your stand is.'

I replied, 'I am for the merger, but only if the conditions are satisfied. You leave it to me. I will talk to the finance secretary and sort out the matter.' I rang up Ajit, who was my batchmate.

'Ajit, what is it you are trying to do with ICICI?'

He explained that the finance minister was annoyed with the RBI for delay in approving the merger and that he wanted the matter to be sorted out by him. My advice was that he should tell the the MD of ICICI to discuss the matter with the Reserve Bank and finalise the merger proposal satisfactory to the regulator within a month or two. He could advise RBI to expedite the process. Ajit Kumar was happy to go along.

The result of the meeting was that Kamath came back to Mumbai and called on me. Presumably he got a clear sense of the stand of the government and governor.

Kamath and I had detailed discussions. SBI had, in its possession, a large amount of government securities in excess of what was obligatory under our regulations. ICICI had commercial assets outside the SLR. A swap would not disturb the markets, and it could be negotiated at market-related rates. It could take place with effect from day one of the ICICI merger with ICICI Bank. He accepted that it would be possible for ICICI to swap some assets with SBI. Jalan was satisfied with the outcome.

A few months later, N. Vaghul, chairman of ICICI, met me in Washington, D.C., where I was executive director in the IMF. Vaghul expressed his gratitude to me for insisting on all the prudential requirements being met from day one. Apparently, there was a run on ICICI Bank some time after the merger. RBI had to and was in a position to give a statement of assurance to the depositors in the market about the soundness of ICICI's financials. This was facilitated by the fact that all prudential requirements were met by ICICI from day one.

My relationship with Jalan was somewhat complex. He had been and was my boss. Though he respected my professionalism, he felt that I was not accomplished in understanding political factors and bureaucratic machinations and that I was too rigid. I respected his brilliance and judgement. We shared not only our successes but also frankly discussed our failures. Both of us had no hesitation in arguing our respective positions. The net result was that our relationship was one of trust and affection at a personal level, but one of occasional tensions at official as well as professional level.

My longish tenure with Jalan was peppered with possibilities of exit from time to time. I recall that in 1998, soon after Vajpayee took over as prime minister, I received a call from Mohan Guruswamy, advisor to Finance Minister Yashwant Sinha. He asked me whether I was willing to be considered for appointment as finance secretary in the Government of India to succeed Montek Ahluwalia. I said that I was willing. After a few days, Guruswamy called me and said that I was cleared for appointment as finance secretary in a meeting between the prime minister, deputy prime minister and the finance minister. However, the next morning, the principal secretary to the prime minister apparently rang up the finance minister and informed him that the prime minister had changed his mind.

In 1999, I got a call from Vijay Kelkar, who was the finance secretary, asking me whether I was willing to be considered for the position of executive director (ED), IMF. I gave my consent. The governor appeared inclined to relieve me if I were appointed as ED. Kelkar himself was appointed as ED, IMF.

I was thinking of equipping myself for activities after retirement, in addition to academic interests. So, I got myself included in the panel of arbitrators maintained by the professional body for it (Indian Council of Arbitration). I sought and obtained permission from Jalan to join a correspondence course for master's in business law at National Law School, Bengaluru.

Jalan looked at the application form and then at me and said, 'Venu, are you mad?'

'I want to have fun. I have always liked law,' I told him, but after one semester and a study of course material, I realised that the programme did not excite me and I discontinued it.

In 2000, Jalan asked me whether I would be willing to be considered for the position of director, Independent Evaluation Organisation, a new post created in the IMF. I told him that I would be quite happy to be considered for the position since both my children were already in the US and I was due to retire soon. I was given to understand that at the instance of Governor Jalan, my candidature was supported by the government. I was invited to Hong Kong for interaction with a representative of the firm that was retained by the IMF for providing a shortlist of candidates. With Jalan's permission, I participated in the interaction. I also learnt that I was included in the shortlist of about ten candidates along with Montek. However, when the final selection took place, it was Montek Ahluwalia who was selected for the position for his standing in a multilateral institution setting.

A few months before my due date of retirement, in August 2001, I indicated to Jalan that I was not interested in reappointment. Jalan had no objection. He started consultations about my successor. But, due to unexpected developments, both Jalan and Sinha changed their mind. They wanted me to continue because a decision was taken by the government to appoint a Joint Parliamentary Committee to examine what was famously known as the Ketan Parekh Scam.

Ketan Parekh, a stockbroker, built a network of companies. These companies borrowed funds from various banks by offering shares as collateral. He traded these shares within the network of his own companies. He could manipulate the share values, finally resulting in huge losses to a network of cooperative banks in Gujarat and Global Trust Bank in Hyderabad. Jalan wanted me to continue for at least one more year with the Reserve Bank to make the necessary presentations before the parliamentary committee. He felt that my background, in particular, my experience in dealing with parliamentary committees, would be helpful in assisting him in preparing the position of the RBI. He added that Finance Minister Yashwant Sinha was also keen that I should continue and handle matters relating to the JPC. I consented and he showed me the letter he wrote to Sinha. The letter placed on record the fact that I wanted to leave; that it was initially agreed; and that I was being persuaded to accept reappointment for valid reasons. It was a very faithful account and, indeed, very generous of both the governor and minister.

The submissions of the Reserve Bank to the JPC and related work were completed by early 2002. At that stage, I mentioned to Jalan that it was time for me to plan my departure from the Reserve Bank since I had fulfilled my obligations related to the JPC.

Jalan responded, 'What is the hurry! Wait for a few more months.'

And I did.

18

INTERLUDE

'So, someone is trying to get rid of you,' Governor Jalan said when I told him about a phone call from C.M. Vasudev, secretary, Economic Affairs. Vasudev had asked if I would be willing to be considered for the executive director's position in the World Bank or the IMF, and, if so, what was my preference. With unconcealed alacrity, I had chosen the fund.

Jalan continued, 'Venu, why were you in such a hurry to say "yes"? Do you know how they select an executive director in the government? Either for services rendered to those in power or to get rid of you. You did not serve anybody's interest.'

'I was going back to Hyderabad in any case. My son, daughter and grandsons are all in the US. I am happy to go, if I get it,' I said. Jalan did not stand in the way. Soon after, I received orders to take charge as ED, IMF.

I made a trip to Delhi to meet officials in the finance ministry[1] and friends. I called on Yashwant Sinha, who had by then moved to external affairs. I wanted to thank him for all the support that he had extended to me. He was pleasant and affectionate, and recalled our working together rather fondly.

'Venu, you may be knowing that I wanted to get you as finance secretary. It didn't happen,' he said.

I simply smiled. We chatted some more, and Sinha wished me well.

I was looking forward to my stint in the IMF. It would be nice to be close to the children. In addition, the IMF was not an uninteresting place to work in.

I joined the International Monetary Fund as executive director in August 2002. The IMF as an international organisation with a membership of about 190 countries now works mainly to foster global monetary cooperation and secure financial stability. Member countries (governments) contribute funds to a pool through a quota system from which countries experiencing balance of payments difficulties draw money. In a way, it's a cooperative, which tries to enforce rules on the membership for common interests in global finance and trade, and provides assistance to countries in difficulties. All countries are represented equally on the governing board, but the voting strength differs, and in many ways is related to quotas. The affairs of the IMF are managed by the board of executive directors, who number a little over twenty. Countries elect executive directors, and most of the executive directors represent a group of countries.

The most important function of the IMF is to oversee the international monetary and financial system, called global surveillance. It also analyses and oversees the policies of member countries, including aspects relating to their spillover impact on the global system, and this is called bilateral surveillance. The board approves financing to countries facing balance of payments difficulties. In the process IMF establishes 'conditionalities' in coordination with the authorities of the member country concerned. These are considered integral to receiving a financial package. The executive director performs multiple roles and the effectiveness depends on several factors related to the voting strength of the countries he or she represents, backing of the countries, whether the country concerned is a borrower from the fund, and the skills as well as stature of the person holding the office. In addition to being part of governance of the board, the executive director functions as an ambassador to the IMF from the countries that he or she represents and advises them in enhancing the benefits that accrue to them out of membership of the IMF.

The ED from our constituency is the nominee of the Government of India, though the constituency that formally elects the ED to the board consists of Bangladesh, Bhutan, India and

Sri Lanka. In view of its voting power reflecting its importance in the global economy, India captured the most attention in my representing the constituency. But I was especially careful in all my dealings with other countries to make them feel that due attention was being given to each one of them. I made it a point to visit all the capitals and call on the heads of state or government, in addition to finance ministers and governors of central banks. As ED, my primary loyalties had to be to the IMF. But as an elected representative of the countries of my constituency, I needed to protect their interests and was accountable to them. What happened when the interest of the IMF was hard to reconcile with the interests of the member countries? This was a challenge, but also an opportunity to facilitate reconciliation.

In one such situation, I had to draw upon my diplomatic skills in representing Bangladesh. Bangladesh wanted funding from the IMF but it could not be processed due to some hitches. I was approached by the Government of Bangladesh to do something about its relations with the IMF. I was clear in my mind that I should not go into the substantive issues. I called the director, South Asia Department, for a chat on many subjects over lunch, and Bangladesh was the main subject. I mentioned that I had an assurance from the minister that he was keen from his side to give a fresh start to the relationship. I was assured by the director that the fund would also be keen to take a fresh look at ties with a new team. I requested the minister to visit Washington and meet the director and deputy managing director concerned to personally assure a new and more positive approach. He did that, and I was deliberately not present in the meetings of the minister, though I arranged for them. The finance minister, in an unusual gesture, called on me in my room during the process to assure me of his commitment to the programme. To reinforce the good relations, I made a visit to Bangladesh. The Bangladesh programme was processed and approved in record time.

Sri Lanka also had a programme to be negotiated. Their relations with fund staff were cordial. The programme was being processed smoothly. All that I had to do was demonstrate to all concerned in the fund on every possible occasion that I was firmly supporting the stand of Sri Lanka. I made a trip to Sri Lanka and was treated with warmth. Similarly, my visit to Bhutan was deeply appreciated, as a not-so-usual event. In the banquet arranged by the finance minister, as the event commenced, I became breathless. A doctor was summoned. It was concluded that it was due to lack of oxygen, in view of the altitude. After some rest in an adjacent room, I joined the formal banquet.

The management represented by the managing director, three deputy managing directors, and directors of various regional and subject areas are generally keen to have the support of executive directors, particularly those who have significant share of voting power. The Indian executive director is taken seriously as the voting power is not insignificant and officials at senior levels are deputed to the fund as executive director. In addition, I had some advantages in my role as ED. The IMF's mandate is closely related to the functions of the member countries' central banks. As deputy governor, RBI, I had interacted with other central bankers, and therefore, my credentials were known to the other EDs through their central banks. I had also interacted with the professional and senior management of the IMF and they were familiar with me. Other directors appreciated my broad-based and diverse experience at the state level, in the Union government and in the central bank. Further, my reputation in the Bank for International Settlements, with other central banks, was useful since EDs often get instructions from their central banks. So, both management and executive directors were interested in exchange of views with me. My emphasis was on mutual understanding and rarely on promoting a particular view. Most of the interactions with them took place outside the formal meetings of the board, while the formal position was stated in the board.

In the board meetings, I preferred circulating our stand in written form in advance, as is customary. My advisors were adept at detail and drafting as well as analysing, and I confined myself to guiding them on substantive aspects or relationship angles. My preference was to take a firm stand only when our stand was likely to make a difference to the outcome, or the management or executive directors sought my support. If a fundamental principle was involved, I put it on record. I intervened (that is, spoke during the discussions) only when the direction of discussions warranted some course correction. Abbas Mirakhor from Iran, who also represented Pakistan, was the dean, being a long-standing director on the board. I drew upon his wise counsel on both substance and procedures. Anne Krueger was the most influential at the senior level as first deputy managing director. I had met her at seminars when she was teaching in Stanford University and I was deputy governor in the RBI. We became friends and developed mutual admiration and affection. Geetha was very pleased when Anne told her about my presence in the board.

Anne said, 'Venu speaks rarely in the board. But when he does, people sit up and listen.'

I learnt important lessons from the board meetings and experience with lending to several countries during this period. First, the cost a country would pay if there were a crisis on the external front was huge, not only in terms of economic costs, but also in terms of policy independence, though both are interrelated. Second, the IMF conditionalities associated with programmes for different countries varied depending on not only macroeconomic conditions but also geopolitical conditions: the IMF is a creation of governments with unequal voice and strength in the organisation, and governments are political animals; so a creation of such governments cannot be totally apolitical. Finally, one can never be sure that the programmes of the IMF will succeed. Often, the programme is a medicine for a highly complex disease, which, even with the best of intentions and capacities, would be greatly difficult to address. This process is influenced by the ideological predilections of the dominant membership. Of course, these insights were not new to me. Yet, they had special significance in the context of the dominant preference for the liberalisation of capital account and deregulation of the financial sector. With these experiences at close quarters, I did become even more cautious than before about the liberalisation of the capital account in particular and liberalisation of the financial sector in general.

Some time in the end of May or June, Anne Krueger discussed

with me the replacement for Kenneth Rogoff, the economic counsellor. The economic counsellor is a very senior position which provides critical inputs to the assessment of the world economic outlook and economic research as well as policy in the fund. It appeared that US and European governments could not agree on candidates from their countries. The tradition has been that together they call the shots for that appointment. She wondered how I would react to Raghuram Rajan as a possible candidate for the position. The three of us had participated in some conferences on the Indian economy. I told her that I had invited him to visit and take a seminar on banking in the Reserve Bank when I was deputy governor. I said that I could back him, meaning that our constituency would back him and I would work for support for him in the board. I asked her: 'Does he hold an Indian passport?' She was not sure. Thereafter, Rajan called on me. He confirmed that he was an Indian citizen. He wanted my advice and I encouraged him to express his willingness to the IMF.

In early July, 2003, the managing director formally informed the board of his intention to appoint Rajan as economic counsellor. I called Jalan and informed him. I wrote a letter to Jaswant Singh, giving the email ID of Rajan so that he could be congratulated by him. I could take the liberty with him since he had signalled his trust in me from the first meeting that we had when I joined the IMF.

I was delighted that Rajan was chosen for this important and prestigious assignment. I had met him earlier in a common friend's home when I was visiting Chicago. I was very impressed with the young economist. I requested him to notify me when he was visiting India. This was followed up with an invitation to him to take a session in the RBI, addressing the professionals dealing with economic research and regulation of banks. His performance in the session was outstanding. I had also witnessed the respect he commanded in a couple of international conferences relating to the Indian economy. With this background, I was naturally enthusiastic about his candidature.

I met the finance minister, Jaswant Singh, for the first time, as executive director, in Washington, D.C., when he attended the annual meetings of the IMF and World Bank in September 2002. In the one-on-one meeting in his hotel, he asked me: 'Why should the Government of India not issue sovereign bonds and raise money to finance our development? There is a lot of interest.' I explained in detail the case for and against the proposal. This included an examination of countries which went in for such a bond with a vulnerable fiscal position, especially with deficit on revenue account. I explained the risks to our economy and banking system if our government bonds were in foreign currency and open to foreigners. These risks outweighed the advantage of bench-marking for foreign debt and additional resources for us. He listened carefully and thanked me.

On all my subsequent visits to Delhi, including those in transit to Colombo or Dhaka or Bhutan, he granted me interviews, and I was very brief in my reviews. He was extremely courteous, gracious and pleasant, whether we met in his office in North Block or in Parliament House. His basic message not stated explicitly was: 'I look at the big picture. I trust your knowledge and judgement on details. You have my mandate and support. Tell me only if it is essential or you need me to do something about it.' I got the impression that he had a high regard for Governor Jalan. It was a smooth, comfortable, indeed, luxurious and rewarding period for me in IMF as executive director. But such good times seldom last long.

While coming to IMF was a surprise in 2002, going out of it in 2003 was a bigger surprise. In April 2003, I was in India and made the customary call on Jaswant Singh. Out of the blue, he said in a matter-of-fact tone: 'A vacancy may arise in the Reserve Bank of India in the governor's position in the near future. We are considering your candidature also.' I said: 'Sir, I have a three-year term in the fund. I went there a few months ago. I am happy and settled in the fund.' There was no response from him. I added: 'I am already sixty-two years old. I am not very keen to be considered, sir. But I will finally obey the government's orders.' He changed the subject. I was intrigued by the inquiry since Jalan's term was up to December 2004. I promptly called Jalan and mentioned the conversation. He did not seem surprised at all, and said: 'Keep it to yourself. I may leave well before the end of my tenure.' On my return to Washington, D.C., I mentioned this to my family. They felt that I should have been firm in indicating my lack of interest in moving out of the fund. I told them that I could not afford to displease the government beyond a point. I could not even continue as executive director, if I defied the government. In any case, the offer itself was an honour. So, I said that the only practical way for me was to convey my preference and comply with the final decision of the government. I was confident that there were several contenders and my opting out of the race would embolden them to pursue their efforts.

After a month or so, I was appointed as the RBI governor, though by this time I was settled in Washington, D.C. and was enjoying spending time with my children and grandchildren. Yet, the orders were passed and I left for Mumbai soon after.[2]

19

CENTRAL BANKING IN CONTEXT

GOVERNOR JALAN AND I ENTERED THE BOARD CONFERENCE ROOM on the eighteenth floor of the new RBI building on Mumbai's Mint Street. In the past, the RBI governor assumed charge by signing in an official roster. It was a simple, closed-door affair. For the first time, Jalan arranged for a public signing ceremony. The boardroom was crowded. There were RBI officials and journalists and photographers jostling for space. I gave the first statement as the governor of the Reserve Bank of India in the glare of the relentless flashbulbs.

The statement was a general one and it reflected the approach to my work as governor. 'Even reform is a continuous process. Continuity and change will be mixed appropriately depending on the context.'

But what was to be continued and what was to be changed? I did not want continuity for the sake of continuity or change for the sake of change. When appointed, I was given the maximum legally permissible tenure of five years, instead of the recent norm of an initial three years. Also, the government had given no specific mandate. These reflected the government's trust in me. That was a source of confidence to take a long-term view of my work, balancing continuity and change.

I had no preset agenda. Yet, convictions and beliefs which had been garnered from accumulated experience, value sets, and knowledge of theory and practice would be guiding forces. These convictions and beliefs provided the framework for policies, functioning, and interactions.

In policy-making, arriving at an appropriate solution is both a science and an art. Ideology, theory and convictions are helpful in the search for solutions, but they are not solutions by themselves. Corner solutions (either one way or the opposite way as the solutions) often oversimplify the reality and so balance is needed and appropriate balance itself is often contextual.

Economists often advocate the desirable. Bureaucrats focus on what is feasible. It is possible to begin with the search for the desirable, then move towards the feasible, while at the same time assessing the costs and benefits of the distance between the two. This is a way of reconciling and balancing the feasible and desirable, always keeping the desirable in view. Similarly, starting from international best practices, one can assess how the Indian situation is different. The goal should be to move towards policies that are tailored for our requirements, while being consistent with international best practices. Or put another way, match the international best practice, but in our context.

Beliefs do influence priorities. Inclusive growth and an emphasis on risk mitigation, given our socioeconomic vulnerabilities, all played a role in my approach to policy making.

It is natural for central bankers to consider finance as a matter of supply and demand for money or credit. But finance should also be a service. It should cater to the needs of the common person. A migrant worker should be able to send money to his home with ease and least cost. A housemaid should be able to keep her cash safe and away, perhaps, from a demanding husband. Someone with seasonal employment should have access to credit for consumption smoothening (credit to finance consumption in the intervals between two streams of income from seasonal employment). This belief in finance as an essential service led to the RBI becoming the pioneer in financial inclusion – a concept that was first used in the Annual Monetary Policy statement on 28 April 2005. By 2008, one could see the servant and his employer in the same queue in front of the same ATM to draw money at no cost from any bank. As part of financial inclusion and as a means of efficient disbursement of government funds, direct benefit transfer from the government to the beneficiaries was initiated in Andhra Pradesh. It was later adopted in several other states. Now, this has become a national endeavour.

External sector balance continued to be a matter of highest priority for me. This was based on experience in managing the crisis in 1991, which was reinforced by observation, during my time as executive director in the IMF, of the impact of external sector imbalance on some countries. At that time, I recognised that the exchange rate and stability were being influenced more by capital account than current account. Adequacy of forex reserves had to be determined as an insurance against volatility in capital flows.

My first action on joining as governor was to ban investments through overseas corporate bodies (OCBs) of NRIs since their beneficial ownership was unclear. OCBs were undermining the integrity of our financial system.

Another early move on taking charge as governor was to build capacity for intervention in forex markets to manage capital flows. For this purpose, we devised a unique mechanism for sterilisation (mopping up of rupees injected into the system while buying foreign currency). We called this innovation the Market Stabilisation Scheme (MSS). With MSS, we could take advantage of the then ample capital inflows to build forex reserves. With strong inflows and reserves, we could now afford selective liberalisation of capital outflows. The liberalisation was focused on households and corporates in non-financial sector, but extended to financial intermediaries judiciously. Preference was not for self-reliance in the traditional sense, but minimal reliance on foreign savings to finance our investments while pursuing active engagement with global trade.

As articulated by my predecessors, C. Rangarajan and Bimal Jalan, the relative emphasis between the objective of price stability and growth or credit availability depended on the circumstances. However, I was aware of the limits of monetary policy in influencing both price stability and growth in our country. Growth is constrained more by supply rigidities that can be resolved by the government than demand constraints that can be managed by the RBI. International trade cannot, by its nature, fully mitigate all supply side issues in our country. Government policies had an impact on investment climate more than interest rates. Similarly, oil prices and food prices account for a dominant part in the price indices. Oil prices were virtually administered, and there were large elements of subsidies and taxes. Food prices are influenced by the Minimum Support Price, which is a part of government policy. So, the RBI was not in a position to accept full responsibility to deliver on inflation. Yet, inflation expectations had to be addressed, and I announced a self-imposed flexible target in April 2007 in the Annual Monetary Policy Statement (2007-08). The policy noted, 'The Reserve Bank had articulated a self-imposed medium-term ceiling on inflation at 5.0 per cent. There are indications supporting the belief that this approach has had a salutary effect on inflation expectations and the socially tolerable rate of inflation has come down. In recognition of India's evolving integration with the global economy and societal preferences in this regard, the resolve, going forward, would be to condition policy and perceptions for inflation in the range of 4.0–4.5 per cent. This objective would be conducive for maintaining self-accelerating growth over the medium term.'

The level of inflation intolerance in India, that is, the level at which political leadership reacted with special measures, was close to 10 per cent till then. In reality, during my tenure we had to battle the effects of elevated oil prices on inflation without succumbing to the temptations of the appreciation of rupee. Yet, regrettably, high inflation became a matter of serious concern during the final year of my tenure.

In my view, the RBI's contribution to growth can be significant if it ensures the availability of adequate savings and thus of lendable resources. Growth percolates to the disadvantaged with a lag, but instability impacts them instantly; and their risk-bearing capacity is limited. Financial markets may correct, but when they do correct themselves, the losers may not be those who gained in the upswing. In exercising my judgement, savers got greater weight and stability received significant attention. As it turned out, during my tenure, household financial savings were high and so was credit.

Credit is important for growth, but its availability is more important than its price. Initially, the problem we in the RBI faced was lazy banking and credit growth was tepid. Soon, we were faced with crazy banking. Credit was growing too rapidly for our comfort. The fear was that it was flowing for financing of asset bubbles. We had to curb that. At the same time, agriculture was starved of credit, and we doubled the flow of credit to agriculture during this period.

Unfortunately, towards the end of my tenure, I had to be privy to the waiver of loans to farmers. Another cause for regret is that we were hoping to reduce the cost of financial intermediation, that is, the difference between the return to the saver and the cost to the borrower. But it proved to be a vain attempt.

A regulator has to be respected and, perhaps, feared by the regulated, but not liked too much. This was made clear to the regulated. I told them that our instrument was a constraint on them, and that their freedom was a constraint on us. We had to recognise this and work together. I was not satisfied with mere regulatory compliance, but desired a comfort for the regulator that banks were being run in a trustworthy manner. Governance standards in banks are critical to ensure effectiveness of regulation as well as competition. As we wanted to be assured and wanted to assure all stakeholders that banks are owned and controlled by those who are fit and proper to do so, we mustered the support of the government by making governance standards a part of the budget announcement in 2005. The rigorous pursuit of compliance with the standards helped in an unprecedented shake-up in several private sector banks. We succeeded in our efforts in all but one case.

The urban cooperative banking system was in a state of highly depressed sentiment. In this context, we weeded out some urban cooperative banks and encouraged others. This was done with cooperation from state governments. A bank knows a lot about its customers, but a customer knows very little about her bank. We wanted to fill that asymmetry. The penalties levied on banks for violations were till then a secret. We put them in the public domain. We could get rid of one very large deposit-taking non-banking finance company, Sahara, after several years of relentless pursuit, since we were uncomfortable with its business practices. All deregulation should be, we believed, accompanied by intensive monitoring, both for feedback and oversight.

Banks are special. There are several reasons for this. The most important one is that savers who are risk-averse put their money in banks. The primary responsibility for us is, therefore, to protect the interests of the savers. We discouraged the funding of risky activities by banks such as venture capital, concentration in exposures, and cross-ownership among banks. We were aware that in India, effective legal mechanisms for loan recovery are conspicuous by their absence. Borrowers repay their loans more out of moral obligation than due to legal compulsion. So, the risk weights and provisioning requirements for determining adequacy of capital of a bank had to be more stringent than the global standards.

Just as 'trust' is critical to banking, integrity is critical to markets. Integrity broadly defined means that the players are recognisable, rules are observed in letter and spirit, and the infrastructure is robust. Market-oriented approaches are not always the same as market-friendly approaches. These beliefs were reflected in the RBI's pursuit of changes in money and government securities markets. To illustrate, we were hesitant in allowing derivatives. We were averse to corporate bonds in repo-market since we were not fully comfortable with the integrity of the market as reflected in the large share of private placements and low levels of trading.

The advantages of globalisation in trade are undeniable. But globalisation of finance undermines the policy space available for public authorities. In particular, globalisation of finance makes regulation difficult and diplomatic pressures are not unusual. By the time I joined as RBI governor, the government had decided to allow foreign banks to take over our banks. I did not agree with that. Our financial system was not yet ready for their entry. My experience with the operations of foreign banks was that they enjoyed political and diplomatic clout that undermined effective regulation. The RBI and the government finally settled for a roadmap for the entry of foreign banks to take over our banks.

With regard to space for public authorities to act, the law requires certain functions to be performed and prohibits certain actions. Between the two, there is a large space available for action. This is where desirable policies can be pursued. A desirable policy can be implemented, even if it is not yet incorporated into the formal legal framework. Its successful implementation gives additional comfort for people to transform the policy into law. However, good policy can be firmly put in place only if a good legal framework is established, and that should be the eventual goal. For example, some of the amendments to the RBI Act and Banking Regulation Act were actually the policies that were already under implementation. In other words, if a good policy is not prohibited by law, the policy maker does not need legal sanction to do it. The policy maker has a resonable unoccupied space between what is prohibited and what is allowed by law.

Beliefs and priorities are personal. But they are filtered through the dynamics of the institution that the policy maker works in. During my stint in the RBI, there was a continuous interactive process in which I shared my beliefs and thinking with the professionals in the RBI, and my beliefs and thinking were honed by them. A priority as governor was my relationship with the professionals in the RBI.

Outside experts bring new thinking to an institution. But they may also bring discomfort to existing professionals. In the context of the RBI, the costs and benefits had to be weighed. As governor, I was not keen to induct external expertise. Instead, the RBI invited, consulted, and learnt from outside experts.

There was much to learn, not only from outside experts but also from each other. On New Year's Eve 2004, I sent my first letter, a letter of greeting, to the officers and staff of the RBI, saying that we should build teams and not hierarchies. For example, a committee of deputy governors was formally constituted which had to consider all matters going to the board, and all important issues with governments and markets. Every deputy governor was fully involved in attending to major policy issues. It ensured coordination and enhancement of appreciation of the 'big picture' by senior management. It also developed wide ownership of the policy decisions.

Another way to blur hierarchies was through the use of vernacular languages. Speaking a local language introduced a level of informality and personal connection in discourse. I can speak Hindi, Telugu and Tamil, and I took every opportunity to converse with my colleagues and staff in those languages. In fact, I made it a point to regularly read the Telugu (my mother tongue) newspapers to get a sense of what the common person thought. I had popularised a few Telugu phrases to describe my preferred approach to policy making.

Diversity of views certainly improves the quality of analysis. Ultimately, many decisions of the central bank imply distribution of gains and burdens over several sections of institutions and interests. It is, therefore, important to understand the perceptions of various sections. We instituted several committees within the RBI, drawing upon professionals in the bank and outside experts. This did not mean that decision-making was diffused. In many instances, the decision finally rested entirely on the governor, in law and in practice. Yet, in taking important decisions, one should have the benefit of the collective wisdom of a group of people representing a variety of interests. The general approach of relying on small groups representing a spectrum of disciplines, expertise and views enhanced the quality of decision-making at all levels in the organisation. The most important instance of this approach was with the Technical Advisory Committee on monetary policy. We wanted to have inputs from distinguished people from relevant disciples, including economists, representatives from financial markets and institutions, former central bankers, and, importantly, select members of the RBI board.

The central board of the RBI is unique. In many countries, the central bank board consists of economists. In the RBI, the board consists of not just economists, but also eminent persons drawn from several walks of life, for example, social workers, scientists, industrialists. This provides a window to the societal concerns at large. In the RBI, we drew upon the advice and support of the board.

I sought active participation from the central board of the RBI, both at formal and informal levels. We introduced two new practices in our central board meetings. I gave a briefing of global developments. This exercise made me prepare for the board meeting and the board could appreciate the role of the global economy in our policies. A discussion on the state of the Indian economy followed, based on a presentation by a deputy governor. The formal agenda was taken up after the big picture was discussed by the board. We gave every board member a book at every board meeting. Often, we selected the book depending on the personal interests and expertise of the member. Usually the book reflected some issue that we were grappling with.

Getting the Reserve Bank on board was important. But in all countries and at all times, it is the relationship between the government and the central bank that is critical. Sometimes, these interactions can be like walking on a razor's edge. The relative emphasis between autonomy for the RBI and accountability to the government is difficult to define and complex in practice.

Soon after I took over, a journalist once asked me, 'Governor, how independent is the RBI?'

'I am very independent,' I replied. 'The RBI has full autonomy. I have permission of my finance minister to tell you that.'

In all seriousness, is the RBI indeed independent? The RBI is independent, but within the limits set by the government. There are three overlapping spheres of activity in the RBI-government relationship: operational issues, policy matters, and structural reforms.

When it came to operational matters, I insisted on having the freedom to decide. On policy matters, I was particular about consultations to avoid discord and ensure harmony in policies. On structural issues, I believed in very close coordination with the government. While interacting with the government, I had to sometimes take a firm stance on important issues. If there were persisting differences of views, I was prepared to annoy, or even irritate and frustrate the sovereign, if necessary. But I was not inclined to defy.

In the final analysis, the sovereign is the sovereign. In extraordinary situations, it is the sovereign which has the primacy. Also, the law provides for the government to give written directives in the public interest. In the case of the RBI, however, prior consultation with the governor is mandatory. On critical issues where there is difference of opinion, often the choice is for the governor to concede to the sovereign with or without a written directive. By tradition, both the government and the governor avoid recourse to any written direction.

Towards the end of my tenure, I was asked whether I believed in a single objective. I knew they were referring to price stability.

'Yes,' I replied. 'My single objective is to protect the Indian economy from the Government of India.' In some sense, that is the reason for the existence of the RBI. The government created the Reserve Bank of India to moderate its temptation to take a short-term view on matters relating to money and finance.

For a central bank, there is no such thing as blanket independence. The extent of autonomy exercised by the RBI depends on the function being performed by the bank and the nature of the relationship between the RBI and the government, particularly the relationship between the finance minister and the governor.

The independence of the RBI also faces certain structural constraints. The government is the dominant owner of the banking system in India, and the banking system dominates the financial sector. The jurisdiction of the RBI over public sector banks, relative to private sector banks, has been restricted by law. The exercise of its regulatory authority is constrained in practice. Moral suasion addressed by a central bank to the banks is not uncommon globally. But the RBI cannot exercise such an option unless the government, which is the owner of public sector banks, tolerates it. The transmission of monetary policy may be constrained if the finance minister is perceived to be guiding the bankers differently. Traditionally, the RBI is expected to play an active role in economic development, particularly in matters of credit. These expectations are long-standing and almost universal. Distribution of responsibilities and authority between the government and the RBI in the complicated process of financing development, particularly in regard to rural areas, is a genuine source of overlap and tension. In addition, the RBI is not merely a monetary authority, but performs several other functions in the service of the government, including that of being a debt manager and a banker to both the Union government and state governments. Hence, there are multiple areas requiring close interface between the RBI and the Ministry of Finance, while its role as a monetary authority warrants some independence from fiscal authority.

The relationship between the governor and the finance minister is necessarily an unequal and complex one. A central bank is not expected to be subordinate to the government. Yet, as a legal construct of the government rather than a constitutional authority, the RBI can never be equal to its creator. Still, the RBI is expected to be independent in the conduct of monetary policy while performing several other functions in close coordination with the government.

The role of the RBI, and hence its scope for independence, has also been evolving. During the plan era, especially after the nationalisation of banks, central banking had to be subordinated to plan priorities. The economic reforms initiated in 1991 sought to change the balance in favour of the RBI. By the time I joined as governor in September 2003, the ecosystem of the financial architecture in India had transitioned from government dominance to market orientation. It was during my tenure that the government had reached a critical phase in the implementation of structural reforms where it had to cede ground to both the markets and the RBI. Therefore, the relationship between the RBI governor and the finance minister took on increased significance in recent years.

When I took over as governor, the Reserve Bank had every reason to be proud of the record under the leadership of my predecessors. Each governor brings to the table her unique priorities, perspectives, styles and beliefs. I believe that during my tenure also, the RBI instituted significant changes, focused on new directions, and brought about important innovations. As an organisation, the RBI evolved into an even more professional institution. The governing philosophy of continuity with change was a guiding principle through my tenure also.

Being governor meant some changes in my personal life. I moved into the governor's bungalow on Malabar Hill. It was a huge building with dark wood panelling and sprawling lawns that had decades-old trees. It was an unimaginable luxury – but the big house for Geetha and me could also get lonely. Often, I missed the sounds of children playing and their parents chatting on their evening rounds in the open spaces of the apartment building in which I had lived when I was deputy governor. Sometimes, I would go to the old apartment complex for my evening walk and my old friends – the children playing there and their parents – would greet me and the children would ask me to throw them a ball.

As governor, my daily routine did not change too much. I woke up early morning, anywhere between 4 and 5 a.m. I liked to work on important matters, including speeches, in the early morning. This was followed up with a walk or exercise, including a massage, and morning coffee till 7 a.m. Diligent reading of the newspapers was a daily ritual. Like all my officers and staff, I went to the office in the morning and was back in the evening, often around 7 p.m. If I reached home early, I would go for a walk. I went to bed around 9.30 p.m. Geetha and I had only a few friends in Mumbai, unlike our large social circle in Delhi or Hyderabad, so the evenings were pretty uneventful. Occasionally, I used to go and enjoy English plays for which Mumbai is famous.

It took about three months for me to persuade my mother to join me in Mumbai because I would be there for five years. To my delight, she settled down and stayed with me in Mumbai. No doubt, she missed her large circle of family and friends. She was virtually bedridden and ill, but she was proud to see me as a governor.

It was my daily ritual to go to her room to read the newspapers. We would also gossip about old times. On return from my office,

I would sit with her for some time and chat. This made her very happy. Unfortunately, after a year she fell sick and soon became completely bedridden. She had to undergo treatment that caused great pain. Finally, in April 2005, I had to take her back to Hyderabad, since she wanted to be closer to her familiar surroundings. She passed away in September 2005. I always regret that she had to undergo prolonged suffering. I remember she always used to say that she wanted a first-class ticket.

'The first-class ticket is a heart attack. With that, you are fine, enjoying life, then next minute, you are gone. When I go up, I want to go on a first-class ticket,' she would tell everyone. But no one has a choice in matters like this.

Amma was an extremely dynamic person. She gave us all a sense of pride and dignity in working and serving others with cheer and affection. She was generous to a fault and never lacking in energy. With her departure, my link to the village – the wider community and larger family – disappeared. For most of them, I would always be known first and foremost as Ammanamma's son, and only then as RBI governor.

20

INTERESTS AND INTEREST RATES

MONETARY POLICY IS ONE CRUCIAL WING OF ECONOMIC POLICY, and an important part of the RBI's work. Its key focus is to assure price stability through the use of instruments called money supply or interest rates, which are difficult to define, and which have a variety of connotations.[1]

M. Narasimham, who was a former RBI governor himself, once spoke to me of Dr Manmohan Singh's visit to his home some time after the latter became finance minister in the early 1990s. Apparently, Mrs Narasimham asked, 'Manmohan, you say that inflation has come down. But, when I buy vegetables, I still have to pay higher prices than before.'

He, who had himself been an RBI governor, replied, 'In fact, my wife Gursharan also asks me the same question. And I tell her that I really find it difficult to answer!'

As governors, both knew how complex it is to measure inflation, an index of change in the general level of prices as distinct from relative prices (the price of a commodity in relation to the price of another commodity or the ratio of two prices). Reduction in inflation only means that the rate of increase of the general level of prices has come down. It does not mean that the general level of prices itself has come down.

I faced a tricky question in a similar vein when I was deputy governor.

My mother asked me: 'Venu, why is it that the bank is giving me a lower interest rate than before on my deposit? They tell me it is because of the Reserve Bank.'

I told her that actually she was getting a higher real interest rate than before. She looked at me, puzzled, and said: 'What is unreal about the interest rate? It is a rate and it is money that I get as interest.'

I tried to tell her that the real interest rate is a nominal interest rate with a correction for the effects of inflation on the resources available for money during the relevant period. I could see that that might sound complicated to her. This is just to warn the reader about the complexities in the conduct of monetary policy, an important area of the RBI governor's work.

Monetary policy seeks to influence the course of events, but in reality, the course of events also drives monetary policy actions. In modern days, interest rate is associated with monetary policy just as fiscal policy is associated with taxes. In both cases, policy actions result in gainers and losers.

Any monetary policy action results in more gains for some, less gains for some others, and, maybe, losses for others. Likewise, the risks to their incomes and standards of living over time will also vary. There are interested parties who exercise influence through media or other means, to form opinions in favour of a specific policy action. At times, it may simply be the prevailing ideology or beliefs that drive assessments that precede decisions.

Governments, especially in democratic systems, cannot but be subject to such lobbies – be they domestic or global. But governments are conscious that money and finance are matters of trust on the one hand and an assessment of longer-term effects of policy alternatives on the other.

The governments in market-oriented economies want central banks to appear to be independent and apolitical. The philosophy is that the authority that creates money should ideally be independent from the authority that borrows and spends money, namely, the government. That is an important rationale for the autonomy of a central bank.

But the governments insist on accountability, and that gives legitimacy to governments to oversee the central banks. In addition, since there are losers and gainers in any monetary policy action, political economy considerations are inevitable. The interest rate should ideally balance the needs of savers and those of borrowers or investors. The interests of savers as a class is in favour of higher return on the deposits, that is, higher interest rates. The borrowers, on the other hand, would prefer lower rates so that the cost of borrowings is minimised. The distinguishing feature in India is that the savers are dispersed, and they are mostly a very distinct class from the borrowers.

Under the circumstances, a short-term view of the problem to spur investment will tend to favour lower interest rates for borrowers or investors than would be warranted under the circumstances.

The preamble to the RBI Act (as it was during my tenure) stated '...that the objective is generally to operate the currency and credit system of the country to its advantage.' The goals of monetary policy in India have been set through interpretation of the preamble and the Act. They have been set as price stability and growth, with relative emphasis depending on the evolving situation. The RBI has been emphasising ensuring of financial stability as an important and additional consideration in monetary policy in recent years.

Although monetary policy is the core function of the RBI, it is not the only function that the bank performs. It acts as a banker to the government, manager of public debt, and, of course, lender of last resort in the system. It is also endowed with powers and responsibilities under separate legislations. Examples are: regulation of banks and foreign exchange management.

This characteristic of the RBI makes it a full service central bank, as distinct from central banks whose sole responsibility is only monetary management. The RBI has been conscious of the need to bring about structural reforms in banking and the financial sector. Reforms of monetary and financial system are closely related to each other.

Policy measures and reform measures are also intertwined in practice. My first policy statement was, therefore, christened 'Annual Policy Statement' for the year 2004-05, replacing the earlier tradition of calling it 'Monetary and Credit Policy'. In the pre-reform period, these were called Slack Season Credit Policy and Busy Season Credit Policy. The Annual Policy Statement contains a review of domestic and external developments, stance of monetary policy, monetary measures, financial markets, prudential measures, institutional developments, currency management, payment and settlement systems, and so on. But the main focus remains monetary policy; and the processes reflect this.[2]

The annual statement generally made in April/May is followed by a Mid-Term Review. I added a Quarterly Review from July 2005, but it was confined to monetary policy only. Monetary measures may be taken at any time, but the preference was to make them part of annual policy and periodically review the statements.[3]

I began my tenure on 6 September 2003 with huge goodwill and more important – an enviable legacy. Bimal Jalan left behind a robust and well-functioning economy.

The macro-economic environment was benign with positive outlook for growth and price stability on both domestic and external fronts. There were signs of pickup in credit from a low base. The distinguishing features for the rest of the year were the large capital flows and addition to forex reserves. This was welcome for the political leadership but a mixed blessing for monetary management.[4]

Anticipating large capital inflows, we put in position an innovation called the Market Stabilisation Scheme (MSS) in March 2004, which was operationalised along with a revised Liquidity Adjustment Facility. Details of how these innovations were brought about with good coordination between the government and the Reserve Bank will be narrated later.

A few days before the assumption of office by Dr Manmohan Singh as prime minister and P. Chidambaram as finance minister, the Annual Policy Statement for 2004-05 was made on 18 May 2004.

The outlook for growth and stability continued to be positive, though we had to manage large capital inflows. The growth prospects improved further by the time of the Mid-Term Review of the policy on 26 October 2004, but there were early signs of pressure on global and domestic prices. In the external sector, the new downside risk was on account of the persistence of uptrend in global oil prices. We had to stabilise inflationary expectations. For the first time since April 2001, we had to increase the policy interest rate.

The uptrend in global oil prices triggered differences between the government and the RBI. The government was inclined to assume that the increase in oil prices was temporary, or just a supply shock, and so, monetary actions would not be called for. We were not willing to proceed on an initial assumption that the oil price increase was entirely a short-term phenomenon or a supply shock, and was likely to be reversed very soon.

In the absence of any action by the central bank, we had to make a judgement about the impact of an oil price increase on the inflation expectations. No doubt, oil prices were administered (that is, subsidised by the government) but that could not be unlimited or forever. The government's fiscal management with high oil prices also puts pressure on inflation. Increased oil prices require us to pay more foreign currency to import the same amount of oil, putting a strain on our balance of payments.

The global interest rate assumed increasing importance in the conduct of monetary policy and external sector management. We faced difficult choices in formulating the Annual Policy Statement for 2005-06 (announced on 28 April 2005). Excess liquidity and firming up of international commodity prices warranted further tightening of credit policy. At the same time, credit was picking up after a prolonged period of sluggishness and hence a neutral stance was justifiable. On balance, tightening of liquidity and increase in the policy rate became inevitable, particularly because the non-food credit during 2004-05 recorded its second highest growth in fifty-five years.

The idea of excess of credit growth was new to the political leadership and to the public since they had generally been experiencing shortage of credit.[5] Perhaps, the most demanding was the formulation of the annual policy for 2006-07, announced on 18 April 2006. In the domestic economy, non-food credit growth, deposit growth, and money supply growth were all higher than our projections. Asset prices registered a substantial increase. Downside risks to the global economic outlook became evident. These warranted action, but we desisted. Soon, in the statement on 25 July 2006, we flagged the issue of unprecedented growing current account imbalances in the global economy and record highs in oil prices globally, but we still did not act.

I decided to go public with my concerns, more directly than through my speeches. I invoked the word 'overheating' in the Mid-Term Review of the annual policy for 2006-07, dated 31 October 2006.

I referred to indications of growing demand pressures and potential risks from rapid credit growth, strains on credit quality and elevated asset prices, high levels of monetary expansion, the evolution of the liquidity situation, and need to look for signs of risks to inflation.

I concluded, 'At the current juncture, for policy purposes, the two major issues that exert conflicting pulls are exploration of signs of overheating firming up to warrant a policy response, and the impact of lagged effects of earlier policy action on the evolution of macroeconomic developments. This was meant not only to justify the tightening in the past, but alert public opinion and the political leadership.

The use of the word 'overheating' triggered a major reaction from the government, with statements from the finance minister. This was perhaps the beginning of differences in perceptions coming into the open. Yet, we could pull through tightening in October 2006, and again in January 2007.

The idea of overheating of economy was something virtually unknown at that time in the context of monetary policy in India. Overheating occurs when growth is above the inherent capacity of the economy to expand. In the normal course, it expresses itself in inflationary pressures due to growing aggregate demand. In our assessment, on the basis of telltale signs and fragmentary data, the Indian economy was growing beyond its normal capacity. There were significant bubbles being built up, particularly in real estate.

The popular view was that in the absence of acute inflationary pressures, we had no reason to tighten the monetary policy. In the RBI, we did not agree with the dominant view.

We took actions on the regulatory side also, mainly in the banking sector, which dominates our financial system, to check excesses in lending. Some of the members of the board who shared the popular view started expressing reservations about the policy measures being taken.

According to them, I was acting merely on some vague fears which not many were willing to share. So, I ordered for twenty copies of a book on economic crises, to distribute to the members of the central board. However, on second thoughts, I decided not to distribute it to them since there could be a press leak about my actions, leading to unpredictable reactions. I decided to give a few copies to select persons and gave one copy to Finance Minister Chidambaram. He took it, looked at it, and kept it aside. Later, when I called on Prime Minister Manmohan Singh, I told him that I had given Prof. Charles Kindleberger's book *Manias, Panics and Crashes: A History of Financial Crises* to Chidambaram to read.

Singh looked at me intently, paused and said, 'Is it not outdated?'

I replied, 'Sir, I gave the latest edition to the FM.'

Charles Kindleberger was an economic historian. His book on speculative stock-market bubbles was published in 1978. It was reprinted in 2000 after the dotcom bubble. He used a narrative approach to knowledge and not mathematical models to prove his point.

I was trying to convey that there were scholarly contributions that supported my understanding of what was happening. Later, I gifted a few copies to select media persons. I was concerned about the risks to the global economy and the potential impact on India. I was also worried about our committing the same mistakes and making ourselves vulnerable. We were making two points to the government. There were signs of excesses and imbalance in the global economy and to some extent in our economy. So, I was seeking support for restraints on capital inflow and tightening monetary policy. The policy makers in Delhi were unwilling or afraid of resisting capital inflows beyond a point.

We had no choice, therefore, except to aggressively intervene to buy dollars and sterilise the purchases to reduce the rupee liquidity. But there were costs of sterilisation. The RBI and the government suck in liquidity through the issue of bonds, which they cannot use, and thus they bear the cost of sterilisation.

We had to distribute the costs of such sterilisation between the RBI up to a point, and the government through MSS beyond that, and in the final stages, the banking system by increasing the CRR. When the CRR is raised, banks have to deposit the amount with the Reserve Bank and they get no remuneration, though they are paying interest on deposits. Banks have to bear the cost of what may be called 'killing money'.

We decided reluctantly to reactivate the use of CRR, which had not been touched for years, to dampen liquidity in December 2006. Increase in CRR was in violation of the medium- to long-term objective of reducing such burdens of financial repression. But the RBI did not have enough room in open-market operations to do that and the government was not keen to expand the limits of MSS. The CRR was raised on several occasions between December 2006 and May 2008, though the banks and the owners of the banks, including the government, were not happy.

Some analysts point out that our assessment and policy actions were ignoring the fact that our higher growth was on account of good policies and higher productivity. They held that it was not merely a bubble or a part of upward movement in the business cycle. Many in the government shared this view. So, I felt it appropriate to explain we were conscious that there were both structural and cyclical elements. In the Annual Policy Statement of 24 April 2007, I conceded that there was evidence of structural changes, but there was also the cyclical component in the strong performance of the domestic economy. The structural changes (lasting changes) included a step-up in the investment rate supported by domestic saving and improvements in productivity in industry and services.

There were cyclical factors (movements that are likely to reverse) too, namely, robust global GDP growth, the persistence of high growth in bank credit and money supply, the pick-up in non-oil import growth, and the widening of the trade deficit.

Cyclical forces were also evident in the steady increase in prices of manufactures, resurgence of pricing power among corporates, indications of wage pressures in some sectors, strained capacity utilisation, and elevated asset prices. Perhaps, cyclical pressures were not felt so intensely in the economy in the past.

The government had a distinct preference for low interest rates and high credit growth, but when a strong pressure on prices was observed, the government tended to react immediately and preferred stronger monetary measures than might be warranted if a medium-term view was taken.

This is reflective of the short-term view of governments in general, while the central bank is expected to take a medium-term view on these issues. Further, transmission of monetary policy occurs with a time lag and hence monetary measures try to anticipate developments and act, rather than react, to events, which is what governments may be inclined to do.

Financial stability was a matter of concern for us, but the government exhibited a benign indifference. It was more interested in reforms in the financial sector. Actually, in our underdeveloped financial system with large presence of the public sector, the government had no particular reason to focus on the issue of financial stability during this period. At the same time, the financial markets, which also have generally a short-term view, tended to ignore the importance of financial stability in the medium to long term. There was little awareness of financial stability issues in the past, as the financial sector was underdeveloped and, in any case, wholly dominated by the public sector. Naturally, the possible impact of financial instability in the global economy on us was not taken seriously in the government and the financial markets.

The first quarter review announced on 31 July 2007 pointed out the danger of our economy being affected by the repricing of risks by global financial markets, and the danger of downturn in some asset classes.

'The immediate task for public policy in India, therefore, is to manage the possible financial contagion which is in an incipient stage with highly uncertain prospects of being resolved soon,' I said in the statement on 30 October 2007. It was evident that

With my family in 1957. I am in the centre with (from L to R) Pramila, my sister; Ammannamma, my mother; Ramesh Konda Reddy (seated), my youngest brother; Yaga Pitchi Reddy, my father; and Madhusudhan Reddy, my younger brother, who passed away in 1970.

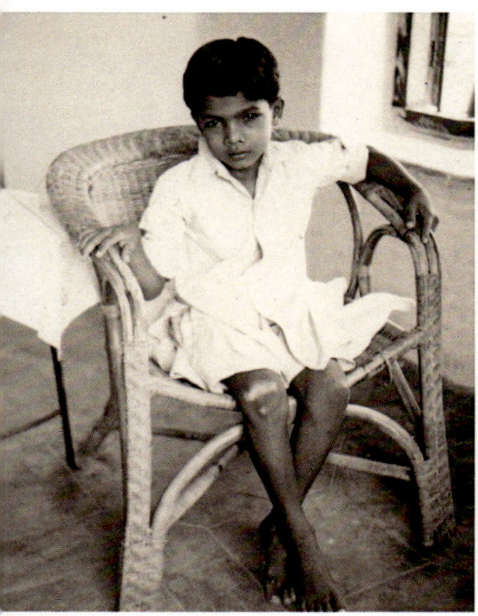

Shy as a nine-year-old, in 1950.

As Second Lieutenant, a commissioned officer, in 1963.

With President V.V. Giri at Ongole railway station, where he distributed pattas (land rights) to the landless at my request in 1969.

At the Institute of Social Studies, The Hague, Netherlands, 1968.

Addressing the Republic Day Parade in Nalgonda district as Collector and District Magistrate in 1974.

In step with Andhra Pradesh Chief Minister N.T. Rama Rao in 1985.

With my wife Geetha at Christmas dinner at the International Monetary Fund, Washington, D.C., in 2002.

All smiles with President A.P.J. Abdul Kalam at the inauguration of the Currency Museum, Mumbai, in November 2004.

As Executive Director, IMF, escorting Finance Minister Jaswant Singh at the annual Fund-Bank meeting in September 2002.

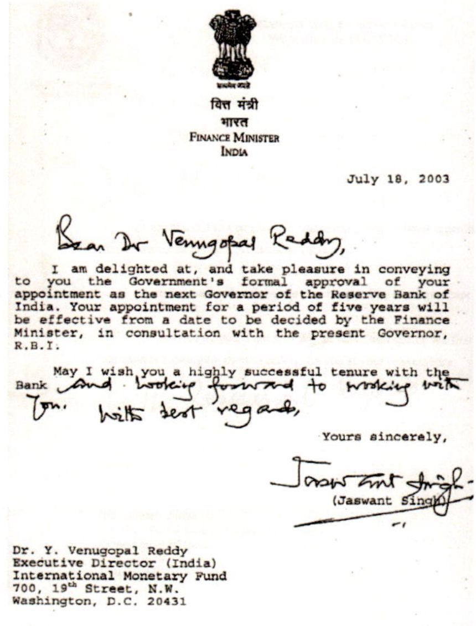

वित्त मंत्री
भारत
FINANCE MINISTER
INDIA

July 18, 2003

Dear Dr Venugopal Reddy,

I am delighted at, and take pleasure in conveying to you the Government's formal approval of your appointment as the next Governor of the Reserve Bank of India. Your appointment for a period of five years will be effective from a date to be decided by the Finance Minister, in consultation with the present Governor, R.B.I.

May I wish you a highly successful tenure with the Bank and looking forward to working with you. With best regards,

Yours sincerely,

Jaswant Singh
(Jaswant Singh)

Dr. Y. Venugopal Reddy
Executive Director (India)
International Monetary Fund
700, 19th Street, N.W.
Washington, D.C. 20431

The letter from Finance Minister Jaswant Singh dated 18 July 2003 informing me of my appointment as Governor of the Reserve Bank of India.

With five former RBI governors in March 2006: (L to R) S. Venkitaramanan, C. Rangarajan, Manmohan Singh, M. Narasimham and Bimal Jalan.

With the RBI Board of Directors in 2008.

Sharing a light moment with Finance Minister P. Chidambaram at the RBI board meeting in New Delhi in 2005.

With Tamil Nadu Chief Minister J. Jayalalithaa during my visit to Chennai as chairman of the Fourteenth Finance Commission in December 2013.

With my best friends in the financial sector: S.S. Tarapore, former Deputy Governor of the RBI, and M.G. Bhide, former Managing Director of the SBI and former Chairman of Bank of India, in 2004.

On my last day at the RBI in September 2008 with (L to R) Leeladhar, Usha Thorat, Shyamala Gopinath and Rakesh Mohan.

With Jean-Claude Trichet, President of the European Central Bank, in 2011.

Delivering the Per Jacobsson lecture to a gathering of central bank governors in Basel, Switzerland, in June 2012.

With Sir Howard Davies, Director of the London School of Economics and Political Science, in July 2008.

Receiving the Padma Vibhushan from President Pratibha Patil in 2010.

With my family in 2016. Standing (L to R): Hari Buggana, my son-in-law; Kavitha, my daughter; Pranav, their son; Swetha, my daughter-in-law; and Adithya, my son. Seated (L to R): Rohan, Hari and Kavitha's son; myself; Uma, Adithya and Swetha's younger daughter; my wife Geetha; and Diya, Adithya and Swetha's elder daughter.

the most important issue for India would be the possible impact of global financial market developments and policy responses by central banks in major economies. We were aware that on the domestic front, aggregate demand conditions had remained firm and on the uptrend. However, our judgement was that no further tightening in interest rates would be needed at that juncture; since the actions taken in March 2007 should be allowed to work themselves out. However, the cash reserve ratio had to be consistently increased from December 2006, and intensified from April 2007. Tightening of liquidity was thus preferred to increasing the interest rates.

The upside inflationary risks in the period ahead were evident by January 2008. I was afraid that domestic monetary and liquidity conditions were likely to be amplified by global factors. We had no choice but to keep tightening the monetary measures, both through policy rates and tightening of liquidity, while being prepared to take both conventional and unconventional measures. When I referred to the unconventional measures in the policy statement, I was asked in the media as to what these were. I replied that such measures were unconventional to meet unforeseen specific circumstances and so by definition I could not have a preconceived notion. At that time, the words 'unconventional measures' were not in fashion.

As it turned out, I had to take at least one important measure.

The chairman of the Indian Oil Company (IOC) came on television in May 2008 to announce that the oil companies did not have enough money to import oil. The company had to import oil at elevated prices but sell it at administered prices. The government was to provide subsidies but issued bonds in lieu of subsidies. The bonds were special, however, in the sense that they were IOUs rather than tradable bonds at that stage. I did not want panic to grip the system as a reaction to the IOC chairman's statement.

As soon as I went to the office, we discussed internally and announced special market operations (SMO). The RBI bought the bonds with rupees and simultaneously exchanged them with US dollars. The announcement pre-empting panic said that it was done in view of systemic implications.[6]

Chidambaram expressed displeasure since I did not consult the government. But he backed the decision. The move invited criticism from many circles, as people assumed that we in the RBI did it at the behest of the government and that it undermined the independence of monetary policy, exchange rate management, and balance sheet of RBI.[7] It was ironic that analysts criticised us for obliging the government while the government was unhappy for not being consulted in advance.

In June 2008, we were all very concerned at the price increases, and hence the government considered a package of policies to tackle the issue. As part of the package, I was advised to increase the policy rates outside the calendar of monetary policy statements. I pleaded that the monetary actions already taken were under transmission and further increase would have adverse effects.

I was advised very seriously and urgently to consider it, and the media was made to understand through the finance secretary, Subba Rao, that the RBI would act.

I made a statement from Pune explaining my assessment, and simultaneously convened an extraordinary meeting of the Technical Advisory Committee on Monetary Policy to have the benefit of their views. I wanted to strengthen my hands with additional inputs before deciding. I was informed by Rangarajan of the strong feelings of the government in this regard, irrespective of my views and that of the Technical Advisory Committee.

I obeyed.

Did we, in the RBI, achieve the objectives of monetary policy?

The growth in GDP was at a record high during my tenure, with an average of 9.5 per cent in three of the years. Inflation was contained in the range of 4.4 per cent to 6.6 per cent, though it shot up towards the end of the tenure and reached 8.1 per cent in 2008-09, the year of the global financial crisis. Growth was enabled by the high level of investments financed almost wholly by domestic savings, with a record performance in household financial savings and fiscal consolidation. The indicators of external and financial sectors pointed to stability.

There were several criticisms in regard to the conduct of

monetary policy. First, the growth in GDP could have been higher but for the uninterrupted tight monetary policy. Second, the credit growth was at a prevailing historic high, despite tight monetary and credit policy, sowing the seed for non-performing assets in future. Third, the pressures on inflation in 2008-09 could have been avoided if timely action had been taken since the tightening happened too late and too little, and close to the onset of the global financial crisis. Finally, there were several prevailing beliefs in global circles to which we did not contribute.

The popular belief was that there should be a target for inflation to ensure effective monetary policy. Assignment of such a target, it was held, would enable clear accountability and exercise of independence by the RBI. The belief was that a commitment to such a target would enhance both the effectiveness and credibility of monetary policy.

In the RBI, we felt that arguments in favour of inflation-targeting were not relevant to India, and even if considered necessary, it was not operationally feasible here. We did not have a record of very high inflation in the past that warranted a review of the existing approach. The RBI had a reasonable track record of delivering price stability which lent credibility to it. The issue of accountability of an autonomous technical body did not arise since RBI was not de jure independent in the first place.

The governor, deputy governor, and all members of the board are appointed by the government of the day and full-time members of the board can be removed without assigning any reason. Further, the RBI has been endowed with several other responsibilities, including banking regulation, debt management and exchange management. It was not a mere monetary authority, and so its performance could not be judged with reference to monetary policy alone.

Traditionally, the RBI had given importance to provision of credit to enable growth, and people looked up to it for a role that was not exclusively concerned with inflation. Even if it was assumed that inflation targeting was appropriate to India, we felt that the RBI would have serious difficulties in delivering such a target. Its credibility would be eroded if it accepted a responsibility that might be difficult for it to deliver on its own. The appropriate measure for targeting inflation was the Consumer Price Index, and a single index was not available. Inflation includes prices of energy and food, but both are vulnerable to shocks. In our case, energy prices depend on the price of imported oil and food stock on monsoon conditions. Some countries target 'core inflation' that excludes the prices of oil and food items.

In our case, such a core inflation would exclude major commodities in the consumption basket of most people, which were energy and food. More generally, the causes of inflation in a country like ours have more to do with supply bottlenecks then demand management. The RBI's tools, however, address mainly the demand side.

The huge borrowing programme of the government implies a large demand from it on the resources, in a dominant and inflexible manner. Such a fiscal dominance does impede the operational effectiveness of monetary policy.

The transmission of monetary policy is hampered by the prescription of interest rates by the government, that is, administered interest rates for savings and lending. The ownership of a large part of the banking and insurance system by the government also has the potential to hamper transmission because the entities may be guided more by government directions than signals from the RBI.

We were, therefore, opposed to the idea of being accountable on a matter where the RBI was not in a position to deliver, with a potential for it to become a scapegoat or find its credibility eroded. At the same time, I saw merit in the idea of a transparent commitment to the cause of price stability through an indicative, self-imposed target. Such a commitment helped anchor inflation expectations, and hence we moved in that direction. I decided to articulate what may be called a self-imposed desirable range of inflation, appropriate to our economy, but aligning it broadly with global inflation over the medium term.

The finance minister was comfortable with the idea of articulating a self-imposed desirable level of inflation, but was uncomfortable with the range indicated, which was considered too low to be achieved. The articulation of the expected level of inflation for the RBI, I believe, anchored inflation expectations more firmly than before.

It became a forerunner of the idea of flexible inflation targeting. I also realised that expectations of inflation among the people at large is extremely important for the conduct of monetary policy.

Some countries have their own inflation expectation surveys. We decided to adopt a system of inflation expectation survey which was used initially for internal purposes and over a period put in the public domain.

Who should have the authority to finally decide on the stance of and measures related to monetary policy? When I joined, making the monetary policy was the governor's responsibility, with the implicit guidance of the central board and overt consultation with the government.

I was aware of the recommendation of an advisory group, headed by former governor M. Narasimham and with S.S. Tarapore as a member, with regard to bench-marking of our system with international standards and codes. It recommended constitution of a committee of the central board for discharge of monetary policy functions. We (the Committee on International Standards and Codes with the secretary, Economic Affairs, and me as co-chairs) endorsed the recommendation. I saw some merit in the committee system.

We studied international practices relating to the composition, functions, periodicity of meetings, openness and communication of such committees. My interactions in the BIS, especially with some of the governors, helped me appreciate the nuances of their functioning. With the benefit of such consultations, we took a view on what suited India best. We decided to establish a committee on monetary policy, though the law does not mandate it or provide for it; but the law also did not prohibit it.

I did not formally consult the government before taking the decision since the committee was advisory to the governor, but kept Chidambaram informed of my thoughts and actions. To make sure that the committee was beyond the formal purview of the government, I used the words 'technical' and 'advisory' in the nomenclature (it was christened as Technical Advisory Committee on Monetary Policy – TAC), making it abundantly clear that it was not a policy body and was not taking any decisions.

The membership included, apart from the deputy governor, four outsiders representing monetary economics, central banking, financial markets, and public finance. Two members of the RBI central board were subsequently added to the TAC. As governor, I worked out the composition and the terms of reference, in consultation with the RBI board.

The TAC arrangement was unique at that time in subjecting the RBI governor to the discipline of some sort of committee system. I did it partly because I felt that responsibility on a single person for taking monetary policy decisions was too onerous, and advice from outside experts would add value. At the same time, having two members of the central board ensured legitimacy to the arrangement since the authority to conduct the affairs of the RBI vests with the central board. Yet another reason was to preempt the government from taking hasty decisions and to mandate a committee to fall in line with global practice.

My fear was that such a mandated committee system only for monetary policy did not fit in well with the existing system of a central board that governs multiple functions of the RBI. I felt that the law can always, in due course, legitimise and mandate any good practice that has proven benefits. The working methods of the committee were discussed in the committee itself since we were still experimenting. Some refinements were made from time to time, particularly in periodicity and transparency.

This process of forming the TAC introduced an element of challenge to the professionals in the RBI since they had to make presentations similar to those in other countries which had monetary policy committees. Above all, the meetings of the advisory committee helped me in my discussions with the finance minister on monetary policy measures. I was in a position to fortify my arguments with the variety of inputs that I had received. I used to keep the minister informed about the membership of the committee, their stature and standing. I was also keeping him informed of the broad trend of the discussions in the meetings, without attributing a particular point of view to a member. Coordination of policies is important, I felt, which in a way ran counter to the view that monetary policy should be independent.

What were the instruments that the RBI had to achieve its objectives, and how did it operate them? A little background will help.

As a monetary authority, the RBI can take recourse to managing the quantity of money especially through credit allocation called direct instrument, or it can take recourse to using the indirect instrument, that is, interest rate, to influence the aggregate demand, and thus achieve its goal of price, output, and financial sector stability.

Direct and indirect instruments are not mutually exclusive, and the relative emphasis varies from time to time, depending on the structure of the economy, state of the financial sector and monetary conditions. So, these issues are reviewed at intervals.

Monetary authorities periodically ask questions such as what is money? How can it be measured? Does such money matter? How to influence the quantity or price of money, and for what purpose?'

This was analysed in the Indian context in detail by the third working group on money supply under my chairmanship. The group, which was constituted by Rangarajan in 1997, submitted its report in June 1998. It recognised that the monetary targeting approach, the use of quantity of money for achieving the objective of policy – was progressively becoming less effective than before. The analysis helped the evolution of the multiple indicator approach to assess monetary conditions and a movement towards Liquidity Adjustment Facility (LAF). LAF involved the process by which the monetary conditions are influenced by the policy instrument, namely, injecting or absorbing liquidity at appropriate rates of interest. Initially in 1999, we had Interim Liquidity Adjustment Facility in the RBI, which was converted into full-fledged LAF a year later, combined with a time path for making the call money market purely interbank, and for making improvements in the payments and settlement system. I was associated as deputy governor in preparation for the movement to full-fledged facility.

When I came back as governor, we were working on reviewing the LAF afresh. In its original form the LAF came to be overburdened with sterilisation of large capital inflows, which was not anticipated in designing it.

We got a working group to make recommendations on LAF and another group to study instruments of sterilisation. We realised that if capital flows tended to be very large, the exchange rate would gain more importance and mere improvement in the LAF by itself would not suffice.

We concluded that there was a need to distinguish between normal liquidity management on the one hand and surplus liquidity generated consequent upon intervention in forex markets (to mop up foreign currency inflows consistent with exchange rate objectives) on the other.

When huge capital inflows or huge capital outflows occurred, we might have to buy up dollars or sell dollars in large quantities if we were to smoothen the impact on the exchange rate. For example, large inflows mean that we put large quantities of rupees in the system to buy dollars, which results in excess liquidity. When we buy up such excess liquidity due to forex intervention, it is called sterilisation. To suck rupees from the system, we sell bonds. No doubt, the Liquidity Adjustment Facility was effectively used as an instrument of sterilisation also till then, but there were limits to this. The stocks of government securities available with the Reserve Bank to sell were not unlimited.

Under the system we proposed and as agreed with the government, it could issue market stabilisation bills or bonds under the MSS for mopping up liquidity from the system on account of extraordinary capital inflows. The amounts so raised would be credited to a fund created in Public Account. The fund would be maintained and operated by the Reserve Bank in consultation with the government. The fund could not be drawn upon by the government except for repayment of bonds and bills issued for sterilisation under the MSS.

The normal tendency for any government would have been to reject a proposal like the MSS. The bureaucracy would be averse to take fiscal burden (paying interest on borrowings that cannot be used by the government, which is what MSS does) to manage liquidity in the monetary system, a legitimate responsibility of the RBI.

Economists would argue that monetary management is the responsibility of a central bank, and the arrangement with proposed limits from time to time circumscribes the autonomy of the central bank. Critics said that the arrangement was messy, non-transparent and vested discretionary powers in the monetary authority. My view was that if the 'impossible trinity' could not be resolved, it had to be managed, however messily.

The 'impossible trinity' states that a fixed exchange rate, free capital movement, and an independent monetary policy cannot all coexist. Policy makers are advised in theory to choose any two options. We had to devise mechanisms for managing the trilemma. We devised a system that was not considered in theory to be difficult to practise and could be mounted without a change in legal provisions.

For the system to work, a central bank that was supposed to be independent from the government, and the government had to work together closely.

We chose neither free nor controlled capital movements but managed capital flows; not fixed or freely floating but market or some sort of managed floating and monetary policy that is independent with constraints due to fiscal dominance. It was complex but we saw no practical alternative.

We recognised that the fiscal policy, monetary policy, and the regulatory policy have to supplement each other, and sometimes, one set of policies has to make up for excesses in the other.

We know that the fiscal policies are determined by the government. It borrows what it budgets for, or sometimes even more. Therefore, the monetary policy has to take into account the existence of fiscal dominance, and not assume otherwise. Under the circumstances, the banking system has to be used by executing powers of regulation to ensure a smooth borrowing programme for the government. We did not want to think or act in silos.

The finance minister fortunately embarked on a path of fiscal consolidation during this period, taking advantage of the boom conditions. Together, the government and the RBI took the opportunity to rationalise both external debt and public debt obligations of the Centre and the states, making use of the liquidity and low interest rates globally and domestically.

There were occasions when it was said that we were making it easy for the government to borrow and, thus encouraging it. I clarified that we as a central bank could protest till the government decided to borrow, but after a decision was taken, we as the debt manager to the government had to make the process as smooth as possible.

We did not subscribe to the view that there were conflicts of interest or perverse incentives involved in a coordinated approach; on the contrary, we were particular about coordinated formulation and implementation of our policies, whether they be in banking regulation, foreign exchange management or monitoring public debt.

Communication from the central bank, especially the governor, is also an important instrument of influencing the monetary environment in the desired direction. The dominant philosophy held by the US and UK was that there should be forward guidance by the central bank to the financial markets. The European central bank, however, did not believe in forward guidance. The RBI's communication policy was to share with the markets and other stakeholders the data and the inferences, and the thinking, but a refusal to give forward guidance.

We clarified that I did not know the future to be able to give guidance and, therefore, I could only share our thinking process about the past and the current developments.

I had also argued that the market players might be tempted to underprice risks based on the guidance of the central bank. The critics argued that my policy framework was not transparent. I responded that various elements of policies can be discerned from three sources, the policy statements, policy actions and policy outcomes, when read and understood in an integrated fashion.

'Dr Reddy needs no introduction; he needs only a conclusion,' was a popular quip in financial markets. On several occasions, I was accused of giving confusing signals. I responded by saying that I was faithfully sharing my confusion. Sometimes I had to be ingenious. Defending increase in policy rates, I said: 'You are paying more than before for vegetables, petrol, and clothes. The price of everything is going up. What is wrong if I increase the price of money also? That may reduce the price of clothes.' It appealed!

On one occasion, I had to explain in great detail why I was doing nothing in terms of policy actions at a particular juncture to prove that it was what I called, 'thoughtful inaction'.

Extracts from a policy statement I made in the First Quarter Review, on 26 July 2005, illustrate our approach.

'Factors such as increased global uncertainties, high and volatile international prices of oil…could prompt a change in the stance of policy.

'In favour of continuation of the stance, it could be argued that the oil price hike has been managed well with a combination of monetary and fiscal measures…global inflation during 2005 is projected to be moderate despite high oil prices…

'The considerations in favour of status quo are evenly matched by those for change in stance, but the balance of convenience at this juncture lies in continuing with status quo while monitoring the unfolding constellation of uncertainties, especially in the global arena.'

This quote illustrates the non-quantifiable trade-offs involved in the conduct of monetary policy. In the final analysis, judgements are often called for, and judgements do involve assessment of consequential risks. We had to consider the consequences of our assumptions and judgements going wrong, however remote it might seem, because the capacity of most people to bear financial risk is limited. So, the stance of the monetary policy depended not only on careful assessment of macroeconomic developments in the domestic economy, including the impact of developments in the global economy, but the overall balance of risks.

Communications from central banks often give an impression that the decisions are based on deep insightful analysis. That is true, but that is not the whole truth. We have to weigh several factors, some of them conjecture and some of them mere gut feeling. The scientific part of monetary policy is analysis, but the art of it lies in the judgements and balancing of risks.

In retrospect, the biggest challenge I faced was increased uncertainties.

The economy was growing rapidly, the financial sector was growing even more rapidly, and our pace of integration with the global economy was unprecedented. This was at a time when the global economy was heading towards a crisis. I faced the problem of data systems in India lagging behind these developments.

Once, Ruchir Sharma of Morgan Stanley said to me that a policy decision I had taken was inconsistent with the data.

I told him, 'In India, not only the future but even the past is uncertain.'

The problem is that variations between estimates and revised estimates are large, and further revisions are made very often.

When Timothy Geithner of the Federal Reserve visited India, I gifted him *Complications* by Atul Gawande, and told him that it was the best book I had read on monetary policy, though it was a narration of a surgeon's experiences. In periods of crises or rapid change, the conduct of monetary policy becomes more of art, though not less of science.[8] Personally, I was somewhat amused about the dramatic shift in challenge to monetary policy between the day I joined the RBI in 1996 and the day I left in 2008. We started to wrest autonomy for the RBI by restraining fiscal dominance in the conduct of our monetary policy. We ended up fighting dominance of a more capricious source, global capital. That fight is the main theme of the next chapter.

21

THE PROBLEM OF THE RUPEE

DR BHIMRAO AMBEDKAR WROTE A SCHOLARLY BOOK TITLED *THE Problem of the Rupee: Its Origin and Its Solution.*[1] He started his career as an economist and he made a name for himself as a monetary economist. Dr Ambedkar wrote this book in 1923 (and updated it in 1947). He gave a memorandum to the Hilton Young Commission (Royal Commission on Indian Currency and Finance) in 1925 on the exchange rate of the rupee. At that time, the Indian national opinion and business in India were almost unanimous in favour of a depreciated rupee as an instrument for our growth. The government had a different view which provided incentives to British exporters. Ambedkar is reported to have said in his statement before the commission: 'At the outset, it is necessary to realise that this controversy involves two distinct questions: (i) should we stabilise our exchange? and (ii) what should be the ratio at which we should stabilise?'[2] The two distinct questions raised by Ambedkar continue to be relevant even today.

'I do not know,' was my answer to a question on my opinion as governor on the prevailing exchange rate of the rupee. There was a follow-up question: 'How can the governor intervene in forex markets to influence the market-related exchange rate without knowing what is the right value?' I responded: 'I cannot define God. I can recognise the devil. We can see excess volatility or an out-of-alignment rate of exchange when we see it happening.' That summed up our view on management of the exchange rate.

'Venu, you should get some respect for our rupee. I have to pay forty rupees to buy a dollar; rupee is shamefully weak,' one of my friends advised me. I told him, 'The Japanese have to pay double that amount of their currency, yen, to buy a dollar; and surely, Japan is not weak.'

He retorted, 'The yen is a strong currency as it has appreciated in the past compared to the US dollar.' I asked him, 'Does it become a strong currency for appreciating in the past or for expected appreciation in future, based on the past?' I added that sometimes, the rupee depreciated vis-à-vis the US dollar, but most other currencies also depreciated similarly. That might reflect strengthening of the dollar in general, rather than weakening of the rupee in particular. My friend got bored with the conversation. Many of us feel that we are patriotic if we advocate a strong rupee, but strong in what way? More important, who determines the exchange rate? How does it come about?

The exchange rate is also a price. The difference is that in goods and services, the exchange takes place between a currency and a good or service. In the case of exchange rate, the exchange is between two currencies.[3] When the exchange rate is left to forces of demand and supply in the market, it is treated as flexible exchange rate. If, on the other hand, the government decides the price, then the demand and supply will have to be at that price, and the government should be willing to enforce the fixed exchange rate.

The demand and supply of foreign currency can arise from the earnings of exporters and demands of importers of goods and services called trade account. The demand may arise for reasons such as tourism or overseas education or medical and health treatment or even payment of interest on loan taken. These are called invisibles. Together, these are called current account transactions. When an investor takes a loan or invests in another country, it is considered a capital account transaction mainly because the obligations arise in regard to a future payment. The exchange rate is determined by the supply and demand for both current account and capital account purposes. Speculation (and derivative market transactions) play a major role in foreign exchange markets when their quantum is huge. Illustratively, as per BIS data, about $5 trillion per day is traded on foreign exchange markets. This amount is vastly more than what is needed (a) for international trade of goods and services (about $24 trillion per year) or (b) for foreign direct investment (which is about $1.0-1.5 trillion per year).

The supply and demand of currency for use and for speculation are reflected in trades in the forex markets, and our exchange rate is determined by the market. The RBI influences demand and supply at a system level by regulating the current account transactions and capital account transactions. This is supplemented by buying or selling foreign currency in the markets from time to time. When a central bank buys or sells foreign currency, it is described as intervention in forex markets.

The RBI's intervention in the market is possible to the extent it has enough currency to do it. It can generate rupees, but it needs a stock of foreign currency to intervene, hence foreign exchange reserves. Thus, reserves are only those foreign currency assets that are readily available for use by the monetary authorities. The capacity of the RBI to intervene, and its effectiveness, depends on the level of reserves. But keeping foreign currency assets has costs as against the benefit of comfort. Any addition or depletion to foreign currency reserves through the market by the RBI affects the demand and supply of foreign currency and impacts the exchange rate. The balance of payments position of a country is reflected in a statement that contains transactions in current account and capital account (showing a surplus or deficit in both) and change in the level of forex reserves.[4]

Movements in exchange rate are as important as the level. A good way of understanding movements in our exchange rate would be to treat it as a reflection of movements in the external value of the rupee, just as inflation or upward movement in the general level of prices is a reflection of the changes in the internal value of the rupee – the goods and services it can buy.

The movements in the internal value of the rupee and that of the internal value of the dollar are reflected by inflation in India and in the US. It is not unreasonable to expect that the exchange rate between the two currencies will, at some stage, also reflect the differences in inflation. Also, the price of money, that is, the interest rate prevailing in the two countries, will influence demand and supply for the two currencies. In a globalised world, several currencies are traded freely and that makes our understanding difficult. It also opens up opportunities to speculate on future movements, which in turn affects the demand and supply.

The exchange rate in the market is thus a product of several factors. The rates keep changing, but if the changes are too large and too often, those who export or import may face too many uncertainties. In countries like ours, the facilities for insurance against such large changes are not adequate, or too expensive. Such wild and frequent movements are what we describe as excess volatility. The RBI's policy has been to intervene to reduce excess volatility.

Once, I was asked: 'What is excess volatility?' My reply was: 'Volatility is a state of mind. What was volatility yesterday becomes flexibility tomorrow, as the market participants get to experience it and markets develop to offer products for hedging the currency risk. So, volatility in currency markets has to be seen as a dynamic involving attitudes and institutions also.'

As in the case of interest rates, there are gainers and losers when a currency appreciates or depreciates. Interests and emotions do govern views on the exchange rate. In India, governments seem to favour an overvalued rupee, as a sign of national pride perhaps, and there are beneficiaries. Any depreciation or devaluation is seen as a sign of weakness. An overvalued currency tends to make imports cheaper and could possibly moderate inflation. Corporates who borrow heavily from external sources favour appreciation since their liabilities in rupee terms get reduced. Foreign investors also favour it since their income in terms of foreign currency increases. But they also realise that beyond a point, appreciation would be counter-productive, and might result in a crisis. Yet, they often bet on the depreciation occurring after they exit. There are also interests that favour undervalued currency, such as exporters, because it makes their products more competitive abroad. A depreciating currency is also advantageous to local business and economic activity since imports may cost more. On the downside, the domestic prices will go up.

The interest rate and exchange rate are also related because the interest rate differentials between currencies (adjusted for inflation and country risk) influence capital flows and thus exchange rate. A currency that is perceived to be overvalued will at some stage depreciate, and the currency that is undervalued will at some stage appreciate. The level and the direction of the changes, the magnitude of change and the pace of change in the exchange rate do affect players differently. The players exercise their influence over the market, both through their participation and through representations to the government. Market players and, to an extent, governments tend to have a short-term outlook. Our policies had to consider the impact that goes beyond short term, recognising that we have limited knowledge of the uncertain future and limited instruments in an interactive financial world.

In a way, therefore, several judgements were involved in agreeing on (a) the exchange rate that could be considered to be out of alignment with the fundamentals; (b) the extent of volatility in forex markets that was acceptable; (c) and effectiveness as well as costs and benefits of intervention by the RBI in forex markets. The tensions in exchange-rate management mainly arise out of the judgements involved, in particular, in regard to the quasi-fiscal costs (that is, costs on account of financial transactions not included in the budget but with similar effect on fiscal policy) and benefits from intervention in the forex market and build up of forex reserves by the RBI.

Intervention in the market to mobilise forex generates rupee liquidity and excess liquidity can be mopped up by a combination of measures, such as, (i) open market operations of the RBI with impact on its balance sheet; (ii) changes in the cash reserve ratio, implying a burden on the banking system; (iii) issue of bonds under Market Stabilisation Scheme (as explained in the previous chapter), which involve a fiscal burden on the government. Getting agreement on burden sharing is not easy.

The contours of the exchange rate regime are determined by

the government in close consultation with the RBI. However, the actual conduct of exchange rate policy is left to the RBI. The broad approach during my tenure continued to be as it was before my time, namely, to allow market forces to determine the exchange rate, subject to the RBI intervening to avoid volatility. But the challenges do not remain the same.

I was aware of the different types of challenges faced by my predecessors in management of the external sector. R.N. Malhotra conveyed his worries about the impending balance of payments crisis but was helpless in the absence of political will to do anything. Venkitaramanan handled the balance of payments crisis, the likes of which we had never seen before. Rangarajan had to build a framework for reformed external sector management, but towards the end of his tenure, had to battle the Asian Crisis in 1997. Jalan continued to fight the battle successfully and managed the shocks emanating from the sanctions on India following the nuclear tests. The challenge for me, as it turned out, was that it was not just an event, but a paradigm shift in the state of affairs that most of us in India were not very familiar with at that time. I did not expect such a dramatic shift in the external sector environment.

My tenure was unprecedented in external sector management. We were opening up our economy. That by itself would not have been a problem if the financial sector was not growing too rapidly. Many believed that the financial sector would lead growth. Global liquidity was at an unprecedented high. By early 2007, the IMF realised that it was not able to generate income to fully meet its expenses! Those were interesting times.

I must confess that my approach to managing the external sector was considerably influenced by my experiences in the past. First, I had had bitter and humiliating experiences as a common person in foreign exchange transactions for personal purposes. Second, our country faced three types of shocks, on the external front, oil prices, monsoon conditions affecting food supplies and volatile capital flows. So, we had to reckon with potential external and domestic shocks, which could occur together. Forex availability is also an important element of security considerations. Third, if we faced problems, our needs would have been too large for the IMF to come to our rescue. Geopolitical considerations too might result in lack of support for balance of payments when needed.

I was wary of hasty liberalisation of the financial sector, both for inflows and outflows. I was aware of the volatile nature of such flows. I was also aware that data showed that a majority of such flows took place through tax havens. Further, some were conduits for round tripping; that is, residents illegally took the money out and reinvested it in India. The regulatory framework was undermined by investors whose identity or beneficial ownership was difficult to establish.

The objectives of exchange rate management were to moderate excessive volatility; build adequate level of reserves; and develop forex markets in a calibrated manner. In the process, it would be possible to rely less on active management of the exchange rate, and more on markets.

The movements in exchange rate are critical for policy just as movement in prices is. One way of capturing the movement in exchange rate is Real Effective Exchange Rate (REER). The RBI calculates Real Effective Exchange Rate and puts it in the public domain. This index is different from the nominal exchange rate that we use in day-to-day transactions. REER tries to capture the relative effects of inflation on the rupee exchange rate in terms of select countries with whom we have significant trade and a relevant basket of currencies (of those countries). Expressed as an index, when it is more than 100 it reflects overvaluation and an index of less than 100 reflects undervaluation.

My predecessor Jalan stated that REER was not a reliable guide. I felt, however, that some indication of what our inclination was on the appropriateness of the exchange rate, without committing to a level, would be suitable. We tried to signal that we were looking at REER in our policies, though were not bound by it.

We noticed in 2005 the growing importance of trade between China and India. Hence, we replaced the prevailing five-country indices with a new six-country index, comprising the US, Euro-zone, the UK, Japan, China, and Hong Kong. To signal the importance we were giving REER, the methodology of computation was published in detail in the *Bulletin*, a monthly official publication of the RBI.

I reproduced Jalan's language on the exchange rate in all policy statements for record, but we were guided by REER in practice, as a starting point to assess the alignment of the prevailing exchange rate in the market with economic fundamentals. The rule of thumb was: movements within 5 per cent of the rate as per REER would be welcome. Movements between 5 and 10 per cent warranted close observation and intervention if the volatility was higher than normal. Deviation of more than 10 per cent warranted intervention unless there were good reasons not to do so, for the moment. Prolonged stability at a rate also warranted our attention and on occasion intervention. We felt that the markets were also comfortable with this arrangement.[5]

We had to work in close coordination with the Ministry of Finance to ensure that the capital flows were not significantly in excess of our capacity to absorb and manage. We worked together to build the reserves initially, and later to maintain an exchange rate that was competitive. We had to undertake sterilisation as appropriate. Most of the build-up of reserves is on account of intervention in forex markets by the RBI to purchase dollars. Naturally, sterilisation became necessary. The more we built up the reserves, the more we needed to sterilise, and consequently we had repeatedly approached the government to enhance the ceilings on outstanding bonds under MSS and approvals were granted despite the additional fiscal burden.

We were in a difficult situation during calendar year 2006. Capital flows were large and restrictions on their inflow went against the reform credentials of the government. To maintain a competitive exchange rate, intervention and sterilisation became necessary. This was imposing a fiscal burden. The RBI was not in favour of allowing outflows through financial intermediaries; and we had already liberalised outflows for households and non-financial corporates for acquisitions.

Having reached a comfortable level of reserves, perhaps, more than a comfortable level, the government wanted to risk appreciation of rupee rather than restrict capital flows with their attendant limitations or incur fiscal costs for sterilisation. We were against appreciation in view of its possible adverse impact on our competitiveness. There was an impasse by the last quarter of fiscal year 2006-07.

We noticed in early 2007 that the signals emanating from the ministry reflected hesitation on the part of the government to incur the fiscal cost of sterilisation. At the same time there was reluctance to contain capital flows, which could have reduced the appreciating pressure on the rupee, the need for intervention, and costs of sterilisation. Clearly, the government wanted to attract foreign investments, and take advantage of the plenty that was on offer. They were aware that exchange rate objectives would be compromised under these circumstances of hesitation and reluctance. Perhaps, the government was convinced that the 'hands-off' policy on the exchange rate advocated by some influential economists was appropriate. There was no formal change in the position of the government, but the actions and statements in the media gave us the unmistakable signs of a change in attitude.

Once we realised that our capacity to intervene and sterilise was constrained by the ceilings under MSS, the manoeuvrability of the RBI to maintain the exchange rate within the parameters of REER set for itself was reduced. We did not want to wait till we exhausted our capacity to sterilise before we moderated our operations. We could not afford to be caught without instruments to intervene and thus make the rupee vulnerable to speculative attacks. I, therefore, decided that we should allow the exchange rate to appreciate by simply not intervening, though we were aware that the movement might not be gradual. In any case, I felt that it would have been very difficult to pursue an exchange rate intervention policy that was undermined by the actions or inactions of the government. As expected, the exchange rate appreciated. The government, perhaps, became conscious of the repercussions of exchange rate appreciations after these occurred.

The net result was that the government enhanced the ability of the RBI to sterilise by enhancing the outstanding limits to MSS/bonds. We were also informed that we should resume the intervention in the forex markets that we had interrupted in view of the lack of full backing by the government in the past.

On 16 September 2003, after office hours, we issued a notification stopping fresh investments into India through overseas corporate bodies (OCBs). The OCBs that were hitherto permitted to freely invest in India and repatriate earnings could henceforth only sell and could not make fresh investments. This restriction would not apply to non-resident Indians in their individual capacity. This was a follow-up on recommendations of the joint parliamentary committee on the Ketan Parekh scam. My predecessor had been working on follow-up in consultation with the government, though I had to take the final decision. OCBs were funds whose beneficial ownership was suspect, and often, they were a conduit to resident Indians to take black money out and then bring it back to India. We did not know to whom the money really belonged. OCBs were one of the two channels identified for special attention by the joint parliamentary committee; the other was participatory notes. This was a subject with SEBI and they were not banned. However, Finance Minister Jaswant Singh did not object to the decision to ban investment by OCBs.

Soon after the new government headed by Dr Manmohan Singh was formed in May 2004, I explained to the finance minister that I was hoping for a ban on participatory notes at the time when we banned investments by OCBs. He was not keen to discuss the subject in detail. When I pushed the subject, he appeared a little annoyed. He said, 'Venu, a greenback is a greenback. We need investments and we should get them for our development.' My contention was that like OCBs, participatory notes were unhealthy flows, and that banning them would replace the unhealthy with healthy flow. More important, I was anticipating large capital inflows, and hence this was an opportune time to ban them.

Since all my efforts to restrain excess capital flows and put a ban on participatory notes were not bearing fruit, I thought it appropriate to provoke an academic and policy debate on the subject. I flagged the issue on 12 January 2005 in connection with the release of India Development Report in Mumbai.[6]

I must confess that I was aware of the possible consequences of my statement in the speech. As per my normal practice, I had discussed the draft with all the three concerned heads of departments in the RBI. Two of them pointed out that a statement regarding capital account measures could be very sensitive, and advised me against making it. However, I chose to go ahead and told them that this was my decision. I was aware that this would be provocative, but I felt that I had to flag it as a matter of concern for us. I did not, however, anticipate a virulent attack from market participants, specially the electronic media (TV). Finally, since ministers' assurances did not pacify the financial markets, I was compelled to call for a meeting with the media in the night and issue clarifications. Further, I had to make changes to one sentence in the speech that was already on the RBI website, the same night.[7]

Chidambaram felt strongly that the issue of participatory notes should be settled and the matter clarified. Therefore, he appointed a committee under the chairmanship of Dr Ashok Lahiri, chief economic advisor, with membership which included a nominee of the RBI.

The expert group on 'Encouraging FII's flows and checking the vulnerability of capital markets to speculative flows' submitted its report in October 2005. There were serious disagreements between the nominee of the RBI and the rest, generally on encouraging FIIs at a time when we were keen to moderate capital inflows and volatility; and specifically on the continuance of participatory notes. The recommendation of the committee on participatory notes was particularly disturbing. It said: 'The current dispensation for PNs may continue. SEBI should have full powers to obtain information regarding the final holder/ beneficiaries or of any holder at any point of time in case of any investigation or surveillance action. FIIs may be obliged to provide the information to SEBI' (para 153).

In an unprecedented gesture, the nominee of the RBI appended a note of dissent. We wanted the issue to be put in broader context of capital flows. The note of dissent suggested that in view of macroeconomic implications, impact on financial stability, especially on exchange rate, and fiscal vulnerability, apart from monetary management, a special group may be constituted to study measures to contain large volatility in FII flows as a priority. The note of dissent added that the Reserve Bank's stance had been that the issue of participatory notes should not be permitted. The note pointed out our main concerns regarding the issue of participatory notes, namely, that the nature of the beneficial ownership or the identity of the investor would not be known, unlike in the case of FIIs registered with a financial regulator. Trading of these notes would lead to multi-layering (a series of transactions to put veils around the real owner or the beneficial owner) which would make it difficult to identify the ultimate holder of the notes. Both conceptually and in practice, restriction on suspicious flows enhance the reputation of markets and lead to healthy flows. The note, therefore, reiterated that the issuance of participatory notes should not be permitted. The government was not happy with our note of dissent and proceeded with the idea of encouraging FII inflows through these notes, but with some safeguards.

Full convertibility on current account was adopted by us in August 1994. There was a global fascination for full convertibility on capital account even as I entered the RBI in 1996. To consider the issue, a Committee on Capital Account Convertibility (Tarapore Committee I) was appointed by the government, and it gave its report in June 1997. It recommended, wisely, a gradual movement towards full convertibility in three phases. We followed up with capital account management based on the Rangarajan Committee and Tarapore Committee.

Prime Minister Singh, in a speech at the RBI on 18 March 2006, requested us (the finance minister and I) to revisit the subject of capital account and 'come out with a roadmap based on current realities'. He prefaced this with the words 'there is merit in moving towards fuller capital account convertibility within a transparent framework'. Within two days of the PM's suggestion, in consultation with the finance minister, the RBI appointed a committee to set out the 'Roadmap Towards Fuller Capital Account Convertibility' with Tarapore as chairman. It was to give its report on 31 July 2006.

I felt it appropriate to signal the RBI's view on the subject in the Annual Policy Statement on 18 April 2006. While the prime minister was referring to moving towards fuller capital account convertibility, I said that 'continuation of the gradual process may warrant some hard and basic decisions are taken in regard to macroeconomic management, in particular, monetary, external and financial sector management'. I addressed the committee on 6 May 2006. We got the report on 31 July 2006. It recommended a five-year roadmap with three phases in timing and sequencing of measures. Low inflation, low non-performing assets of the banking sector, and low fiscal deficit were key to fuller convertibility.

I must confess that I was consulted about the speech that the prime minister was delivering. The draft sent to me in advance said 'full' convertibility. Full convertibility somehow gave an impression or expectation that there would be no restrictions at all. I did not consider full convertibility as popularly understood feasible in the foreseeable future and hence we did not want to build expectation. My suggestion to use the word 'fuller' was accepted. Fuller could mean that it was short of fullest! I did not want the impression to go round that it was a destination since we believed that it was a process. Dr Singh confirmed his trust in my judgement.

What is the appropriate level of reserves for a country? My position as governor was that it was difficult to define such a level since months of import cover, a traditional indicator, had become less relevant due to other liabilities. I was willing to learn from anyone who could claim to know.

In my view, the appropriate level of forex reserves should be viewed from several angles and in a dynamic fashion. As deputy governor, I had identified four sets of indicators to assess adequacy of reserves, namely, money-based, trade-based, debt-based and liquidity-based.[8] My conclusion was in favour of exploring a national balance sheet approach. Such an approach takes into account total external assets and liabilities both public and private, and considers reserves as a component of national external assets readily usable by public authorities in forex markets. In any case, my reputation of being a proponent of active capital account management and in building adequate foreign exchange reserves preceded me when I joined as governor.

Was our level of reserves adequate? When I joined, they were less than comfortable, and by the end of the tenure, they had reached a very comfortable level. However, they were not excessive if we looked at them as a national balance sheet of external assets and liabilities. Basically the reserves were built on excess capital flows and not excess of, say, export earnings over import needs. Hence, additional external liabilities were the source of reserves for us. The nature of the external liabilities, that is, the preponderance of portfolio flows which have the potential to be volatile, had to be kept in mind in assessing the comfort level of our reserves. In brief, we did not have excess of reserves to be invested in commercial undertakings.

Foreign exchange reserves are managed by the RBI, consistent with the provisions of the Act. The appropriate level of forex reserves, the deployment and the use of such reserves are matters in which consultations between the government and the central bank are essential. We did not have differences regarding deployment, but there was a serious issue about the use of forex reserves.

The parameters of deployment are discussed by the governor assisted by a deputy governor with the secretary (Economic Affairs), and chief economic advisor. The finance minister is invariably kept informed. Successive ministers left the issue of deployment of reserves to the best judgement of the team, consisting of finance ministry and RBI officials.

Forex reserves are deployed in various instruments denominated in reserve currencies. Deployment of forex reserves takes into consideration safety of the investments, the liquidity associated, and the returns anticipated. The currency composition of deployment of reserves is also an important consideration in preserving the overall value of the assets.

In managing the reserves, the overriding consideration is reputational risk. As a central bank, we cannot afford to invest in any institution or instrument that could be associated with any wrongdoing. Of the three considerations, namely, safety, liquidity, and return, safety is given high weight, especially when the reserves are not excessive. Liquidity continues to be important and becomes less important as the level of reserves rises to and goes beyond comfort level. Return gets higher weight as the level of reserves moves up on the comfort level. When the reserves reach a level beyond which they do not serve the purpose of reserves (namely, being readily available for use by public authorities to intervene in the market), they can be treated or carved out into a Sovereign Wealth Fund. They become long-term investments. As the level of reserves increases, for a country like ours, the quasi-fiscal costs of acquiring and holding the reserves increases, while the benefits may be decreasing.

In 2004, there was a proposal that the RBI should use its forex reserves for funding infrastructure. The surprise was that such a proposal emanated from economists in the government.

Once we use the reserves to lend to domestic entities, they cease to be reserves since they are not readily available for use. Of course, they can be used to meet forex needs by taking them out of reserves. But the infrastructure does not need much of forex. So, if we release forex to infrastructure projects, they will sell it in the market and the RBI would have to buy it to maintain the exchange rate. In any case, the government could buy from the RBI and lend, since it is not legitimate for the bank to evaluate commercial projects for investments.

Apparently (as I came to know in 2006 from Dr Arjun Sen Gupta, chairman of the economic cell of the Congress party), the proposal to use the reserves to fund infrastructure was included in the manifesto of the Congress, which was elected to power in 2004. The advantage of this approach was that the government would be able to lay its hands on reserves without adding to the fiscal deficit. Dr Rakesh Mohan, who was secretary (Economic Affairs), explained to the finance minister that the objective to fund infrastructure would be served with the creation of a public financial institution for the purpose without any reference to the use of reserves. This was accepted and the India Infrastructure Finance Company was announced in 2005. But the use of reserves was not deleted from the agenda.

Larry Summers, noted economist, visited India in March 2006 at our invitation to deliver the L.K. Jha memorial lecture. Summers explained that the level of reserves in many countries far exceeded the traditional measures of reserve levels required to guard against a foreign exchange crisis. Professor Summers suggested the creation of an international facility by the two multilateral institutions, the IMF and the World Bank, under which the countries could invest their excess reserves without taking domestic political responsibility for the process of investment decision and ultimate outcome. In turn, the modest fee charged by these two institutions could support the concessional and grant aspects of global development. This idea appeared to provide a way by which our reserves could be used for infrastructure in our country, avoiding political responsibility and overcoming the RBI's objections. India was likely to be the most important potential user of the proposed facility. The proposal appeared to serve the intent of the government too.

Not unsurprisingly, Summer's proposal was included in the programme of seminars in Singapore in connection with the Fund-Bank annual meeting in September 2006. Among the lead speakers were Summers and I. Summers elaborated on his proposal. I accepted that the option was interesting, but would be relevant only if the level of reserves was above what I called the comfort level. I listed the factors that influence degree of comfort and how the options are linked to the comfort level. I made a specific mention of the emerging risks and added that 'at this moment, the global economy has not been tested on the eventuality of a not-so-orderly correction of the current global imbalances'. Even assuming that there were reserves to spare and higher return was sought, the critical issue, I pointed out, would be the professional expertise of the proposed entity in terms of assuring an acceptable reward equation. As it happened, the proposal was not pursued.

Basically, I questioned the legitimacy and expertise of multilateral institutions operating as asset managers to central banks. The Bank for International Settlements (BIS) provided such services (that is, investing our forex reserves), though I did not mention this in the speech.

In this seminar, I referred also to the proposal made in 2005 by Eswar Prasad and Raghuram G. Rajan of the IMF for controlled approach to capital account liberalisation for economies experiencing large capital inflows and excessive addition to forex reserves. The proposal combined three elements: capital account management, financial sector development, and level of foreign exchange reserves. I explained that the proposal would be attractive only under some questionable assumptions and gave a central place to cross-border financial intermediaries. As it happened, this proposal also was not pursued.

The government revived the proposal for use of forex reserves in 2007. The finance minister announced in the budget speech of 2007-08 that forex reserves would be used for infrastructure development in India on the advice of the Deepak Parekh Committee report. Hence, the Reserve Bank devised a scheme of providing funds to a subsidiary of a Government of India entity to be located in London to be a conduit for such financing. Such an arrangement was necessitated by the legal provisions and best practices governing the RBI in such matters. Though the government guarantee was extended, we suggested that we would refinance specific investments made by the proposed entity since we wanted to be assured that the resources of the RBI were put to the intended purpose.

The government was not happy with the refinancing method to use reserves. They wanted the funds to be invested in the proposed entity in London. At the board level, in December 2007, it was agreed to accept the proposal of the government, while conveying our concerns. There was no doubt high drama, both before and during the meeting.

The second half of 2006 witnessed the beginning of my fears of a dark side to the future. I expressed it to industry and banking leaders in India to resist pressures to liberalise the financial sector.[9] I shared my anxiety about the vulnerability of the global economy with other governors also on various occasions, in particular, in the meetings in the BIS. William White, the economic advisor and head of the Monetary and Economic Department at BIS, shared my concerns about the vulnerability. The chairman of the ECB, Jean Claude Trichet, was foremost in sharing his agreement with my fears. At one stage, the subject of global imbalances and vulnerabilities was discussed with Alan Greenspan, chairman, Federal Reserve in Washington, D.C., when he invited about ten of us for a breakfast meeting in his office. The main concern was about the vulnerabilities in the global economy and, in particular, the future of the dollar. Greenspan did not seem concerned and Trichet was worried. The meeting ended inconclusively with no inclination for corrective action by anybody, including China. For my part, I indicated that we did not contribute to global imbalances because we did not have excessive deficits or surpluses, but we would be affected if there were disorderly correction.

Around this time, Axel Weber, the governor of Bundes Bank, visited the RBI. He was very clear in his mind that the housing bubble in the US that had started unravelling was of enormous magnitude. He foresaw very serious consequences. In a private conversation, he admitted to me that the regulators were almost afraid of taking actions that would annoy global financial conglomerates.

As the housing bubble intensified in the US in 2007, a meeting of select governors and heads of global financial conglomerates discussed the issue. Some of us wanted to know how much and for how long the financial markets would require the support of central banks. They indicated that we would have to support them as long as they needed it. They were not in a position to give any estimate of the amounts needed or time. However, a suggestion was made by them that the accounting standards could be changed by the regulators to show an improvement in the profitability. I recall that Trichet was furious and he said: 'We see that there is a patient with a fever. We have to give some treatment. You are advising that we should change the thermometer and declare the patient as healthy. How does that help?' To this, they said, 'If the thermometer is changed and the patient declared normal, there is a good chance that the patient will feel more confident. Hence, the patient may recover. Our suggestion is to soothe the nerves in the market, and improve the market sentiments.' It was clear to me that the global financial conglomerates, such as Goldman Sachs, Citibank, HSBC and so on, would be calling the shots. It was time for me to be prepared for the crisis that was on the horizon.[10]

My instinct told me that there could be capital outflow from India since threats to global financial health were imminent. I wanted to say in a subtle manner that we in the RBI were prepared for that eventuality. I spent hours in drafting the main message in the concluding para in the speech delivered on 3 January 2008. Finally, it read as: 'While the immediate focus is on managing the excess capital inflows and some volatility in regard to the excess, I believe that it will be prudent not to exclude the possibility of some change in course, due to any abrupt changes in sentiments or global liquidity conditions, despite strong underlying fundamentals of the Indian economy. Strategic management of capital account would warrant preparedness for all situations, and the challenges for managing the capital account in such unexpected turn of events would normally be quite different.' The warning went unnoticed.

We prepared detailed contingency plans and kept them ready within the Reserve Bank. They detailed the measures that would have to be taken as and when there was a serious stress due to large-scale capital outflows. We prepared plans for three contingencies, sudden massive capital outflows, sustained large outflows, and slow continuing outflows. Draft press releases were also kept ready in the custody of the deputy governor in charge of financial markets.

We were prepared for a crisis from January 2008. The global financial crisis broke out eight months later.

My tenure was generally good for the external sector, and a lot of it had to do with the favourable global environment. We did not waste the opportunities to take advantage of it. The exchange rate of the rupee vis-à-vis the dollar was remarkably stable in nominal terms from 2003-04 to 2008-09; in the narrow range of a high of 40.2 and low of 44.1. There was a two-way movement of the exchange rate, compared to the unidirectional depreciating trend in the past. There was a sharp movement in the rate only on one occasion, in March 2007. More important, the current account deficit was contained in the range of 0.4 to 1.3 per cent of GDP, except in 2003-04 when there was a surplus, and the year of global crisis 2008-09, when it was higher. The global financial crisis that struck in September 2008 (soon after I retired) was very disruptive to most economies. The forex reserves, which were less than 100 billion dollars when I joined, reached a level of well over 300 billion. We had prepaid some of the loans taken by the government. The external debt to GDP ratio was maintained in a range of 17.2 to 18.5 in all the years except the crisis year, and short-term debt liabilities contained. The share of equity flows increased.

I am fortunate in my involvement in the management of the external sector almost continuously for over eighteen years (1990-2008) in several capacities. We had entered into the psyche of 'valuable foreign exchange' and persistent depreciation in our currency in 1957. During the balance of payments crisis of 1991, I went through the agony of managing the crisis by pledging gold. I assisted governors Rangarajan and Jalan, who built strength in our external sector, brick by brick. We, the government and the RBI, had moved together from the agony in 1991 to comfort in the external front by 2003. In the five years when I was governor, by September 2008, we moved further from comfort to confidence in the external sector.

The crisis of 1991 was essentially because of vulnerabilities in the Indian economy, such as high fiscal deficits, huge current account deficit, and high short-term debt and low forex reserves. Global developments, in particular, a spike in oil prices, triggered a liquidity crisis at a time when there were political uncertainties. In 2008 it was very different. India had a very strong and resilient external sector (high forex reserves and low current account deficit) while ensuring that the financial sector, especially banking, remained robust. Yet, the impact of the global financial crisis was felt since the transmission occurred through the global trade channel, capital flow channel, and sentiment channel. In 2008, we were well equipped to deal with the crisis since we were prepared to meet such a contingency, specially in the RBI. Necessary policy instruments were available with the RBI in monetary, regulatory, and external sector management because of precautionary measures and also caution in adopting newly emerging sophisticated finance. In view of the fiscal consolidation that had taken place during the good times before 2008, there was enough fiscal headroom to undertake stimulus to manage the crisis.

Above all, there were no political uncertainties in 2008 unlike in 1991. Thus, relative to most other countries, India can claim to have come out of the global crisis relatively unscathed and without recourse to special financing.

In 2013, we faced a serious stress, but not a crisis. It warranted special financing arrangements for balance of payments support. This was the second time since reforms in 1991 that we took recourse to special financing. Special financing refers to public policy initiatives to put in place extraordinary mechanisms to make up for shortfall in normal capital flows. We raised NRI bonds through the SBI in 1998, to manage the impact of US sanctions against India. The recourse to exchange guarantees (by the central bank) was eschewed while raising NRI bonds in 1998. Exchange guarantees assure exchange rate at a future date, thus assuming exchange risk. In 2013, the rupee was under pressure in exchange markets due to the disruption in the global financial markets caused by an indication from the US Federal Reserve that the monetary policy would be tightened. The RBI took recourse to a form of extending exchange guarantees for mobilising foreign currency through NRI deposits. In both cases, there was some accounting jugglery.

Another important question to ask is whether there are risks of a future crisis. The state of external sector in 2015-16, compared to 2007-08 as per indicators, is not a matter of serious concern, though the external position now is not as strong as it was in earlier years. To illustrate, for the years referred, the ratio of external debt to GDP increased from 18.0 per cent to 23.9 per cent. The foreign exchange reserves to external debt ratio decreased from 115.6 per cent to 71.9 per cent. The external debt, which was $172.4 billion, increased to $475 billion. The percentage of external reserves to gross external liabilities decreased from 64.3 per cent to 38.5 per cent. The year 2015-16 was very benign for India, mainly due to low oil prices in that year.

There are three important sources of vulnerability for India – fuel price, food price and heavy dependence on portfolio flows on capital account. Going forward, lesser reliance on imported energy, that is, lesser dependence on import of oil, should be of some help. This warrants attention to energy policies. Food prices can potentially be a source of vulnerability as a consequence of climate changes globally, including in India. In 2006, we faced a problem when the oil prices reached high levels. Corn was used as an alternative source of energy. Around the same time, there was drought in Australia affecting the supply of wheat. Therefore, from India's point of view, the emerging global linkages between climate change, oil prices, and food prices are a source of serious concern. The most important source of vulnerability for India in future would certainly be the magnitude of volatile capital flows and external debt, especially short-term debt.

22

THE FINANCIAL SYSTEM

OUR EFFORTS TO IMPROVE THE FINANCIAL SYSTEM HAD MIXED results. With public sector banks we tried, but we failed. With private sector banks, we tried, and we succeeded. Similarly, with rural cooperatives, we failed, and with urban cooperatives, we succeeded.

We explored specific strategies for improvements in each of the components. Public sector banks dominated our thinking, but the RBI's manoeuvrability was limited by legal provisions that empowered the government. Private sector banks required improvements in governance and we in the RBI had the scope to achieve results. Foreign banks had few branches, but were keen to penetrate deeply into our system. However, we successfully resisted premature onslaught. The cooperative system was relevant for a large number of people, but it suffered from several weaknesses arising out of politicisation of the system. Non-banking financial companies was a large but nebulous segment within the jurisdiction of the RBI. Two of them with large public deposits posed problems that we could resolve. There was a large segment of the semi-formal financial system that was undertaking banking-like activities. These included chit funds, trusts, non-governmental organisations, and self-help groups. They were out of our jurisdiction. In brief, we in the RBI had to be conscious of the scope for and limits to our contribution to the financial system. But reforming, regulating, and supervising such a diverse segment has been a fascinating personal and professional experience.

The overall performance of the financial system depended on the functioning of the public sector banks which accounted for more than two-thirds of banking business. The standards of governance depended on the manner in which the government exercises its powers under the legislative provisions by which several banks were nationalised. The RBI's oversight of public sector banks was focused on prudential regulation.[1]

Public sector banks had some strengths as well as some weaknesses. They had a large network of branches. They had a large workforce, which at the time of recruitment was skilled. Their familiarity with the society and local businesses was unparalleled. Their functioning in a modern competitive environment was constrained by several factors. The officers and staff were lacking in incentives to perform. They were subject to parliamentary oversight, to the jurisdiction of the CBI and the Central Vigilance Commission, which should ideally concentrate on those issues which arise in performing sovereign functions and not commercial activities. Also, accountability to Parliament and influence of individual parliamentarians and bureaucrats are often indistinguishable.

The nominations to the boards of the banks were governed, to a significant extent, by political affiliations. The official nominee of the government on the board represented both the sovereign and the shareholder and thus exercised disproportionate power.

The chances of privatisation of public sector banks or similar reforms were, in our judgement, very dim. Their medium-term future was unclear for the entities themselves. A budget announcement to reduce government shareholding below 51 per cent by Finance Minister Yashwant Sinha had not been followed up. The government had no specific strategy on the future of public sector banks. I did not expect either a dilution of public ownership or an end to dual control by the government and the RBI over them. We made some attempts to improve their standards but with disappointing outcomes. I will narrate them to show how the system works.

We wanted the directors nominated by the government to the public sector banks to satisfy the 'fit and proper' criteria on par with those prescribed by the RBI for private sector banks[2]. The government was not averse at a formal level to the RBI recommending or commenting on the 'fit and proper' aspects of the proposed nominee directors from the government. In practice, it did not welcome our intense due diligence. A proposal to create a roster of competent professionals who could be nominated on bank boards was made but was never responded to. After a while even the formality of a reference to the RBI when the government nominated non-officials to bank boards was done away with.

The chief executives of banks were appointed by the government, as per the legal requirement. However, a committee headed by the governor recommended the names. The committee had representation of the government and an expert nominated by it. My contention was that a regulator could accept or reject a choice but could not recommend to an owner who ought to be appointed. The government's nominee is involved both in the process of recommending and approving. We pleaded for total exclusion of the RBI's role in recommending chief executives by exempting the bank from participation in the process of selection. At the same time, we sought the government's voluntary acceptance of the RBI's role in giving clearance to CEOs selected by the government. This was in consonance with procedure in respect of private sector banks. Our proposal was not accepted by the government.

An important issue in governance is conflict of interest. Hence, we did not want our officials to be on the boards of public sector banks. We proposed amendments to the relevant laws which mandated such nomination. However, I was informed by the finance secretary that the parliamentary standing committee was keen to continue to have RBI official in the boards. I suggested that, as a compromise, the law could provide for nomination of a person with experience in financial regulation. The suggestion was accepted. So, the legal amendment did not bar the nomination of RBI officials while removing the mandated nomination of RBI officials. During my tenure, I proposed the names of retired officials of the RBI.

The government expressed policy preference to bring about

consolidation in the public sector banks. Our view in the RBI was that consolidation should not be an end in itself. It should be driven by appropriate assessment of synergies by the enterprises concerned. Experience showed that many cases of consolidation of banks had failed globally. My view was that increasing size through consolidation would not solve the basic problems of the public sector, namely, standards of governance. We suggested that the government, as owner, should assess overall benefit to it as a result of the proposals for consolidation of individual cases or consolidation should be part of an overall well-worked-out strategy. Despite our advice, divestment, and consolidation were considered by the government in parallel, without much progress.

In contrast, we had excellent support from the government in improving the private sector banks, which were a mixed lot of good and bad ones. The old private sector banks were relatively small, and in the nature of community banks. Some of them had been captured by investors with doubtful credentials. The newly licensed private sector banks started off well, embracing new technologies and modern banking practices. Over time the segment became a mixed bag, with a couple of super-performers, and some causing discomfort. Two of the super-performers, ICICI Bank and HDFC Bank, were promoted and incorporated in India, but the majority of ownership was foreign.

There were several small private sector banks which did not satisfy the minimum capital adequacy requirement prescribed under the new guidelines. Several stratagems were adopted to ensure that either they increase the capital within a specified time or they get merged with a healthier bank on a voluntary basis. The RBI actively encouraged consolidation in the private sector banking system, mostly through voluntary mergers or acquisitions. Consolidation happened mainly due to enforcement of fit and proper criteria on ownership and governance. In one case, however, merger was imposed, and it was a challenging task.

Soon after I joined as governor in September 2003, I had to take a view on cleaning up of the balance sheet of GTB for the financial year 2002-03. The inspection by the RBI in previous years found that there was significant misclassification of assets and other accounting irregularities to understate losses significantly. After making the corrections, the financial statement for 2002-03 showed an overall loss, but a small operating profit for the year. The balance sheet had to be in the public domain before the end of September. The proposal before me was that the RBI should issue a statement welcoming the clean-up of the balance sheet by GTB which, no doubt, was at the instance of the RBI. The danger of issuing a statement was that markets might treat it as a certificate of sound health and good conduct, which certainly was not true. At the same time, the case for issuing a statement was to ensure that there was no serious loss of confidence and consequent run on the bank as a result of the disclosure of the significant misclassifications made in the past. We issued a statement of assurance just in time, on 30 September, so that we could consider a line of action in due course, at a time of our choice. However, GTB continued to be on the list of problem banks to be carefully monitored by the Board for Financial Supervision.[3]

In this background, the RBI was keen that the bank should be adequately capitalised and the governance in the bank improved. The GTB was not in a position to attract additional capital, but there was an offer to inject capital from a private equity firm. However, the offer sought some temporary relaxation of regulatory prescriptions. We felt that we could not start rebuilding trust and confidence in a bank with relaxations in regulations. Hence, we sounded leading private sector banks if they could take over GTB. Surprisingly, they did not evince interest. We decided to act before it was too late, and at our request, the government imposed a moratorium on withdrawal of deposits on 24 July 2004, a Saturday evening. I was confident that once we put a moratorium on encashing of deposits, the interested parties would be emboldened to express their interest in a merger. We had in parallel identified banks which might have synergies for a merger. In the process, we had to handle an unprecedented challenge: to restrict the withdrawals from ATMs dispersed all over the country, in addition to making available sufficient cash in all branches spread over the country. These required extensive logistical efforts, but in total secrecy.

By Monday, 25 July forenoon, we could choose one of the two banks that were interested in a merger – the Oriental Bank of Commerce. The message to the banking community was loud and clear – the RBI would be prompt, severe, and effective in corrective actions in respect of any bank or banker that came to our adverse notice.

There were several criticisms of our action. One view was that shareholders suffered, but I was clear in my mind that depositors' interests were foremost. Some complained that it was over a weekend, but then it was deliberate. A third criticism was that the public sector bank was informally forced to merge. That simply was not true. In fact, Finance Minister Chidambaram, on being informed over phone minutes ahead of public disclosure of successful identification of the bank that was to merge, said: 'Is it with the State Bank of India?' That was the expectation on the basis of precedents, but it was the Oriental Bank of Commerce.

Suggestions were made that we should consider the issue of new banking licences as a means of strengthening the banking system. Our stand was that the emphasis should be on improving the large number of private sector banks already existing and also consolidating them as vibrant units. Additionally, we insisted that issuing of new bank licences could be considered after amendments that we had proposed to the existing Banking Regulation Act were approved. They were meant to strengthen the RBI's capacity to enforce appropriate fit and ownership criteria and governance. New banking licences could not be approved during my period, pending passage of the relevant laws.

Foreign banks had a small share of the banking business, but had significant, in fact, critical presence in select segments of finance, such as forex markets and government debt markets. They were keen to expand their presence in India through inorganic growth, that is, by taking over control and management of existing private sector banks. They operated across borders, and across markets, through multiple organisational layers within a conglomerate. They had a network of non-banking arms operating in parallel in India. Operations in India accounted for a major source of profits for many of them for a variety of reasons, one of them being their expertise in and access to modern technology. They had a special place in financial markets, in addition to skills and competitive strengths. Cross-border presence gave them an opportunity to move financial assets across the border to take advantage of differences in regulation, taxes, and interest rates. They were also important for flow of investments that public policy seeks. In brief, the branches of foreign banks did a lot of good to public policy, but they could also undermine public, policy, especially regulation, without necessarily breaking the law.

The most important issue at the time I joined related to increasing the presence of foreign banks and raising the limits to foreign ownership in our banks to 74 per cent. Such a policy was announced in the budget speech of the finance minister. I was uncomfortable with giving priority to larger presence of foreign banks in advance of reforming the domestic banking sector. We had to work with the government on resetting priorities. We succeeded in convincing the government to defer immediate increased presence of foreign banks and to adopt a gradual approach through a roadmap.

In effect, we reset the priorities and that is a long story.

In September 2003, when I joined as governor, I found that there was only one important item in the agenda for reform before the government. That concerned increasing the permissible share of foreign ownership in Indian banks, and permitting foreign banks to acquire Indian private sector banks. The government was keen to implement the policy and was in readiness to process the legislation in the budget session of 2004 in fulfilment of the announcement in the February 2003 budget speech. The existing legislation did not deter foreign banks from setting up 100-per-cent-owned subsidiaries, though a policy to facilitate them was not in place. To acquire existing private sector banks, or to have subsidiaries with less than 100 per cent of ownership, amendment to the law was needed to allow for foreign banks to exercise voting rights in proportion to the ownership.

I opined that policy constraints on our banks should be addressed urgently, before opening them up for deep presence of foreign banks. Hence, my preference was to increase the number of branch licences of foreign banks well beyond the commitment made by us to the WTO for the present. However, the government made it clear that it wanted to implement the decision announced. The task before us was to find a way of fulfilling the commitment made in the budget speech of 2003, but ensure that in the actual sequencing of reform in banking, improvements in domestic banks took precedence.

On the basis of consultations with us, the government issued a press note, on 5 March 2004. The FDI limit in private sector banks was raised to 74 per cent under the automatic route, including the investment made by foreign institutional investors. The major input that we gave to the government was that a foreign bank should be permitted to have only one form of presence. Foreign banks, according to the press note, would be permitted to have either branches or subsidiaries, not both. They could operate in India through only one of the three channels – (a) branch/es; (b) a wholly owned subsidiary; or (c) a subsidiary; further aggregate foreign investment up to a maximum of 74 per cent in a private bank was permissible. The press note mentioned that the guidelines in this regard would be issued by the RBI. We were required to issue guidelines on liberalising foreign investment, as per the press notification in March.

As a first step, I focused on governance in our banking system. So, the Annual Policy Statement of 18 May 2004 indicated that keeping in view the special nature of banks it was necessary to articulate in a comprehensive manner the policy in regard to ownership and governance of both public and private sector banks. We put in public domain a draft with three elements, namely, (a) criteria for significant shareholding, that is, beyond 5 per cent; (b) for being a member of the board, and (c) additional requirements for chief executive. The guidelines were equally applicable for foreign investors under the liberalised regime announced in March 2004. We provided for transition arrangements where the existing ownership structure in any bank did not satisfy the requirements specified. The guidelines asserted the RBI's intention to undertake independent verification of 'fit and proper' test conducted by banks. We did not have specific legislative provisions to enforce these guidelines, so we formally invoked powers conferred by Section 35A of the Banking Regulation Act, 1949, and gave directions 'in public interest'. We got our point of view on the reforms in banking sector, in a draft form, in public domain, so that our view became the starting point for feedback from the stakeholders and consultations with the government.

The professionals in RBI worked closely on several drafts in consultation with market participants and the government. In the final stages, I had detailed discussions with Chidambaram. The result was a comprehensive agenda for reform and development of the banking system in India. This was set out in the budget speech of 2005-06. It said: 'the RBI has prepared a roadmap for banking sector reforms and will unveil the same. While most proposals will be implemented by the RBI on its own authority, some legislative changes would be required to be made.' (Para 82)

In his budget speech Chidambaram added: 'In consultation with the RBI, I proposed to introduce amendments to the Act: (a) to remove the lower and upper bounds to the statutory liquidity ratio (SLR) and provide flexibility to RBI to prescribe prudential norms; (b) to allow banking companies to issue preference shares, since preference share capital can be treated as regulatory capital under specified circumstances as per Basel norms; (c) to introduce specific provisions to enable the consolidated supervision of banks and their subsidiaries by RBI in consonance with the international best practices in this regard. I also propose to introduce amendments to the Reserve Bank of India Act, 1934 – (a) to remove the limits of the cash reserve ratio (CRR) to facilitate more flexible conduct of monetary policy; and (b) to enable RBI to lend or borrow securities by way of repo, reverse repo or otherwise.' (Para 83).

This is perhaps the most comprehensive package of reforms in banking ever announced by a finance minister. The language reflects the fact that the minister and governor thought alike on this subject.

Soon after the budget speech, in fact, the same day, RBI released three documents that reflected policies already agreed with the government: a roadmap for presence of foreign banks in

India; guidelines for setting up wholly owned banking subsidiaries; and guidelines on ownership and governance in private sector banks. The roadmap was divided into two phases: in the first phase, up to March 2009, foreign banks could establish by way of setting up wholly owned subsidiaries, or conversion of the existing branches into such subsidiaries. Detailed guidelines were given for establishment of such subsidiaries. The second phase was to commence in April 2009, after a review. Guidelines on ownership and governance for private banks emanated out of the draft put in public domain for feedback and consultation with the government.

The RBI's approach to reform of banking sector was captured in the preamble to the roadmap for presence of foreign banks in India. It said: 'The banking sector in India is robust and its standards are broadly in conformity with international standards. In further enhancing its efficiency and stability to the best of global standards a two-track and gradualist approach will be adopted. One track is consolidation of the domestic banking system in both public and private sectors. The second track is gradual enhancement of the presence of foreign banks in a synchronised manner. The policy decisions announced on 5 March 2004 on FDI, FII and the presence of foreign banks will be implemented in a phased manner. This will also be synchronised with the two-track approach and will be consistent with India's commitments to the WTO.'

In parallel on the same day, we announced a liberalised policy for overseas presence of Indian banks and foreign banks' presence in India, to express our intent for an element of reciprocity in the process. The policy of issuing branch licences to the foreign banks, consistent with our obligations under WTO, was codified with specific indication that due weight would be given to the treatment of Indian banks in the home country.

For the RBI, and for me, the set of guidelines issued in February 2005 counts as the most satisfying service to our banking sector.

In the process of devising our approach, my relationship with foreign banks was not smooth. In fact, the *Financial Times* of London commented on my attitude on 1 September 2004.[4] But the global financial crisis, in some ways, indicated my approach. My experience with foreign banks in India led me to speak in Basel in June 2012, before a gathering of governors, and say: 'In the prevailing environment of global financial markets, some large global financial conglomerates are larger and, perhaps, more powerful than some of the central banks.'

'Cooperation has failed, but it must succeed' is a statement that I read for the first time over fifty years ago. The concept is too appealing to be taken lightly. We wanted cooperatives to succeed. We tried and spent money on rural cooperatives and failed. In the case of urban cooperative banks, we merely innovated and succeeded. How and why?

The rural cooperative system with large nationwide network was critical for credit dispensation in rural areas, and most of them were not functioning satisfactorily. Some of them had negative net worth, meaning they were not solvent, and yet they were permitted to accept deposits and dispense credit. Their functioning in terms of prudential supervision was carried out by a separate body, National Bank of Agriculture and Rural Development (Nabard), though the regulation part was left with the Reserve Bank. There was close coordination between Nabard and the Reserve Bank.

Urban cooperative banks, on the other hand, were both regulated and supervised by the RBI. Urban cooperative banks stood discredited after the Ketan Parekh scam involving a few of them. Some of the urban cooperatives had to be wound up and the claims from the Deposit Insurance Corporation were the highest recorded in our history. Some of them were defunct. Some of them were weak. Most of them were stagnant.

The rural cooperative banking system was expected to provide a range of banking services, in particular, deposit taking, short-term lending, and medium- to long-term loans and investments for agriculture-related purposes in rural areas. A countrywide network of cooperatives with a federal structure consisting of village-, district- and state-level cooperative banks had been developed over time. However, it was plagued with serious problems, particularly due to politicisation of cooperatives with the connivance of the state governments concerned. There had been several attempts in the past to revive the dormant cooperatives in the system and revitalise them. They were not successful. The government appreciated the need to make another attempt. We were committed to improving the banking system, particularly for the rural areas and the common person. But how?

The government appointed a task force on cooperative credit institutions in August 2004 under the chairmanship of Professor Vaidyanathan to recommend measures for revitalising the cooperative credit system. It made several recommendations and the government provided budgetary support to implement its recommendations. The major players for bringing about changes were the state governments. They were keen to avail of the funds provided for revival of the cooperative credit system, but less than enthusiastic about bringing about necessary changes in governance structures and practices to revive the system. The Union government while providing finances was compelled due to political circumstances to gradually dilute the conditionalities that were proposed by the task force. Initially, I was chairman of the implementation committee that became defunct soon. In most parts of India, cooperative banking has become a captive of political parties, and the Union government and the RBI worked together to use fund allocation as a leverage to improve the system but political compulsions prevailed. Not much has changed in most parts of our country.

In contrast, the initiatives that we took in the RBI on the urban cooperative banking system have been successful – thanks to state-level innovative arrangements for voluntary collaboration among the stakeholders. The urban cooperative banking system was virtually in a mess by 2004. The weaknesses were exposed in 2001 with the outbreak of a scam in which Gujarat cooperative banks were significantly involved.

The representatives of urban cooperative banks met me and explained that many of the sound banks were being penalised due to these legacy problems. They convinced us that many of them were well run and provided finance to small- and medium-sized businesses. We accepted their contention that there were many banks that needed to be encouraged; that there were some which had the potential to become viable; and there were a few which should be wound up. We were willing to review our regulatory prescriptions and even support enhancement of skills as well as technology upgradation, if they ensured closure of bad banks and adoption of a reform package for potentially viable ones. The industry association agreed to collaborate, but solutions need the involvement of state governments.

If the cooperation between the state government and the Reserve Bank of India was essential, I concluded that it had to be a state-specific solution. In other words, the RBI had to devise an institutional mechanism within the legal framework that would promote urban cooperative banks in states which were willing to support and encourage healthy banks and discourage unhealthy ones. Despite serious reservations within the RBI, I suggested that we enter into a formal memorandum of understanding with those states which were willing for coordinated action to improve the urban cooperative banking system. Under this memorandum, an advisory committee with representatives of the state governments, RBI and the urban cooperative banks themselves was constituted for each state. This unique experiment in institutional arrangement for coordination succeeded beyond everyone's expectations.

Andhra Pradesh and Gujarat were the first to sign the agreement in a competition between their chief ministers. The signing in both cases reflected their personalities and styles.[5] That was how the urban cooperative segment which was on the verge of collapse was saved; it has survived, and it is thriving.

To serve the needs of local areas, there was a network of regional rural banks jointly owned by the Government of India, state governments, and nationalised banks. They were allowed to survive through periodic infusion of capital. Local area banks, an experiment akin to RRBs, but in the private sector, was virtually given up.

For us, the major challenge was in dealing with deposit-taking NBFCs. In the NBFC sector there was a category called Residuary Non-Banking Finance Companies. This category raised several concerns with regard to their deposit-taking activities, and compliance with the 'Know Your Customer' criteria. The business model itself was unviable unless inappropriate banking practices were adopted. We took a decision to tighten the regulation to an extent that the category would cease to exist. We also felt that it was necessary to provide them an opportunity to exit from this model to avoid disruption. Out of five RNBCs, three quickly exited and two were remaining. These two (Peerless and Sahara), however, accounted for over 60 per cent of the total NBFC sector.

One of them planned for gradually moving out of this business as per a mutually agreed path. The second one, Sahara, had been dragging its feet, which finally resulted in a legal battle that went up to the Supreme Court. Some, though not the whole of the drama in our dealing with them, has been chronicled in a book titled *Sahara: The Untold Story* by Tamal Bandyopadhyay. At one stage, I received a hand-delivered letter, purported to be from the chief of the company, saying they had heard that I believed my life was under threat from them. I was assured that there was no basis for such fears. I handed the letter over to my deputy governor and told him to keep it, and forget about it. However, the objective of virtually eliminating these companies, which were a threat to the integrity of the financial system, has been successful.[6]

A memorable case involving NBFCs was linked to a chit fund that was part of a media empire, namely, the Eenadu group. The case had political overtones. It began when a complaint was received from a customer of a chit fund (an HUF registered under the chit fund act) that agents of an NBFC within the group were compelling chit-fund holders to invest in deposits with the NBFC, though the latter was forbidden by the RBI to take deposits. The NBFC was taking cover under an ambiguous wording in a letter from RBI. By this time the deposits of this NBFC had ballooned to over Rs 2,500 crore. The choice before the RBI was difficult. Effective action against such unauthorised acceptance of public deposits was clearly warranted. But any such action could have resulted in the large number of depositors being hurt. Any precipitative action would have made it impossible for the management to refund the deposit even if they had adequate assets. On the other hand, not moving against the errant behaviour gave an impression that the regulator was not enforcing the law. A decision was made to make the group agree to refund the deposits as and when they matured and not accept new deposits as a pre-condition for not precipitating action.

It was also necessary to recognise that the RBI's reputation was itself at stake since it did not take action when this activity was growing phenomenally over several years. Taking advantage of some of the High Court judgements in dealing with non-banking financial companies, it was decided to give greater weight to the interest of the depositors. So, RBI was content with prompt return of all deposits on maturity and immediate exit from deposit taking. However, the state government concerned was clearly in favour of severe action against the errant conglomerate. It tried unsuccessfully to take legal action against the entity.

Promoting an NBFC for development of infrastructure was one of the last acts of the RBI in founding institutions for development. The company was meant to be an institution predominantly funded by the government and the RBI but effectively managed as a non-government company mainly to promote infrastructure financing. I was an enthusiastic supporter of this idea, and in fact, the organisation was designed by a committee under my chairmanship in 1996. I noticed, as governor, a discomfort in that RBI was a partial owner of an NBFC which it was regulating. These concerns became accentuated once the company decided to get its shares listed in the stock exchange as part of a public issue. We took a stand that such an approach would make it a profit-seeking institution and it would be inappropriate for the RBI to continue to be an owner. The RBI also had reservations about the capacity of the institution to discharge its developmental functions once it became a profit-seeking institution. Since the government overruled the objections of the RBI about the initial public offer, the RBI decided to offer to transfer its shareholding to the government, which it accepted.

Towards the end of my tenure, I realised that despite all our efforts to expand the role of credit through formal channels and micro-finance entities, the credit needs of the widely dispersed informal sector could not be met in the near future by the formal financial system. If moneylenders were inevitable, the system should be able to utilise them, but with sufficient safeguards. I was aware of the legislation on moneylending in many states. I was also aware that the laws were not well formulated and were seldom taken seriously. It was essentially a state subject. If there were a reasonably effective law, regulation and enforcement at state level, we could use the moneylenders also as a part of the financial system. In a way, we had already favoured multiple, but competing, channels of outreach of financial services. Our idea was to push supply of credit through multiple channels and thus provide ease of access.

I mentioned my intention to consider the option in one of my informal conversations on the financial system with Prime Minister Manmohan Singh. I was afraid that he would dismiss it outright, but he was willing to briefly discuss the pros and cons. That was enough for me to announce the constitution of a working group to recommend a model money-lending legislation for consideration by the state governments. The working group had representatives of select state governments. The model legislation was sent to all the states for consideration. I was disappointed, but not entirely surprised that the model law was universally ignored.

As mentioned, between the government and the RBI, we settled on an agenda of reform of the banking sector. Together, we did our best with mixed results. But an important component of the financial system is capital markets and the banking system has a stake in it. The government and the RBI had difference of opinion, especially during the second half of my tenure, on the relative emphasis between banks and capital markets in the development of the financial sector. The government, in alignment with prevailing beliefs and global wisdom, focused on the development of equity markets and corporate bond markets. It wanted banks to participate and contribute to the process. It wanted derivatives to be encouraged. It wanted greater scope for global conglomerates in our financial markets. We were not comfortable with the emphasis on capital markets that could potentially inject risks into the banking system instead of diversifying risks.

We were keen to maintain the integrity of money markets, a crucial market for transmission of monetary policy. We were mainly concentrating on development of money, government debt and forex markets. We were cautious in integrating them through nexus products often described as B-C-D (Bond-Currency-Derivatives). Derivatives in forex markets should ideally help corporates hedge their forex exposures. But we were not sure whether our corporates had adequate inhouse expertise to assess the usefulness of such derivatives. So, while permitting banks to offer such products, we said that the banks should be convinced that customers were made aware of the implications. We put the onus on the banks to ensure consumer awareness. Yes, we were less than enthusiastic about sophisticated products. Our approach was: people should understand financial innovations or banks should be able to make people understand them. But we could not approve products that people did not understand.

The government was keen that the banks should play a more active part in capital markets. The belief was that the capital markets have to be developed to enable economic development. We, however, felt that our banks, particularly public sector banks, were not yet equipped to participate in capital markets actively. We also felt that the purpose of capital markets is to develop non-banking intermediation and thus diversify risks. The banks had expertise in providing working capital, and there was shortage of working capital for most of our economic agents. As such, we felt that banks should focus on their core competence. The statutory preemptions restricted the capacity to compete with other forms of intermediation. Therefore, the priority should be to remove the policy constraints on the banking sector. In particular, opening up of our financial markets to foreign players without removing the constraints on our banking sector would make our banking unviable. Finally, the confidence of most of the savers was in the banking system. The activity in capital markets in our country is dominated by foreign institutional investors and domestic insurance and mutual funds with marginal involvement of households. Mutual funds themselves had to depend on bank finance. Despite increased volumes in the capital markets, the participation of retail investors continued to be low in the capital markets. In brief, we resisted the attempts to use the bank deposits as the main instruments for development of capital markets.

We had no hesitation in restricting the total exposure of banks to capital markets. We took recourse to raising the margins for lending against shares, depending on the movements in markets. We suggested that policies be approved by the board.

Development of the corporate bond market was another area of priority for the government in the belief that financing of infrastructure would be enabled through the bond market. We also were keen to develop the corporate bond market. One of the suggestions was that the RBI should allow corporate bonds to be used as instruments in the repo markets. The repo and reverse repo market being the most critical element for conduct of monetary policy, we gave the highest importance to the integrity, reliability and robustness of the money markets. We had discomfort with regard to the corporate bond market because most of it was privately placed and even if listed, the trading was very low. Hence, it was difficult to assess the liquidity as well as the market price of many of the corporate bonds. The RBI was therefore keen that the corporate bond market should first become genuinely market based before it became eligible for repo.

Chidambaram said in his budget speech 2006-07, 'A sound banking sector meeting international norms has emerged.' There were, no doubt, differences of opinion on the relative roles of the capital market and banks, and their linkage. The government was keen to enhance the flow of foreign savings to accelerate development and viewed the financial system as the best channel. The RBI took the view that over 90 per cent of our investment was financed domestically and hence we were focused on appropriate level of domestic savings. In addition, we were of the view that the financial sector only facilitates but does not lead development, and that globalisation of finance should be managed with caution than enthusiasm. An influential part of the intellectual opinion and that of global financial conglomerates favoured a path that was different from what we in the RBI believed. The government was also sympathetic to this alternate approach as illustrated by the appointment of the Percy Mistry Committee and Raghuram Rajan Committee.[7]

The role and functions of the RBI in the financial system became a matter of intensive discussion. The issue of carving out of regulatory functions, in particular banking, was raised. The RBI felt that at the current stage of development, there was merit in keeping the regulation of banks with the monetary authority. Similarly, we took the view that the regulation of government securities market should continue with the RBI till the government was in a position to complete its borrowing programme without financial repression (that is, prescriptions that require holding securities at a level beyond the prudential considerations). In fact, we wanted these to be clarified in law, by suitable amendments. We were in favour of divesting the public debt function from RBI, but only after debt levels and fiscal deficit were brought down to a reasonable level.

The critical issue that stalled progress in the financial sector had less to do with ideology and more to do with structural imbalances in the macroeconomic situation in India and the institutional rigidities within which the financial sector was operating. As explained in detail, structural imbalances relate to the fiscal deficit which necessitated financial repression. The banks continued to be compelled to hold government securities. The rigidities in institutional structures relate to the constraints under which the banking sector, notably, the public sector banks, have to operate. Large capital inflows further constrained our capacity to reduce the statutory preemptions. Financial sector reforms racing ahead of the reforms in macroeconomic management and institutional structures had the potential to destabilise the economy and make the banking system vulnerable.

I had narrated at the beginning of the chapter the assessment of the financial system in 2003. We, the government and the RBI, did redefine priorities for reform of the banking sector, and focused on improving the domestic financial sector. Broader issues relating to the role of the banking sector in the financial system came to the fore. Legislative actions to strengthen and modernise the policy environment were initiated and many, including one on the payment system, were enacted. But most of the basic structural issues of the financial system, especially that of the public sector component of the banking system, remained unaddressed. I am disappointed; but had the satisfaction that we reset the priorities in the reform of the financial sector, especially the banking sector, and strengthened private sector banking.

23

FINANCE AND THE COMMON PERSON

'SIR, DO YOU WANT ME TO ANSWER AS RBI GOVERNOR OR AS A citizen of India?' That was my response to a question put to me by a group of parliamentarians soon after I took over as governor.

The question was whether I was in favour of a single regulator for the financial sector, with the Reserve Bank confining itself to monetary policy. A separate but single regulator for the financial sector was the model in the UK, where the Financial Services Authority was established in 1997. Consequently, the Bank of England became responsible only for monetary policy.

'Both, as governor first and as citizen next,' was the demand.

I responded to them by saying: 'I welcome as governor such separation, sir, as that would make my task of monetary policy focused. My goals will not be diluted. I will be spared of regulating banks, which are a retail business – full of hassle.' Then, I added: 'As a citizen, I am scared of the prospect of such a separation. Banking is very important. We have a pretty safe record with the RBI so far. It is trusted. Actually, the prestige and authority of the Reserve Bank gives comfort to banking, especially depositors.'

The idea of separation of regulatory functions and monetary policy functions was not pursued in India. The RBI continued as a full-service central bank and thus as a regulator too. In the UK, there was a reversal of separation, after the experience of the global crisis in 2008.

Regulation of the financial sector is different from regulation of goods and other services.[1] The nature and functioning of the financial sector has been changing rapidly. As a consequence, regulation of the sector has also been evolving. Despite impressive globalisation of finance, regulation of the sector remained national. Rangarajan and Jalan, my predecessors, believed in gradually aligning our standards of prudential regulation with global standards, though the pace of alignment depended on our circumstances. Similarly, we accepted the need to increasingly rely on market discipline as part of our reform. I was clear that deregulation in the financial sector to achieve competitive efficiency does not mean no regulation. As the financial sector becomes more evolved, the process of deregulation must continue, but in such a manner that all categories of financial institutions are strengthened and financial stability of the overall system is safeguarded.

Jalan made it a practice from 1998 onwards to present the nature of financial sector reforms being undertaken by the RBI in the Annual Policy Statement. I was used to this practice when I was deputy to Jalan from 1998 to 2003, and as governor, I continued with this practice of communicating in detail every half-year the nature of regulatory and development measures taken by the RBI from time to time. They encompassed regulation of money, forex and government securities markets, prudential measures, credit delivery and institutional developments.

During my tenure, there was some refocusing of priorities in regulatory and developmental policies. First, we felt that effectiveness of regulation should be ensured. Second, in view of the unusual exuberance, counter-cyclical regulations should accompany monetary policies. Third, financial inclusion was evolved as one of the objectives of regulation to supplement the twin objectives of consumer protection and stability. Fourth, the reasonableness of charges levied by banks was included in the remit of regulation. Finally, there was an effort, though unsuccessful, at evolving a conducive credit culture.

The Reserve Bank had a policy of not disclosing the adverse findings during inspections and even the penalties levied for violations under the Banking Regulation Act. In this, the regulator and the regulated were on the same side; non-disclosure of penalties. I felt that the customers of banks had a right to know what we found out about the bank and wanted disclosure of the penalties levied by the RBI on the banks. There was a resistance to this proposal from within, on the grounds that it was unprecedented in India and that it would erode the trust of the people in the banking system. Further, it was argued that disclosure of penalties might involve violating laws relating to banking secrecy. My argument was that the penalties are provided by the law and were being levied by the regulator under the law, and hence the public could not be kept in the dark about this. However, I had no objection to being governed by some guidelines on the nature of details that could be put in the public domain, so that the policy relating to banking secrecy of details of the customer was continued. Finally, it was agreed that we put a brief note on penalties levied in the public domain without disclosing the identity of the bank's customer.

The idea of a forensic audit was adopted for the first time in the RBI, based on the experience with a residuary non-banking company (RNBC). We had information, through our market intelligence unit, that a particular RNBC was being used as a conduit for transactions in unaccounted money. In the Board for Financial Supervision (BFS), a suggestion was made that we could employ specialists for forensic audit. But, under the provisions of law, only officials of the RBI could inspect the accounts. So, we initially used forensic auditors available with a leading multinational audit firm to assist our inspecting teams. They found that in one single address in Delhi, there were a few hundreds of deposits in fictitious names and in small amounts deposited in cash. The matter was reported to the government. Based on this experience, the supervisory staff of the RBI were subsequently imparted training in forensic audit. We understood, through this method, the importance of going beyond the papers produced before the inspection team to ascertain the truth.

The auditors of banks are, in a way, an extended arm of the regulator, since we depend on their findings to know the state of affairs. In the context of our inspection findings of misclassification of accounts in the Global Trust Bank, the complicity of the auditors, one of the globally renowned firms, was established.

The RBI sent a letter to the Institute of Chartered Accountants, complaining about the conduct of the auditors. No action was taken for a long time. When we wanted to know what action had been taken, we were told that the RBI did not file a formal complaint in the prescribed form. We then decided to bring to the notice of all the regulated entities our discomfort with the said audit firm. It had the effect of blacklisting the firm. The auditors went to court, but they were on weak ground since we did not formally blacklist. After some time – two or three years – the firm withdrew the petition with a request to us to withdraw the adverse observation since they were already penalised. We withdrew the circular since by then the firm had suffered some punishment through loss of business with entities regulated by the RBI.

We felt that some financial intermediaries were tending to be too large with activities that encompassed the jurisdiction of more than one regulator. So, in consultation with the chairman, SEBI, and chairman, IRDA, the policy statement of November 2003 proposed to establish a special monitoring system for Systemically Important Financial Intermediaries (SIFIs) that would encompass a reporting system on financial matters of common interest to the RBI, SEBI and IRDA; in particular, of intra-group transactions. Mechanisms for the exchange of relevant information among RBI, SEBI and IRDA were formalised. India did not have huge financial conglomerates in the private sector yet, but we thought that we as regulators should monitor system-wide stability issues.

The remuneration of the chief executives of the private sector is subject to approval by the regulator. I was keen that the remuneration should be linked to the work on hand and instruments such as signing-in bonus and termination bonus should not be approved. We had two considerations: the remuneration packages in the system as a whole, and the dangers of remuneration other than salary influencing the decision-making process. There was resentment in the market, apparently, because of lack of binding guidelines for our approach.

Banks are exposed to many types of risks, more importantly, credit risk in credit portfolio and market/interest rate risk in the investment portfolio. The investment fluctuation reserve was intended to protect the investment portfolio against market risks (this went beyond the call of Basel norms of that time). Banks have been maintaining capital charge for market risk as envisaged under the Basel norms since end-March 2006. In the case of risk arising in credit portfolio, the new norms introduced were provisioning[2] even for standard assets and creation of floating provisions. The provisions for standard assets were revised progressively in November 2005, May 2006 and January 2007. The provocation for actions was the continued high credit growth in the real estate sector, personal loans, credit card receivables, and loans and advances qualifying as capital market exposure. Further, a higher default rate with regard to personal loans and credit card receivables emerged as a matter of concern.

Credit expansion is generally associated with economic growth, and more of it is often believed to be better. That is normally true, but too rapid an expansion should also be viewed with scepticism; especially when there are no clear signs of demonstrable credit penetration to new areas or activities. We noticed in November 2003 rapid growth in credit; what we called 'crazy banking', that followed the earlier 'lazy banking' or lull in credit growth. I was conscious of the well-known dictum that the seeds for the bad times of banks are always sown in the good times. I suggested in the policy statement that banks should quickly build up the investment fluctuation reserve, something that was already in place, but we added a sense of urgency to this counter-cyclical measure and accelerated the process. The objective was to ensure that banks build reserves in their balance sheets in good times, which could be drawn upon when the environment turns adverse. My preference for counter-cyclical policies was made clear in my first policy statement in November 2003. Despite severe criticism and contrary to global wisdom, we persisted with our approach relentlessly.

We debated whether India had a housing bubble, since returns on housing were much steeper than those on any other financial instrument, and if so, whether it should be pricked. Our concerns were that financial markets in India were still in their infancy, having embarked on liberalisation just about a decade earlier, and were not as deep as those in the US. A miscalculation could harm the development process of the markets. If indeed there was a bubble, and the RBI did not recognise or address it, then inaction would damage the credibility of the regulator and supervisor of the banking system. On the other hand, if there was no bubble, and banks were lending with due diligence, given that housing is a robust collateral, then it would unnecessarily expose the balance sheet of the banking system to scrutiny and could hamper the credit-creating mechanism of the banking sector.

I had been watching the global housing markets carefully, and was already cautious in not permitting derivatives in the Indian market. It was then that we raised the cost to banker, of lending to housing, above a prescribed limit. We did it in a phased manner. We also advised the banks to reduce exposure to the housing sector immediately to safer limits, and that fresh loans to the housing sector would have to be sanctioned carefully. The bankers were unhappy. One banker asked as to how, in the absence of data, we raised risk weights.[3] In response, I wondered how the banks could price the risk in lending to housing without data. But we followed up with other similar measures that could be described as counter-cyclical policies.

The investment portfolios of our commercial banks were to some extent insulated by prudent regulatory practices such as building up of an investment fluctuation reserve within a period of five years (announced in 2002), progressive relaxation of investment under the held-to-maturity (HTM) category, or restricted investment in non-government securities. With an embryonic credit derivatives market as well as limited pursuit of the 'originate to distribute' models, we had near-zero exposure to the toxic assets which originated in the US subprime mortgage market. Under the Indian accounting practices, marked-to-market valuation was applied in a conservative manner. It was applied in a non-symmetric manner whereby banks are required to value their investments under held-for-trading (HFT) and available-for-sale (AFS) categories at fair value and at periodic intervals so as to provide for net losses but ignore the net gains.

In brief, we contained banks' exposure to risky assets. We calibrated the risk weights of certain classes of risky assets (for example, real estate) for the purpose of capital adequacy. Even within the standard assets, loans and advances to personal loans, capital market, real estate, and systemically important non-banking finance companies (NBFCs) were subject to pre-assigned limits. Above all, prudential limits were placed on the extent of inter-bank liabilities for the banking sector, thereby nipping the problem of 'too-interconnected-to-fail' in the bud. Prudential regulation and counter-cyclical policies serve the financial sector but they are not enough to assure that the common person benefits. That required simultaneous and parallel actions.

'I am emphasising service to common person because I am a selfish person. I will retire in a few years, and then I become a common person. So, I am trying to serve my future interests.' That was my response when asked about references to 'the common person' in my first monetary policy statement made on 3 November 2003.

Customer service and consumer protection have traditionally been a major concern of the RBI. Measures announced in my first policy statement were not new, but they changed the orientation and emphasis of both the banks and the RBI in favour of the common person.

We added access to finance to all common persons as one of the objectives of regulation in India; and indeed as one of the important purposes of reforms in the financial sector. We started with several measures out of concern for the common person. Commitment to a cause, proactive thinking and appropriate measures culminated in adopting and implementing the new concept called financial inclusion, which eventually became a movement. A piece by D. Murali in the *Business Line* on 8 November 2006, titled 'Financial Inclusion: Financial Strategy for Banks,' captured it as it was happening. He concluded: 'There is every possibility that banks may grudgingly take to financial inclusion, to comply with the diktat from the Mint Street.'

We in RBI did not start financial inclusion merely as a diktat but through orientation and persuasion. We encouraged Indian

Bank to survey the coverage and use of banking in Puducherry. It was found that the public sector bank's staff, especially officers, were apprehensive about their being burdened with work beyond their core duties. But technological developments were in our favour, and we encouraged the Institute for Development and Research in Banking Technology (IDRBT), promoted by the RBI as our technology arm, to collaborate with the government of Andhra Pradesh to facilitate direct transfer payments. Within the RBI I found many, if not all, who became equally involved in this orientation. As for my part, the policy statement of April 2005 was the first detailed articulation of our concern at financial exclusion, in particular of those employed in the unorganised sector. We urged banks to align their existing priorities with the objective of financial inclusion. We said that we would incentivise banks appropriately.[4]

Financial inclusion was dealt with in detail in the policy of October 2005.[5] It referred to what we were doing for the credit disadvantaged section of society. It referred to 'no frills' accounts that were suggested as a means of extending financial accessibility to all sections of the population. Thus, a commitment to make the financial sector accessible as an essential service was translated into measures, articulated as a policy, and added to the objectives of regulation. However, we approached provision of credit as part of inclusive financing cautiously, though it was part of financial inclusion.

The financing of micro-finance institutions (MFIs) by the banks was encouraged by us. The idea was that the MFIs will be able to reach a wider population and have the necessary flexibility in operations though they may be charging interest higher than what the banks would charge. We expected that the hold of the moneylenders in the local areas would be dented with the presence of the MFIs. At that time, the MFIs were organised essentially as non-profit institutions, usually in the form of trusts or non-profit companies registered under Section 25 of the Companies Act. The MFIs did expand significantly under this dispensation, especially in select states.

Problems arose when the non-profit companies got converted

into for-profit companies and were listed on the stock exchanges, pushing them towards profit maximisation. I was reminded of Prof. Muhammad Yunus, the Nobel laureate, who told me when he visited the RBI: 'For profit MFIs are no different from moneylenders.' We were aware of the dangers of giving a push to credit to the common person, especially subsidised credit. Unlike the government, we were focusing on institutional mechanisms for accessing financial services, and credit is one component.

Paul Volcker, the legendary central banker, said: 'The most important financial innovation that I have seen in the past twenty years is the Automatic Teller Machine. That really helps people and prevents visits to the banks and is a real convenience.' He added that the machine is 'in fact more of a mechanical innovation than a financial one.' (*Wall Street Journal*, 14 December 2009).

The Reserve Bank could take credit for extracting impressive benefits for society from this innovation. We made use of the ATMs of all banks free for withdrawals of cash and balance enquiries. That was not easy. How did we do that?

We made a survey of the charges being levied by banks for various services, in response to some complaints. We found that the charges were varied. Further, the basis of levying charges was not clear. Hence, I announced the appointment of a working group on 18 April 2006 in my Annual Policy Statement to study and report on the issue. It included a nominee of the Indian Bank's Association and representatives of customers. The working group was mandated to formulate a scheme for ensuring reasonableness of bank charges and to incorporate the same in the Fair Practices Code. The compliance of each bank with such a code would be monitored by the BCSBI. The board was a self-regulatory body to monitor whether banks were rendering the services that they assured the customers. The board was an RBI initiative, operationalised in February 2006. The report of the working group was put in public domain on 15 September 2006. The working group recommended broad principles of reasonableness for bank charges.

We monitored the charges being levied by all major banks with reference to those principles. The banks were not forthcoming regarding the costing and the variation between banks was inexplicable. There was a visible sense of exercise of pricing power by banks over captive customers. The RBI prepared an approach paper and placed it in the public domain to get comments. Armed with these inputs, we announced that all ATM transactions would be free.

The circular announcing free ATM services dated 10 March 2008, inter alia, stated: 'International experience indicates that in countries such as the UK, Germany and France, bank customers have access to all ATMs in the country, free of charge, except when cash is withdrawn from white label ATMs or from ATMs managed by non-bank entities. There is also a move, internationally, to regulate the fee structure by the regulator from the public policy angle. The ideal situation is that a customer should be able to access any ATM installed in the country free of charge through an equitable cooperative initiative by banks.'

I was approached by some bankers through the government that it was causing a burden which was heavier on banks that had more ATMs. I explained that large banks have many other advantages of scale. I added that if it became inevitable, the RBI would subsidise the banks in case of serious losses. I was justified in the offer because the RBI had to deliver cash through a bank counter at our cost, and so why not at an ATM. In fact, the RBI might save on the cost of currency operations if the ready availability reduced total need for cash for transaction purposes.

Thus, payments to bank customers through ATMs were mandated by the RBI to be free for the customers, irrespective of the ownership of the ATM (all ATMs were owned by banks only). No limit was prescribed for availing this facility. With regard to inter-bank transactions, the banks concerned were free to fix any charges to each other, but they could not be passed on to the customers. To enable this facility without excessive burden on profitability of banks, switch facilities for use of ATMs of one bank by the customers of another bank were provided free of cost by the IDRBT.

The underlying philosophy with regard to regulation of charges in banks is that the licence for banking is a privilege that is granted. There is a sort of monopoly over payment services granted to them. They are also permitted to accept non-collateralised deposits. Hence, there is legitimacy in the regulator demanding some services in the public interest. Further, financial services are considered to be in the nature of a public utility and approval of tariff should not be ruled out, provided it does not undermine competition or efficiency.

The ATM was also considered to be a great leveller in the sense that all the customers have to stand in the same queue in the ATM, unlike in the banks where the privileged customers might get faster service. This has special significance in the socio-economic setting of India, characterised by practice as well as perceptions of discrimination among various social groups.

We had credibility in pushing this programme through because of the background of what we in the RBI did on the payment system: by not only funding but also by bringing about legal, institutional and technological changes. Jalan started the practice of the RBI releasing a Payments System Vision document for the medium term, which I continued. In early 2000, we envisaged a law to enable and bring in an effective modern payment system. We built the system in 2005, and the law was passed in 2007. We took full advantage of the IDRBT and Clearing Corporation of India. We worked on setting up the National Payments Corporation of India by 2008, transferring part of the work that we were doing at RBI to it. Thus, investments in technology served a dual purpose – servicing the financial sector and servicing the common person.

The availability of credit in adequate measure at reasonable cost in a timely manner has always been the dominant concern of the RBI. In 2004, the finance minister announced his intention to double credit to agriculture in three years. We achieved it. The government wanted to announce a massive scheme of loan waiver with respect to farmers in the budget speech in 2008. I opposed it on several well-known grounds. It was clear to me that a decision had been taken and that what was left for me was only to work out the modalities of implementation of the government's decision. I put forward two conditions for implementing the decision: firstly, there could not be cross subsidisation within the banking system, secondly, the total amount of the waiver should be paid by the government on behalf of the farmers. Basically the taxpayer had to bear the burden. It meant that those who had nothing to do with loans had to pay on behalf of those who failed to repay. It made those who repaid appear foolish. This was not the first, nor the last of such waivers, but it was massive, and inconsistent with the logic of reform, and indeed the health of the financial sector.

The full benefits of financial inclusion require a strong credit culture that inspires confidence among lenders and borrowers. While it is a matter of satisfaction that financial inclusion has been recognised as a worthy goal, the credit culture has been further undermined, despite my best efforts, I said in a speech in January 2004. Credit culture is a question of sense of fairness in India, since people repay loans out of moral compulsion, I went on to say. There are difficulties in forcing borrowers to pay, in view of the complications and delays in legal processes. Now, if we do not ensure a sense of fairness, this moral compulsion may be eroded. We should apply our mind to the issues of credit culture in addition to institutional and legal changes and policy initiatives. We have to work towards evolving a conducive credit culture and perhaps the critical factor on which it anchors is fairness. Are we fair to savers? Are we fair to borrowers' interests? Are we fair to all employees? Are we fair *inter se*?

Nothing much could be done, despite my initiatives. No doubt, non-performing assets as a proportion of lending were among the lowest at that time, but that could be partly because the base increased rapidly.

As regulators, we want to know and quantify the value of assets of a financial institution, and whether it has sufficient assets plus capital to meet its obligations to depositors and other liabilities.

Non-performing asset is a concept used by regulators, especially banking regulators. When the interest or principal due remain 'past due', it means there is a problem of recovery for the lender. The internationally accepted norm is that anything due beyond ninety days is considered NPA. We in the RBI adopted the global norm, with effect from 31 March 2004. Earlier the norms were less stringent. We could reach that level gradually over a period. For agriculture, we used two harvest seasons as the time frame for an asset (loan) to be treated as NPA.

Non-performing assets are further classified into three categories, based on the period for which the asset has remained non-performing and the realisability of the dues. An asset is treated as a sub-standard asset if it remains an NPA for a period not exceeding twelve months; a doubtful asset is one that has remained sub-standard asset for twelve months; and loss assets are those where the loss has been identified by the bank or its auditors. If the amount has been written off, it will not be an NPA, usually. Regulators may temporarily relax these conditions.

There is no bank that does not have an NPA. There is always a risk, when a bank lends, that someone may not be able to repay, for genuine reasons or otherwise. The issue is whether the NPAs are properly accounted for, promptly reported and put in public domain, and are within the limits acceptable to the regulator.

It is not that all NPAs are a result of fraud. There are many reasons or combination of reasons for NPAs, namely, incapacity to assess risks or deliberate mis-assessment while lending and borrowing.

High transaction costs, delays in resolving disputes, and structural judicial processes make the lender or bank weak, relative to the borrower, especially large, rich and powerful ones (who have the resources to delay processes).

Sometimes, the commercial bank misclassifies in connivance with the auditor and gets away with it till it is found out, often thanks to unanticipated development in the market or administrative or judicial interventions. The borrower may start with a genuine intent, but the moment things appear bleak, she will start defaulting on the payments. The borrowers or managements know more about what is going on in the business than the bank. The bank will avoid precipitating a problem because forcible recovery involves transaction costs, time and uncertainty.

The soundness of the banking system depends on a conducive credit culture. High level of non-performing assets as well as debt write-offs go against this.

24

TEAMS AT WORK

'The governor's job is, perhaps, the loneliest job in the country,' were Dr Manmohan Singh's words, when I called on him upon my appointment as governor of the RBI. He was in the Opposition then. He had said this before, in fact, when he was governor two decades before me. He was right. It was lonely, but I was seldom alone.[1] Most of the time, I was in a team.

As governor, I was personally responsible for whatever happened in the Reserve Bank, in the eyes of the public, in the view of the government and in the belief of the Reserve Bank itself. I was conscious of the heavy responsibility for all the decisions taken or not taken. In all my previous jobs, the position was different. As deputy governor, my word was not always final. Most often in the government, I was one among the few that shared their responsibilities. The governor does his work by leading a team or by being a member of the team, and sometimes, he can create a team. He is, in the ultimate analysis, a part of the teams at work. The working of a governor is best appreciated with reference to the style and substance of his dealings in a variety of themes in different teams. First, I would like to cover teams in external relations, followed by teaming within the bank.

For example, the International Monetary Fund is the multilateral institution with which the national central bank is functionally connected. At a technical level, the RBI and IMF interact closely, but it is the finance minister who represents India on the board of governors. I was the alternate to the minister as governor. Whenever the finance minister was present in the Fund-Bank meetings, I only assisted him. On the rare occasions when I lead the delegation as requested by the finance minister, I would interact with the other finance ministers, in addition to the governors.

At an institutional level, my approach was that India, as an important shareholder of the IMF, would be interested in what the IMF was doing. I was aware that our influence in the IMF was not insignificant. I did not expect infirmities in the governance of the IMF to change in any meaningful manner in the near term for lack of agreement on changes. The ideological biases in the IMF were well-known, and they impacted its operations, but there were dissenting opinions within the fund which I tried to focus on. I was keen to benefit from the analysis of the IMF, especially about the global economy and, to some extent, our economy. I was very clear that the IMF's advice on what we should do was less important than their analysis.

We have not given credit that is due to the IMF in terms of the analysis that they have been doing continuously – on India in particular. We have also benefitted from the assistance the IMF provided and the endorsement that it gave to our policies at the time of crisis and our reforms. Yet, the IMF is a good friend as long as you are not in need, and make sure that the IMF knows that.

Among the managing directors, I had constructive interactions with Rodrigo de Rato and Dominique Strauss-Kahn. Rato, managing director of the IMF, visited the RBI, as was customary. I was happy when he made a public announcement supporting the stand of the Reserve Bank in regard to the use of forex reserves, and expressing his strong reservations on the proposals made by the government. I had met Strauss-Kahn before he became MD, IMF, and he knew about me through his brother, a central banker. Precisely for that reason, I made it clear at the lunch that this was an exception to the rule that there was no free lunch. I insisted that no business should be conducted over lunch. This helped us engage in a very informal and uninhibited chat, to the delight of everyone, in particular some directors of the central board.

My relationship with the IMF continued even in the later years for purposes of independent evaluation. In a meeting held in April 2016, its former managing director, Jacques de Larosiere, enquired whether India was working towards including the rupee in the Special Drawing Rights (SDR) basket of currencies.[2] Since China's currency had been included in SDR recently, and the global consensus was in favour of expanding the currency basket, he felt that India was the natural choice for the next addition. My response was: 'What do we gain?' I went on to explain that I was yet to see any gain for China, except in terms of national prestige. Even in China, many observers believed that the purpose of joining the SDR basket was to strengthen the forces of reform within the country by appealing to national pride. In the informal exchange on the subject with some others in the gathering, I persisted that in the absence of gains, I saw no reason for India to do anything in this regard. When the world needed the rupee to be included in the basket, the demand would come from the global community.

After retirement, I was asked by a journalist whether I missed being the RBI governor. I replied that I did not, but the only thing I missed about being a governor was not being able to attend the monthly meetings of the Bank for International Settlements. We used to meet almost every month in Basel, Switzerland. On each occasion, there were three meetings in sequence on Sunday evening, forenoon of Monday and afternoon of Monday. The governors would fly in on Sunday and fly out the next evening.

The BIS is virtually a club of central bankers. It was an exclusive and very West-centric institution for a long time. India was admitted to the club in 1997. However, by the time I joined as governor, India was being invited to a smaller group of governors with a substantial presence in the global economy. In the small group that discussed recent economic and financial developments, there used to be exchange of views on the global economy, especially the policies of the major countries and emerging issues. I was very keen to understand what other important countries were doing since their actions affected us. I was not giving any advice about what they should do. I used to make interventions on broader issues when warranted, and would limit myself to briefly presenting the position of our economy and its prospects. This did not go unnoticed. In the farewell meeting to me, the chair said: 'Dr Reddy's intervention has always been precise, concise and comprehensive, which no one could match.' More than formal meetings, my interactions with individual governors on the sidelines, which was common, was a great source of obtaining insights into their personal thinking and beliefs on central banking and political economy.

I took interest in the work of the central bank governance group of the governors in BIS. This was one group where there was significant mutual learning about governance in central banks, both at formal and informal levels. For example, in implementing the Right to Information Act in our country and in constituting an Advisory Committee on Monetary Policy, I sought insights from the discussions in this group.

The governors of advanced economies, the G-7, used to meet separately on Sunday evening, and a corresponding forum for the governors of emerging market economies was started in 2006. This was extremely useful in exchanging experiences among the developing countries in a very frank manner with full understanding of the technicalities. I was able to play an active role in this group, partly because of my long experience in central banking relative to many others. Zeti Akhtar Aziz of Malaysia, Guillermo Ortiz of Mexico, Heng Swee Keat of Singapore and T.T. Mboweni of South Africa were among the governors with whom I developed professional and personal relationships. Naturally, bilateral visits between us were frequent.

In the monthly meeting of the BIS, there was an all governors' meeting which picked up subjects of current importance. This provided up-to-date thinking in the central bank community about these issues, and was open to all governors.

I made it a point to brief the deputy governors and other officials concerned in detail about what I heard, learnt and contributed in these meetings. In addition, as mentioned earlier, I used to give a briefing to the central board.

There is an annual meeting of select central bank governors and experts in money and finance, in Jackson Hole in the US. After attending one of the conferences, I suggested Rakesh Mohan, deputy governor, participate in it.

The Asian Consultative Council is a body of governors from Asia serviced by the Hong Kong office of the BIS. This was a useful forum for bringing together governors from the Asian region. Along with Zeti Akhtar Aziz, I took special interest in the exchange of views. I would have liked India to be part of the Chang Mai Initiative,[3] but for a variety of reasons beyond our control, it did not happen.

The G-20 is an informal group of finance ministers and governors of twenty large economies of the world and was constituted in 1999. It was created after the realisation that the crisis in developing countries may affect the global economy as it happened during the Asian Crisis. The origin can be traced back to the G-22, which met in Washington, D.C., in 1998 after the Asian Crisis, which had a spillover affect. This was quickly wound up and replaced by the G-33, which met in Bonn, Germany. G-20, along with the Financial Stability Forum (FSF), was the outcome.

I represented the RBI in all these meetings, and participated in G-20 meetings as deputy governor and once as executive director from the IMF. I have two interesting memories. Between the forenoon and afternoon meetings of deputies of G-20, there used to be a formal lunch. Central bank deputies assemble for lunch in one room and finance secretaries in another. The IMF official lunches with central bankers and World Bank deputies with finance secretaries. That was in a way an assertion of the autonomy of central banks. On 18-19 May 2001, in Istanbul, Turkey, I found the seat by my side vacant. In the lunch of central bankers, such absence is unusual, and in fact, punctuality and protocol are strictly observed. Stanley Fischer from IMF was expected to sit there. We were informed later that a banking currency crisis had erupted in Turkey and he had to rush to Ankara.

India was not included in the Financial Stability Forum, but we were associated with the development of international standards and codes. I have some memories of these deliberations. Both the G-20 and the FSF had no power or direct influence. They were deliberative bodies, assembling periodically. At best, these bodies provided inputs to the processes of decision making in the institutions concerned.

With the growing importance of India in the global economy, external relations became an important part of the governor's job. I did not have the background or temperament to adopt the sophisticated style of western-style governance. I had great difficulty in addressing others by their first names: and others could not address me by my first name, because I did not have one. I had many. So, I was called as 'YV', 'Reddy', 'Venu' and 'Yaga'. That did not matter while promoting our external relations.

The most pleasant and productive relationship for me has been with the governors of the South Asian region (SAARC). I became good friends with the governors of Pakistan (Ishrat Hussain) and Bangladesh (Fakhruddin Ahmed), both of them being from the Pakistan Administrative Service of 1964 (I am IAS 1964) and economists as well.

Ishrat and I exchanged visits. We wanted to establish commercial bank presence. We agreed in principle. Both governments approved. However, the specific bank sponsored by Pakistan was not acceptable to us. But our friendship continued and Ishrat used to visit India as an educationist. Fakhruddin in 2007 became chief advisor (head of the government) of the non-party (interim government). That did not change our personal equation.

In Sri Lanka, I had a plethora of friends, thanks to old ties from the time I was in the executive director's office in the World Bank and later in the IMF representing Sri Lanka also. The relationship between the RBI and the Central Bank of Sri Lanka was always special and close. Among the governors I worked with, A.S. Jayawardena was a family friend for two decades, while his successors, Sunil Mendis and Ajith Nivard Cabraal, were also friendly to us. Developments in our economy affect Sri Lanka, like Bangladesh, and I felt that we should be in touch to understand their concerns and reassure them. With Nepal, we had a special relationship because our currency, the rupee, is legally permitted. One problem that we wanted to solve was the remittance facilities for Nepalese in India to send funds to Nepal. We tried together, but our success was less than what we hoped for.

An interesting feature of my tenure was the large number of visitors to the RBI due to the growing importance of the Indian economy. I made it a point to invite the directors of our board for a lunch or dinner whenever there were distinguished visitors. Of particular significance was the acceptance of a lunch invitation from me by the US secretaries of treasury John William Snow, and later Henry Paulson. Understandably, both were most interested in the progress of liberalisation of the financial sector and access to foreign banks. Timothy Geithner, as chairman of the Federal Reserve, also visited the RBI. We had known each other when he was working in the IMF, and hence there was some informality in our relationship. He covered ground similar to that of Snow and Paulson, but was a lot more circumspect in referring to liberalisation of the financial sector. He added that he was aware of and could appreciate my position vis-á-vis the banking sector.

A large number of central bankers visited us in the RBI and, no doubt, there were lighter moments too. The governor from Russia found that the interpreter was fumbling, so he spoke in Russian and then he himself translated his speech into English! We developed special ties with governors in Asia, Africa and Latin America.

I had invited Paul Volcker to join me for a dinner when he was scheduled to visit Mumbai. He regretted, saying that he was skipping Mumbai and proceeding to Delhi since he had accepted a dinner invitation from Manmohan Singh, the prime minister. However, a few days before the scheduled date, I received a message that his programme had changed and that he would be available to have dinner with me. I was delighted to organise a dinner in his honour and invited a few distinguished people, including some from the media, for the dinner. Chairman Volcker did not mince words when extending his full support to my firm stand in resisting inflation. In passing, he mentioned to me in private that the dinner invitation from Delhi was withdrawn to him, presumably on account of his authorship of the UN Report on oil trade in Iraq in which some leaders of the Congress party were named.

The cult of governors conceals the intricate organisational structure of the RBI that brings a diversity of views and depth of knowledge into decision making. There are teams at work, at different levels. Most of them are internal while some of them include academics, market participants and the government.

Among the public institutions in India, the Reserve Bank is unique in many ways. It has strong technical competence and professional skills. Over the years, it has preserved institutional memory. Though it is accused of being conservative, it has demonstrated adaptability to changing times. Above all, the professionals take pride in their integrity. No wonder, a finance minister is reported to have commented: 'Whomever we send as governor, the Reserve Bank's technocracy captures him.' The image of the governor created by the media masks the fact that the governor's effectiveness draws on the strengths of the institution. The leadership of the governor makes a difference where judgements and difficult issues are involved, engagements with markets and government are sensitive, and credibility of policy communications is at stake. In times of structural transformation, the governor's vision and values do matter.

Some hold that central banks are being run by a bunch of technocrats, with no democratic credentials or societal concerns. That is not true of the Reserve Bank. The Reserve Bank's affairs are governed by the central board of directors, and the directors are appointed by the government. The board was broad-based, with eminent persons drawn from different backgrounds, while economists were in a minority.[4] The directors conveyed the concerns of society at large. The committees of the board, especially those dealing with financial supervision and payment system, provided deep insights. Informal chats on the sidelines of the board or its committee's meetings were as valuable as those in the board. For every board meeting, we made a presentation on the state of the economy. I briefed the board on what I could gather from the meetings I had in global fora.

I made one innovation in my relationship with the board. Usually, I gifted a book to each member in every meeting of the board. Sometimes I gave the same book to all and at times I requested the staff to research the interests of various members of the board and identify an appropriate book for each one of them. They were excited in doing something like this because they had to consider the background of the individual board members and the books that might be of interest to them. Dr Ashok Ganguly mentioned that in his house, there was a bookshelf devoted to books gifted by the governor. A committee of the board met every week (usually at noon on Wednesdays) and a non-official member constituted a quorum; the governor presided over it unless he was out of town. Among the committees of the board, the Board for Financial Supervision, which met every month, was a source of great support and guidance to us. Especially so, as it had an economist, a social worker, a chartered accountant, and an industrialist from the board as members. It was not a bunch of mere technocrats that were overseeing our bank regulation and supervision.

The apex management consisted of all deputy governors and they could seek my advice as and when needed. All important issues had to be considered by the committee of deputy governors. I was fortunate in having an excellent team of deputy governors. Kishori Udeshi received me with unconcealed warmth when I arrived in Mint Road to take charge as governor. She was a very efficient and effective head of the Exchange Control Department when I was the deputy governor. Our interaction resulted in her appreciating the logic of reform and my appreciating the importance of control through monitoring. She was enthusiastic in her orientation towards the common person. She was our natural choice to be the first head of the Banking Standards Codes and Board of India.

Udeshi as deputy governor had, perhaps, the most difficult task of managing changes in the approach to regulation. The RBI had recommended buyback of shares by the government in some banks but that was discontinued at my instance. Both of us had to explain to the professionals the reasons why we were reversing our stand and to convince them that it would not be held against them. The approach to foreign investment in our banks and the presence of foreign banks took a 'U' turn during her tenure with me. The complex operation relating to the merger of GTB was done under her charge. With her long experience and excellent rapport with officers in the RBI, she was ready to argue her case forcefully. She made initial contributions to the orientation of our policies towards the common person.

Vepa Kamesam, a deputy governor, was retiring at the end of the month when I joined. A three-month extension was given to him at my request. I had known him when he was managing director and I was on the board of the State Bank of India. He was my colleague as deputy governor and I assisted him in his commendable work in currency management in some ways. In the short period available, he gave a push to the Real Time Gross Settlement project, and wound up the Optional Employees Retirement Scheme, which was successfully implemented during Jalan's period. His vacancy could be filled only after nine months.

Dr Rakesh Mohan had taken my place as deputy governor, in charge of monetary policy. We had known each other professionally and as friends. After a couple of months, Rakesh made a powerful plea for a particular course of action. I told him, 'Rakesh, I can vividly remember a scene when I was sitting in your place and Jalan Saab was sitting in this chair. I recall how vehemently I argued and how patiently Jalan Saab disagreed because some judgements were involved. I understand that scene better now.'

The biggest challenge Rakesh Mohan faced was to manage the capital account under extraordinary circumstances. He never tired of mentioning that we could add hundred billion dollars to the forex reserves, amounting to ten per cent of the GDP in 2007. This involved constant interface with the government. He had to take the burden of interface with the government on many fronts. In the initial stages, he had to resist a proposal by the government to use foreign exchange reserves for purposes of infrastructure. After joining the government, he played a critical role in ensuring that the Indian Infrastructure Finance Company Limited (IIFCL) was created with a view to avoid specific mention of the use of reserves. Similarly, he played a very important part in resolving the deadlock between me and Chidambaram in his capacity as secretary to the government. He was instrumental in conveying the logic of reforms in the banking sector and incorporating it in the budget speech of February 2005. At some stage, the Ministry of Finance believed that he was Reddy's plant in the government. He came back as deputy governor in July 2005.

I was not in favour of a symbol for the rupee, like the $ sign for the dollar and the £ sign for pound. I felt that we should wait for some time and not appear to be showing off. He insisted and felt that it adds to our self-esteem. I told him that he was abroad for some years, and he should know better. We went through the process of competition and selection of a sign which was ultimately accepted by the government.

He, along with Shyamala Gopinath, played an important role in legal changes in the Reserve Bank of India Act and Banking Regulation Act. At that time, I wanted the RBI Act to be amended to remove the debt management function of the RBI on the grounds that we had enough and let the government have its way and face the consequences. He persuaded me that it would be risky as financial stability was ultimately our responsibility. I conceded the point.

Another challenging task in which we had to work together closely along with Shyamala and Usha, who was the moving spirit, was the Market Stabilisation Scheme. It was exhausting work for several people at many levels, but none of us regretted sweating on it. Rakesh had the unpleasant task of explaining to the finance minister the circumstances under which the remuneration for cash reserve ratio was removed. It was removed through a legislative process after due consultation with the government and discussion with the Parliamentary Standing Committee. Yet, since the commercial banking community was extremely unhappy, he had to face their wrath. His permanent contribution has been the monumental work he did on self-assessment under the Financial Sector Assessment Programme. In the process, almost a hundred professionals, most of them from the RBI, were imparted the skills of understanding the global standards and applying them to the Indian conditions in all aspects of financial sector policies.

Shyamala Gopinath was a natural choice to succeed Udeshi and she joined on 21 September 2004 along with V. Leeladhar. We worked together briefly on a complex matter during the balance of payments crisis of 1990-91, and developed mutual respect and affection when I was working as deputy governor. I have memories of multiple occasions when she guided me on the intricacies of banking regulation and supervision, and subsequently in reserves management. She made a mark in the IMF where she worked for two years, before returning to the RBI as executive director.

There is virtually no area in banking in which Shyamala was not involved closely since she is versatile and seeks perfection. Her initial exposure was to regulation and supervision, but I had requested her to move to reserves management when I was deputy governor. She had the advantage of being closely involved in negotiations with the WTO. She provided the logic for differing with the government's view on our commitment to the WTO in financial services favouring a negative list. Negative list means that only some items listed by us will not be liberalised by India, but all others would be free for entry. Our argument was that it is difficult to enumerate in advance the type of financial services that would feature in it because the list is amenable to continuous innovation. Our preference was to give a positive list so that we could keep adding to the list of services that we were willing to liberalise as we progressed.

The depth of her knowledge and her technical competence made her indispensable in all serious matters involving central banking. One of her significant contributions was in the area of financial markets and foreign exchange reserves. Similarly, along with Rakesh Mohan and Usha, she had to be a partner in exchange rate management. At the height of the problem in 2007, she, along with Rakesh, had to take on the burden of managing the stand-off between the government and RBI after the sudden and steep appreciation of the rupee. Much of the counter-cyclical policies adopted during my tenure were on account of Shyamala's deep insights and Leeladhar's understanding of the actual working of commercial banks. She was of great help in resolving the differences with the government on the applicability of service tax to RBI. To the extent international experience was relevant, Shyamala's inputs on fit and proper criteria became critical. No proposal for legislative amendments was cleared by me unless it was vetted by Shyamala; and the list of legislative actions during the period we worked together is perhaps unprecedented.[5]

I made enquiries from informed people and decided to request Leeladhar, then president of the Indian Banks' Association, to join me as deputy governor. I was surprised when he responded by saying that he was comfortable continuing as a commercial banker. He met me and explained that he was working on an important merger proposal. He added that he was not confident about working in the central bank. Obviously, he was not willing to give up the status and perquisites available to a bank chairman. I did not give up. I rang up N. Sisodia, secretary in the Ministry of Finance, with whom I had excellent personal rapport, and requested him to persuade Leeladhar to join me. Sisodia told me that he had discussed the matter with Leeladhar and advised him to reconsider and meet me again to convey his final position. He did come to me. I received him in my room and for some reason I assumed that he would give his consent.[6] I warmly welcomed him and told him that I looked forward to working with him, and that we should do well together. He said that he was honoured by my offer and accepted it.

Leeladhar's strength was his familiarity with the banking industry and with the existing governance in each one of the banks. Having been a long-standing chairman of public sector banks and also chairman of the Indian Banks' Association, he knew about the private sector banks also like the back of his hand. The consolidation of smaller banks and weaker banks, which was a laborious process involving powerful interests, required not only knowledge but strategy and tactics which Leeladhar had displayed in ample measure while maintaining a low profile. The programme of eliminating RNBCs including

Sahara and a chit fund-linked non-banking finance company required a combination of diplomacy and firmness. Being a former commercial banker, he knew how to be an effective bridge to reach the goal with minimum disruption to the system. He also took forward and shaped the regulation of systemically important non-deposit-taking NBFCs. He initiated the process of signing of MoUs with state governments in regard to urban cooperative banks, though the subsequent work was carried out by Usha Thorat. Having been an engineer with strong background in banking, he was the right man at the right time for strengthening of the RTGS (Real Time Gross Settlement) and NEFT (National Electronic Fund Transfer) system, setting up state-of-art data centres, making effective use of ATMs and, above all, the whole payment and settlement system. He led the RBI to the goal of reaching global best standards in banking technology. Rakesh Mohan and Leeladhar, the two engineers among four deputy governors that I had, made a strong combination for effecting these changes.

I had worked with Usha Thorat on several subjects, and she had a formidable reputation as a central banker and excellent communicator. But there was no vacancy, since a fourth vacancy of a deputy governor provided in law was traditionally kept vacant. Both Chidambaram and Manmohan Singh agreed to my request to fill up the fourth post with an internal candidate from the bank.

Usha Thorat was executive director first, and became deputy governor in November 2005 with a five-year term, as was the norm. Her contributions to the work on the RBI balance sheet and reserves management and debt management were recognised. Yet, we brought her into regulation and supervision to bring a breath of fresh air. She, along with Udeshi and Shyamala, was an expert in working on the fit and proper criteria for banks' ownership. The problem was that our Banking Regulation Act stipulated that voting rights be restricted to ten per cent, irrespective of ownership. There was circumvention of this rule through artificial slicing of the ownership by creating several entities. This had to be remedied over a period through persuasion. The RBI was giving 'acknowledgement' as a precondition for transfer of ownership beyond five per cent, but there were no clear-cut guidelines, and we had to evolve them. Along with Shyamala, Usha undertook the challenging and onerous task of identifying legal provisions and practices for appropriate criteria in other countries.

In the end, we introduced policy without explicit legal sanction, but by interpretation of existing provisions of global practices. In addition to being involved in evolving the criteria over several months, she had to take on the task of actually applying these. Usha had to take follow-up actions after the committees were formed in several states. She exhibited special skills in negotiation with the states. We wanted to introduce the banking correspondent model as an extended arm of the bank, subject to regulation by the bank concerned. This was contrary to the philosophy of the RBI for decades, since this amounted to banks engaging agents for banking business. The Legal Department had reservations on the proposal. Usha had to overcome internal resistance.

The concept, design and implementation of the variety of measures taken, leading to financial inclusion, was done under Usha's leadership. Her interaction with the IDRBT was helpful in developing the technological aspects of financial inclusion. She was especially sensitive to societal needs and consumers' interest.

The most frustrating aspect for both of us related to depoliticisation of the appointment of directors on the boards of public sector banks. We tried several ways, but the government was not willing to take our inputs before processing or before sending out orders of appointment or even after appointment.

When Rakesh Mohan went as secretary (Economic Affairs), we had to look for a successor. I requested Raghuram Rajan to join me as deputy governor when he happened to call on me in Mumbai. We had known each other professionally when I was deputy governor and executive director, IMF, and he was with the University of Chicago and later in the IMF. I explained to him that we would require somebody like him so that the country could avail of his valuable services over the long run, virtually hinting that he could one day be the governor. He agreed to give a thought to it. However, after going back to the US, he expressed his regret. Finally, Rakesh Mohan himself expressed the desire to return to the Reserve Bank from the government. I was happy to welcome him back.

The senior management team included Dr R.B. Barman for the entire period of my tenure. He was a valuable asset for the organisation, not only in matters relating to data, financial statistics and computer applications, but also in establishing a modern payment and settlement system. Dr Narendra Jadhav exhibited extraordinary qualities of leadership in addition to his scholarly contribution to central banking. Though not a formal member of the management team, Ms Alpana Killawala was exceptional in public relations, not merely in relations with media.

Among my professional colleagues, Kanagasabapathy has been a friend and a guide who spared no effort to stop me from doing anything too risky or too far from conventional wisdom or current global practice. I continued to depend heavily on his knowledge and wisdom as governor too. There were many others who joined the management team on invitation, depending on the subject under consideration; be it executive directors, advisors, or any other functionary, irrespective of the rank, but based on acknowledged expertise.

A couple of years into the job, I was told about the prevailing view in the Ministry of Finance. It was: 'In the RBI, not an ant moves without the permission of Governor Reddy.' But I believe that I had a consultative approach. How do I reconcile the two views? One explanation was that even if Dr Reddy wanted discussion, the officers in the RBI were not forthcoming, out of respect or out of being 'overawed'. I have a different explanation, namely, our new work methods in dealing with the Ministry of Finance. Officers in the RBI were good at penning their opinions, but hesitant in asserting them in meetings with the ministry. I encouraged them to write their comments on the subject in advance, preferably after insisting on a note on the agenda for the meeting. The minutes of the meetings are generally prepared in the ministry. A good record of our initial views was ensured only by sending our views in advance. In a way, this required the ministry to acknowledge each one of our arguments formally.

Our approach to policy changes or reform generally commenced with extensive consultations, both within the RBI and outside. Once a final decision was taken, we stuck to the goal, and there was no compromise or dilution, but we were willing to negotiate the paths and make the transition as smooth and non-disruptive as possible. My draft speeches had to be seen and commented upon by the heads of departments concerned with the subjects. When I decided to comment in favour of Tobin tax, two out of four officers advised me against such a reference. They anticipated a reaction. I decided to stick my neck out. I might have overruled them, but seldom failed to seek the advice of professionals in the RBI. In fact, the first book I published as deputy governor was dedicated to the talent and commitment of professionals in the RBI.

The bank has a pool of highly qualified professionals. Among the officers, forty-six were PhDs and seventy-eight MBAs in 2003, and the number increased to sixty-four and 171 by 2008. Rangarajan had introduced a scheme of Golden Jubilee Scholarship, under which four scholars are funded for advanced studies in overseas universities. Ninety-six scholarships were availed in aggregate by 2008. Most of them continued to work in the RBI, while a few did move out to BIS, IMF and World Bank.

That we had excellent professional skills relative to other public institutions did not deter us from seeking advice from several sources. We explored two ideas to strengthen our abilities – lateral entry at higher levels and giving substantive weight to merit in promotions. In an institutional milieu where mobility is not common, we have to weigh the negative impact on the vast majority of professionals against the contribution of a few who are brought in from outside or moved up. I encouraged outward mobility as a first step to inward mobility. We allowed deputation up to five years on an automatic basis. We allowed deputation to the private sector also. We permitted people to retire while on deputation. Prospects for going on deputation had a good effect on performance. Excellence was recognised and encouraged, but not necessarily through out-of-turn and accelerated promotions within the hierarchy.

Do the governor and finance minister constitute a team? My answer is that they have to be a two-member team sometimes, and adversaries at other times, but never antagonistic. The governor is accountable to the Parliament through the minister, and is expected to function autonomously from the government, which is represented in the persona of the minister. A governor in our scheme of things could not be subordinate, and never equal to the minister. That makes the working of the team interesting. The succeeding three chapters give a glimpse of how I worked with Jaswant Singh and P. Chidambaram, as a team.

25

A GENTLEMAN AND A STATESMAN

THE WAY POLICY IS IMPLEMENTED DEPENDS GREATLY ON THE people involved. Dealing with Finance Minister Jaswant Singh during the first nine months of my tenure was a pleasure. When I joined as governor, the state of the economy was on the uptick, the outlook was bright. The policy interest rates were easy, with a view to encourage credit growth. The external sector was strong and the global environment was benign. There were no hard choices to be made or difficult trade-offs to be considered. The prevailing economic conditions, and the good personal equations the minister and I shared, resulted in a conducive atmosphere.

Singh did not hesitate to speak his mind. He did not delve into details. He had clear views on directions for the economy. In one of his books, Singh writes that he had worked in the 'D, E, F' of Indian leadership – Defence, External Affairs, and Finance. Of them all, I had often thought that his heart was not in finance. But he put his confidence in people who he believed had a strong background in finance. He used the considerable clout that he had with the top BJP leadership, Prime Minister Vajpayee in particular, to extend his support to those of us who commanded his trust.

Singh had given me a full five-year tenure as governor. It was a bold move on his part. His support for me would be called to test sooner than he expected.

On the morning of 17 September 2003, just eleven days after I took charge as governor, I woke up to find that the finance minister had called. I had woken up unusually late that day and it was 7.30 a.m. when I returned the call.

'Governor,' Singh said, 'what is this about banning non-resident deposits? Many people are worried about it. They have been calling me.'

After office hours the day before, the RBI had issued a notification prohibiting capital inflows through the accounts of overseas corporate bodies (OCBs) owned and managed by non-resident Indians. OCBs had been allowed to freely invest in India and repatriate the earnings. With the RBI notification, they could now only sell existing investments but could not make fresh ones. This restriction would not apply to NRIs in their individual capacity.

'Sir, this is based on the JPC report,' I was quick to point out. OCBs had been identified by the Joint Parliamentary Committee instituted to investigate the Ketan Parekh stock market scam of 1999-2000 as possible sources that had enabled the scam. It was also the conclusion that my predecessor had reached.

Singh said, 'But people are worried that stock markets will crash. They feel that it will result in a drop in capital inflows.'

I said, 'Sir, it is true that stock markets will be adversely affected, as an immediate reaction. But that will be temporary. Markets will not crash. What will happen is that the unhealthy flows will stop. That is good for us because very soon, healthy flows will increase and replace the unhealthy flows.'

'Why are you so sure OCBs are unhealthy flows?' Singh asked. The beneficial ownership of OCBs was suspect. We did not know where the money originated; it could have been, for example, from smugglers. OCBs were often a conduit for resident Indians to take black money out of India and bring it back into the country.

'I agree. We should not encourage that type of money,' Singh said. 'We should stop that. But we cannot afford a stock market crash.'

'Sir, trust me. Unhealthy flows will be more than replaced by healthy flows. I guarantee it. We just have to be a little patient. The fact that we do not want unhealthy capital flows into our country will itself encourage healthy flows,' I said.

'I trust you, governor. But what do I tell all these gentlemen who are complaining?' Singh asked.

'Sir, please tell them what I explained to you.'

'Thank you. I will tell them what you told me. And I will convey to them that you told me. Keep me posted on the developments,' Jaswant Singh said. Once convinced, Singh did not revisit the issue, despite, I imagine, facing considerable pressure.

OCBs were not my only concern on this issue. I was equally concerned about participatory notes (PNs). PNs are financial instruments issued by registered foreign institutional investors (FIIs) to overseas investors who wish to invest in India's stock markets without registering themselves with the market regulator in India. Without adequate information on the participants in PNs and OCBs, regulatory oversight was hampered. PNs, like OCBs, had been introduced as instruments to attract investments from abroad, but I believed that both OCBs and PNs undermined the integrity of the financial system.

The JPC report on the Ketan Parekh scam had identified not just OCBs but also PNs as a possible source that had enabled the scam. But what to do about them? One view was to regulate these entities strictly. But regulating foreign entities from India would be extremely difficult and the information they provided would be from interested intermediaries. Therefore, the other view was to ban them. This was the view I supported. When I took over, we implemented the OCB ban in a surprise move. We had to act with speed and secrecy, since we were sure that powerful vested interests, if they suspected action, would work to prevent the OCB ban. However, once it was done, it would be difficult for them to get a reversal.

Though we could ban OCBs, we could not do the same with PNs as they were not in the jurisdiction of the Reserve Bank – they were in the jurisdiction of SEBI. But the integrity of the financial system was in RBI's mandate, and in that capacity, I requested the chairman, SEBI, to ban PNs, too. He agreed. However, the ban on PNs did not happen.

Although not extensively, I had interacted with Singh a few times at a personal level. Once, when he had been finance minister during the short-lived BJP rule of 1996, Singh invited Geetha and me, along with a few other senior officers, for an official farewell dinner. This was unusual to begin with: spouses are hardly ever invited by ministers for official dinners. Geetha remembers him as a stately and extraordinarily courteous man.

To some people, Singh came across as perfunctory and dismissive in his interactions. They felt he was almost arrogant – in a typical feudal style. I did not find this to be so in my interactions with him. I found him extremely formal, but never arrogant. We had a mutual respect. This allowed us to work together on issues that had far-reaching consequences.

After the action on OCBs, I turned my attention to an issue of enormous importance relating to foreign banks.

In the budget speech of February 2003,[1] Jaswant Singh had announced: 'For facilitating the setting up of subsidiaries by foreign banks, as well as for inviting investment in private banks, this limit will be raised to at least 74 per cent.' Singh added, 'The voting rights of any person holding shares of a banking company are restricted to 10 per cent, irrespective of his/her shareholding. The Banking Regulation Act, 1949, will be amended to remove this limitation.' The budget announcement by the finance minister had two elements, namely, allowing foreign investments in private sector banks up to 74 per cent, and making amendments in the relevant Act to enable foreign banks to acquire ownership in our private sector banks.

The government had obviously decided to open up our banking sector to foreign investment and subsidiaries of foreign banks. The policy, in my view, ignored the need for structural reforms of the domestic banking sector to which it was committed for the past twenty years.[2] To rescind the commitment would be virtually impossible, but we could delay the measure till our banks were sufficiently competitive. To do so would mean a long and sustained struggle and we would have to move in several directions at once.

I decided, as a first step, to go public with my views. I did not make a direct reference to the government's decision, but carefully articulated my thinking in a speech, which I gave on

11 December 2003, three months after I joined as governor. The title of the speech was 'Towards Globalisation in the Financial Sector in India'. In it, without referencing the budget proposal, I explained that the approach implicit in it was neither consistent with global obligations nor the global best practices.[3] I concluded this speech with an emphasis on our strengths in the global banking industry.[4]

I linked the implementation of the budget announcement with obligations to the WTO and global consensus on the subject[5] in the speech. All over the world, even in developed economies, banks were considered special. Licensing and opening up of banks to foreign ownership and allowing their branches were treated with caution. Our regulatory regime was not yet attuned to opening up. Instead of removing the constraints on our banking system and improving its efficiency through reform, we were inviting foreign banks to run our system. Therefore, my view was that our banking systems needed to be improved first and then opened up, and that too with caution. Besides, the advantages of foreign ownership had not been established conclusively. There were often diplomatic pressures to contend with. In addition, foreign banks often undermined regulatory effectiveness. Importantly, it was irreversible. Once we opened up, it would be practically impossible to go back. Anyway, I did not see the urgency since our commitments to the World Trade Organisation were limited to giving licences to twelve branches of foreign banks per year and we were already giving licences in excess of that.

Every item announced in the budget is to be followed up with the Parliament a year later, with a note on the action taken on that item. Singh had made his announcement in February 2003. The update would have to be given in February 2004.

A few weeks earlier, I met the finance minister. Singh asked me to update him on the action taken regarding his announcement on foreign banks. I mentioned, briefly, that I had reservations about implementing the announcement in the budget. He heard me out. He pointed out that the announcement had already been made. Parliament had to be informed of action taken.

I said that the RBI had concerns.

Singh insisted that action should be taken and reported to Parliament. He asked me to discuss my concerns and work out the details with his secretary, Banking, Narendra Sisodia. I could see that Singh had many matters on his mind, as the budget itself had thousands of important items that he had to attend to. Besides, he must have been preoccupied with the elections that were to be held soon. In any case, this suited me well. Sisodia was an outstanding but low-key and sincere officer, who had the full trust of the finance minister.

Sisodia pointed out the case that was in line with current thinking both in India and abroad – that foreign banks would make our banking systems more efficient, increase financial innovations, deepen markets, provide access to global capital and manpower, etc.

I made my case.

'Sir,' Sisodia said, 'I see your point. It is valid. But the government has already committed to the policy of allowing foreign shareholding up to 74 per cent.'

'Okay. Let that be announced by the government. But let it also be announced that it would be subject to guidelines to be issued by the RBI.'

'Yes, sir. That should be possible.'

My strategy was to link the guidelines for foreign shareholding in Indian banks to the broader issue of shareholding by all investors, and thus seize the initiative. I bought time and an opportunity to link the issue of guidelines to foreign investment with regulating all investments in all banks, and in fact, on several other aspects.

'Sir, I have some concerns about the policy on foreign bank presence,' Sisodia would say.

'Come for lunch,' I would tell him.

Over lunch, we would discuss the implications of the presence of foreign banks.

'A foreign bank should have only one form of presence,' I insisted. This meant that the foreign bank could have a branch, a wholly owned subsidiary or a subsidiary – single form of presence, rather than multiple forms. My reasoning was that most of the foreign banks that were interested in a presence in India would already have a branch. Therefore, they already had their single form of presence. This clause made the entry of foreign banks difficult.

In the end, a press note was issued by the Ministry of Industry and Commerce on 5 March 2004, technically complying with the budget commitment but reflecting agreement with Sisodia. This was merely the start of a battle, which had to spill over to Chidambaram, who succeeded Singh.

But it was a tough battle. We were going against the thinking and ideology of the time. Even within the RBI, some senior officers were inclined to the opening up of the banking sector to foreign banks and foreign ownership. They had committed to it, and were disinclined to rescind. But there were some others who were willing to consider what may be called a system-approach, allowing the presence of foreign banks along with improvements in our system. We had to work on the new approach for several months.

During this period there was an attempt by a foreign bank, HSBC, to take over UTI Bank.[6] It was called a 'palace coup', and we had to put in place policies that would prevent HSBC from circumventing the upcoming policy guidelines.

By November, the idea of going in for elections to the Lok Sabha was in the air. The focus was on showcasing the achievements of the government that finally led to the 'India Shining' campaign. Jaswant Singh asked me when we could reach a hundred billion dollars in foreign exchange reserves. A good-sized reserve, he felt, was important for our economic security. It was also a feel-good factor in the run-up to elections.

I told the finance minister, 'No problem. When do you want it?'

'By March.'

'Well before that, sir. I will tell you when we reach the figure. You can make the announcement on that day.'

That day was 20 December 2003. Singh made his announcement.

Singh, in his announcement, said, 'It marks a period of great confidence... Self-reliance, for which we worked for decades since Independence, has been reached.'

The *Hindu Business Line* dated 21 December 2003 said, 'The credit for this stupendous achievement by any standard goes to four governors', and added that 'Dr Y.V. Reddy, the fourth governor, has the good luck to report the news to the finance minister and the country.' Though forex reserves are in the RBI's balance sheet and are managed by it, I felt it important that the minister broke the good news.

Singh was happy. It was satisfying for me as well. Yet, I was concerned. These inflows of capital were comforting for us now. But when significantly in excess of what our economy could absorb, I was concerned that they might become too large for comfort. We had moved out of starvation, but I was worried that we might move to indigestion.

When capital flows are in excess of the normal demand the exchange rate may appreciate beyond what is desirable. In such a situation, the RBI purchases US dollars and adds to the reserves. When it purchases dollars to add to the foreign currency reserves, rupees are injected into the system. The RBI would often purchase the rupees to mop up the liquidity injected at the time of intervention. In the process the interest has to be paid to the bondholders who parted with their money. This is the cost of sterilisation, and it is not fully compensated by the returns on investments made from foreign exchange reserves. Normally, the Reserve Bank would have to bear the costs, but I had suggested that the magnitudes of flows could be too large for RBI to incur the cost without its own balance sheet going into the red.

In case of large inflows, my proposal would add to the fiscal burden of the Union government up to the limit decided upon by it. This meant that the government had to approve the proposal. I met with Jaswant Singh.

'Governor Reddy,' Singh said in his rich baritone, 'the government and the RBI are both our public institutions. If you think it is in the best interest of our country, we will approve it.'

I said, 'Sir, this is very important. Before I send the proposal to you, you may like to get the informal approval of the prime minister.' Nothing like this had been done anywhere in the world, the stakes were high, and it had implications on the fiscal burden of the government. Therefore, I did not want to take the risk of it being later reversed by the prime minister.

'Governor,' Singh said, a few days later, 'There are some reservations.'

'Sir, what are they?' I asked him.

'The chief economic advisor was not in favour,' he said.

'I'll discuss with him,' I said.

The chief economic advisor said that my proposal implied an erosion of independence of the central bank in managing the exchange rate.

I said that, on this important matter, I did not want central bank independence. What was the point of independence if, in the case of extraordinary magnitudes, my balance sheet did not permit me to have the strength to be independent on this issue? My proposal would allow the RBI to act beyond the limits of its balance sheet. The markets knew the RBI balance sheet limits and the proposal would signal that the government and the RBI were acting together. The fact that the government could set the limits in excess of RBI balance sheet limits, depending on the need, would allow the RBI greater latitude and effectiveness in sterilisation and intervention in forex markets. Ironically, while technically restraining my independence, I was actually strengthening the effectiveness of our operations.

Now I had to convince the finance minister. I had explained to Singh that we, in India, did not need to go by the textbook idea of central bank independence.

'Especially in extraordinary situations, sir, we can be innovative,' I said.

'The issue is whether the costs of adding to the forex reserves should be shown in the balance sheet of the government or the RBI. The government is already in the red. The Reserve Bank is not. If the government bears the cost, it will add to the fiscal deficit. If the Reserve Bank bears it, its balance sheet could turn from surplus, which we give to the government in any case, into deficit. We can have both the RBI and government balance sheets showing deficit, or only the government's, which is already in the red. It is good to make a central bank balance sheet a healthy one. It can serve the government better.'

Jaswant Singh said, 'I will do nothing, in any way, that undermines our central bank. I want our central bank to be strong. It should command respect. We will approve your proposal.'

That was how the innovative Market Stabilisation Scheme was approved by the government.[7] This instrument was crucial for managing large capital inflows, maintaining a competitive exchange rate, and building forex reserves. This scheme, by virtue of its counter-cyclical nature, also became extremely valuable five years later in 2008, when there was a reversal of capital inflows.

Soon after MSS was launched, in a meeting of the Bank for International Settlements, some central bank governors from other countries could not believe it. How could you convince your minister, they asked. I could convince him, I explained, because he was willing to be convinced; Singh was willing to take a broader, holistic view of public institutions in the public interest and did not view the government and the RBI in a compartmental fashion.

Any government's natural tendency is to avoid fiscal burden when it can be borne by the central bank. Yet, Finance Minister Singh and Prime Minister Vajpayee took on the burden, despite bureaucratic and economic advice which they most likely would have received. Approval of the MSS scheme was an act of statesmanship by Singh and Vajpayee. The other governors in the BIS meeting were right to be surprised. There are very few world leaders I can think of who would have acted with such trust and foresight.

On the evening of 19 February, Jawant Singh was in Mumbai and I had gone to call on him. Singh was scheduled to address a gathering of industrialists. We were in an elevator on the way down to the meeting.

'Governor, what do I tell these people?' Singh said. 'These meetings have become tedious. We keep repeating the same thing. I want to say something different. Something that will make them feel good, something that will spur them.'

I explained that he could allow corporates to freely acquire companies abroad to do business. I said that we are confident about inflows and we can afford to liberalise outflows for our industrialists to acquire companies abroad.

He said, 'That is all right. But how about the average person? I want our people to feel that they are free to take money out. Tell me, how can we do that?'

The lift doors opened. We began to walk through the corridor.

I said, 'Yes, sir, we will allow our citizens to take money out – no questions asked. But within limits, say a few thousands of dollars. Certainly not millions.'

We started down the stairs to the meeting hall where top industrialists were waiting. 'Shall I make the announcement now?' Singh asked.

I said, 'Sure, go ahead. We can afford it. Capital flows cannot be a one-way street. There should be inflow and outflow also.'

The minister told the gathering that it was time for Indian industry to go global. 'Go and conquer the world, we will be your supporters.' He added that our people could take out liberal amounts of money that they wanted, no questions asked.

Pointing to me in the audience he said, 'I have consulted the governor, Reserve Bank. He is agreeable. He is sitting here.' There was applause.

We prepared a draft press release and notification within a day or two. I called the minister over the phone and briefly explained the limits I had in mind. He wanted the limit for individuals to be 25,000 per head per year, to which I readily agreed. This is a 'no questions asked' window and was in addition to all the existing facilities. I asked Singh whether I should, as in the normal course, wait for a formal approval from the government, or whether I should issue the orders and inform the government. I did not want this important proposal to be lost in bureaucratic processing. I pointed out that the minister had announced a decision in a public meeting in Mumbai.

He said, 'You go ahead. You have the approval of the government. Go ahead.' That was a historic decision in the annals of India's economic history. The oppressive forex regime that had haunted individuals in India since 1957 was put to an end on 19 February 2004. For several months, industrialists did not comprehend the enormous significance. This is one measure of liberalisation which was not sought by any corporate in India. They simply had not yet felt the need to go global nor did they ever expect that it could be possible. There was a case where a chairman of a bank refused to believe it. How could the law become so liberal overnight, he wanted to know. He concluded that it had to be a misprint.[8]

Though there was no real push, I was keen and the minister was enthusiastic. Our interests converged.[9]

Jaswant Singh was frank in mentioning cases of political pressure on him so that I could appreciate his compulsions. I could explain my dilemmas also. One day, on the eve of the Lok Sabha elections, Singh asked me for my opinion. A commercial banker was being considered for appointment as deputy governor in an existing vacancy. What did I think of him?

I told him, 'There is nothing negative about him. There is nothing very positive either. I am not comfortable.'

As usual, we were both sitting on the sofas in his office. Singh picked up some papers from a file lying between us on the table. I assumed he was looking through some correspondence on the candidate. I could see he was uncomfortable, his eyes did not meet mine, and his voice lacked his usual confidence.

'He is highly recommended by many people,' Singh said. It was evident that many senior leaders were backing the candidate.

I told him, 'Sir, I have no objection if you appoint him. I cannot recommend him, because he is not senior enough nor capable enough to be a good deputy governor.'

Singh responded, 'What would be the reaction of people?'

I said, 'Sir, that appointment will not bring credit to me if I recommend, and will not be to your credit either.'

Singh put the papers and the file aside. He smiled, and looked directly into my eyes, 'Governor, I will not do anything that will not bring us credit. Please forget the matter. We will bury this for some time.'

No appointment was made, despite what would be, I imagine, intense pressures due to the forthcoming elections.

One of the determining factors in cordial relations between the minister and governor is not only the minister but also his position in the cabinet, particularly vis-à-vis the prime minister. Jaswant Singh had enormous clout with the prime minister. He also had a high standing in Parliament, including with senior members of the opposition. It was said that with a joke or well-turned phrase, he could persuade Parliament on an issue. This enabled him to be bold and effective.

In the aftermath of the Lok Sabha elections held between 20 April and 10 May 2004, the crisis management skills that I learnt from governor Jalan were of great help. On 13 May, the National Democratic Alliance led by the BJP conceded defeat, but the new ministry was sworn in only on 22 May. On Monday, 17 May, from about noon the Sensex dropped precipitously in financial markets at the prospect of the UPA forming a government with the presence of left parties in the coalition. Trading in stock markets was temporarily stopped by SEBI. There was significant selling pressure from FIIs which led to pressure on the rupee exchange rate. One view was that we should intervene in the forex market promptly as a pre-emptive measure, that is, sell foreign currency and simultaneously issue a statement, to avoid panic in markets. The other view was to wait and time the intervention and statement strategically to make sure that we would succeed, taking the risk that things could get worse as time passed by.

I subscribed to the second view and convinced others since I was keen that to maintain credibility we should intervene with minimal risk of failure. We waited for some more downward movement in the value of the rupee to take place, and then intervened heavily in forex markets at a time when we felt that there were some players who thought that the fall in the value of rupee was 'too much'. So, we waited for the beginning of some sentiment among market participants that enough depreciation has taken place. This sentiment though weak was strengthened by initiation of our heavy sale of foreign currency. But, we did not want to lock into a stance till we had assessed the possible impact of our intervention. When we found that our intervention was not ineffective, we issued a statement that the RBI would continue to sell dollars, directly as well as through banks to moderate volatility. In addition, we said that the banks acting on behalf of FIIs were free to approach the RBI for supply of dollars at prevailing market rates. Whenever there are large and unexpected outflows, there could be a pressure on availability of rupee liquidity also, especially for stock exchanges and settlement banks. Hence, the RBI was in touch with them to ensure smooth settlements and followed it up with a statement the same day about availability of rupee liquidity for them, as needed. They were also advised to be in touch with the task force led by the Executive Director, Shyamala Gopinath. The Financial Markets Committee which I had initiated when I was deputy governor was in continuous session.

I called Jaswant Singh and assured him that we were closely watching the developments and would take appropriate action as needed.

He said, 'Governor, I am no longer in government.'

I said, 'Sir, as far as we are concerned, you are our finance minister till the new government is sworn in. If you consider it necessary, you may brief Congress party leaders. I report to you only, for now.'

He said, 'Thank you, governor, I wish you all the best.'

The panic situation in forex markets was managed by the RBI in a state of temporary political vacuum; and both outgoing finance minister and incoming political leaders left the situation's management to the central bank. In the global community of central bankers, this episode was highly regarded.

It was October 2005. Jaswant Singh was now Leader of the Opposition in the Rajya Sabha. Singh called me over the phone. He said that a US delegation headed by Under Secretary Nicholas Burns had called on him. He said that during the discussions, the American ambassador, David Mulford, was rather critical of me, and that they complained that I was not cooperating with the government in reforming the financial sector.

'I told them that I know you well, and that I respect you,' Singh said. 'I was blunt and told them that you would do nothing that was not in public interest. But I was surprised at their vehemence.'

Singh paused. I was quiet. I wanted to hear everything before reacting.

'Could you please explain it to me when you visit Delhi next? In the meantime I am writing to you formally, about my meeting.'

Singh sent me the letter dated 22 October 2005. The letter gave the gist of Singh's discussions with the US delegation. Singh had pointed out in the letter that he had told the US delegation that I could not but be governed by the basic policies of the government. The letter was typewritten but at the end, Singh had added, in his handwriting, 'I had, short of objecting explicitly to such unwarranted observations, told Mulford and Burns of the respective roles and functions of finance and RBI plus the regard and personal equation that I have with you.'

A detailed account of this meeting between Jaswant Singh and the US officials, the version of their ambassador to India, was released as part of Wikileaks.[10] That version was in consonance with what Jaswant Singh wrote to me and narrated to me.

A year after I retired on 20 September 2009, Singh gave me a copy of his book titled *Jinnah: India–Partition–Independence*. In it he had penned a personal message: *For a wise counsel, a great guide, the Statesman sans-pareil of the country's Central Bank and a great helpmate: Governor Y.V. Reddy. With highest regards and warmest good wishes.*'

It was full of warmth, an expression of his regard and trust. I reciprocate every sentiment fully.

26

WORKING WITH CHIDAMBARAM

Autonomy is seldom granted; it has to be taken. This was the suggestion I made to C. Rangarajan in 1997, when there was a political vacuum in the government. It was now May 2004, and I was in a similar situation.

The Annual Policy Statement had been slated for 18 May 2004, assuming normal transition, but the transition was delayed. With the surprise election results, we had to wait for some time for the new Congress-led United Progressive Alliance government to be sworn in. If I did not postpone the date of the announcement, it would mean that we would announce an important policy without the customary consultations with the finance minister in position.

We could have waited. After all, announcing the policy without prior consultations could have annoyed the incoming leadership. Besides, it is reasonable for newly elected formations to expect that the policies of the RBI should have the benefit of their advice. But my view has always been that a central bank should be seen to be in full command, performing apolitically, especially during periods of uncertainty. This reassures the financial markets, too. We also thought that this was a good time to highlight the benign macro-economic environment, which would provide comfort at a time of change. We decided to go ahead with the statement on the due date. Of course, we were careful to announce a policy which would not be unacceptable to the political leadership. In the end, no controversy arose.

Since the circumstances of my appointment were well known, I was not identified with any political party, personality or ideology. Therefore, I expected that my statements and policies would be viewed in that light. In addition, I had a good equation with the outgoing government and I expected to have one equally with the new government as well, since I had worked closely with many of the economic stalwarts whom I expected to be part of the incoming government, such as Manmohan Singh and Montek Singh Ahluwalia.

On 22 May 2004, the new government was sworn in and the new finance minister was P. Chidambaram. I had worked with Chidambaram before. The economic situation continued to be positive, with indications of even greater pick-up in credit and a strong external sector. I expected that I would have a good working relationship with the new finance minister, as I had had with the old one.

I called on Chidambaram on 25 May.

'Vango, vango,' he said in Tamil, as I walked in. Come in, come in.

We recalled our previous association. I updated him on the current work of the RBI. In particular, I briefed him about the monetary policy statement and there was an implicit endorsement of the statement by him.

Over coffee (with us, it was always south Indian filter coffee), he narrated the circumstances under which his appointment as finance minister was announced. It was a short visit. I could see that Chidambaram was immensely happy to be back in his den.

A civil servant is normally expected to brief the incoming minister about the state of various issues. A governor of a central bank is also expected to brief the minister. There are several ways of briefing the minister. One is to disown the previous policy directions and endorse possible new directions, in order to cement cordial relations with the incoming government. Another is to skirt the issues where there may be disagreements and leave it to the minister to take the initiative. The third is to explain the circumstances under which important decisions were taken and the rationale behind the decisions. My preference is the third.

Usually, I have found that the political leadership is open to understanding the rationale behind the decisions.

In my preliminary briefings with Chidambaram, I detailed five crucial policy decisions taken by the previous government concerning the RBI: the banning of OCBs, the liberalisation of the investment regime for Indian corporates to make acquisitions abroad, the freedom for individuals to remit funds overseas, the Market Stabilisation Scheme, and shifting of external commercial borrowings approvals to RBI. I was keen to obtain the minister's support for continuing these policies, and Chidambaram was supportive of them to varying degrees.[1]

The elephant in the room was the policy relating to opening our banking system to foreign ownership, in particular, to enable foreign banks to acquire Indian banks. I suspected that the new government was keen to implement the budget announcements of Jaswant Singh in this regard. I was opposed to continuity in this policy. In our initial meetings, I did not raise the issue with Chidambaram and he did not raise it with me.

But my views were known. Within two months of the new government formation, I made a speech in which I was unusually forthright. I deliberately titled it, 'India and the Global Economy'. In the speech, I dealt with economic integration, financial integration, and the role of banks, in particular foreign banks, in financial integration. The thrust of my argument was that in both industrialised and developing countries, the supervisors (in our case, the RBI) evaluate the benefits and risks of licensing foreign banks in the context of the specific country, according to 'fit and proper' criteria using guidelines that are judgement-based and evolving. In India, I explained, we would evaluate the foreign banks on a case-by-case basis, while keeping in mind the broader picture, such as domestic banking sector consolidation, our obligations under the WTO, and other considerations.[2]

There was no immediate reaction, but it did come after some time. One evening, Chidambaram called me over to his house. It was in a leafy street in Lutyens' Delhi. The two of us sat in the living room. He was, as always, pleasant and warm.

Chidambaram had the file on this matter with him. I saw that he had flagged, with numbered references, all important points on the subject. Nothing had been left out, all datelines and sequences were highlighted, even the smallest counter-argument had been anticipated. As usual, Chidambaram had done his homework and was at his convincing best. Before the court, he is known to make his arguments systematically on an almost equal footing with the judge. With me, he usually moved from formal to informal, businesslike to joking. In this case, he spoke with unusual gravity. It was very clear that this issue was of great importance.

With the file in his hands, he spoke at length pointing to the sequence of events that would leave no room for me to disagree or demur. It was an undeniable settled policy and both the major political parties had subscribed to it, he pointed out.

'Governor,' he concluded, 'this is a national commitment made to the global financial community. How do we justify a reversal of such a policy? Is it just because there is a change in the incumbency of the governor? Do we review our commitments every time a governor of the RBI changes? On what basis do we reverse this decision?'

I said, 'Sir, as I explained, it has serious irreversible consequences. I believe that it is better to go back on our commitment at this stage, in national interest.'

Chidambaram said, looking up from the file, 'But I believe that it is in our national interest.'

I thought for a few moments and asked him, 'Does the prime minister believe that it is in our national interest?'

He said, 'Yes. The prime minister also believes that it is in national interest.'

I paused, and said, 'Sir, if the prime minister and the finance minister believe that this should be done in national interest, it has to be done. I agree. Let me think how to go about it.'

I went back to Mumbai. I thought about it deeply. When I was deputy governor RBI, I had had a telling experience with diplomatic pressures to protect the interests of foreign banks. In the case of a legal dispute between the British ANZ Grindlays Bank and the National Housing Bank (of which RBI was the owner), we were forced to go for arbitration, despite our strong case before the Supreme Court. Experiences such as this indicated that, in the light of political realities, the regulation and supervision over foreign banks in India would be more difficult than in the case of domestic entities. This feeling was further strengthened during my stint as executive director in the IMF. In literature, as well as in some cases that I knew of, it was clear that the benefits of the increased presence of foreign banks were uncertain. Our obligations under the WTO did not require it, and we could not allow ourselves to be distracted from important and painful banking reforms that we still had pending. The governance standards in the domestic private sector banks needed to be improved first. The regulatory framework for bank ownership in general was yet to be developed, and I felt that the foreign ownership issue had to be a part of the overall criteria for 'fit and proper'.

Above all, I was shaken by my experience during the Fund-Bank (World Bank and International Monetary Fund) Spring meetings in Washington, D.C. It was April 2004. Normally, the finance minister leads the Indian delegation. At that time, Jaswant Singh was still finance minister, but he nominated me to lead the delegation as he had other pressing matters.

In Washington, D.C., a senior official of Citibank called on me.

He offered to provide assistance to the RBI in preparing the guidelines for the entry of foreign banks. Elections have been ordered and a new government is yet to take a position on this matter, I informed him.

He asserted that Citibank was confident of ensuring the implementation of the policy, whichever government came to power. I was taken aback. 'Whichever government comes to power': to me, such an assertion indicated the influence that the global financial conglomerates could exercise over the political and decision-making processes in our country. I resolved that we simply could not afford it. In any case, I was convinced that on merits and in terms of proper sequencing of the reforms, inviting the larger presence of foreign banks in India should be back-loaded, and this conversation only strengthened my conviction.

Nothing that Chidambaram had argued before me in our meeting, months after the incident, diluted my resolve.

I called Rakesh Mohan, secretary, Economic Affairs, who had joined the Ministry of Finance in October 2004, and had been my deputy governor previously.[3] I narrated the exchange between Chidambaram and me.

'Rakesh,' I told him, 'it is better I leave the job. I believe that the issue is very critical to our national interest. I think opening up of foreign banks should not be done at this stage at all. Still, if the government feels that this has to be done, it has to be done. But I will not be able to put my heart in it.'

Rakesh was listening to my outburst patiently.

'Even if I do my job in implementing the decision, the government will not have confidence that I am doing it sincerely, since I made no secret of my opposition. Also, if there are difficulties in implementation or some adverse consequences, the government may suspect my motives. So, better I quietly leave the job.'

'I don't think there is a need for that,' Rakesh insisted.

'I will not make an issue of it. I will simply get admitted in a hospital, and after a few days seek retirement on health grounds. I am quite old and a diabetic, so it will be convincing. I do not want to embarrass the government, yet I cannot, in good conscience, open our banking system to foreign banks at this stage.'

'There is no need to precipitate anything. Let us meet,' Rakesh said. I agreed.

It was fortunate that Rakesh Mohan, who I had worked with earlier, was now heading Economic Affairs. He would play a critical role in resolving the issue.

After a few days, while I was in Hyderabad attending a social function, I got a call on my mobile phone. It was from Chidambaram.

'Venu, we have considered your views,' he said. 'We are keen to honour the commitments made on foreign banks by the earlier government. We will not go back on them. We would like to make a formal policy statement to that effect. But I know you have your concerns and you may propose a roadmap that will take care of them. We should announce our policy commitment through a clear-cut, timebound roadmap. Step by step. Send us a draft, as soon as possible.'

I was greatly relieved. We drafted a roadmap and sent it to the minister. He went through it and called me promptly.

'It's all right, Venu,' he said. He suggested a minor change in the language and a reduction in the period of the roadmap.

Our divergence on this matter had been noted in the public domain.[4]

It must be acknowledged that Chidambaram took personal interest, not only in regard to the foreign bank policy, but in every detail of improving the governance and policy environment of the banking sector as a whole.

The RBI constituted study groups for all important policy changes and reform measures in the banking sector. Chidambaram ensured that the government gave inputs to the study groups, which proved productive.

Our joint commitments were incorporated in the budget speech in February 2005. In it, he pointed out that the 'RBI has prepared a roadmap for banking sector reforms' and that the 'RBI' would 'unveil' them. He said that most proposals would be implemented by the RBI 'on its own authority'. Required legislative changes would be made 'in consultation with the RBI'. To note was the emphasis in the language on the centrality of the role of the RBI in the process.

The close association with the budget was not only on the foreign banks issue in 2005. Chidambaram and I worked together on four budgets, from 2004 to 2008. In the finance minister's room, it would be just the two of us, he with his laptop, reading out each paragraph relevant to the financial sector, and we would discuss them one by one. (In the later years, there were a few cases when I was not entirely comfortable. I was aware that he was annoyed with my resistance to some budget proposals for the reform of the financial sector, especially financial markets.)

From the beginning, Chidambaram and I had many extensive discussions on the state of the banking system. We gave highest priority to it, as the banking system is at the heart of the country's financial system.

Throughout our years of working together, Chidambaram shared my concern on the functioning of public sector banks. These banks form the dominant part of the banking system. He was generally supportive of structural and governance changes. But, I could recognise his political constraints in reforming the public sector banks.

As regards private sector banks, I expressed my concern at the governance in and functioning of some private sector banks, and the level of capital adequacy (the minimum reserves of capital that the bank is required to have available). Improvements in the private sector banking system had to be brought about by public policy as soon as possible. He assured total support and delivered on his promise.

Soon after I joined, Chidambaram said that he would drop by to see me at the RBI guest house in Delhi where I was staying. He wanted to chat about a few matters. The finance minister generally summons, calls or invites the governor of a central bank and it is extraordinary for the minister to visit the governor for a one-to-one chat.

Chidambaram turned up around 11.00 a.m. on a weekend. He was clad in his usual white dhoti. For a while, we talked about general issues, politics, his recent trip to Sri Lanka. It was time for lunch and the minister stayed back for an impromptu meal.

'Venu,' he said, as we enjoyed the fluffy chapatis at the guest house, 'let us talk about your proposal on the selection of chief executives of public sector banks.'

The government has the power to appoint CEOs of public sector banks.[5] The appointments are made based on recommendations of a committee,[6] in which the RBI governor is the chairman. There are also representatives from the government, the finance secretary, the banking secretary, for instance, as well as an expert. I was clear: I did not want to be in the committee that selected the CEOs of public sector banks.

Instead, my proposal was that the government, as the largest owner, select CEOs; RBI would then approve the candidate based on 'fit and proper' considerations.[7] This was the case with private sector banks, where the owner chooses the CEO, and the regulator – the central bank – then approves the appointment based on 'fit and proper' criteria. This method was in consonance with the global best practice.

'I am convinced about the logic behind your proposal,' Chidambaram said.

But he requested that I not press for the proposal. He was worried that selections done without the governor's association could politicise the process.

'Let me give you an assurance,' Chidambaram volunteered. He said that he would not, directly or indirectly, influence our committee's recommendation. He would be fully supportive of the independence of the committee. I accepted his advice and did not press the matter, and he honoured his promise.

The carving out of the RBI's public debt management function, to avoid possible conflict of interest with its monetary management functions, was an issue that had been on the anvil for years. Chidambaram supported it. I argued that it was premature: it was desirable objectively, but the system was not yet ready. So we did not put it in fast track.[8]

On the regulation of the government securities market, Chidambaram strengthened our hands with various regulations. On this there was both ideological and policy convergence.[9] Chidambaram and I also worked together to shed RBI's ownership of several developmental financial institutions (DFIs).[10]

Ideologically, I was greatly committed to viewing finance as a means to serve society. All measures proposed by the RBI to serve the common person were fully supported by the finance minister (as well as the prime minister). In the annual policy of 2005, I used the term financial inclusion for the first time. As a part of financial inclusion, Chidambaram's support for the business correspondent model – where a resident of a community that is underserved by banks is authorised to perform limited and basic banking services at the doorstep – was enthusiastic. When the RBI sought to inject growth in the micro-credit segment and give a stimulus to micro-finance institutions, we had Chidambaram's unconditional support.[11]

Another area where I actively sought Chidambaram's

support was the expansion of the banking ombudsman scheme (the ombudsman is an official appointed to resolve customer complaints) of 2006. I remember I met him at a transit hotel between flights. He looked through every line of the banking ombudsman scheme with great interest. Again, though it was an RBI scheme, his support was valuable.

There were some areas where Chidambaram did not need my active support, but sought it: such as in the bid to improve the cooperative credit system.[12] From the efforts to reorganise regional rural banks,[13] to the flow of credit to agriculture,[14] Chidambaram and I worked closely together.

The most satisfying part of my working with Chidambaram was the manner in which he successfully managed to get legislations for reform approved in the government.[15]

Operationally, Chidambaram continued the tradition of consulting the governor in the appointment of directors on the RBI board. In fact, all appointments were done after the two of us had discussed them and agreed. Every deputy governor appointed was on the basis of my recommendation as governor. However, the proposals were made by me after consultations with the minister and with the knowledge of the prime minister, in addition to Rangarajan at an informal level.

True to the tradition, I had one-to-one meetings with the minister and on rare occasions he called the secretaries concerned (Economic Affairs, Banking, Revenue and Expenditure) or the chief economic advisor to assist him. We met in his room in North Block at least once a month. Our meetings lasted, on an average, from half to one hour. That was the length of time needed to satisfy his passion for precision and detail. Chidambaram went into the legal position, the economic logic, the institutional arrangements, and implementation aspects. Our discussions, whether we were in agreement or not, sharpened my thinking. In the end, our discussions improved the quality of decision making significantly.

I had a long-standing working relationship with the prime minister, Manmohan Singh. At Dr Singh's suggestion, I would brief him about the global economic situation as well as the Indian economy; the prime minister was keen to track the developments in the world of central bankers. (I made certain that the finance minister was updated of these briefings). Dr Singh had been a central bank governor himself. He had also been a finance minister and understood the story from both sides. Interestingly, Chidambaram and I had to contend with an unprecedented configuration of leadership in economic policy in our country. In addition to Dr Singh, Chidambaram and me, there was Dr Rangarajan, chairman of his economic advisory council, and Montek Singh Ahluwalia, deputy chairman, Planning Commission. The five of us used to have frank discussions and, therefore, in some ways, the relationship between the minister and the governor was also impacted by the inputs from these occasional high-level meetings.[16] In fact, the five of us were described as original reformers and felicitated at an *Economic Times* awards function in Mumbai on 6 October 2006.

Also, the Manmohan Singh government had support from parties with left leanings. This political geography lent weight to what was perceived as an ideological convergence between their approach and my tilt in policies relating to financial and external sectors.

Chidambaram and I also worked well in multilateral settings – mainly the IMF, International Monetary and Finance Committee (IMFC), G-20 and G-24. Our working relationship was the envy of others, and it lasted all through my tenure as governor. In one gathering, someone commented on the conflicting signals they were getting from the RBI and the finance ministry. Chidambaram said, 'I promise growth. I deliver it. Governor assures stability and he is delivering it. What is the problem?'[17]

In these multilateral meetings Chidambaram dominated the show. With his legal background, he was quick to grasp the essentials and argue his case eloquently and effectively.[18] In those gatherings, I usually stayed silent, unless my inputs were sought by Chidambaram. For his part, the minister made it a point to seek out my advice in the meetings.[19]

We shared a memorable experience in the meeting of G-20 in Beijing. All members of G-20 – finance ministers and governors – were to be introduced to the president of the country. We were shepherded into a huge hall. We were made to stand in a long queue, each pair in one row, in an alphabetical order. We were told that each country's representatives would be ushered to meet the president. We were all advised to restrict the time for pleasantries. We had to keep standing for the whole ceremony, lasting, perhaps, an hour. The message was clear: their time was important. In the alphabetical configuration, the last pair in the queue was the most unfortunate. It turned out to be US Fed Chairman Greenspan and Treasury Secretary Paulson. We were left in no doubt: we were having an audience in the Imperial Court of China.

Chidambaram and I recognised that our relationship was necessarily complex: in the global arena, the minister represents the country, and the governor assists him. Within India, the RBI governor is not a subordinate though never equal to the minister.

Chidambaram and I worked together amicably most of the time. But that seldom makes news! We disagreed sometimes, and we disagreed intensely. When we agreed, we did so equally intensely.

27

CREATIVE TENSIONS

HOW DOES THE FINANCE MINISTER INTERACT WITH THE governor? The answer is, it depends.

Monetary policy is the core function assigned to the RBI. The issue of autonomy and accountability of the RBI becomes critical here. The RBI is a lender of last resort to the financial system as a whole, and is, therefore, responsible for the financial stability of the system also. While the RBI is the first line of defence in times of stress, the sovereign assumes the big risks in times of crisis. The RBI act also specifies that the RBI is the banker to the government and its debt manager.

The Banking Regulation Act that came later assigned functions of regulation to the RBI. In the Indian context, public sector banks account for a majority of the banking system and the government is the majority owner of the public sector banks. Even more interestingly, the government is also the owner of the RBI itself. This means that the government, as the RBI owner, regulates itself as the owner of public sector banks. In a convoluted maze of ownership, accountability, and autonomy, the RBI must regulate the entity that is owned by the government, and is accountable to the owner of the regulated entity.

If that were not complex enough, the Foreign Exchange Management Act is a separate act that empowers the RBI to manage the external sector, while the forex reserves are on the balance sheet of the RBI. But since the interactions are with the external world (foreign countries), it is impossible for the RBI to work without the close cooperation of and coordination with the government. In many developing countries, the central bank is a repository of expertise related to money and finance. India is no exception. Governments tend to draw heavily from this expertise; making the RBI an advisor to the government.

RBI's responsibilities include the payment and settlement system, distribution of coins and management of currency. It functions as banker, debt manager, and advisor to state governments.For these reasons, the relationship between the RBI and the government is multifaceted, dizzyingly complex, and sometimes circular.

In addition to this, the personalities of the governor and finance minister matter. In the case of Chidambaram and I, both of us were known to go into excruciating detail (sometimes excruciating to each other) and we had a reputation (entirely well-earned) of being stubborn. In this spicy mix, we also had a prime minister who was both a former RBI governor and a former finance minister and knew the tricks of the trade of both sides. I sometimes wondered if the PM would have a quiet chuckle to himself while observing the back and forth between Chidambaram and me.

The monetary policy deals, essentially, with managing the supply of money, credit allocation, interest rates, and exchange rate, to achieve defined objectives such as inflation and growth. In India, the monetary policy is announced annually (usually in April/May) and mid-term (October/November). During my tenure, we introduced quarterly reviews also. Normally, monetary measures are taken as part of the policy statement.

Technically, monetary policy is decided by the RBI. However, it is customary to have consultations with the minister. During these consultations, the first step is to reach an agreement on the direction in which the monetary policy should move: whether to tighten, loosen, or keep the policy status quo. We take into consideration domestic and global factors. We take a view on both present circumstances as well as the future path (as these measures impact the economy with a time lag). Then we take a view on which instruments to use: whether to tweak interest rates or change the supply of money.

Reforms and measures in monetary, financial, external, and fiscal sectors have to be mutually consistent. Every decision impacts different interests (for example, importers vs. exporters, savers vs. borrowers) differently. Therefore, Chidambaram and I had a lot to discuss as we debated the implications of each decision.

I had to contend with a further complication. Even as we were having consultations on monetary policy, there were occasions in which Chidambaram would express his opinions in public. This meant, first, if I were to announce measures that were contradictory to the minister's public statements, it would send confusing signals. Second, it would mean that, by the time my policy was announced, his statements had already influenced expectations – and therefore my policy then became less effective. That was not all. After every important policy statement, Chidambaram would convene a meeting with the chief executives of public sector banks and give guidance to them on all aspects of policy. Invariably, given the timing, the guidance included follow-up actions on the monetary and regulatory policy and developmental measures announced in the statement. The transmission of my policy – which was mainly through public sector banks – was diluted by the minister's guidance.

Early on, I raised this issue. I urged Chidambaram to be circumspect about expressing his opinions before the monetary policy statement.

'I agree,' he said. 'I sympathise with your point of view.' But, he pointed out, in a democracy, it is legitimate for the finance minister to express his opinions on important economic policies, including those having monetary implications.

I had no choice but to leave things at that. However, though he continued to express his views, perhaps there was some moderation in the light of my concerns. Therefore, while designing the monetary policy, I had to take into consideration possible statements that Chidambaram would likely issue.

In the early part of my tenure, there were occasional disagreements, but I would not consider any of them to be serious.

They were part of the usual differences of views and philosophies between the RBI and the government.

The first sign of serious difference surfaced with the tightening of policy on 24 January 2006 due to global imbalances, oil price scenario, booming levels of credit and asset market activity in India. The perceptions on growth prospects and pressures on prices differed significantly.

In the Mid-Term Review of policy on 31 October 2006, I mentioned that there were signs of overheating. I raised the repo rate and said that it is only a signal that borrowing from the central bank would be expensive. I added that we had complaints about fairness and transparency in regard to the housing sector.

On 1 November, Chidambaram said that there were no signs of overheating, though he justified the Reserve Bank's decision to hike repo rate by 25 basis points as 'well intended'. He added, 'And if they had not taken action, I think some sectors have shown some signs of overheating.'

To be fair to Chidambaram, in public, he was muted in his unhappiness about my using the economic term 'overheating'. His reaction in private was strong.

He said, 'What are you doing? For decades since Independence, we have been dreaming of double-digit growth. Now that we are almost there, you want to spoil everything. Where is the evidence that there is overheating? What is overheating for that matter?'

After this conversation, I decided not to use the word 'overheating' but continued with policies to moderate asset bubbles and excessive credit growth. I was merely responding to Chidambaram's guarded criticism of my approach.

Chidambaram's reaction in private was strong in another instance, namely, on the self-imposed inflation target that I had proposed in April 2007.

I said, 'For the medium term also, the RBI has lowered its inflation target to 4 to 4.5 per cent from 5 per cent earlier.'

Chidambaram promptly called me over the telephone and said, 'What is this target? It is too ambitious a target. I don't agree.'

He did not go public on that view, for understandable reasons.

He was disinclined to appear to be against low inflation but was in favour of high growth, as all finance ministers are.

Closely related to the monetary policy and an important source of complexity in the relation between the government and the RBI is exchange rate management. Its management till the end of 2006 enabled not only orderly and two-way movement in the rate, but added significantly to our forex reserves. Perhaps, this is unprecedented in our country since Independence. The tendency has been one way, and towards depreciating. By early 2007, there was a perception in the government, in particular Chidambaram, that we had reached more than a comfortable level of reserves and that at that juncture, the cost of intervention was unsustainable and allowing the currency to appreciate might be a better option. While this was the view of the government, the view of the RBI was that capital flows, particularly through External Commercial Borrowings, could be tightened, and thus the need for intervention could be moderated, rather than allowing the exchange rate to appreciate. The government was not inclined to restrict capital flows, and preferred appreciation rather than sterilised intervention.

The finance ministry was sending out clear and strong signals to the market that they would not be uncomfortable with appreciation of the rupee, and that they were inclined to avoid the fiscal cost of intervention and sterilisation. There was enough evidence in the public domain to believe that the finance minister was also giving similar signals to the market participants. I mentioned to Chidambaram about the signals from the ministry, but he did not react.

I got a signal about the reluctance of the minister when he wanted to discuss the issue of enhancing limits to the enhancement of the Market Stabilisation Scheme (MSS) with me rather than approve the proposal from the RBI, as was customary.

The RBI had proposed enhancement of the prevailing limits prescribed for the issue of bonds under MSS to the ministry in order to continue forex intervention. Approval of this request was kept aside for discussion. Consequently, the capacity of the RBI to sterilise was constrained and its ability to intervene in the forex markets was limited. Our fears about the adverse impact of an overvalued exchange rate were communicated to the ministry and by me in person to the minister. Chidambaram was not forthcoming in his reactions, perhaps because he felt that I was unbending. The signals to the media that the government was not uncomfortable with an appreciating rupee intensified and I surmised that the minister had allowed such impressions to persist.

A stage was reached thereafter when I felt no purpose would be served by my formally raising the matter with the minister. He had not raised it with me. I felt that it was better to fall in line with the intent of the minister and the ministry on the exchange rate.

What did I do? I ordered in March 2007 that there should be no more intervention in the forex markets to resist appreciation. Intervention in forex markets in this context meant purchase of foreign currency by the RBI to resist appreciation of the rupee. Since purchase of foreign currency results in addition to rupee liquidity, it is accompanied by sterilisation, namely, issue of bonds to drain the liquidity. Simultaneously, the circumstances under which this decision was taken was explained by the RBI in a detailed letter to the ministry. The letter contained reference to a series of media reports as well as pending approval of enhancement of limits to the Market Stabilisation Scheme. As expected, there was a steep appreciation of the rupee consequent upon cessation of intervention in forex markets.

The finance secretary, A.K. Jha, a fellow IAS officer from the Andhra Pradesh cadre, came to Mumbai thereafter and met me at my home. He said that he had been instructed to personally convey to me that the RBI should continue its policies in regard to forex intervention as was being done in the past, and that the government would be fully supportive. He clarified that this instruction was given jointly by the prime minister and the finance minister after a discussion between them. Thereafter we resumed intervention in the forex market to some extent. Many scholars attribute the exchange rate movements in 2007 to a change in the RBI policy on the rate, but in fact, it was due to the unusual circumstances.

The government felt that the forex reserves were enough, and I could not dispute that. The government preferred appreciation to save fiscal costs and to moderate prices at a time when inflation pressures were evident. I gave a high priority to external sector balance and so wanted to intervene to maintain a competitive exchange rate and sustainable current account deficit.

A similar problem of tensions arose in regard to the use of forex reserves to provide finance to domestic entities. The Ministry of Finance asked for the comments of the RBI on a proposal made by Montek Singh Ahluwalia, who had by then become deputy chairman of the Planning Commission. The proposal was that RBI should use a part of the forex reserves available with it to provide funds for development of infrastructure. A detailed note was sent by us to the Ministry of Finance explaining that such a proposal was neither desirable nor feasible.[1]

The subject came up for discussion in the Ministry of Finance when the budget for 2005-06 had to be formulated, and by then Rakesh Mohan, who was earlier deputy governor in the RBI, had joined the ministry as secretary (Economic Affairs). He was, therefore, in a position to explain in detail to the minister the implications of this proposal that was examined by him while he was in the RBI. The issue was deflected by creating a 100 per cent government-owned entity to obtain finances outside government budget and fund infrastructure. Thus there was a vehicle, Indian Infrastructure Finance Company Limited (IIFCL) which could, but was not obliged to, seek funds from forex reserves. But, there was no more discussion about the use of forex reserves.

The subject did not get buried there. The use of forex reserves for investment in infrastructure was mentioned to me by Chidambaram in connection with the discussions on the draft budget speech in February 2007. He wanted to make a reference to the acceptance of recommendations of the Deepak Parekh Committee on infrastructure financing, which included a proposal for the use of forex reserves. Deepak Parekh is a leader in the area of finance, an impartial expert who traverses private entrepreneurship and public policy.

I told him, 'Sir, I read about this report in the newspapers a few days ago. I am not aware of the existence of this committee or its recommendations. So, how can I say anything about it?'

Chidambaram said, 'I myself got this report only a few days back. I can show it to you.'

He walked across to his office table, picked up the report, brought it and showed me the recommendations. One of these was that the forex resources should be lent to the IIFCL for onward lending to the infrastructure companies in India.

I reminded him of the discussions that were held on the subject earlier, in 2004-05, when the question of use of forex reserves to fund infrastructure was mooted.

I said, 'Sir, we went over this ground before and it was settled.'

His reaction was frank. He said, 'We have to do this. We have no choice. It does not matter whether investments made in our infrastructure are a formal part of the reserves or not. We have enough forex reserves. So let us agree on a draft.'

I must admit that there was change in the situation in 2007, compared to 2004 (US$199 bn by end-March 2007 compared to $113 bn by end-March 2004). We had reached a comfortable level of reserves. Further addition to reserves was mainly to maintain stability in exchange rates. So, we could afford to have little less of readily usable reserves. Hence, as proposed by the minister, we agreed on a draft that was incorporated in the budget speech.

The budget speech of 2007-08 recalled the recommendations made by the Deepak Parekh Committee and added: 'Government proposes to examine the legal and regulatory aspects of the recommendation in consultation with the RBI, in order to find an innovative method of enhancing the financial resources for infrastructure.' There is nothing objectionable in the statement since the government would consult the RBI and explore innovative methods.

We prepared a detailed scheme for refinancing by the RBI of forex loans extended by a 100 per cent subsidiary of IIFCL to be located in London to infrastructure companies in India. This procedure amounted to 'round tripping' to circumvent the legal and regulatory provisions. The scheme was approved by the board on my encouragement and it was forwarded to the government promptly within a few weeks of announcement in the budget. Chidambaram did not discuss this issue with me and so I presumed that the government was comfortable with the scheme. There was no reaction from the ministry for several months.

After some months, we received a communication from the government that they wanted investments for infrastructure financing in the London-based company upfront, rather than refinancing of loans extended. We in the RBI took the position that investments were not possible as per our policy, since end use monitoring was difficult. The RBI was keen on refinancing so that it could be assured of utilisation of its funds as loans to the intended beneficiaries.

I received a call from the finance secretary, D. Subba Rao, in November 2007. He explained that the finance minister was unhappy with our stand in this regard, and that he was keen that the mode of financing should be through investments in the London-based company. I explained our position in the matter, and added that if the minister insisted I would have to take the revised proposal to the board. Subba Rao came back to me after a couple of days and told me that the FM was unhappy, and was wondering why it was necessary to take the matter to the board. He added that the FM mentioned that the board was appointed by the government in any case. I explained to him that having obtained the board's approval on the earlier proposal, I would like to go back to it. I assured him that the matter would be brought before the board very soon for its meeting in Kolkata in the early part of December.

The matter was taken to the board. The members of the board were individually briefed by the government. Despite my reservations, having due regard to the wishes of the government as expressed by Subba Rao to the members of the board, I encouraged it to accede to the suggestion of the government. However, the reservations of the board to approve the proposal were also communicated to the government along with the approval. In view of the urgency and sensitivity, the resolution of the board on this subject was approved in the meeting, to enable prompt communication to the government. The tense moments were behind me.

Was the finance minister or the government unreasonable? In some ways, yes; but they observed due process and respected the diverse views. There were some instances in other countries where governors were summarily dismissed precisely because of their resistance to attack on forex reserves by governments. It is significant that neither of us talked to each other about this event after the budget speech of February 2007.

The accumulation of reserves was not unrelated to the capital account management. I thought it appropriate to provoke an academic and policy debate on the subject as soon as I experienced difficulties in resisting large capital inflows. I flagged the issue on 12 January 2005, in connection with the release of the India Development Report in Mumbai. I made a reference to Tobin tax in passing in the context of volatile capital flows. Tobin tax is defined as a tax on all conversions of one currency into another, and it is intended to put a penalty on short-term capital flows.

Within an hour from the time of the delivery of the speech in the evening, I received a call from Chidambaram on the reference to the tax in my speech.

He said, 'You have referred to the Tobin tax. I am getting lot of enquiries. What did you say in your speech?'

I responded by saying, 'Sir, this speech is in the context of medium-term prospects and challenges of the Indian economy. I referred to the issue of discretionary and non-discretionary price-based measures for capital account management. Tobin tax is one of them. It was an academic forum.'

Chidambaram said, 'I will tell the media that you made a statement only as an academic matter. I will tell them that I have consulted the governor. I will also assure them that there is no such proposal before the government. Honestly, Venu, I think you should not have made a comment relating to a fiscal matter.'

I clarified that I had to explain the position in the speech in the context of medium-term issues of the Indian economy and, in particular, destabilising capital flows, and that I illustrated various options in this regard.

I concluded, 'But certainly, sir, you should say that you have sought my explanation, and I clarified that it was meant to be only an academic debate from my side.'

I must confess that I was aware of the possible consequences of my statement in the speech. As per my normal practice, I had discussed the draft with all the three concerned heads of departments in the RBI. Two of them pointed out that this statement regarding capital account measures could be very sensitive, and advised me against making it. However, I chose to make it and I told them that it was my decision. I was aware that this would be provocative, but I felt that I had to flag it as a matter of concern for the central bank. I did not, however, anticipate a virulent attack from market participants, in particular, the electronic media. Finally, I was compelled to call for a meeting with the media late in the evening and issue clarifications. Further, I had to order changes in one sentence in the speech that was already put on the RBI website, the same night.

Tobin tax was not the only issue on which we had differences in regard to capital account management. The issue of participatory notes stands out, since they have been associated with black money. Participatory notes are financial instruments through which overseas investors invest in India without revealing their identity to the regulators. Hence, they provided a mechanism for round-tripping, that is, taking money illegally out of India and then investing in India thereby escaping taxation. A decision was taken by RBI in September 2003 to stop investments by OCBs in India to avoid such round-tripping. However, my attempts to persuade the government to impose a similar ban on participatory notes had not been successful. Chidambaram felt strongly that the issue of participatory notes should be settled and the matter clarified. Therefore, he appointed an expert group under the chairmanship of Ashok Lahiri, chief economic advisor. A nominee of the RBI was a member.

The expert group recommended an approach to participatory notes which we in the RBI considered to be excessively liberal. The representative of the RBI was, however, isolated in the expert group. The draft, therefore, contained the recommendations acceptable to all other members. I instructed the RBI nominee that he should not sign unless the reservations of the RBI were incorporated in a dissent note.

In view of the pressure from the government that the nominee of the RBI should sign the report since it contained the recommendations of the expert group, I decided to ring up the finance minister. I explained to him that we had serious reservations on the recommendations, and if the RBI nominee on the expert group had to sign, he could do so only with a note of dissent. I explained that a note of dissent by the RBI nominee in a government-appointed expert group would be unprecedented and it was better that such a situation was avoided. I suggested that the committee could give an innocuous report and leave it to the government to decide.

Chidambaram said, 'No. The matter should be settled. If a dissent note is inevitable, so be it.'

I pleaded with him to think over it for a couple of days and then call me back with his decision. I would abide by it. Presumably, out of regard for me, he agreed to it. After a couple of days he rang me up.

Chidambaram said, 'Venu, I thought about it. Let the report be signed with or without dissent note.'

I told him, 'Sir, the RBI nominee will definitely sign with a dissent note.'

The report was finally submitted by the chairman along with the dissent note. The dissent note explicitly brought on record the serious concerns of the RBI in this regard to perpetuating participatory notes.[2] A standoff like the one in PNs was the exception than the rule in our interaction.

The finance minister made an announcement in the budget of 2007 that housing mortgage insurance companies would be permitted in the Indian financial markets. The announcement came in the background of such guarantee companies failing in developed economies. The RBI was called upon to draw up the guidelines for setting up the companies. We were aware of the weaknesses in their operations in other countries. So, we drafted detailed guidelines, taking care to ensure that the companies would be strong and not vulnerable. The guidelines were to be approved by the government, before they were notified by the RBI. The government mentioned that the guarantees invoked by banks on default of the mortgage loans underwritten by the companies would be paid only after the banks had exhausted all avenues available for recovery and there was a final shortfall. The government felt that the minimum capital adequacy ratio of fifteen per cent suggested for guarantee companies by the RBI in the draft guidelines was on the high side. The global financial conglomerates that were keen on this business felt that our stipulations, especially on capital adequacy, were unrealistic, and Chidambaram appeared convinced about their stand. The government finally approved the guidelines as drafted by the RBI, and on the same day the RBI issued the final guidelines. Chidambaram did not take up the issue with me at any stage, but his annoyance was conveyed to me.

I was surprised to learn in August 2007 that the Foreign Investments Promotion Board had cleared investments by global conglomerates in a holding company that was to be established in order to bring ICICI and all its subsidiaries under one umbrella. However, for purposes of operationalising the approval, the RBI had to issue a letter of approval. We in the RBI did not yet have any established policy in this regard. We did not have a regulatory framework in position. We formed a working group under the chairmanship of an executive director to consider the desirability of holding structures and the appropriate regulatory framework for permitting such companies. The intention was that the follow-up action on the approval of the Foreign Investment Promotion Board could be taken by the RBI after the regulatory framework was finalised. This took considerable time because of the complexities. I suspect that I was not consulted because my opposition to the proposal could have been anticipated. Chidambaram did not raise the subject in our discussions.

I opposed the proposal made in February 2008 to write off loans to farmers amounting to Rs 60,000 crore. I argued my case before the finance minister, and at one stage before the prime minister accompanied by the finance minister. Economic logic including preservation of credit culture was in favour of the RBI's position. During the discussions, references were made to precedents of periodic write-offs in the past, urban-rural divide in growth, social unrest and farmers' suicides. The arguments advanced were on the following lines. Fifty per cent of the population dependent on agriculture had to be content with 15 per cent of GDP. Worse, their capita incomes were growing at about two per cent, while for the rest it was a multiple of that. This was a threat to social order unless immediate concern was demonstrated. Loan waiver was the best fit for this.

I could see the government was acting out of broader concern for the welfare of farmers. I suggested that the government should pay the money to the banks on behalf of the farmers. This would help spare the banking system from any financial burden. Since the fiscal position of the country did not give enough room to provide for the expenditure from the budget, we suggested that the banks could be compensated by providing budgetary support over two financial years, but within a period of six months. I added that we could take this into account and provide for an enhanced transfer of surpluses from the RBI to the government. The scheme was implemented accordingly. I believe that as governor, I could advance arguments from the point of view of money and credit, but I had no legitimacy to question the judgement of the government on social order.

Monetary policy and management of the external sector are considered within the parameters of economic reforms. Chidambaram and I were in agreement on the broad directions of the reforms in the financial sector, that is, broadly rebalancing in favour of markets and designing a monetary regime and a financial sector that would serve the country in terms of higher growth with stability. However, we had differences of opinion and in judgement on the sequencing of reforms across the sectors, that is, finance vis-à-vis other sectors of the economy. There were also genuine differences in regard to the priorities for reform within the financial sector, especially between banking and capital markets.

Consistent with the prevailing beliefs, Chidambaram was keen that the financial sector should lead the process of reform. I had, however, taken the view that there should be reasonable amount of market elements in the real sector. For example, severe restrictions on access to trade in goods, infrastructure and non-financial services undermine genuine competition. Premature liberalisation of financial markets might result in misallocation of resources and induce distortions in the markets. The financial sector can facilitate and enable growth of the real sector but cannot lead or induce economic growth. He was of the opinion that the reforms in the real sector were not a pre-condition and, in any case, such reforms would take a long time. Hence, he felt that the financial sector reform could not wait and it might even induce reforms in the real sector.

The state of finances of the government was in urgent need of improvement, and fiscal consolidation was considered important by both of us. It meant that ideally current revenues should meet current expenditures (elimination of revenue deficit) and borrowings by the government (fiscal deficit) may be restricted to a reasonable level. I was particular that the fiscal consolidation should take place before, and the financial sector reform should follow rather than precede consolidation in the fiscal sector. Chidambaram demonstrated considerable consolidation in the fiscal arena and felt that reforms and liberalisation in the financial sector were slower than the progress in fiscal consolidation. While I deeply appreciated the progress that was being made in fiscal consolidation, I felt that the pace of the financial sector reform had to take into account the possible fiscal slippages in view of the political economy (namely, persons and groups with common interests using politics to affect changes beneficial to their sectional interests) considerations in our country. It is extremely difficult to roll back progress in financial sector reform unless there is a crisis, while the fiscal position can easily slip, and hence I wanted a firm and convincing evidence of fiscal consolidation to accelerate the pace of financial sector reforms significantly.

I pointed out that the level of financial repression in India with continued existence of cash reserve ratio and statutory liquidity ratio at elevated levels put the financial institutions at a disadvantage compared to the financial institutions outside the country if our financial markets were opened up excessively. Above all, I was clear that the public sector banks were vulnerable in view of their limited capacities to participate in sophisticated financial market operations. While Chidambaram could appreciate many of these arguments, his major concern was maintaining the reform credentials and the pressure from various quarters to expedite the financial sector reform. Yet, after detailed discussions, we could arrive at a path that moved forward in reform on several fronts, without taking unacceptable risks. All measures in this regard were announced by Chidambaram after deliberations between the two of us, with a few exceptions.

Within the financial sector, I felt that the reform of public sector banks was most critical since banking dominates the Indian economy and public sector banks dominate the whole banking system. However, the skill levels in the organisations and the governance arrangements were not in a position to respond appropriately to the reforms of the financial sector without serious damage to their balance sheets. He was inclined towards consolidation in the public sector banks as a route to efficiency. I was not equally enthusiastic with consolidation because I felt that the issues in regard to public sector banking had more to do with the structure of governance and political economy, and not the size. In regard to all the improvements of the public sector banks that were possible under these circumstances, we were on the same page.

Chidambaram was also totally supportive of merger of weaker private sector banks with other banks, preferably other private sector banks. Thus, the banking system could virtually get rid of almost all banks with which there was a regulatory discomfort. This process is usually resisted by the political leadership till a crisis occurs, but Chidambaram provided unstinted support in this regard. Formal approvals of the government were needed for several actions which had to be obtained in utmost secrecy and great urgency. He obliged us even outside office hours.

Improvement in standards of governance in banks was given priority by my predecessor. I continued with the policy and this was also supported.

A major area of disagreement between us related to the development of financial markets. Chidambaram was keen about development of bond currency derivatives in an integrated manner. I explained that there were other priorities for financial sector reform. I was particular that the integrity of financial markets was important. In regard to debt markets, my position was that most parts of the debt markets relate to the government securities and the government securities market provides the basis for many benchmark rates. Hence, the development of the government debt markets had to be given a priority, and on this there was an agreement between us. We also agreed that the report of a committee headed by R.H. Patil should be the basis of reform in corporate debt markets. There were differences only in respect of sequencing of elements of reforms relating to corporate debt. Most of the corporate debt was privately placed or listed, but seldom traded actively, which were areas of concern.

After the budget of 2007, in the latter half of the year, Rangarajan wanted my suggestions for the position of chairman, Thirteenth Finance Commission. I offered myself as a candidate and I told Rangarajan that I would be happy to leave the present position since my relations with the minister were not as smooth as I would have liked them to be. After a few days, Rangarajan told me: 'I mentioned to the finance minister that you are keen to go to the Finance Commission. The minister said that he was not willing to release you. Chidambaram said: "Even if Venu wants to go, I would like him to stay."'

Despite the unwillingness of the finance minister to relieve me, I felt that there was a growing distance between us as the months passed by. His image as a reformer pushing for double-digit growth was, in his view, being dented by my caution to the extent of resisting implementation of some of his policies. At one stage, he said that he was cancelling his foreign tour because he could not face foreign investors with nothing to report on reform. His frustration was confirmed later, I think in early 2008.

I got a call from the Prime Minister's Office to say that I should travel to Delhi and meet the prime minister urgently, that too on a Sunday. Normally, the prime minister would not entertain visitors on a Sunday. I flew to Delhi not knowing what it was about, and after arrival, I rang up the finance minister, as I usually did, and informed him that I had been asked by the prime minister to meet him, and that I did not know the subject. I wanted to know whether he would like me to keep anything in mind, but he said: 'There is nothing from my side.'

I met the prime minister in his house. He told me that he was having a fever. He was looking tired, and somewhat tense. He said: 'Venu, the finance minister is very upset with you. I do not know what to do. I cannot be taking sides between Chidambaram and you. I am very worried about this.' I responded: 'Sir, you have many worries. You have many important issues. You please take care of your health. You need not bother about this problem. I will take care of my relations with the minister.' He thanked me profusely. From the PM's residence, I called Chidambaram over the phone and said that I would like to straightaway drop by at his home. He said, 'There is no need for you to come.' I replied: 'Sir, I am coming, and I will not take more than a minute.' I put down the phone without waiting for the answer and reached his home on Safdarjung Road, right around the corner from the PM's house, within a few minutes.

I had called him on impulse but I did not think of what I would say. I could discuss with him and sort out the differences, so that we could work together, but I did not think that it was possible for both professional and personal reasons. I could resign and quit on health grounds, but that would be letting down the prime minister, who was always positive with me. It would not be fair.

I recalled the book release event in Mumbai in mid-June 2007. Chidambaram was releasing his book titled *A View from the Outside: Why Good Economics Works for Everyone*. I bought a copy of the book and took it to him for his signature. He wrote on the flyleaf, 'For Governor Y.V. Reddy, one of my Economic

Gurus.' I felt that I should be warm and pleasant to a person who expressed such regard, despite our differences at the official level.

I decided that I would render an unconditional apology for offending him in the past, and do nothing more. I could keep the option of retiring any time.

When I met Chidambaram he was unusually formal. He felt that while he was very supportive, the RBI was not adequately reciprocating by progressing with reforms. I expressed my unconditional apology to him and conveyed that I would keep in mind the issue of being supportive.[3]

A couple of months before the end of my tenure, Rangarajan told me that Prime Minister Manmohan Singh was considering reappointing me as governor. I told him that I was already sixty-seven years old and, in any case, my relations with the minister were not great. He said that prime minister was thinking of a two-year and not one-year reappointment. Apparently, the PM was not sure about the political developments in the near future and wanted to secure the financial sector. Rangarajan asked me for my reaction to convey to the PM. I thought for a while and said: 'Sir, I want to be relieved. But you can say that I will accept a three-year extension.' I said this with the intention of politely conveying my rejection of the offer. Nothing happened after that.

As my tenure was coming to an end, there was a rumour that I might accept an extension if it were offered. I had written in my New Year message to all officers and staff that I would be retiring that year. I wanted everyone, including me, to be assured that I would not continue beyond my current tenure. I conveyed to those interested that I had already sought and taken farewell at BIS, Switzerland, in July.

The board met on 14 August 2008, and by that time no orders were issued about my successor. Rumours continued that I might have to postpone my departure. To convey that I would not continue as governor beyond the current tenure, I gifted the members a book titled *The Last Lecture* by Randy Pausch and Jeffrey Zaslow. The book, based on Pausch's lecture on 17 September 2007, literally his last one, is described as a one-of-a-kind last lecture that made the world stop and pay attention. I wanted to convey to the board that it was indeed the last board meeting I would attend. Farewell speeches were made by the members thereafter.

Chidambaram and I worked closely for over four years. Most of our tensions could be described as constructive or as discord that ultimately gave rise to better ideas or outcomes.

I moved out of the RBI on 5 September 2008. Chidambaram left finance and became home minister soon on 30 November.

28

WE PLAN – GOD LAUGHS

There is a quote by Woody Allen: 'If you want to make God laugh, tell him about your plans.' Apparently, the original is an old Yiddish proverb: 'We plan. God laughs.' I am reminded of this whenever I recall my life after being governor of the RBI. I was ready to move to vanaprastha, a transition from the centre of action to detachment from worldly concerns.

I was resurrected from vanaprastha as a fallout of the full-fledged global financial crisis that struck within two weeks after my retirement.[1] If the crisis had occurred a few months later, my work in the Reserve Bank might have gone unnoticed. If it had occurred while I was in office, I might have been battered. But in the events that followed, I came into the limelight to be labelled as a 'saviour' and a 'wise man'.[2]

Early in October 2008, my consent to be a member of the Commission of Experts of the president of the UN General Assembly on Reforms of the International Monetary and Financial System was sought. Professor Joseph Stiglitz was chairman, with sixteen members, from a diverse set of countries, background and perspectives. I agreed because I could continue to live in Hyderabad; it was honorary; part-time and I felt that it was an honour to me. Most important, it was a recognition of the growing stature of the Indian economy in global governance.

Work on a global monetary and financial system in the Stiglitz Commission was intellectually rewarding. It lasted for almost one year, till the end of 2009. Members included serving and former governors as well as finance ministers and eminent academics, but financial market participants were represented by only person. Those not holding official positions were more regular in their attendance at meetings, and the deliberations took us to New York, Geneva, Kuala Lumpur, Berlin and The Hague.

We in the Stiglitz Commission raised some questions about the global crisis and tried to answer them. What went wrong? Flawed economic philosophies and policies; and flawed institutional arrangements especially at international levels, facilitated a process of globalisation that led to instability. What had been done? Unprecedented global cooperation to stimulate the economies; emergence of G-20 as a forum for such cooperation; and commitments of international financial institutions to reform. What should be done? There was a broad agreement on a range of reforms in the monetary system, financial architecture and regulation of the financial sector. The criticality of provision of global public goods for the welfare of all was emphasised to strengthen the regulation of the financial sector.

The value of the report lies in that there was agreement on some common themes. Growing inequalities in most countries have contributed to weak effective demand. The crisis has to be seen as global and responses too, therefore, have to be from a global perspective. There are large asymmetries in the economic order. The financial sector has failed to perform its key role of allocating capital and managing risk. Economic globalisation outpaced the development of political institutions required to manage it well. In particular, globalisation of finance and incentive structures favouring excessive risk taking in a deregulated financial market led to the failure of markets.

What were the recommendations? The recommendations were in favour of increased role for public policy and inter-governmental coordination. We were conscious of the needs of developing countries, the dangers posed by growing inequalities, the impact of policies on environment, and the inadequacies of the international financial architecture. Simply stated, our recommendations tilted strongly in favour of what was desirable rather than what was feasible. Their value lay in the comprehensiveness of approach to reap the benefits of globalisation without its financial costs. We focused on the importance of global public goods and global institutional structures to deliver the benefits. The recommendations reflected broad agreement but there was no unanimity.[3]

What happened to the recommendations of the commission? The report was discussed in the UN General Assembly in June 2009, ending with the issuance of a statement. The president of the Assembly likened its influence to that of the moon upon the tides – it pulled the debate away from manifestly superficial concerns towards systemic issues. The report had no formal official status, in the sense that the commission was appointed by the president despite reservations among several member states. The IMF and World Bank were uncomfortable with initiatives from a large and politically oriented United Nations on matters in their jurisdiction. By then, G-20 came into prominence as an influential voice in matters relating to the crisis.

For me, work with the commission provided an opportunity to exercise my personal freedom to travel, think, interact, learn, express at will and, above all, acquire valuable and lasting friendships. During deliberations, they often sought from me what they described as wise counsel on contentious issues, perhaps, implying that knowledge in depth was not my strong point!

Who was sleeping at the wheel when the global finance was cruising towards a crash? A core mandate of the IMF is to assess the risks and vulnerabilities that the member countries' economies face. The mechanism of surveillance by it has been devised to facilitate such assessment. How did the IMF perform in terms of its surveillance, in the run-up to the financial and economic crisis? In 2010, the Independent Evaluation Office (IEO) of the IMF undertook such an evaluation of the surveillance from 2004 to 2007. In view of the complexity of the task, the IEO constituted an advisory group to discuss preliminary findings, conclusions and recommendations. The group had ten members, almost all of them former central bank governors, while William White was a former chief economist of the BIS. Three of us, E. Sakakibara, known popularly as Mr Yen, former vice minister in the finance ministry of Japan, and I were common to the Stiglitz Commission and the advisory group. The group broadly agreed that the fund failed to warn its members about the risks and vulnerabilities. What were the reasons?

Analytical weakness was one of them. The fund had not analysed the link between the financial and the real sector. Despite concerns expressed by some of us in emerging economies, the fund assumed that there could not be a crisis in advanced economies. Further, the fund assumed that advanced economies, in any case, know how to manage their risks. The governance structure of the IMF, dominated by the advanced economies, especially the US and Europe, encouraged such presumptions. That pressure was exerted by major countries in the surveillance work, both bilateral and multilateral, was evident. The mentality of the professionals in IMF to think in silos added to the problem. Recommendations of the evaluation followed the diagnosis, but the most important message of the report, which was strongly endorsed by us, was to encourage the professionals to 'speak truth to power'.

One message of the advisory group, which reflected my strong views, was that the fund should change its culture towards greater candour in its assessments, and greater openness to alternative views. My main contribution to the discussions was sharing my experiences in dealing with the fund, which tended to collaborate with the government in defending the prevailing orthodoxy, especially in the management of the external sector. The Evaluation Report has since been put in the public domain.[4]

The fund under the leadership of Oliver Blanchard, economic counsellor, took up for serious consideration the major issues of analytical weaknesses in the fund that led to its failure in understanding what was going on in the global economy. The IMF hosted a conference on 'Macro and Growth Policies in the Wake of the Crisis' in its headquarters, on 7 and 8 March 2011. There was a galaxy of economists such as Joseph Stiglitz, Michael Spence, Dani Rodrik and David Romer to share their thoughts. Former bank governors and former finance ministers participated to share their experiences and render advice. The aim of the conference was to distil the policy lessons of the global financial crisis and advise member countries on economic and financial policies. My paper was titled 'Financial Crisis and Financial Intermediation – Asking Different Questions'. After the crisis, if the same questions as before were posed, it was possible that the answers would be the same or at least within the fundamental beliefs that existed before. Asking a different set of questions or the same questions put differently could give new insights.

I suggested that reform of the financial sector should address the role it was intended to play, especially in terms of social benefits and cost, and consider the diversity of experiences in different countries – as for example the US, Canada, Australia, China and India. We did not know in advance which standards were good and which were risky. In this light, we should set the limits to setting rigid international standards of regulation. I emphasised the links between financial sector policies and other policies, in particular, monetary and fiscal policies – my pet theme. I flagged the issue of capture of regulation by the market participants that could draw support from political elements. Basically, my question related to re-balancing between state and market, real and financial sectors, and also between national and global approaches.

The summing up by Oliver Blanchard was brilliant, which was on the following lines: The pendulum has swung somewhat from markets to the state. Macro-economic policy is a game with many targets and instruments. We cannot ignore the political economy issues that surround the use of macro-economic instruments. A pragmatic and a step-by-step approach to policy reform is called for. We should keep our hopes in check.[5]

It was clear from the deliberations in the Stiglitz Commission and our discussions in IMF that the international monetary system is not in a position to cope with the challenges of increasing globalisation of finance. The G-20 leaders also agreed in their meeting in 2010 in Toronto on the common goal to build a more stable and resilient monetary system. Three eminent persons associated with global monetary management, Michel Camdessus, Alexandre Lamfalussy and Tommaso Padoa-Schioppa, took the initiative to convene a group to explore avenues for reform of the existing system. This was christened as the Palais-Royal Initiative. The conveners, informally designated as the troika, were all from Europe. Camdessus was chief of the IMF for a long time, Lamfalussy was economic advisor in the BIS at a critical period of its evolution and Padoa-Schioppa played a crucial role in the design of the European Central Bank, and was later finance minister of Italy. (He was elected as chair of the International Monetary and Finance Committee, for which Chidambaram was also a contender). They had international stature to assemble a group of eighteen former ministers, central bank governors and officials in national and international institutions for the purpose. Paul A. Volcker, chair of the Federal Reserve, and Horst Koehler, former MD of the IMF and former president of Germany, were also members and took active interest in the work.

I agreed to join the group. A major reason for the initiative appeared to be the fact that France was chairing the forthcoming G-20 in 2011, and President Sarkozy was keen on reforms in the global economic order. In the prevailing non-system, the US dollar was performing the function of global money with the attendant adverse impact on the global economy, and this initiative was a renewed effort to promote an alternative, namely, Special Drawing Rights.

Some explanation about the prevailing monetary non-system may be in order. Most of the global trade is denominated in US dollars. The financial assets are denominated in it. A major part of forex reserves by central banks are held in dollars too. In the absence of a globally acceptable currency, the dollar is doubling up as the national currency of the US and as global currency. The monetary authority of the US is required under its mandate to regulate the supply of currency to serve the interests of the US. But the demand for the currency is on account of both the needs of the US and of the global economy. When the interests of both the US and the global economy converge, there is no problem, but that may not always be the case. Some in the US feel that it is in a privileged position to print money that is used as currency globally while others feel that such a privilege also means that global demands on its currency affect the conduct and effectiveness of its policy. It may be tempting for the US to incur deficits. This in brief is the global monetary non-system, where the dollar is performing a function that it is not designed to do. The objective of the group was to suggest a feasible alternative.

In an increasingly globalised world, the non-system contributed to ineffective global adjustment processes, financial excesses, destabilising capital flows, volatile exchange rates that often deviated from fundamentals, and excessive expansion of global reserves. The challenge before the Palais-Royal Initiative was to design a system that would create a currency to replace the dollar as international reserve currency. Such a system would need to be backed by arrangements to increase or decrease the supply of the currency. The governance of the IMF, which has legitimacy to evolve such a system, has to be reformed to enable acceptance of it.

The leadership in China and Europe were keen to replace the dollar. Opinion was divided in the US on whether it was a privilege or a burden, but on balance it preferred the status quo. A common summing up of the US attitude is: 'My currency. Your problem.' The objective of the initiative was to present a package of reform that transcended such narrow national considerations, in favour of the larger good of a globalised world. The package had to address five basic issues, namely, ensuring effective surveillance by IMF; appropriate exchange rate regimes, a level of global liquidity that was neither excessive nor deficient, enlarged role of SDR and an acceptance of governance arrangements. The group of common friends and colleagues did come up with a package that represented consensus, but most of us were not very optimistic about the outcome. As Padoa-Schioppa said: 'Ours will appear a Utopian task to those who still dream of a simple marginal adaptation of the status quo.'

The suggestions of the Palais-Royal Initiative are a mix of exhortation and practical steps. It urges member countries to follow policies conducive to stability, support the surveillance, enforce compliance, especially by the systemically relevant countries, and develop positive incentives to compliance. The IMF is urged to develop globally consistent exchange rate 'norms' from which each country is expected to refrain from deviating. It suggests that the IMF and BIS should work towards a shared analytical approach. Central banks of systemically relevant economies are urged to conduct their macro-prudential policies taking account of the need for global liquidity conditions. It accepts the need for capital controls to prevent disorderly exchange rate movements. It wants the IMF to work with relevant government mechanisms akin to a global lender of last resort. It suggests a greater role for SDR in the international monetary system.

On the composition of the SDR basket, it reiterates the requirement that only currencies widely used in international payments and financial transactions should be part of the SDR basket. On governance, it proposes a three-level integrated architecture, namely, heads of government or states, finance ministers and central bank governors and executive directors.

I had no difficulty in going along with the thrust of suggestions. I was enlightened by the discussions and deep divisions between the Anglo-Saxon and the European view. Tomasso Padoa-Schioppa passed away a few days after the penultimate meeting; but the hope was that the initiatives would be considered seriously, coming as they were from people familiar with the difficulties of reconstructing the system. I did not share the optimism, and it was a fond hope. I suspect that many others were also in agreement with my reservations, but we simply had no better alternative.[6]

As mentioned earlier, the G-20 had emerged by 2010 as an important forum for coordinated action among major economies of the world to avert severe economic depression. It commenced deliberations on new directions for global economic cooperation, going well beyond managing the crisis. It was perceived by many non-G-20 countries as an enlarged version of the G-7, a group of advanced economies that coordinated their positions on global issues. In a way, it was serving a useful purpose but lacked legitimacy and representative character. So, a group was constituted at the invitation of the French president, the chair of the G-20 meeting for 2011, but at the initiative of Jean-Paul Fitaussi and Joseph Stiglitz. It prepared an agenda for global governance for the twenty-first century.

My contribution to the preparation of the agenda was on cross-cutting issues. I took the position that the G-20 was rightly contextual, and its importance would and should diminish in due course as the compulsions to coordinate receded. The G-20 was, thus, no substitute for the needed reform in monetary and financial non-systems, in particular, the IMF and World Bank. The recommendations of the group, described as 'An Agenda for Global Governance for the Twenty-first Century' did not reflect my approach.[7]

The global financial crisis is sometimes described as the North Atlantic crisis since the crisis of 1997 was described as the Asian Crisis. In my view, the crisis of 2008 is global in the sense that there is now a worldwide recognition of the need to rethink economics as a discipline; the way it is being practised and taught. One of the initiatives to encourage such a rethinking was the establishment of the Institute for New Economic Thinking (INET). I participated in its conferences and was also on its advisory board. The main promoter of the institute was George Soros, the much-hated currency speculator who caused massive damage to the Bank of England, but that did not deter us as far as our work was concerned. But new economic thinking had to be on the long haul. I could learn a lot from the conferences.[8]

I had to cancel some engagements, take recourse to video conferences in a few meetings and moderate my travels in 2011 and 2012 in view of uncertain health. I concentrated on academic work, but continued with participation in conferences convened by institutions with diverse ideologies. Some of my speeches were published as compilations to reflect my understanding of the global economy and its functioning during the post-crisis period, till 2012.[9]

There were many reasons for the crisis, and each institution emphasised the set of causes that suited their ideological dispositions best. The reforms proposed were also similarly divergent. My approach was to point out to them that some rebalancing of their views on how the global economy functions might be warranted, and in any case, the post-crisis world would be very different from the pre-crisis one. My effort was to explore in what ways it could be different, though I did not anticipate fundamental changes in the global monetary and financial systems.

Climate change and environmental concerns were high in the agenda for financial regulation reform advocated by the Stiglitz Commission, but I did not devote attention to them because I had no expertise or experience. However, I was drawn into the subject by accident. One of the key decisions taken at the UN Conference on Climate Change in December 2010 was to set up a Green Climate Fund (GCF) at the global level. The GCF was to be the new institution to manage long-term finance mobilised to enable developing countries to address climate change. The GCF was to support projects, programmes, policies and other activities in developing country parties. The fund was needed to finance the efforts of developing countries to shift to more efficient energy use as well as less carbon-intensive energy generation and thereby reduce greenhouse gas emission. The task of designing the GCF was to be achieved through a transitional committee with a membership of forty persons drawn from representative countries.

I was persuaded by the Government of India to be on the transition committee. Amongst the forty members finally nominated by the governments, only three of us had association with their central banks, while one of the three chairs, Trevor Manuel, was finance minister in South Africa earlier. My comments and suggestions were mainly on the governance structure of the GCF. During the deliberations, some of the key questions that emerged dealt with the relation that the GCF would have with multilateral development banks. Apparently, India played an important role in securing the agreement on the establishment of the Global Climate Fund. I was pleasantly surprised to learn that the final design of the fund that was operationalised had benefitted from our inputs. But, the fact remains that advanced economies abandoned some of their commitments, in respect of money or otherwise.

I was invited to deliver the Per Jacobsson Lecture on 24 June 2012 at the annual meeting of Central bank governors in Basel, Switzerland. I spoke on 'Society, Economic Policies and

Financial Sector'. I selected the subject since I viewed money and finance as one element of economic policies which are meant to serve the society at large. My initial background was general administration from where I moved to focus on economic policies before becoming a central banker. I will sum up the main message in this speech, which was in the nature of a swan song from me.[10]

It was: the central banks are expected to ensure trust and confidence in money and finance, and avoid the pitfalls of regulatory capture (capture of regulator by the interests of the regulated), while the common person seeks inclusive finance. Central banks need to preserve space for public policy at the national level consistent with their obligations to the global economy. The financial sector may draw lessons from global coordination in other industries, especially in managing networks. Better regulation warrants effective regulation. Consideration of regulation, competition and ownership in an integrated manner, enhanced monitoring of financial market activities and the use of fiscal tools to supplement regulation could be helpful in this regard. Central banks have to ensure that bank managements and the financial sector in general serve the masses, and not merely the elite or the financially active.

29

GAME CHANGER

THE FOURTEENTH FINANCE COMMISSION WAS APPOINTED IN A political flux, and no wonder, its report turned out to be a game changer. By 2012, several chief ministers had acquired political stature to bid for the position of prime minister. By then, the decentralisation in political clout was countered by an increasing centralisation in planning and fiscal relations. Mechanisms like the National Development Council became virtually non-functional and the Inter-state Council had a birth defect as it was located within the home ministry. In the Union government, executive authority and political authority were vested in two different persons. The Planning Commission, a critical institution, in Union–state fiscal relations, was increasingly identified with the Union government. The political system was yearning for a thorough rebalancing in Union–state relations.

In India, the legislative domains of the government are divided between the Union and the states. Their responsibilities and sources of revenue are also allocated as per the Constitution. It mandates the periodic establishment of a Finance Commission by the president, at least once in five years, mainly to recommend sharing of taxes collected by the Union, between the Union and the states. The commission's ambit includes the principles that should govern the grants-in-aid of the revenues of the states from the Union government. All the taxes collected by the Union are shared with the states, normally as per the formula recommended by the finance commissions from time to time. Cesses and surcharges levied by the Union are not divisible. The work of the commission lasts for about two years, and the commission has a heavy schedule of meetings, including with each of the states, many ministries of the Union government, and local bodies.

The meetings with the local bodies in each state are a recent feature, due to the 73rd and 74th Constitutional amendment that deals with grants-in-aid to states by the Union, to help the states support local bodies. Other issues may also be referred to the commission 'in the interest of sound finance'. These are spelt out in the presidential order constituting each finance commission, and hence reflect what the president wants the commission to consider. The recommendations of the finance commission, which are in the nature of an award, are generally valid for a period of five years, that is, until the next finance commission gives its recommendations.

I received a telephone call from R. Gopalan, secretary, finance ministry, seeking my formal consent to be chairman of the Fourteenth Finance Commission (FFC). I was not keen to accept the onerous responsibility. I was advised to convey my response in person to the prime minister, who was then holding the finance portfolio also.

I called on Dr Manmohan Singh. After the usual exchange about the state of the global economy and the prospects for our own, I mentioned to him about the offer of chairmanship of the finance commission and said that I had not given my consent to be considered.

Dr Singh smiled and quipped: 'I gave the consent. Finance Minister Pranab Mukherjee formally proposed your name. I gave the consent on your behalf.'

I mentioned about the stress on my health, and the fact that I was very well settled in Hyderabad. So, I wanted his guidance as to what I should tell Gopalan about the offer. He said: 'Please say yes to him.'

I conveyed my consent.

I did not hear anything more about the matter from anyone for several months. In November 2012, Chidambaram, who had become the finance minister, sought my formal consent to be the chairman of the commission. A notification constituting the Fourteenth Finance Commission was issued on 2 January 2013, with a term up to October 2014.

M. Govinda Rao, a global authority and indisputably the foremost expert on fiscal federalism in India; Sudipto Mundle, a development economist with experience in the Ministry of Finance and the Asian Development Bank; and Sushama Nath, a highly respected IAS officer with experience in finance at the highest levels, both at the Union and the state, were appointed as members. Abhijit Sen, who was a member of the Planning Commission, was appointed as a part-time member of the commission. I had professional and personal relationship with all the economists, while both the prime minister and the finance minister spoke very highly of Sushama Nath. A.N. Jha, a senior officer, was appointed as secretary, and Pinaki Chakraborty was selected by the commission to be the economic advisor.

The terms of reference of the Fourteenth Finance Commission reflected the fundamental changes in the approach to Union–state relations triggered by the political context and economic compulsions. No doubt, the core mandate remained the same, but there were four significant departures.

First, there was no specific mention of the need to treat gross budgetary support to five-year plans as a committed liability of the Union government. Thus, our Finance Commission was not obliged to treat plan expenditures to be beyond the scope of the commission.

Second, in the past, the commissions were obliged to take the base population figures of 1971 in all cases where population was a factor. This time, an opening was created by the terms of reference which said that in addition to the 1971 population, we could take into account demographic changes. This was a significant departure from commitments made earlier before the Parliament on the subject.

Third, the other terms of reference normally included a reference to public enterprises and cost recovery in the states. Now, the reference was not confined to states, and so even-handed treatment of Union and states by the commission was facilitated.

Fourth, we were also required to make suggestions to amend fiscal responsibility legislations.

The game changer was as much the terms of reference of the commission appointed by the UPA government as the acceptance of the recommendations by the NDA government.[1]

Apart from the political context the development debate acquired a new and unprecedented dimension when we commenced our work. There were claims that the Gujarat model or Bihar model, or Kerala or Tamil Nadu model, worked best. This debate demonstrated that many states had acquired institutional capabilities to design and implement their own priorities. It was also a reflection of change in balance between state and market, whereby the policy environment to facilitate private investment at state level played a bigger role than before, relative to fiscal transfers from the Union. The expectations of people on the level and quality of public services varied significantly between states, and the scope for centralised determination of provision of public services was increasingly unacceptable at state level.

Structural changes in the Indian economy also warranted a review of Union–state fiscal relations. The Indian economy was increasingly integrated with the global economy. The Union government had to accept international obligations on subjects in the domain of state governments, such as environmental concerns and Millennium Development Goals. The government required the necessary policy space to undertake counter-cyclical policies and meet challenges arising out of shocks to the global economy. States, depending on their exposure to the external sector, faced the impact of changes in the global economic environment. These structural aspects were not entirely new, but came into sharp focus when we in the commission commenced our work.

The macro-economic outlook at the time when we started our work was uncertain, since the global economy was yet to fully and convincingly restore normalcy or settle for a new normal after the financial crisis in 2008. But, there were enough grounds to conclude that the worst was over, though revival was weak. The fiscal positions of the Union and the states presented an unusual picture. The Union government could not meet its obligations under fiscal responsibility legislation, and had to revise its interpretation and ceilings. In contrast, the state governments as a whole consolidated their fiscal position and emerged stronger. Interestingly, the fiscal expansion of the Union government was not to meet its constitutional obligations under the Union list but substantively on subjects in the state list or concurrent list. The fiscal position of the Union did not leave much scope for increasing the share of the states in aggregate transfers.

We were faced with a dilemma. At a time when the states were demanding greater share and policy space, the finances of the Union government were not in a position to permit enhanced transfers. There was, however, a strong case made by the state governments that legitimate fiscal space to them should be restored both on grounds of efficiency and the spirit of the Constitution. The challenge was to enhance the policy space available to states as demanded by them without significantly enhancing the aggregate transfers from the Union government to the states (aggregate transfers meant all transfers, both on account of the Finance Commission and others).

The work of the commission was divided into three phases. In the first phase, we searched for the right questions to ask and analysed the issues. The second phase was listening and learning, especially from the states, and ministries of the Union. The third phase was deliberating and agreeing on the recommendations. We decided that we would seek the opinion of experts and sponsor studies as was done in the past. We wanted to focus on a study of experiences, in particular of other major emerging markets, such as South Africa, China, and Indonesia.

In the first phase, we focused on discussing emerging issues. First, how deep should we go into the ramifications of the proposed goods and services tax, in view of its political sensitivities and persisting uncertainties? Second, what are the implications of growing global economic integration and policy obligations, such as the environment or Millennium Development Goals, on Union–state fiscal relations? Third, what are the implications of cyclicality in economic management of the fiscal policy space for Union and state? Finally, should the Finance Commission be made a permanent body and should its remit extend to all grants from the Union to states?

Simultaneously, the commission sought data on fiscal and economic and demographic variables from the Union, states, and the comptroller and auditor general on the trends in the past. We also sought the projections of their finances from the Union and states. The secretariat was fully pre-occupied with these, while the commission was exploring answers to the recurring and new questions. We in the commission knew how to conduct business in English and Hindi, the official languages of the Union, but many states have their own official languages. Some political representatives and almost all representatives of local bodies speak in their respective state's official languages. We have fourteen national languages, but official languages at the state level number 39. Among the states with more than four official languages are Jammu and Kashmir, Meghalaya, and Sikkim. We have states which are bigger than half the countries in the world, in terms of population or area. The diversities in the levels of development, religious and cultural practices, geography and attitudes are well recognised. We were aware of all these, but what we did not anticipate was the difficulty in the language of communication.

It was no surprise that a strenuous part of the work in the Finance Commission was in the second phase. We had to visit twenty-eight states, which increased to twenty-nine during our tenure.[2] We spent a couple of days in each state, holding at least four meetings in every capital; with the government, political parties, elected representatives of local bodies and members of trade and industry.

A meeting with the state government where the chief minister presents the views of the state is naturally the most significant. The cabinet and senior bureaucracy would be present to assist the chief minister. In these meetings, sometimes issues well beyond our scope were raised, but we had to respect their concerns also. Sometimes they made what appeared to be unreasonable demands, but we could not sit in judgement on the spot and, in any case, had to listen carefully. Many of them, in particular chief ministers, made representations to us mainly to inform their constituency about what they were demanding from the commission – no matter whether it was fair or relevant or not. We were there to listen, and if we wanted clarifications, we sought them through our officers separately.

Chief ministers come from different backgrounds and views, temperaments, styles and substances. Each has his or her unique strengths and weaknesses, some of which could be gathered or discerned. I made it a point to study the curriculum vitae of the chief ministers – with a focus on their background and experience in public service. That helped not only in my being well prepared for both formal and informal conversations with them, but also in briefing the commission about what we should be sensitive about.

Many chief ministers had experience in Parliament, some of them as ministers in the Union. One of them had entered Parliament in 1962. A large number of them had been chief ministers before the current term. A few of them had dealt with three finance commissions before us, and could give us a lesson or two. One of them had been a chief minister in the 1970s. Several of them had experience at three levels of the government, local, state and national. A few of them had been in more than one political party. There were some who had been imprisoned during the Emergency or in connection with political activity. One of the chief ministers had won elections three times in a row, every time with an increase in majority. In general, those chief ministers who headed a regional party or had strong local political standing tended to be significantly well equipped to make their presentations. The female chief ministers were, by and large, very impressive, in terms of knowledge, command and communication.

The chief ministers in the border states were naturally acutely aware of our relations with neighbouring countries and their bearing on the state's economy and fiscal position. Their religious background was varied – Hindu, Buddhist, Sikh, Jain, Muslim and Christian. Their ethnic backgrounds were also varied – at least one of them tracing ancestry to a province in China. Educational background was also varied, one of them having graduated from St Stephen's College in Delhi half a century ago, one from an Indian Institute of Technology more recently, and a few of them were educated in convents or missionary schools.

Chief ministers displayed different personal styles in dealing with the commission; imperious, informal, formal, reserved, and very forthcoming. A few who were very formal and reserved in formal meetings, tended to be totally relaxed over dinner or lunch. One chief minister regaled us with jokes over dinner, while another actively participated in cultural activities on the stage. One chief minister of a north Indian state could speak fluent Tamil. In a couple of cases, they confined themselves to meeting the commission at a formal level only – not over lunch or dinner. In a few cases, there were one-to-one meetings with me.

In our formal meetings with chief ministers, cabinet ministers and officials, we came across an impressive variety in the style of conducting meetings! In one case, the whole cabinet had to sit in the row behind the chief minister; in some others, almost no one else spoke; while, in a few, there was participation. One of the chief ministers conducted the meeting in a manner that a chief executive of a multinational would – except that he spoke in Hindi most of the time. In a few cases, the chief ministers displayed command over the issues that was amazing; while, in a very few cases, there was delegation of this task to senior officials. In one case, there was indifference to the meeting.

The meetings with the political parties reflected three aspects, namely, their ideological position, mainly left parties; their political alignments in the state; and, their relationship with the chief minister. In one state, the opposition parties did not attend our meeting; in another, there were quarrels; and in a few, criticism of the government of the day. But, in a majority of the cases, they stood united in support of the interests of the state, especially in urging the criteria for devolution of taxes. Interestingly, we expected acrimony among the numerous political parties in a state, but we found strong across-the-board support to the state government.

The meetings with select elected heads of local bodies were the most instructive. The heads of panchayats and municipalities were very clear in what they wanted, they were articulate, and they were closest to the people. They spoke in the official languages of the states concerned, and hence we had to depend on translations in some cases.

Narendra Modi was sworn in as prime minister on 26 May 2014. The commission sought appointments with Prime Minister Modi and Finance Minister Arun Jaitley soon after they were sworn in. We were given an appointment with the finance minister. We had an internal briefing and we decided that we would follow 'a listening brief', though we were prepared with the subject matter. The finance minister welcomed us warmly and it was clear that he had also decided on 'a listening brief'. So, we were listening to each other, with no one addressing any substantive issue relating to our work. Naturally, we had a very pleasant conversation. Everyone kept every option open!

As was customary, the deputy chairman and members of the Planning Commission, including Professor Sen, resigned from their positions after the change in the government. It was expected that Professor Sen, who was appointed as a part-time member of the Finance Commission in his capacity as a member of the Planning Commission, would resign from the Finance Commission also. This was the standard practice in the past, without an exception. Sen consulted me, and I said that I would be quite happy if he continued to work in the finance commission and gave us the benefit of his advice. Sen's continued presence in the commission was of great benefit to its deliberations, as also in its interactions with the ministries and the states.

Since there was a change in the government, we were keen to have an updated presentation by the Ministry of Finance. This was of over-riding importance in determining the macro-economic framework and the parameters of a feasible fiscal path for the national economy. We in the commission decided, in order to be realistic, to be broadly guided by the fiscal path indicated by the ministry.

Within the commission, there was never a dull moment; and thank God, none of us in the commission suffered from a bloated ego. There were tense moments, but they too passed. Once, a member was so upset that he walked out and said he would never again attend a meeting. Of course, he was cajoled and he relented. Another time, the seating arrangement was changed to facilitate peaceful co-existence. There were at least four occasions when I, as chairman, retired to my room, when I could not manage an agreement among the members on some issue. I returned to the meeting only when the members came to an agreement. I must confess that, on each of the occasions, my absence helped build a consensus! On a couple of occasions, I commented that my respect for politicians had gone up, after seeing the three economists arguing with each other, with no agreement in sight. On most occasions, Sushama Nath had the last word because she was very pragmatic, forthright and decisive.

The most contentious discussion in the commission was on identifying a set of activities, such as secondary education, among the centrally sponsored schemes, and allocating each one of them to Union or state, as most appropriate. This had to be with reference to the provisions and spirit of the Constitution, as well as the theoretical framework of appropriate level for decision-making. The discussions focused simultaneously on the central issues: defining the boundaries between public, private and merit goods; ensuring need-based and equitable distribution; and evolving a design which could take care of the diversity across states. Our discussions aimed at a framework for classification led us nowhere. So, we agreed, despite initial resistance from a section, that each one of us would give the classification in writing based on their respective beliefs. The responses were tabulated.

We found to our dismay that those who were pro-Union in their statements, turned out to be pro-state in actual application to specific schemes and vice versa. That was a landmark event in determining the course of thinking. Until then, there had been a virtual split in the commission on whether we were five wise men (persons) who could agree on details of priorities and be prescriptive, or we could leave it to processes. After this exercise, we focused on institutions and incentives that would facilitate sound practice of fiscal federalism specific to an activity. We convinced ourselves that we might not be as wise as many others thought!

Heated and prolonged discussions on complex issues was, but, natural. In regard to vertical balance (that is, division of taxes between Union and states) and fiscal responsibility at the Union level, the major issue was the extent of flexibility needed for the Union to increase or decrease deficits. Some flexibility is needed to manage global uncertainties or domestic shocks and to follow a counter-cyclical fiscal policy. Beyond a point, flexibility may undermine effectiveness. The incorporation of flexibility in the relevant law was also an issue – taking account of global practice and our assessment of the political economy. In regard to horizontal balance (distribution of taxes between the states out of the total share in vertical balance), the issue was reconciliation of conflicting considerations of backwardness, reward for performance, and incentive for conducive policies. Several simulations were undertaken and each of the solutions to a problem created new problems. At least one member felt strongly that the commission was giving a wrong signal by not explicitly recognising priority to social sector expenditures and put up a valiant fight, though he fell short of appending a dissent note. The dominant view was that the commission should stay out of sectoral priorities.

There was also a concern that a single uniform target for the states would not be appropriate as their fiscal sustainability levels varied widely. We, therefore, decided to provide greater borrowing space to the states with better fiscal sustainability numbers in terms of debt to GSDP ratio and interest payments to own revenue ratio.

We applied the idea of default option in public policy advocated in the book *The Nudge* by Richard H. Thaler and Cass R. Sunstein. The default option means that if you do not decide or till you decide, what we propose will amount to your decision. We intensively debated whether the state governments should be free to evolve criteria for distribution among the local bodies in each state, or it should be on the basis of the criteria prescribed by the FFC. Ultimately, we gave a formula for distribution of funds among local bodies by a state, which could be replaced once a state finance commission gave its recommendations. We faced complex issues in regard to local bodies because of several incongruities in the constitutional arrangements, precedents and experience gained so far. We were unanimous in supporting the local bodies, and we had to find a simple and defensible way of doing it.

We had intensive discussions on several drafts of chapters from April 2014 and overall, we had come to an agreement on the articulation of views and recommendations. Drafting skills were displayed in an impressive manner by everyone in the commission, as we went through several revisions of each chapter. A final draft of every chapter was submitted by the secretary for comments and approval to each member in the month of November. It was agreed that the commission would sign the report on the morning of 5 December 2014. The secretariat made all the arrangements accordingly, and the report was approved on the 5th with a dissent note dated 4 December.[3]

Our report has been described as a game changer or watershed in fiscal federalism in India mainly because it has fundamentally changed the vertical balance, nature and design of transfers from Union to states. The share of devolution of all taxes collected by Union to states increased from 32.0 per cent to 42.0 per cent (the Thirteenth Finance Commission had increased the states' share from 30.5 per cent to 32.0 per cent and the Twelfth Finance Commission from 28.0 per cent to 30.5 per cent). The increase in tax devolution has enhanced the flow of unconditional transfers to the states. As a result, more than 70 per cent of the total resources transferred from the Union to states will be in the form of untied transfers, instead of less than 50 per cent. This award gave an unprecedented increase in untied fiscal space to the states to design their own programmes for development and not necessarily an increase in aggregate transfers.

A game changer is usually good for some, but not so good for some others. The large increase in vertical devolution has, of course, reduced the scope for financing what are considered by the Union government of the day to be nationally important centrally sponsored schemes. Similarly, not recognising special and non-special category states may potentially have adverse implications on the finances of special category states, depending on how transfers from Union to states outside tax devolution and grants-in-aid take place. By taking aggregate expenditure rather than non-plan expenditure, the Finance Commission has undermined the scope for plan transfers and thus the process of planning.

What is new in our report? We refrained from giving critical policy advice ether to the Union or the states, reduced discretionary elements in transfers and ensured fiscal space for each level of the government to carry out its constitutionally assigned functions. At the same time, we fully acknowledged the role of the Union government's interventions on functions and programmes that have nation-wide externalities. The framework of federalism proposed by us seeks to ensure that central intervention does not result in proliferation of one-size fits all centrally sponsored schemes. We felt that the Union is not bestowed with superior wisdom or knowledge or integrity beyond what was envisaged in the Constitution, though we were aware of the different standards of governance in different states. We did not take account of categorisation of states, that is, special category by the Union government. We, however, suggested that the new institutional arrangement proposed by us should consider the inter-state infrastructure needs of north-eastern states.

For me, a matter of satisfaction is that our report points to a new mindset that should govern treatment of Union–state fiscal relations. Every tier of the government – Union, state, local – should be regarded as equally accountable and responsible for the functions assigned to it. At the same time, the existence of overlapping responsibilities should be recognised and mechanisms put in place for their discharge. Clarity in regard to respective jurisdictions, including overlapping responsibilities, will add to healthy Union–state relations. The Directive Principles of State Policy of the Constitution or national priorities are of equal concern to the Union and state governments. Globally, debt as well as expenditures of sub-national levels are generally increasing as a proportion of general government expenditures and such trends should be analysed in their relevance to our systems. Further, globalisation of economic activity and need for provision of global goods cast special responsibility on the Union. These do have an impact on Union–state fiscal relations. The new economic realities, including globalisation, may warrant greater involvement of the Union government in many ways, but they do not necessarily justify intrusion into the legitimate fiscal space of the states accorded by the letter and spirit of the Constitution.

I must confess to a minor disappointment, namely, the time taken to accept the recommendations, which were eventually acted upon.

As is customary, I called on the finance minister along with the secretary and submitted to him a copy of our report after submission to the president on 15 December. I explained to the finance minister that we had worked hard to complete the report in advance of the terminal date, to facilitate a timely decision that would help both the Union and states to chalk out the transition path, as part of budget exercises which were soon due. We got it translated into Hindi and, thus, provided both the English and Hindi versions in adequate numbers for distribution in Parliament, in case the government took an immediate decision. I urged the finance minister to take an early view on the recommendations of the Finance Commission for a very important reason. I explained to him that the recommendations were far reaching. Therefore, the Union and state governments should have an adequate opportunity to prepare their budgets on the basis of new realities recommended by the commission. The finance minister gave me an impression that he was keen to accept our advice and proceed accordingly in a few days. Jha and I called on Prime Minister Modi also, a few days later. We explained to him the basic features of our report. He appeared to be fully informed of what we recommended and why we did what. However, he gave no indication of his reactions.

The president appoints the Finance Commission and places the Action Taken Report before Parliament. I called on the president before leaving Delhi for Hyderabad on completion of my work. He discussed several details and it was obvious that he read the report and related its approach to his vast experience with several previous finance commissions, six of them, spread over thirty years. We then recalled our past association. He recalled how he was very keen that I should be the chairman of the finance commission and proposed my name when he was finance minister. He expressed that his trust in me was fully vindicated and that I had lived up to the expectations.

As I was taking leave, Rashtrapati Pranab Mukerjee smiled and said: 'Congratulations. You have really addressed very fundamental issues.'

NOTES

1. A WINDOW TO THE WORLD

1. Though the village sarpanch, or the elected representative, was empowered later, it was the postmaster, teacher, karnam and munsif who still held sway.
2. Like many people at the time, Ayya and Amma began to take Hindi lessons through the Hindi Prachar Sabha.
3. Both villages were in Rajampet taluk of Cuddapah district.
4. It was this experience that I drew upon while making recommendations for the Rayalaseema Development Board in 1971. One of the recommendations was to address the issue of depleting water table, which I noted would be a huge problem.
5. I did not mind the spartan conditions and the discipline. I was miserable because I missed home. I was so homesick that I wrote to my father to take me away, and he replied that he would. But by the time he arrived two weeks later, I told him that I had changed my mind. I wanted to stay.
6. When I went to pay my fees at the college, I was dressed in my usual shorts and shirt. The clerk looked up at me and told me I had come to the wrong place: this was the college; the school was across the street. I told him I had come to college.

   'Why is your name like this?' he said. I did not know what to say; it had always been 'Venugopal Reddy, Yaga'. But the clerk did not think it was correct to have my family name last. He entered it in the college registry as 'Yaga, Venugopal Reddy', which is the proper Telugu format. 'Yaga Venugopal Reddy' is now my official name, though confusion still prevails about whether my last name is 'Yaga' or 'Reddy'. Decades later, when I was appointed executive director, International Monetary Fund, my diplomatic status was not granted for a couple of months. The authorities were in a quandary; they could not decide whether the diplomatic status should be given to 'Reddy' or 'Yaga'.
7. That year, Pinamma threw me a birthday party and called all my friends

and had special snacks made. I was unused to all this attention and effort. That birthday remains one of the best I have ever had.

8. It was the most well-known college in the Ceded Districts (so-named since the then ruler, the Nizam of Hyderabad, had ceded Anantapur and other districts of Rayalaseema, Bellary and Davangere to the British Raj in 1800).
9. In my first play, since I was a newcomer, I had to play the part of a girl. I had to don a bright dress. I put on pancake make-up. But I must have performed reasonably well, because in my next role, I graduated to the role of a policeman.
10. Veeranna was centre forward in the Andhra state football team. He kept himself fit with *vyayam*, traditional Indian exercises that incorporated yogasanas and used ropes, clubs and shovels to build strength.
11. One time, when I was at an NCC camp, I took part in a strike against the food in the mess. This insubordination cost me my promotion to lance corporal in the NCC, but did not improve the food much.
12. Ramesh Murthy taught my children and we kept in touch for sixty years, till he passed away recently.
13. The college, too, was not my first choice. When I arrived in Madras to join Loyola, I called on Chinmatrananda Swamiji, a freedom fighter and my old warden from Ramakrishna Mission High School.

    'Benugopal,' he said, 'why Loyola?' He said it was clear that I should join Ramakrishna Mission's Vivekananda College for which he was the treasurer. So it was settled.
14. Of course, I had my hostel warden's permission.
15. One of the most vivid memories I have are of our college tour. We went to Bombay, Delhi and Calcutta. We travelled by train in a third-class compartment and stayed in modest lodgings, but I had a grand time. The Gateway of India, Victoria Memorial, India Gate: these were thrilling, new sights. In Delhi, we met Jawaharlal Nehru (he shook hands with us and gave us an autograph in English) and then President Rajendra Prasad (whose autograph was in Hindi) and Vice-President Radhakrishnan (who did not give us an autograph at all).

2. THE MAKING OF A BUREAUCRAT

1. It was in this journal that I published my first two research papers (one of them, as a co-author).
2. It was my first appointment as a gazetted officer through a notification in the Gazette of India.
3. I also had the privilege of leading the NCC contingent in the Independence Day parade in Hyderabad on 15 August 1963.
4. It was done through a membership in a cooperative society that managed the land, permissions, etc.

5. Buying as well as selling a car was quite a feat. Selling it within five years of purchase required government permission. The waiting period to buy a new Fiat car was eight to ten years.

5. WORK, STUDY AND WEDDINGS

1. Rama Naidu went on to become a famous movie director.
2. And, in fact, drought relief was only one part of the story. Recovery from drought would be even harder. People needed to replenish their health, their incomes, their stock of seed and fodder, long after the drought and drought relief works were, officially, over.
3. Given by the Swedish National Bank.

6. THE ART OF GETTING THINGS DONE

1. The Sribagh pact assured that the capital city of Andhra Pradesh or the high court would be in the Rayalaseema region. Both these were rescinded in order to persuade Telangana to join united Andhra.
2. The reorganisation of the states was to be done on linguistic considerations.
3. The gentlemen's agreement proposed, among other things, that the balance of income after expenditure would be reserved for Telangana; the admissions to the educational institutions in Telangana be reserved for natives of Telangana; administrative and judicial language for Telangana was to be Urdu; also, either the chief minister or the deputy chief minister was to be from Telangana. Some of these were to be reviewed every few years.
4. The Rayalaseema Board consisted of a chairman of rank of cabinet minister, all the legislators elected from the region and chairmen of zilla parishads of all the four districts in the region, namely, Kurnool, Cuddapah, Anantapaur and Chittoor. Two taluks that were transferred to form Ongole district continued to be treated as part of Rayalaseema while parts of Bellary district that were in Karnataka were not included. An executive committee was also constituted to perform executive functions, consisting of the chairman, selected legislators nominated by the government and all chairmen, zilla parishads.
5. B.V. Subba Reddy as a minister requested me to put up a file supporting the electrification of a particular village. I opposed it. Soon, Subba Reddy asked me why.

   'Sir,' I said, 'according to the guidelines it cannot be done.'

   He thought about it and said, 'But I want it to be done since I was there recently.'

   I told him that such an order was not illegal, but it could be questioned in the assembly. He was also setting a precedent and he would get similar arbitrary requests from other constituents.

'I will manage all that,' said Subba Reddy. 'You tell me what I should do.' My role as a civil servant was to advise on legality, propriety, costs and benefits. His role as a leader was to take that into consideration and act.

'Sir,' I said, 'I have to oppose the proposal and I will. You can overrule my advice on file. You can write a note saying that you had visited the village and that you were convinced that it should be electrified on the basis of ground realities.' Within an hour of receiving the note, I passed the order to allocate the funds.

6. Attendees included Dr B. Venkatappiah of the Planning Commission, whose presentation helped put the issues into a national perspective.
7. I had first met Dr Sukhamoy Chakravarty at a conference where there was a discussion of the development of backward regions. I made the point that there were different reasons for backwardness. One region could be backward in terms of health and another in terms of education or water, etc. Therefore, it was not enough to have one metric for backwardness; rather there should be multiple metrics based on different dimensions. This caught the attention of Dr Chakravarty. I was made a member of the task force on multi-level planning chaired by him.
8. Minhas was a blunt, no-nonsense kind of man. He was a towering intellectual. He was in charge of annual plans and we formed an instant bond. Years later, when we got to know each other better, he told me to join politics and that he would canvass for me.
9. Titled, 'Planning and Development of Backward Regions: A Case Study for Rayalaseema'.
10. In addition, the centre had adopted the Gadgil formula where the states were allocated funds according to a fixed formula. States now had more autonomy and the centre had less discretion.
11. Professor Raj Krishna of the Delhi School of Economics is reported to have said that the Fifth Five-Year Plan of the Planning Commission was merely a fifth edition of the same plan. He was obviously referring to the plan document of the Planning Commission, not the Five-Year Plan of Andhra Pradesh, which represented a new approach to formulating a medium-term plan. Vithal took personal interest in the plan and assigned me the responsibility of seeing it through drafting. At one stage, I had five stenographers of the Planning Department at my disposal so I could dictate the final version of the plan document. We prepared technical papers and used cartographic techniques as inputs. We involved consultants from outside the government in a couple of technical papers. We identified a list of service centres or towns and villages which were ideal, central places for locating public service facilities and wrote a technical paper on this. It was accepted by the Reserve Bank of India as the basis for policy for opening of new branches of commercial banks.

12. Some felt that the reason for the resignation of some of the ministers was that they were disgruntled with the land reforms which had been initiated by Chief Minister Narasimha Rao. The land reforms tried to introduce parity with what existed in Telangana.
13. A unit of the army, led by a brigadier was moved to Vijayawada. It was stationed there to be in readiness for deployment in any of the eleven districts. District collectors could seek the assistance of the army to maintain law and order and the district superintendent of police had a critical role. The movement of the army had to be coordinated with the state government internally on a real-time basis. I was available on the spot with the army, representing the state government.
14. Vithal wished me luck in his own inimitable way.

    He said, 'Venu, I do not know what to wish you. If you succeed in your mission, you will come back as deputy secretary in Planning of Andhra Pradesh. If you fail partially, Andhra state will be born and you may become secretary, Planning. If you fail miserably, there will be three states – Telangana, Andhra and Rayalaseema. Then you may become a Planning minister or maybe even a chief minister of Rayalaseema. So, tell me, what should I wish for you?'
15. When the army was called in to assist the civil administration, the purpose was to demonstrate the might and will of the government and to assure the people of their security in times of unrest. The way it was done was with a Flag March, where the army marched through designated roads while people watched through the windows of their houses. The army was not meant to deal with the operations relating to the unrest and agitation. For the firing operations, the Central Reserve Police Force, the Border Security Force, and special paramilitary police from other states were to be used.
16. In President's Rule, the governor administers the state and is assisted by advisors who perform the functions of the cabinet. At that time, there were two advisors: H.C. Sarin, former defence secretary, Government of India, and V.K. Rao, former chief secretary, Andhra Pradesh.
17. In another incident, when I was collector, Guntur, some higher up had asked for a particular set of statistics that were virtually impossible to get. Yet, the officer in charge gave a number with decimal points. When I asked him the basis for the number, he confessed that it had been concocted by his junior based on a guess! When I asked him why the guess had decimal points, he replied it was done to add credibility. Otherwise, he told me, people would get suspicious.
18. According to the six-point formula, the state was virtually divided into six zones instead of two regions, for the purposes of government employment and access to educational facilities. It also involved allocation of special additional funds for development of each of the regions,

specially backward areas of each of the three regions. It is in this context that development boards were sanctioned for Telangana and coastal Andhra on the lines of the one of Rayalaseema.

19. Reddy, Y.V. (1972), 'State Level Planning and Regional Development Objectives', *Indian Journal of Regional Science*, Vol. 4(1): 12-24. Reddy, Y.V. (1974), 'A note on Regionalisation and Regional Development with reference to Multi-Level Plan Process', *Indian Journal of Regional Science*, Vol.6(1): 57-72.
20. The German Foundation for International Development hosted the meeting in Berlin from 24 to 30 June 1974. The panel of about ten people was accommodated in Tegel Palace on the shores of Tegel Lake.
21. Vemana ends his verses with 'Vishwadha Ahbirama, Vinura Vema'. There are several interpretations for this line.

7. A STATE OF EMERGENCY

1. In fact, the MRTP Act was drafted among others by K.V. Raghunatha Reddy, a prominent leader in the left movement. He was a man of extraordinary integrity and was a close family friend. Since my research for the PhD was initially on that subject, he asked me to help him informally, and I did – with enthusiasm. At that time, we thought we were doing the right thing.
2. During my tenure as collector, Hyderabad, I realised that the problems of the rural areas in the district were not receiving enough attention. Hence, I took interest in the proposal to bifurcate the district into Hyderabad, Urban and Hyderabad, Rural. The proposal was approved much later, and Hyderabad, Rural was christened Ranga Reddy district.
3. My family was settled in Hyderabad and Amma was happy to have me around. Besides, I had the time and freedom to attend to my academic work and felt rooted and respected in the state. A Delhi posting was outside my sphere of thinking.
4. I believe that in normal circumstances, Vengal Rao would not have relieved me. But with the furor caused by my work with regard to the land ceiling and bonded labour, perhaps he felt less reluctant to let me go. Also, there was a strong pull from Delhi. The finance secretary was Dr Manmohan Singh, and he made a strong case for me. I had never met Dr Singh, so I was not sure why he wanted me, but it appeared that I had no choice in the matter. (I learnt later that Dr Singh had asked for the top rankers in the eligible batches of the IAS who were students of economics and had a strong performance record.
5. For this purpose, I also facilitated the establishment of a private limited company called Mitra Brindam Enterprises with the help of several friends and relatives.

8. A GLOBAL PERSPECTIVE

1. The World Bank group consists of the International Bank for Reconstruction and Development (IBRD) and its associates, the International Development Association (IDA), and the International Finance Corporation (IFC). The original and principal organisation is IBRD. The World Bank is a cooperative institution, with membership open to all the countries of the world. Capital, part of which is paid up and the rest callable, is contributed by the member-countries and the amount depends on, broadly, economic strength. The World Bank also raises funds from capital markets and uses its own resources (capital, dividends, etc.) as well as borrowed money for lending. Since funds are also raised through market borrowings, the perceptions of financial markets about World Bank operations are important.

   The IFC provides subsidised loans to the private sector, while the IDA provides loans to governments at zero-interest rates or low, concessional interest rates. The operations of all the World Bank institutions are overseen by the board, which consists of members nominated from member countries.

   In the World Bank, the developed economies typically have large voting power. For example, the voting strength of the US is greater than that of Africa, India, and Latin America put together. The World Bank consists of unequal partners. India is a founder member of the World Bank group and continues to be a significant shareholder.
2. My job as deputy secretary (Fund-Bank) had several components. An important charge related to identification, development, finalisation, negotiation and monitoring the implementation of some of the projects funded by the World Bank. This task required interaction with the Planning Commission, the Union ministry concerned, the state governments where relevant, and the project authorities on one hand, and the India desk and sectoral desks in the World Bank, on the other. Projects were pitched to the World Bank for consideration as part of prior agreed conversations between the Government of India, the state government if relevant and the World Bank.
3. The World Bank funded only a part of the project requirements. In some cases, there was co-financing by other donors or aid givers, which complicated the matter further since co-financing could expand conditionalities to justify their involvement in the project.
4. The staff of the World Bank had to convince the board that it had imposed adequate conditionalities to ensure effective utilization of money and maximum contribution to development.
5. Project authorities generally liked to insulate themselves from the uncertainties of budget allocations and other sectoral policies. The

broader interest of the government as expressed by the Planning and Finance departments was to ensure that there were no serious distortions in their sectoral policies merely because the World Bank was funding a part of the costs associated with the sector or project.

6. During the period 1974-77, I sought and was seriously considered on deputation for UNDP assignments as regional planner in Zambia, Iran and Western Samoa. But none of them materialised.
7. In addition, oil prices suddenly increased globally through what appeared to be a cartelisation of oil exporting countries. India was relatively unaffected as we had large remittances from our workers abroad.
8. There was an alternate executive director from Bangladesh who performed functions similar to me for Bangladesh. On policy matters, the Indian executive director consulted alternately the Bangladesh executive director and the Sri Lankan authorities, but the final view was taken by the Indian executive director. At that time, the executive director was Syeduzzaman, who became a friend and we would visit each other in our respective countries over the years. Syeduzzaman was succeeded by Ghulam Kabria, who also became a friend.
9. A vice president of the World Bank flattered Narasimham every chance he got. Narasimham, in turn, helped him in advancing his career. On one occasion, I told Narasimham: 'Sir, he flatters you too much, and so be careful.' Narasimham responded: 'Venu, at my age, there are not many pleasures left. Do alert me if I am going over-board or tripping up.'
10. It was in the IMF that Narasimham played a key role in negotiating an extended fund facility (a large loan) for India. My role was limited to ensuring that the World Bank, in particular the India Division, lent maximum support to the processing of our loan in the IMF.
11. It was, in some ways, a brinkmanship from my side. It was also a calculation of how far the World Bank would push. We could revive the negotiations at a later stage if we were willing, since the World Bank had already invested staff time and cost in formulating the loan proposals.
12. During our time in Washington, D.C. we had many friends and family who visited us. Geetha's parents stayed with us, and to my great satisfaction, so did Amma. She had a wonderful time: we travelled together in first class by air up to London, and from London to Washington, D.C. by the supersonic Concorde. While in Washington, D.C., I took my mother for the Christmas party of the World Bank instead of my wife, for that particular year. She enjoyed it thoroughly. Whenever she recalled her trip, her face used to brighten and her eyes used to sparkle.

9. MY DAYS WITH NTR

1. NTR started his day at 3 a.m. and meetings were scheduled very early in the morning. He expressed his distress when officials complained. He

could not understand how these same senior officers were quite happy to wait outside the houses of previous chief ministers till past midnight, but complained when he met them right on time, and served them breakfast.

2. One of the catalysts for this sentiment was an incident in 1982. Rajiv Gandhi, an MP, and son of Prime Minister Indira Gandhi, was received by the popular Andhra chief minister, T. Anjaiah, at the airport in Hyderabad. It appears that Rajiv Gandhi insulted the chief minister, and Anjaiah, overcome, began to sob, in public, in front of TV cameras. To make matters worse, Anjaiah was reported to have said about his dismissal, 'I came by the grace of madam and I am going under her orders; I don't know why I came, and why I am going.' 'Madam' was Prime Minister Indira Gandhi.
3. It is also rumoured that, initially, all NTR wanted was a political posting and had approached the Congress leadership for a seat in the Rajya Sabha.
4. The Planning Department at state level is expected to take a long-term view of development of the state; formulate medium-term plans in consultation with the Planning Commission and local bodies; finalise annual plans which are operationalised through budgets and advise the Finance Department in sanctioning individual projects and programmes. It acts as a coordinating department for developmental purposes, and it may be assigned specific tasks by the chief minister or cabinet.
5. By the time I joined as secretary, NTR had abolished all three regional boards, but the Planning Department continued to monitor levels of development region-wise.
6. NTR took the view that access to market borrowings for each state government should be based on set principles or a formula (such as the Gadgil formula for central assistance to the states), rather than on an ad hoc basis, which had been the practice. He was also of the view that any borrowings by the Union government beyond what was assumed in the plan should be matched by corresponding increase in the access to borrowings by the state government. At a professional level, we were aware that these were complex issues, while at a political level there was keenness to persist with expression of differences. Behind-the-scenes meetings of administrators were an important part of reaching consensus between politically opposing forces. It was agreed in one such meeting that NTR would not formally oppose the Five-Year Plan, though he would not announce his support either.
7. The chief minister had initially taken a stand against obtaining funds through externally aided projects (such as World Bank projects) on the ground that the Union government was not passing on the concessional element of external assistance to states. I convinced the chief minister that such self-denial, though based on a principle, was not necessarily in the longer-term interest of the state government.

8. I, too, had witnessed a few such short-lived infatuations. Once, NTR asked me to suggest an eminent economist who could be consulted for preparation of the budget of 1984-85. I suggested Prof. Balwanth Reddy.

   'Let us not beat the same bush again. We had consulted him earlier,' he replied.

   NTR also courted Prof. K.L. Krishna, eminent economist in the Delhi School of Economics. Prof. Krishna had already declined NTR's offer of a seat on the planning board. Since Prof. Krishna was my friend, I was asked by NTR to convince him. Prof. Krishna obliged.
9. NTR felt also that the legal system was biased against him. His impression was perhaps not without some basis, since one of his earliest actions was to reduce the retirement age but the court ruled against him, and he had to reverse the decision.
10. It was difficult to make an annual plan without reference to resource constraint since it had to be operationalised through the budget. NTR was, like most political leaders, much concerned with annual plans. Five-year plans were left to the bureaucracy, though individual departments had an interest in including their programmes in the plans. With my background and previous experience, I found work relating to the Seventh Five-Year Plan interesting. The analytics of the plan were sound, and technical quality was impressive, but something was missing. Early signs of plan fatigue were unmistakable. Financial resources for the plan were uncertain; the link between Five-Year Plan and annual plans weak; and the respect commanded by the Planning Commission, both at technical and political levels, moderated.
11. The paper related to the location of the services in the context of formulation of the Fifth Five-Year Plan (Government of Andhra Pradesh, Fifth Five-Year Plan, Technical Papers III, Area Planning Approach 1975).
12. The procedure adopted has been explained in a paper that I wrote in the Indian Journal of Public Administration, January–March 1988; pages 34-45, titled 'Decentralising Administrative Machinery for Development Needs: A Case Study of Andhra Pradesh'.
13. NTR set up a working group for introduction of computer education in the educational system.
14. While in these and other instances, NTR followed our advice, it was not always the case. There were many occasions where my proposals were overruled or my advice not taken. I was not very enthusiastic about the proposal to establish Nizam's Institute of Medical Sciences because I felt that the existing general hospitals should be strengthened, and that such super-specialised institutions on the pattern of the All India Institute of Medical Sciences should be undertaken by the Government of India. Similarly, NTR was committed to the erection of statues on the tank

bund in Hyderabad, but I thought it a waste. He overruled me, and his argument was that the role of the government in matters relating to culture deserved more attention than economists like me were willing to give. There was a proposal to give significant financial support for bringing into existence the Nagarjuna Fertiliser Company. I argued that the state government need not invest money in a fertilizer company since fertilisers can be brought. I was overruled on this also. In the context of allocation of land for Apollo Hospitals, at an informal level, I had indicated that the extent of land that was proposed to be given to the hospital was in excess of the true needs as estimated at that point of time. My advice was not followed.

There was one instance, a rare one, when NTR accepted a proposal that I made, but later reversed the orders. In Andhra Pradesh, perhaps as in other states, printing and supply of textbooks was a state monopoly. More often than not, there were shortages and delays in availability. Since the cost of printing government textbooks was high, increasingly demand was outsourced. I, therefore, proposed that the government should dispense with exercising its copyrights so that non-subsidised textbooks could be made available by the private sector in parallel with the existing system. NTR approved and issued the orders. They were put in public domain. Subsequently, the order was withdrawn, and I was not consulted or informed. Perhaps, NTR felt embarrassed to tell me.

15. While the collector and district magistrate would decide on the projects on the basis of requests from various departments and elected representatives, he/she would be assisted in the process by the district planning officer, who was not associated with any particular executing department. The district planning officer was also answerable to the state Planning Department in ensuring appropriate guidelines that would govern such investments.
16. In one district, the pressure from the legislators to distribute the funds equally among their constituencies was accepted by the collector concerned. The concession made by the collector was that while selecting schemes, the planning officer would ensure allocation of equal amounts to each constituency. The next step in the district was to insist that the schemes selected within the constituency should be as per the recommendations of the legislator concerned.
17. My recollection is that the data at that time had shown that the offtake of food grains in the poorer and backward regions was actually disproportionately small compared to the developed districts.
18. Also, an employment guarantee would provide minimum assured wages to men and women and would have the benefit of empowering women in poor families. In addition, it would alter the poor equations in the rural areas between the landlords and the landless since the landless would no longer be at the mercy of the landlords for daily wages.

19. Betterment levy in this case was levied on the beneficiaries of the proposed irrigation system, in addition to water rates so that a part of the capital cost of the project was met by contribution from the farmers, whose land value stood to benefit by being brought under the government irrigation systems.
20. While I often disagreed with NTR, there was one serious misunderstanding between us. I had done considerable analysis on the annual plan, but NTR was unwilling to see it and launched into a rambling monologue. I was very frustrated. I told the chief secretary that I was planning to leave the state and refused to relent despite many attempts by UB on behalf of NTR. UB acted as a bridge between me and the chief minister and finally, I agreed to meet the chief minister. NTR greeted me warmly and wanted to know what he had done that had so upset me. I told him, and added that what he required was not a professional with twenty years of experience, but a Telugu stenographer. He apologised, and listened patiently to my presentation. That was the end of the matter. NTR did not seem to hold this episode against me in any manner.
21. The ordinarily unsentimental man once showed me a swing, a prized possession that he kept in his home. He said he had shared it with his co-star, Jayalalithaa, in a movie. He had kept it as a memento.

10. RELEARNING POLICY AND PRACTICE

1. Some of the work done in planning has been brought out as a book with Kosal Ram as co-editor: *Multilevel Planning in India: Processes and Perceptions* published by Book Links Corporation (1988). Similarly, in regard to the state-level public enterprises, a book titled *Towards a White Paper* has been brought out with Koteswara Rao and R.K. Misra as co-editors (Book Links Corporation, 1990). Two of my papers incorporating my experience in the Planning Department were published in the *Indian Journal of Public Administration*. These are: 'Evaluating Planning Machinery at Sub-national Level: An integrated framework', Vol. XXXI, No. 1, January-March 1986, and 'Decentralising Administrative Machinery for Development Needs', Vol. XXXIV, January-March 1988.
2. Professor Govinda Rao reminded me of one of my interactions as an honorary consultant to the Government of Andhra Pradesh with the Ninth Finance Commission in 1987, and I quote: 'Perhaps, you do not recall an incident when the Ninth Finance Commission called a meeting of the state finance ministers to discuss the "normative approach" they were required to adopt as per the ToR. There was a background paper prepared by the secretariat of the commission (I was the economic advisor!). My recollection is that nobody from the Finance Department

attended from AP. You came in briefly to the meeting to state that the Union government had no business to tell the commission what approach it should adopt and, therefore, the discussion on any approach paper on the issue is not fruitful. I did not know you much at that time, but I thought it was a brilliant intervention.'

3. In the light of my work in LSE and Templeton College, I wrote articles titled 'Public Enterprise at Cross Roads', edited by John Heath, published in a book by Routledge, London in 1990, and another one titled 'Privatisation in Developing Countries' edited by V.V. Ramanadham, published by Routledge, London in 1989.With Sankar as co-editor, *Privatisation: Diversification of Ownership of Public Enterprises* was published by the Institute of Public Enterprises (1989). In 1990, UNDP drafted a manual on privatisation for the benefit of developing countries. I was invited, as part of a panel, to review and comment on the draft, in a short conference in New York. Incorporating the significant academic exposure that I had to the policy debates, I wrote a book titled *Public Enterprise Reform and Privatisation*, which was published by Himalaya Publishing House (1992). To enable a full understanding of the issues related to privatisation and readily make available the bibliography, I wrote a book titled *Privatisation: Approaches, Processes and Issues*, which was published by Galgotia Publications (1992).

11. THE POWER OF GOLD

1. The title of the chapter is inspired by the book *The Power of Gold: The History of an Obsession* by Peter L. Bernstein, John Wiley, 2016.
2. The finance ministry had three departments: revenue, expenditure and economic affairs, each headed by a secretary, with the seniormost among them usually designated as the finance secretary. Balance of Payments (BoP) was one of several divisions within DEA and comprised two desks: one to handle BoP and the other all matters relating to external commercial borrowings (ECB). The BoP division monitored and made assessments of all foreign exchange inflows and outflows. An important part of the exercise was ensuring availability of foreign exchange for designated purposes, such as import of oil, fertilisers and essential commodities. The division prepared a foreign exchange budget, and released foreign exchange to various government departments especially defence and to official canalising agencies (for example, Indian Oil Corporation). In the old days of import licence regime, issue of any licence beyond a specified level for import of capital goods had to be referred to the division for clearance. The determination of exchange rate was a closely guarded secret. All this may sound anachronistic in the new regime that we have got used to in the last two decades or so, but it is worthwhile recalling

where we started from. My interactions were almost wholly with the governor, deputy governor, finance secretary and chief economic advisor. I was giving inputs, discussing the various options and implementing the decisions taken. I had a direct role in liquidity management of balance of payments, on a monthly, weekly and daily basis. The RBI worked out import compression measures outside the foreign exchange budget while we in the ministry had to take care of big ticket and essential imports, such as defence, oil and fertilisers. Short-term credit facilities were part of my charge.

In brief, I was aware of the macro issues, provided inputs for decisions and was entrusted with execution of policy. All important decisions had to, of course, be taken with inputs from several sources, but as the one on the frontline executing policy, my perspective was sought by the decision makers.

3. Initially, on joining the Department of Economic Affairs (DEA), I was allotted a relatively light and complexity-free domain: The Currency and Coinage Division. This is one of the least favoured work areas in the DEA. The division is responsible for making projections of requirement of coins and currency notes in close consultation with the RBI, and ensuring that the production and delivery targets are met in right denomination, quality and security features. The RBI was responsible for distribution of coins and currency through its own offices and through the branches of commercial banks. During my brief handling of the portfolio, I became aware of how the vested interests of input suppliers and trade unions can influence sensitive matters. I was moved out of the division in a few months. Jalan, then finance secretary, had earlier mentioned to me that I was given the Currency and Coins Division 'for now' – bringing me to the finance ministry to handle a less glamorous portfolio was easier than for a high-profile job. In July 1990, he asked my preference for one of the two openings that were coming up: the division in DEA that handles BoP including managing external commercial borrowings (ECB), and the division that oversees the work of development financial institutions in the Banking Division. The latter dealing with institutions like IDBI and ICICI was considered more 'prestigious' and important. I stated my preference for the BoP division since a crisis was on the horizon, posing intellectual and policy challenges. As mentioned in the preceding chapter, I had taken academic leave and concluded that there was a stalemate in the policy actions and was therefore interested in the subject. This preference eventually proved to be a turning point in my career.
4. By June 1991, we had usable reserves that could last barely for a week. We had to maintain minimum balance with our bankers, and some of our forex reserves were lent to the SBI which could not be encashed.
5. Incidentally, this period was very educational and intellectually rewarding

for me, as I was interacting with the Economic Division in the MoF and the RBI. I interacted with chief general managers and other officials in the RBI and read the relevant manuals of RBI. They told me that it was unusual for officials from the ministry to go to the RBI, especially to learn, and surprisingly meet 'junior officers'. This helped me establish a personal rapport with several professionals and the trust needed to navigate the turbulent times ahead. In addition, these meetings opened my eyes to the professional talent in the RBI.

6. I was joint secretary in the DEA between April 1990 and May 1993. During my three-year stint at the DEA, there were three PMs: V.P. Singh (between December 1989 and November 1990), Chandrashekhar (November 1990 to June 1991), and P.V. Narasimha Rao (June 1991 to May 1996) and three finance ministers: Madhu Dandawate, Yashwant Sinha and Dr Manmohan Singh. There were three secretaries in charge of Economic Affairs, with primary responsibility to manage the crisis as well as the economic reforms at the bureaucratic level: Bimal Jalan (January 1990 to December 1990), S.P. Shukla (December 1990 to October 1991), and Montek Singh Ahluwalia (October 1991 onwards). There were also three chief economic advisors: Nitin Desai (1988–90), Deepak Nayyar (1990–91), Ashok Desai (1991–93) (formally designated as a consultant), and Shankar Acharya (1993 onwards). At RBI, there were three governors: R.N. Malhotra (up to December 1990), S. Venkitaramanan (December 1990 till December 1992), and C. Rangarajan (December 1992 onwards).

7. In this rotation of key functionaries, I was possibly the only senior functionary in the government to provide continuity in risk assessment and for fine-tuning policy initiatives to manage the crisis in the external sector. Among the senior political leadership, I had not personally known any of the prime ministers before and except for Dr Manmohan Singh (whom I worked with as deputy secretary and as director in the Department of Economic Affairs), I had not personally known any of the finance ministers. I worked closely with the secretaries, chief economic advisors and governors in view of the critical balance of payments position. Fortunately, many of them were already known to me. Among the finance secretaries, I had earlier worked with Jalan when he was chief economic advisor, while I was working in the World Bank in early 1980s. I came into contact with Montek when both of us were in the World Bank in 1978. I continued to be in touch with him while he was in the Ministry of Finance and later in the Prime Minister's Office. Among the chief economic advisors, I knew Nitin Desai rather well from the days he was in the Planning Commission in the 1970s. Deepak was known to me as a distinguished development economist, and we had mutual respect and affection. In Shankar I had an admirable and wonderful

friend from the days we were in the World Bank. He had been a friend, philosopher, guide and well-wisher then, and continues to be so. Among the governors, I had worked with Malhotra in the finance ministry for a year and later when he was secretary, Economic Affairs, and I was in the World Bank. I had not worked with Venkitaramanan before, but I had looked up to him as a senior colleague and someone from whom I could learn a lot. At the height of the crisis, we used to be in continuous touch over phone. Sometimes, he would ask my views on subjects which were strictly not within my jurisdiction in the DEA. When I pointed this out, he used to respond: 'Venu, as far as I am concerned, I want your views. I will take it forward in my own way.' I worked with Dr Rangarajan closely during the initial years of my tenure as joint secretary, while he was deputy governor and later member, Planning Commission. My earlier association with them gave me an advantage in handling sensitive matters.

8. There are not too many instances of gold being used by governments, though Italy pledged gold with Bundesbank to secure a loan and Romania used gold as collateral to secure a loan in 1974. The power of gold has been demonstrated after our use of gold also. In September 1999, there was the Washington Agreement on Gold since central banks felt that they need not hold forex reserves in gold to the extent that they were doing before. However, when they tried to sell the gold, it resulted in a downward pressure on gold prices. Therefore, select central banks agreed to limit their aggregate sales each year to the level of not more than 400 tonnes annually. In 2004, this agreement was renewed for five more years. The sale of gold continued. After the global financial crisis in 2008, the situation changed. Central banks stopped selling gold, and in fact, some of them started buying gold. The International Monetary Fund had difficulty in obtaining adequate income to meet their operating expenses. A committee under the chairmanship of Andrew Crocket (2007) recommended the sale of gold with the IMF to raise forex resources for assuring stable income for the IMF.
9. The stock of gold with us was not of standard quality; it was not of acceptable size and was not assayed. So, the buyer had to convert this gold into standard form and quality. When we got the gold after repurchase, we had it as per standard quality. Similarly, gold pledged by the RBI also got purified in the process. We faced a procedural problem in physically transporting gold held in the forex reserves. The law stipulated that not more than 15 per cent of gold held in the issue department could be kept outside India. Gold provided, in the past, a backing for the issue of currency, thereby warranting such caution. We had to send more than what was permitted. So, the RBI moved the gold that had to be sent out to the Banking Department's account to circumvent the limitations.

12. ALL THE FM's MEN

1. V.P. Singh was the prime minister at the onset of the crisis. He had to resign on 7 November 1990. Chandrashekhar took over as prime minister, but he had to depend on the support of the Congress party. The Congress party withdrew support in February 1991. Fresh elections to Parliament were ordered and the Chandrashekhar government became a caretaker government. As the elections were under way, Rajiv Gandhi was assassinated on 21 May 1991.
2. The title of the chapter is inspired by an essay with the same title in Shankar Acharya's book *India's Economy: Some Issues and Answers*, Academic Foundation, New Delhi, 2003. Shankar writes about the half a dozen or so top officials in the finance ministry and the RBI who bore the responsibility for day-to-day economic management. They were critical players in the story narrated here.
3. To the credit of the IMF, Neiss and his deputy David Goldsborough wrote a joint letter to me in 1993, expressing their deep appreciation for my interactions during the crisis, and graciously added that they had learnt a lot from me.
4. I should clarify that much of what has been described was in fact teamwork. The team included K.B.L. Mathur of the Indian Economic Service; R. Krishnamurthy, a professional senior banker from the SBI; Rita Acharya from the Central Secretariat Service; Sanjiv Ahluwalia and Alok Sheel of the IAS. Their professional competence, integrity and commitment were exemplary and they are among the unsung heroes of managing the crisis. I had excellent cooperation and guidance from several other ministries, in particular, the Ministry of Commerce. Jayanta Roy, economic advisor, was a source of strength in discussions with rating agencies and investors. Of course, there were frustrations, especially when they related to individual cases of hardship to some corporates, but no one accused us of nepotism.

13. THE WORLD IS NOT FAIR

1. I was in additional charge as director general of Institute of Foreign Trade (IIFT) for a few months. It was a temporary charge and I decentralised the work processes. Consequently, I attended to IIFT work one day a week. Since I did not stand in the way, the faculty took, I believe, several initiatives that advanced the profile of the institute. Absence of a boss may be conducive to efficiency and innovations – under certain circumstances.
2. There was an agreement between India and the erstwhile USSR whereby the USSR extended into rupee-denominated credit to India. A fresh agreement was entered with the successor government, that is, the

Russian government. The rupee-denominated loans because of these agreements were to be repaid by India through export of commodities to Russia. Importers authorised by Russia could access the rupee balances on authorisation by our government. The main purpose of repayment of our obligations denominated in rupees to Russia was that the incentives required for export against convertible currency need not be extended to exports under the rupee trade agreement. However, over a period, relaxations were made and some incentives were given to the exporters under rupee trade agreement also. Even so, Russia was not in a position to utilise the balances unless we diluted the restrictions. Our view was that we should strictly abide by the agreement already entered into and that we should not give any incentive in regard to export of commodities under rupee trade. If we treated rupee exports and exports to convertible currency on the same footing, the very objective of having a rupee trade agreement would be undermined.

Russia, on the other hand, was interested in diluting the conditions of rupee trade vis-á-vis the foreign currency trade, which would be beneficial to Russia and also help in utilisation of the rupee balances at the disposal of Russia that were parked with the RBI. Under the circumstances, the Russian government proposed that they would like to use rupee balances in their account held in the Reserve Bank towards acquisition of equity in Indian enterprises. There was significant support to this proposal on the ground that it would help utilisation of rupee balances, and it would also amount to inflow of foreign investment. Chidambaram was initially inclined to agree to this proposal. I was opposed to the idea of allowing rupee balances, which were rupee-denominated debt, being converted into equity in convertible currency. There was a double swap involved – debt to equity and rupee denomination to US dollar denomination.

We faced a similar situation later in June 1996. At that time, Chidambaram had taken charge as finance minister. Soon after, he referred to me a file relating to the use of rupee balances of Russia. At that time, I was in the Banking Department and this was not in my purview. Yet, since we had worked together in the Ministry of Commerce on a similar proposal, he asked for my views. My advice was not to support the proposal to permit Russia to utilise rupee balances for acquiring equity in a company in India; this was similar to the advice I had given previously. Chidambaram accepted my advice.

3. I requested Bimal Jalan, who was executive director in the World Bank, to find openings for me. He mentioned to me that he had explored possibilities but nothing worked out. Premchand, my friend in the Fiscal Affairs Department of the IMF, also tried to find me a placement but I was not selected for the position. However, Premchand gave me opportunities for consultancy.

4. I was also happy to be at the top in terms of seniority of those initially empanelled and posted as secretaries in my batch of the IAS.
5. The secretary, Department of Economic Affairs, represented the government on the board of the RBI. The Banking Division performed the functions of the government as owner and functions of accountability to Parliament in matters relating to the RBI, banks and non-banking financial companies. It was understood that the Banking Division would not interfere with the operational autonomy of these institutions. As a general policy, I supported the proposals received by the government from the RBI and other commercial banks, unless there were strong grounds to disagree. In case of disagreement, clarifications were sought to convince the heads of the institutions. If disagreement persisted, intimation about my intended proposals to the minister were conveyed. This helped in clarifying my position to them and an opportunity for them to reconsider. If the minister disagreed with their proposal even after I recommended, I used to call the head of the institution and inquire as to how I could communicate the order of the government. I did not want any communication that would belittle the head of the institution or cause embarrassment to them. My purpose was to be supportive unless there were policy angles or sensitivities that were required to be considered.

   The Banking Division considered all matters relating to legislation and rules in respect of the RBI. This included matters such as appointment of the board of the RBI, the appointment of the governor and deputy governors. There was little scope for analytical inputs since we depended heavily on the advice from the RBI or on other divisions of the ministry in regard to overall economic policies of the government. Yet, the work was not entirely without excitement. Among the memorable experiences were: the process of selecting or appointing non-official directors on the boards of public enterprises, and the appointment of chairmen and other senior executives of the banks and ensuring their accountability to Parliament.
6. A complicating factor in the process of selection of chief executives of banks related to the clearance from the vigilance angle. Often there was an orchestrated effort to bring complaints from a vigilance angle just when the selection process was under way. It was very difficult to distinguish between frivolous cases and serious cases. The chief vigilance commissioner, who had to clear the cases, was also finding it difficult to inquire and take a view on such complaints at short notice. My effort had been to get all clarifications and clearances, to the extent possible, before the interview. On some occasions, I sought the version of the candidate in the interview about some allegations. The candidate had an opportunity to explain his side of the case to the committee during the interview.

14. A CHANGE OF PROFILE

1. In addition, I was in charge of the National Housing Bank at the national level and director general of the Public Enterprises Management Board at the state level.
2. On one occasion, I stayed in Delhi for three days. On the first day, I was given a room in the RBI office from which I could operate while in Delhi. On the second day, I was asked to move to a different room. I was told that the room closest to the governor's office should be occupied by the seniormost deputy governor in the city. Since I was juniormost for some time, I had to move the moment any other deputy governor came to Delhi on work. Similarly, the car allotted to me was changed to a smaller one whenever I overlapped with a senior deputy governor in Delhi.
3. In the 1960s, the RBI had a formidable reputation for scholarship and professionalism. Officers in the RBI were in great demand in multilateral bodies such as the IMF and in many other developing countries. In the 1970s, the atmosphere changed since some of the officers left RBI and fresh recruitment was stalled. Fortunately for the RBI, Rangarajan as deputy governor took initiatives to directly recruit several professionals in 1980. As a result, by the time I joined, we had an enviable professional team.
4. Y. Venugopal Reddy, *Monetary and Financial Sector Reforms in India: A Central Banker's Perspective*, UBSPD, New Delhi, 2000.
5. My predecessors in handling monetary policy were: S.S. Tarapore, a quintessential central banker (1992–96); C. Rangarajan (an authority on money and finance (1982–91); and K.S. Krishnaswamy, an internationally renowned central banker (1975–81). That was reason enough for me to be humble. So, I started with an attitude of 'I want to know', and not 'I know'.
6. I had known the deputy governors also in my capacity as secretary (Banking). Each one of them had unique strengths. S.P. Talwar had a very warm personality. He was always cheerful and dynamic. He had extensive connections in the banking, business, political and bureaucratic circles. The governors depended on him heavily in all matters regarding regulation and supervision. I coined a phrase to describe him: 'Dean of deputy governors', since he was the seniormost. R.V. Gupta, my senior in the IAS, was highly respected for his time management, integrity, impartiality and excellent interpersonal relations. He was particularly strong on developmental aspects. Jagdish Capoor belonged to the RBI, with a very engaging and pleasant approach to work, and was free and frank, though reticent and reserved. Together, we, the four deputy governors, made a good team. The team spirit was well entrenched by the time Vepa Kamesam, former managing director, SBI, and Muniappan, former executive director, RBI, replaced Talwar and Capoor.

7. RBI, established under the relevant Act, performs functions assigned to it under the Act, and also those assigned to it under related legislations, such as those dealing with regulation of banks' foreign exchange management and payment systems. The core functions of the RBI relate to formulation, implementation and monitoring of monetary policy. The objectives of the policy are maintaining price stability and ensuring adequate flow of credit to productive sectors. The RBI manages, to a limited extent, the exchange rate, and the foreign exchange inflows and outflows, in addition to maintaining reserves in foreign exchange. The main objective is to facilitate smooth external trade and payments and a sustainable balance of payments. As regulator and supervisor of the financial system, it prescribes broad parameters of banking operations, including licensing of banks within which the country's banking and financial system functions. The objectives are to maintain public confidence in the system, protect depositors' interest, and provide cost-effective banking services to the public. It issues and exchanges or destroys currency in addition to distribution of coins. The objective is to give to the public adequate quantity of supply of currency notes and coins of acceptable quality to facilitate transactions. It has from its very inception accepted a developmental role. It established several institutions that were precursors to UTI, IDBI, NABARD, etc. It provides important services to the government. As a banker to government, it provides services to both Centre and states. It is also a banker to banks. While the RBI Act gives the right to manage the debt of the Union government to the RBI, all the states have entered into an agreement with RBI to make use of these services.
8. I made a pitch for the liberalisation of gold imports even when I was in the government, but the success was limited.
9. The link between the gold policy and capital account convertibility in India was formally acknowledged by Tarapore, chairman of the Committee on Capital Account Convertibility. In an address at the Gold Banking Seminar in August 1997, he said: 'When the definitive history of India's policy on gold is written up, the speech by Dr Y.V. Reddy will stand out as a watershed as it is perhaps the only speech by a senior Indian official which squarely takes on issues on gold policy and it will be appropriately recorded in history as the forerunner of major policy change. It is by raising pertinent issues that Dr Reddy has paved the way for the committee to come up with specific recommendations on India's policy on gold.' (Tarapore, S.S., *Capital Account Convertibility, Monetary Policy and Reforms*, UBSPD, New Delhi, 2003, p. 24.) Mr Tarapore referred to the speech again in the context of review of progress of financial sector reforms: 'While all this reflected fairly impressive progress, the most outstanding measure was on gold. Lest critics say

that the CAC report is taking undue credit for this important measure, the author would categorically say that this measure owes its origin to RBI deputy governor, Y.V. Reddy's speech at the World Gold Council in November 1996, though what the CAC report did was to set out a phased programme of liberalisation of the gold regulations. This is a major change after 60 years of misguided and purposeless regulation, and the gold regime liberalisation shows that reform can get groundswell support if it is properly articulated and the implementation is worked on patiently.' (Tarapore, S.S., *Issues in Financial Sector Reforms*, UBSPD, 2000, p. 188).

10. The basic framework of liberalised gold policy put in place in 1997 continues, despite occasional, marginal temporary hikes in import duty.
11. We in the RBI had to interact with five secretaries dealing with economic affairs in a span of less than six years of my tenure. I had worked with Montek before, and rather closely. He was succeeded by Vijay Kelkar, whom I had known for decades, an expert in matters relating to trade and energy. E.A.S. Sarma, my colleague and friend in the IAS from Andhra Pradesh, had been additional secretary in the Expenditure Department. Ajit Kumar was my batchmate who had worked in the Finance Department at the state and Union levels. C.M. Vasudev was seasoned and experienced in the Finance Department, both at the Centre and state. We had known each other both in finance and commerce ministries. Shankar Acharya, chief economic advisor, was a source of guidance and strength to me. He was succeeded by Rakesh Mohan, who became a close friend when I was in the Ministry of Commerce and he was in the Ministry of Industrial Development and Policy. I had the advantage, therefore, of free and frank interaction with all the secretaries and chief economic advisors during my tenure as deputy governor.
12. As detailed in chapter 15.
13. As explained in chapter 15.
14. As explained in chapter 15.
15. As explained in chapter 17.
16. As described in chapter 16.

15. THE RANGARAJAN ERA

1. There were two major challenges before us in the conduct of monetary policy. The first was to de-emphasise the importance of using quantity of money as an instrument and to introduce the use of indirect instruments of monetary policy, in particular, interest rate. At that point of time, the bank rate as a signalling rate was virtually non-operative. Finance was being provided by the RBI to institutions for various purposes through refinancing, such as exports and agriculture. The interest rate at which

refinance was being provided varied depending on the purpose. There were efforts to rationalise interest rate structure both on domestic and lending sides since the early 1990s, but with little success. The concept of prime lending rate was introduced in 1974 in the expectation that it would respond to changes in bank rate. The second challenge was to replace the prevailing system of allocating credit and prescribing interest rates on such credit among different sectors or users. The objective was to allow more space for allocation of credit through market mechanisms and pricing (interest rate) of a credit also through such mechanisms. However, the allocation and pricing was to be influenced by the RBI's signalling mechanism on interest rates, and liquidity provision of injection or absorption.

The prevailing feeling in RBI was that the use of bank rate as an operationally significant policy instrument was not feasible unless all financing by the RBI, especially our refinancing operations, were undertaken at that rate. Only ways and means advances to states was being provided at bank rate and none others. Soon after I joined, the governor approved a proposal to constitute an internal working group on credit and monetary policy to prepare a plan for reactivating bank rate and minimising the role of the RBI in credit allocation. The working group recommended that the beginning of the movement to indirect instruments would be possible by announcing that the bank rate would be the anchor, but actual rates could vary till they were rationalised. All sources of financing would be linked to the bank rate, but might be higher or lower than the bank rate initially in consonance with the prevailing rate. This would ensure minimum disturbance to the prevailing rates and avoid resistance to the use of bank rate as the benchmark.

The idea was to pave the way for providing all financing from RBI at the bank rate only, by eliminating the margins for different purposes. Also it was to commit all stakeholders to the final objective, namely, reactivating the use of bank rate for operational purpose, but it could be the anchor rate in transition and the operationally binding policy rate in due course. We hoped that the institutions receiving refinance could be persuaded to accept a gradual elimination of existing premium or discount to the bank rate. At that time, it was also envisaged that in due course, finance to the Union government would also be on similar lines, namely, at bank rate. The major task was to work on the transition.

Shankar Acharya, chief economic advisor, felt that the distortions in the existing refinancing arrangements should be corrected first before announcing the operational relevance of bank rate. He felt that linking several rates to a rate would undermine sanctity of the policy rate itself, ab initio. Acharya added that the prevailing bank rate was not used, and the rate itself was out of alignment with the prevailing policy stance.

However, the governor was able to convince Acharya that it was better to announce the objective of making bank rate an anchor, and move all the rates towards it gradually, so that there was minimal disruption, and general acceptability of universal application of bank rate.

There were two paths for transition. One was to move towards an ideal state in small steps and then formally adopt the new framework. Alternatively, the goal could be defined and movement towards the goal could be made in steps depending on the circumstances. This is in contrast to feeling the way towards the goal. In the instant phase, my preference was to define and commit to the goal while keeping the path open subject to negotiation. Further, by recognising that the prevailing bank rate itself was unrealistic, some movement towards a less unrealistic rate was contemplated as a first step. In the new approach, the RBI would focus on money supply and interest rates, and would accord greater freedom to the banks and corporates in terms of allocation and pricing of credit. The finance ministry did not have strong views on the subject, as long as the priority sector lending and related prescriptions on interest rates were not disrupted.

2. The RBI is enabled by law, to provide finance to the government when required through ad hoc treasury bills which have to be redeemed in ninety-one days. This provision of recourse to treasury bills was meant to provide accommodation to the government to enable it to get over temporary mismatches between receipts and expenditures. This arrangement is somewhat similar to the overdraft arrangements that are available to the customers of the banks. Normally, it was expected that the overdraft would be cleared within the stipulated period. In 1955, the government was not in a position to maintain minimum cash balance with the RBI for a relatively long period. The amount made available through treasury bills was, therefore, accumulating. The Reserve Bank felt that they had no choice except to issue treasury bills, irrespective of whether they had been rolled over repeatedly. The rate of interest charged from 1974 was 4.6 per cent – far below the prevailing market rate. This accommodation by the RBI to the government to enable it maintain minimum balances by taking recourse to the issue of treasury bills became the rule rather than the exception. In popular parlance, the RBI was printing money for the government, and it was printing as much money for the government as it wanted. This was the origin of the limitless availability of money for the use of the Government of India at concessional interest rates. Some creation of money would, no doubt, have been required for enabling economic activity demanded by increasing use of money for transactions and the growth in the economy. However, in the normal course, the required money supply would have been determined by the Reserve Bank on the basis of assessment of

evolving conditions. Here much of the money that had to be created by the RBI was not out of its volition. This, in brief, has been described as fiscal dominance which put a constraint on the capacity of the Reserve Bank to conduct its monetary policy since a large part of creation of money and its cost was not within the discretion of RBI.

3. RBI, like other central banks, has a balance sheet. It is different from the balance sheets of other entities in many respects. A central bank's balance sheet is not merely a statement of account. It is central to the process of money supply. The main assets can be divided into two: net domestic assets and net foreign assets. Domestic assets increase whenever there is an increase in net RBI credit to the government or to the commercial sector, including banks. Money is thus created and infused into the system through this process. Similarly, whenever RBI buys foreign currency, say US dollars by paying in rupees, it infuses fresh money into the system. The created money strengthens the reserves of the banks which then are enabled to create credit and, in the process, they add to the money supply. Changes in the liabilities and assets of the central bank, therefore, lead to changes in the money supply. The operations are driven by policy objectives, and thus the RBI's balance sheet shows the impact of the operations on the balance sheet. In brief, the RBI's balance sheet shows the financial links between the budget of the government, functioning of the banks and money supply. It also has links with the availability of foreign exchange for the country.

   Prior to the initiation of economic reforms, the Reserve Bank's net domestic assets were virtually dictated by the needs of the government for its budget, and the allocation of credit as per plan priorities. However, with the initiation of economic reforms, the position changed. Market orientation of the management of the economy required that the monetary authority, that is, the RBI, be seen as an entity which accepts responsibility for creation of money as distinct from the government, which is the authority to spend the money. Further, the central bank was expected to take a medium- to longer-term view of the economy, while the government with political compulsions might be excessively concerned with the short term. More important, the Reserve Bank had to be endowed with sufficient capital to act as lender of the last resort and absorb systemic risks in times of crisis. It could not afford to run into losses and depend on infusion of capital from the government, without losing its independence. In brief, the logic of reforms warranted attention to the balance sheet both by the policy makers and the financial markets. Fiscal monetary relationship had to change with the onset of economic reforms.

4. The letter dated 2 June 1961 was written and signed by Mrs Indira Gandhi (from the prime minister's residence, New Delhi) and addressed

to the Reserve Bank of India, Bombay, with a copy to the Reserve Bank of India, New Delhi. The letter reads as: 'In continuation of my letter dated May 30, 1961, I wish to inform you that Trinity College, Cambridge, have agreed to admit my son, Rajiv Gandhi, to the Mechanical Sciences Tripos course in October 1962 provided he passes the Mechanical Sciences Qualifying Examination which is compulsory for this purpose. I have secured admission for him with the well known institute of Davies Laing in London as similar facilities are not available in India. This institute will coach him for the Mechanical Sciences Qualifying Examination which he hopes to take in June next year. Necessary certification to this effect from the Indian High Commission in London and the Institute are attached. It is requested that orders regarding the grant of foreign exchange facilities for Rs 8,000 (Pound 600) for one year from 1st August, 1961 to 31st July, 1962 may kindly be issued at an early date.'

5. Here are extracts of the speech: 'There is considerable discussion as to whether the rupee is overvalued or not. As per the REER, it would certainly appear so, irrespective of the base chosen. The overvaluation has got exacerbated with the sharp appreciation of the US dollar against other major currencies, that is, the DM and the yen. The relative "cheapening" of imports may not have resulted in increasing imports and larger current account deficits. This is because imports are relatively less responsive to exchange rate changes and are more sensitive to the level of economic activity. There could be a potential larger current account deficit as industrial activity rebounds – even at the present exchange rates and if oil demand picks up, a correction cannot be ruled out... Thus, enlargement of current account deficit beyond the present level is sustainable...but, the correction, if any, has to be gradual and not sudden...So, some addition to reserves, in my view, would give additional comfort...'
6. S.S. Tarapore, in Noesis column: 'Professor Reddy's discourses,' *Business Standard*, 10 March 2000.
7. It is useful to narrate the background to this issue. India entered into an agreement with Russia to settle the large rupee-denominated debt that was owed to the USSR by India. According to the agreement, rupees were made available every year by the Indian government to the Russian government, and Russia could utilise the rupees to import agreed goods and services from India. It was rupee-denominated debt with a restriction on its utilisation, namely, that it had to be serviced through imports from India. Often, the rupee balances credited by the RBI in favour of the Russian government remained unutilised. These were kept as rupee balances in RBI with credits from the government and had to be paid by the RBI to the exporters from India to Russia. The Russian government used to periodically sell the rupees at its disposal to the importers in

Russia. As it happened, due to exchange rate fluctuations, the rupee liability became onerous on India. The Russian government and the Indian government had significant discretion about what to trade and who would trade under this agreement. Discretion could be for mutual interest, but it also had potential for misuse by either or both to help private gains. There were vested interests in Russia and in India, who took advantage of some provisions of the agreement to the detriment of both the governments. This debt by the Government of India had to be discharged over several years. The amounts were in thousands of crores every year.

17. TEAMWORK ON A CLEAN NOTE

1. The non-official directors are nominated by the Government of India. Unlike most other central banks, the members of the board are not only 'technocrats' or economists, but are distinguished people drawn from diverse backgrounds. They represent broad political concerns, since they are, apart from two or three economists, scientists, social workers, businessmen, and people from industry. The RBI affairs are governed by the central board of directors, nominated by the government. But the governor, who presides over the meetings, exercises concurrent powers, unless specifically restrained by the board.
2. For details, please see the previous chapter.
3. For details, please see the previous chapter.
4. In the landmark policy, the experience with Liquidity Adjustment Facility (LAF) was reviewed and proposal to announce a package of measures encompassing changes in operating procedures of LAF mentioned. The medium-term objectives of LAF were indicated. The four stages through which the call money market would be confined to inter-bank were announced. The roadmap for a negotiated dealing system was drawn up. With regard to development of the government securities market, the initiatives announced related to establishment of a clearing corporation, payment system, public debt office and electronic links among them. A report of the working group on separation of debt management from monetary management dated 1997 was revisited, progress made reviewed and future course set out in the following words: 'In the above context, once legislative actions with regard to Fiscal Responsibility Bill and amendments with regard to the Reserve Bank of India Act are accomplished, it is proposed to take up with the government, the feasibility and further steps for separation of government debt management function from RBI.'

   A decision to adopt a ninety-day norm for classification of NPAs consistent with international best practice was announced in this landmark policy, though effective three years later. Guidelines on banks exposures to individual or group borrowers and revised guidelines on exposure of banks to the stock market in the light of experience gained were announced. Revised prudential measures and a new supervisory structure for urban cooperative banks were detailed. The statement listed the legal reforms initiated as well as contemplated, insofar as they were relevant to the financial sector, including those relating to the Negotiable Instruments Act. We took the opportunity to articulate the previous record and future plan of the RBI to divest itself of all ownership functions. These included shedding of ownership in the State Bank of India, refinance and development finance institutions and Infrastructure Development Finance Company.

5. For details, see chapter 15.

6. Currency management is a statutory function of the Reserve Bank of India. It endeavours to ensure availability of adequate quantities of reasonably good quality notes (and coins) to meet the demand for cash transactions throughout the country. Based on the nation-wide network of Issue Departments and currency chests, the issue and distribution of currency are coordinated on real-time basis. In a vast country like India with its wide geographical spread, predominance of cash as a mode of payment and a high degree of regional variation in income, expenditure and spending patterns, managing currency distribution in an efficient manner is no doubt a challenging task. Among other major activities, disposal of unfit returned notes received from the banking system require significant degree of coordination and care from the RBI's perspective. The RBI has to be vigilant all the time to ensure that returned notes are actually fit for disposal. This feature of disposal function – purely a regulatory concern – demands verification of each and every returned currency notes. Because of its large and growing volume, this exercise is highly labour intensive and there is always a tension with unions to handle this dirty and tedious job. A 100 per cent inspection increases workload of both man and machines. It is also not optimal for the machine due to the risk of failure and huge recurring costs.

In order to address both regulatory and labour union concern, the RBI has been using a dynamic sampling model, particularly for smaller denominations notes. The plan varies by regions and denominations depending on the incidence of occurrence of the non-conformity notes. It is a scientific method based on statistical quality control techniques and termed as acceptance sampling plan. From a known lot size, a sample is chosen randomly and a count of the unacceptable items is made. If the count is lower than a specific number, the lot is taken for disposal; otherwise the lot is chosen for 100 per cent inspection. Both the sample size and specified accepted limit are chosen from the properties of various probability distributions and observed data in the recent past. As the utility of this sampling scheme depends on the proper estimate of producer's average based on non-conformity items, the RBI updates this scheme periodically. This dynamic sampling scheme has been found to be quite effective in dealing with the disposal of currency notes in India.

7. 'During March-April 1992, ANZ Grindlays received nine cheques totalling Rs 506 crore drawn by NHB on the Reserve Bank of India. The cheques were issued in favour of ANZ Grindlays Bank and were delivered by Harshad Mehta's messenger. Harshad Mehta (HM), a prominent money, securities and share market broker of those days, had his current account with ANZ Grindlays. Citing market practice and acting on the oral instructions of the broker's representative who brought the cheques, the bank credited their proceeds to HM's current account. By the end of April 1992, the scam had become public. NHB was a large player in the money and securities market. It had conducted a number of transactions through HM and reportedly with Grindlays (as well as several other banks). The RBI whose subsidiary is the NHB, came to its rescue. Pressure was brought upon the foreign bank to return the money, which it did in November 1992. However, while doing so it sought and obtained permission to refer the matter to arbitration rather than bring it before the courts. An arbitration panel comprising three outstanding judicial brains – the former chief Justice of the Supreme Court, the former chief Justice of the Madras High Court and the former judge of the Supreme Court – was formed. Some of the India's top legal counsel represented the two parties. One presumed advantage of resorting to arbitration was it would render speedier justice compared to judicial proceedings. In the ANZ-NHB case, however, that was not to be. After nearly five years, the award was announced. Through a 2:1 majority award ANZ won what proved to be only the first round. Consequently NHB was directed to return the money to ANZ Grindlays. With interest at 18 per cent, the amount had gone up to Rs 912 crore. NHB went on appeal to the Special Court in Mumbai. Mr Justice A.N. Variava (who has since been elevated to the Supreme Court) set aside the award a year later in 1998. ANZ appealed against this reversal before the Supreme Court. NHB also approached the Supreme Court in 2000, asking for the return of the money from the ANZ group. By this time, their banking operations in India were sold to Standard Chartered. Following the Supreme Court's direction, the ANZ group brought in Rs 912 crore and kept it as an interest earning deposit with the State Bank of India, pending a resolution by the Court. As far as the two litigants are concerned, the matter is settled. Will the resolution of the dispute – blessed by the Supreme Court – be precedent setting? What are the other crucial issues on which the Supreme Court could have ruled and thereby

bring to an end not just one dispute but several others? According to legal experts familiar with the case, the issues are multi-dimensional.' (C.R.L. Narasimhan, 'Resolution without Setting Precedents', *The Hindu*, 10 January 2002.)

18. INTERLUDE

1. I sought an appointment with Jaswant Singh, who had recently succeeded Yashwant Sinha as finance minister, to pay a courtesy call and take a briefing as needed, before proceeding to Washington, D.C. as executive director in IMF. But he was not free at the time, and offered to meet me at the next possible opportunity.
2. At the time, I was transiting through Delhi and at the airport I got a message that I should meet Jaswant Singh before I left Delhi. I did. He was quite brief and said: 'Dr Reddy, I spoke to you earlier about a vacancy in Reserve Bank. I discussed with the deputy prime minister and the prime minister. All of us want you to be the next governor'. After a pause, he continued, 'I understand the inconvenience caused to you. But we feel that you are an ideal candidate. But you need not come back immediately. The date of changeover will be indicated by Governor Jalan.'

   I responded by saying: 'Sir, I am honoured by the trust you are reposing in me. I will obey your orders.' The minister was quick to say: 'No, it is not an order, it is an invitation. We are inviting you to be governor of our central bank.' I expressed my gratitude to him for the kind words. I added that I had a suggestion to make. 'Sir, a good way of publicly demonstrating government's trust in a governor is to give the full term that the Act permits, namely, five years.' On his request, I explained that, in recent years, governors were given a three-year term and the term was extended by a year or two, at a time. He said: 'That is a very good idea. Take it that it is done.' As I took leave, I said: 'I will discuss this with Governor Jalan, sir. I will be in touch with him on further steps.'

   Promptly, I rang up Jalan and narrated the conversation with Jaswant Singh. I called Geetha and informed her. She was very unhappy that we had to leave and wanted me to avoid going back. I told her that I would mention to Jalan. I pleaded with him to mention to the prime minister that my personal preference was to continue as ED. Jalan's response was that my grandchildren would be proud to see my signature on the currency notes. I asked him: 'How many times do you remember your grandfather, sir?' and said: 'Let us forget about all that. Please do me a favour and convey to the PM my preference as a personal favour to me.'

   He said: 'Okay, I will do it. I will tell him your preference. But I will also tell him that you are the best candidate for the job.' I agreed that it was a fair response, and expressed my deep gratitude to him. I got a call from Jalan after a few days, and he said: 'I have conveyed your personal preference to PM. You are off the hook.' I said: 'Thank you, boss.' With that news, there was jubilation on the home front. My son-in-law, who was working in Chicago, planned to shift his base to Washington, D.C. My daughter, Kavitha, notified the school where my grandson, Pranav, was studying, that he would not be continuing the school from next academic year, commencing in September 2003. Adithya and Swetha in Cleveland were delighted. Geetha started to look for an independent house so that we could move out of the apartment. Unknown to me, there were some developments in Delhi.

Surprisingly, in mid-July, in the early hours, there was a spate of phone calls to my home, congratulating me on my appointment as governor. The announcement was apparently made both about the nomination of Jalan to the Rajya Sabha and about my being approved as his successor. Later, I got a message through someone (whom I do not recall) that the finance minister was trying to call me, but could not get through and that I should call him since he wanted to speak to me. I called him. He said: 'I am delighted to inform you that your appointment has been approved. We want to issue orders. But, before I do that, I want to send you a letter of invitation. We will send it to your office by fax.' I said: 'Sir, I am grateful. You called me and invited me. That is enough. No need for letter, sir.' He was curt. 'It is all right, Reddy. I have the letter and it will be faxed to you. Governor Jalan will tell you when you need to join. Look forward to working with you.'

True to his word, Jaswant Singh faxed me a letter dated 18 July 2003. Among other things, it expressed his delight at and took pleasure in conveying my formal appointment. Evidently, the letter was dictated by him. He added in his handwriting: 'May I wish you a highly successful tenure with the Bank and looking forward to working with you.' It was not merely an invitation to me, but a foundation for total trust between governor and minister. This letter of invitation, which preceded the order, is one of my cherished possessions.

Between Jalan and I, we were planning to effect the succession sometime in October, after the annual meetings of the Fund–Bank in Dubai. I got a call from Jalan, I think on 31 August, suggesting that I proceed to Mumbai and assume charge as governor. The Legal Department in the Government of India seems to have opined that Jalan could not continue as governor in view of the presidential notification about his nomination to the Rajya Sabha, without reference to the date of his taking oath as MP. A farewell was arranged in the IMF at a very short notice in a meeting of the board in 3 September 2003.

20. INTERESTS AND INTEREST RATES

1. The Reserve Bank has a large collection of experts in money and finance in the public sector, with over fifty PhDs, and over seventy-five scholars educated abroad with funding from the RBI. The RBI obtains inputs on analysis and options from multiple perspectives and uses these to adopt a multiple indicator approach to help the monetary policy-making process make informed assessments.
2. How does the monetary policy work? As no households and firms have an account with the RBI, monetary policy tends to work through influencing the behaviour of financial institutions in general and of banks in particular. For example, the RBI can provide more money or less money to the system by buying or selling government securities available. Repo or reverse repo may also be used; then it means virtual short-term collateralised borrowing or lending. The interest rate at which it undertakes these operations is linked to policy rate. By announcing a policy rate, the Reserve Bank indicates interest rates at which it will provide to or absorb money from banks. The bank may also prescribe the ratio of deposits that banks should keep with the RBI (CRR) or hold in government securities (SLR), both of which impact (increase or decrease) money available in the system for use. Financial repression occurs when banks are forced to put a part of depositors' money in government securities (currently about 20 per cent). This affects availability and price of credit to borrowers. Similarly, the RBI may prescribe or allocate credit through the banking system. Progressively, there has been a switchover from direct to indirect instruments, especially open market operations and announcement of policy rates.

   How does monetary policy affect the common person? For example, if the RBI lowers the policy rate, a bank can get money from the RBI when needed at a lower rate than before. It can, therefore, afford to charge the borrowers less; but it may also pay less interest to savers since the main source for lending is deposits. So, housing loans may be available at a lower rate, but fixed deposits will get less interest income. But it is not as though changes in policy rates will automatically get transmitted to the consumer. The transmission of policy, that is, the banks following the lead given by the RBI in lowering policy rates, depends on several factors. For instance, if the government prescribes interest rates for use of credit or gives interest rate subsidises, the influence of the RBI on interest rates is muted. If the banks feel that lower deposit rates will make savers withdraw deposits prematurely, they may hesitate to fall in line.
3. How can large capital inflows be a problem, when we are starved of resources for development? First, capital inflows by definition create a right to capital outflows. A large inflow, therefore, means large outflows

in future. Second, some forms of capital flows may be large in a week, and the next week they may flow out. Our exchange rate appreciates when there are larger inflows than normal and depreciates when there are larger outflows. This makes the exchange rate volatile unless the RBI intervenes. As any intervention costs money and has risks, there are limits to RBI intervention. When a central bank buys or sells dollars, there is an impact on rupee supply. Decisions not to intervene also need an assessment of the impact of capital flows as well as the availability of forex reserves with a central bank. Hence, large capital flows complicate monetary management.

4. A sudden rapid and large increase in credit is a cause of concern. It could be a sign of loosening standards of lending, or overconfidence of borrowers or speculation. When the quality of credit is compromised, the repayment will be an issue and non-performing assets will increase, affecting the whole banking system.
5. The statement from the RBI said: 'Public sector oil companies are among the important participants in the money, foreign exchange, credit and bond markets. Consequently, liquidity and other related issues currently faced by these entities arising from the unprecedented escalation in international crude prices have systemic implications for the smooth functioning of financial markets and for overall financial stability.'
6. Extract from an article reads as follows: 'Several conclusions and observations can be made. First, the dire fiscal situation that the central government finds itself in has now sucked the RBI in its vortex, but it is to be hoped that a durable alternative mechanism will be put in place with alacrity to ensure that the SMO is not further resorted to; it can be argued that some of the hard work over the past decade to ensure that the RBI's proximate objective for conducting monetary policy is not compromised – by getting stuffed with government paper – has been undone. Second, we would be hard-pressed to name another country (even among those that subsidise fuel) that has had to resort to the central bank in this manner. Third, praying for international crude prices to adjust sharply downwards soon does not constitute government policy, sound or otherwise. Fourth, the proceeds of the oil bonds upon maturity will be in rupees, hence the RBI, if it wants to rebuild official foreign currency assets to make up for the decline on account of the SMO, will have to intervene in the market at the time and buy foreign currency at the ruling market exchange rate (the central bank shoulders an exchange rate risk if rebuilding foreign currency reserves is an objective.' Urjit R. Patel, 'RBI as an oil spigot', *Business Standard*, 3 September 2008.
7. Geithner noted, 'Y.V. Reddy, India's central banker, gave me a book during the crisis called *Complications: Notes from the Life of a Young Surgeon,* by Atul Gawande. He told me it was the best book I would

ever read about central banking, and the parallels with financial crisis management really are striking. It's about making life-or-death decisions in a fog of uncertainty, dealing with the constant risk of catastrophic failure. It's not a coincidence that after the crisis wound down and I started watching some TV again, I got into *House M.D.*, the series about a misanthropic doctor who leads a team focusing on mysterious medical cases. I could relate – not to the misanthropy, but to the complex problem-solving, the inevitable complications, the team sitting around a table debating diagnosis and treatment'. (Timothy F. Geithner, *Stress Test: Reflections on Financial Crises*, Crown Publishers, New York, 2014).

21. THE PROBLEM OF THE RUPEE

1. Ambedkar, popularly known as Babasaheb, is widely revered as a social reformer working towards emancipation of poor and downtrodden (often from lower castes), and respected as the architect of our Constitution. He battled against discrimination and led a Buddhist movement. He was the first law minister of our country. He earned doctorates in economics from both Columbia University and the London School of Economics.
2. Material on this subject has been drawn from Niranjan Rajadhyaksha, 'Ambedkar, Rupee and Our Current Troubles', *Mint*, 14 April 2015. http://www.livemint.com/Opinion/rMImvbuYNDk4RvWGfcMtQO Ambedkar-rupee-and-our-current-troubles.html;
S. Ambirajan, 'Ambedkar's Contributions to Indian Economics', *Economic and Political Weekly*, Vol. 34, No. 46/47 (20-26 November 1999), pp. 3280-3285.
3. Exchange rate regime is the system that the authorities, government and central bank adopts to establish the rate of its own currency against other currencies. Broadly, there are three types of regimes: fixed, pegged or floating. Most countries have adopted floating regimes with some variations in the extent of managing the floating rate. When policy management of the rupee is extensive and intrusive, the country is accused of manipulating the currency. Most countries have by now adopted some sort of floating regime and India is one of them.
4. IMF defines reserves as external assets that are readily available to and controlled by monetary authorities for direct financing of external payments imbalances, for indirectly regulating the magnitudes of such imbalances through intervention in exchange markets to affect the currency exchange rate, and/or for other purposes. From a policy perspective, the country benefits through economies of scale by pooling the transaction reserves, while subserving the precautionary motive of keeping official reserves as a 'war chest'. Forex reserves are also instruments to maintain or manage the exchange rate, while enabling orderly absorption of

international money and capital flows. In brief, official reserves are held for precautionary and transaction motives keeping in view the aggregate of national interests, to achieve balance between demand for and supply of foreign currencies, for intervention, and to preserve confidence in the country's ability to carry out external transactions.

5. We were aware of the importance of differences in growth of total factor productivity of countries in assessing appropriateness of exchange rate. We were also aware of decreasing importance of exchange rate on trade account due to expanding role of global supply chains and long-term contracts for imports and import capital flows. For our immediate purpose, the REER was better than any other simple guide. REER has direct relevance to current account, while transactions in capital account also matter for determination of exchange rate. We had full convertibility on current account and we were managing capital account.
6. Extracts from the release function of the India Development Report of IGIDR at Mumbai on 1 January 2005.
https://rbi.org.in/scripts/BS_SpeechesView.aspx?Id=175
    - 'First, a view needs to be taken on the quantity and quality of FII flows. While quotas or ceilings, as practised by certain countries, may not be desirable at this stage, there is merit in our keeping such an option open and exercising it selectively as needed, after due notice to the FIIs.'
    - 'Second, there is scope for enhancing quality of flows through a review of policies relating to eligibility for registration as FIIs, and assessment of risks involved in flows through hedge funds, participatory notes, sub-accounts, etc. Strict adherence to "Know your Investor" principle, especially in regard to flows from tax-havens, including beneficial ownership would enhance quality.'
    - 'Third, price-based measures such as taxes could be examined though their effectiveness is arguable and hence may not be desirable.'
    - 'Fourth, FDI flows, as currently defined, also include transfer of equity from residents to non-residents and a disaggregated analysis of FDI through several routes could enable a policy intervention, as appropriate on quantities and quality.'
    - 'Fifth, since there are several routes by which non-residents could hold shares and voting power over Indian corporates, reporting and monitoring arrangements could be considered for assessing the aggregate shares of residents (other than government) and non-residents in larger corporates and those in sensitive sectors in particular. Such monitoring could help timely policy responses on several fronts.'
7. 'FM forces Reddy U-turn', *Business Standard*, 13 January 2005.
8. Special lecture by Dr Y.V. Reddy, deputy governor, Reserve Bank of India,

at National Council of Applied Economic Research, New Delhi on 10 May 2002.
https://rbi.org.in/scripts/BS_SpeechesView.aspx?Id=109

9. I articulated my concerns on the potential for global vulnerabilities affecting us in the context of widespread pressures to liberalise the financial sector, coupled with eagerness to spread financial innovations in India. Some of the observations made in 2006 are worth recalling in the context of the subsequent global financial crisis. First, public policy played an important role in managing the costs and benefits of globalisation. Second, in the context of globalised financial markets, monetary policy faced dilemmas in distinguishing news from noise. Third, financial stability considerations might require the use of both monetary and prudential measures. Fourth, there was an increasing tendency on the part of hedge funds to consolidate the clearing and settlement of their trades through a single firm called the prime broker. The prime brokerage posed some unique challenges for the management of counter-party and operational risks. Further concerns about hedge fund opacity and the possible liquidity risk have motivated a range of proposals for regulatory authorities to create and maintain a database of hedge fund positions. Fifth, there were uncertainties associated with the settling of trades in newer types of over-the-counter derivatives, particularly credit derivatives. Sixth, in view of the wide dispersion of risk, it was necessary to evolve mechanisms to ascertain the size and structure of risk components, the scale and direction of risk transfers and, therefore, the distribution of risk within the economy. Seventh, public policy ought to play a crucial role in ensuring a balanced reform in both the real and the financial sector. Eighth, was price stability an adequate goal for central banks? Finally, the presentation added, 'In the face of the consequent build-up of liquidity, elevated asset prices and soaring consumer indebtedness, is there a dark side to the future?' The speech 'Globalisation, Money and finance: Uncertainties and Dilemmas' was delivered to a joint conference of industry and bank associations of India.
10. On 1 July 2008, I gave a talk in Manchester, UK, focusing on signs of global financial turbulence which were very evident. I ended my presentation with the words: 'To conclude, on the way forward, to exit the current financial turbulence and fortify against future similar episodes, we may need to look beyond reforms within the financial sector and address broader related issues that impinge on the balance between the sovereign, the regulators, the financial institutions and the markets.' Joseph Stiglitz, who was in the gathering, walked across to me, complimented me, and gifted a book signed with the words 'With great admiration'. Of course, I was pleased.

22. THE FINANCIAL SYSTEM

1. The Banking Regulation Act, 1949, bestows powers on the RBI to regulate banks. However, some provisions are applicable to public sector banks while others are not. They remain with the government. The public sector banks have come into existence through several legislations, namely, for State Bank of India for its subsidiaries, for banks nationalised in 1969, and another in 1980.
2. Fit and proper criteria are not set in store, but they imply qualifications, experience, and expertise that inspire confidence and trust of the people in the judgement of the regulator. Initially, the government agreed with our suggestion for giving our view on 'fit and proper' status of candidates for board positions of public sector banks. However, when we received the names of candidates proposed to be appointed by the government on the bank's board, we found that the bio data was incomplete in some cases. We wanted further information from the government or authorisation to seek further information from the potential candidates. The government however took the view that the candidates have been cleared by the Appointments Committee of the Cabinet, and hence it will be inappropriate for RBI to examine further. He suggested that we could give no objection after confirming that he or she had not come to adverse notice of the RBI. The consent of the RBI appeared to be a mere formality.
3. The story of Global Trust Bank (GTB) is a fascinating one. It was one of the first batches of scheduled private sector banks to be licensed as part of reforms after 1991. It had excellent credentials. The main promoter was an experienced economist in the Asian Development Bank, while the active promoter was a professional banker with a reputation for successful growth of a private sector bank. It was backed with investments by the International Finance Corporation, Washington. The board had, among others, as an independent director, a well-known professor from Harvard Business School. It commanded the goodwill of eminent central bankers and won awards for excellence in corporate governance. It adopted the latest technology and had employed professional staff. It had rapidly become systemically important, though not large by any means. Global Trust faced a liquidity crunch and availed of lender of last resort facilities from the central bank in 2000. However, the RBI was keen that the management that brought about such a situation to the bank should be, and should be seen to be, unacceptable. We in RBI felt that this approach was critical to avoiding moral hazard. As mentioned, the central bank's inspections revealed that there was a significant misclassification in asset classification over the years, which had to be corrected in the balance sheet for 2002-03.

4. Relations between Mr Reddy and bankers have plunged. 'I can't recall a time of such dissatisfaction with a regulator,' says a foreign bank executive in Mumbai. They say the RBI chief's approach not only marks a shift from his predecessor in terms of policy and the sophistication of presentation, it is creating divisions within the finance ministry. Extracted from 'Not so fast, Indian regulator tells banks', published in *Financial Times*, 1 September 2004.
5. A note from Leeladhar, deputy governor, who dealt with the subject, gives a graphic description.
   Gujarat: Mr Narendra Modi gave us 20 minutes to explain the concept. I seek permission for making a PowerPoint presentation, only to be told that the CM was aware of it and he will seek some clarifications. First issue was that as per his knowledge, when two parties sign an MoU there will be a give and take. According to him RBI is not giving anything to the state and wants state to give all its powers to RBI. I was clean bowled. I told him, I will stay back, discuss with his officers and see how we can improve the document. He asked me to only leave my deputy in Ahmedabad to work on it and get governor's approval for the changes. After detailed consultations we agreed that the RBI will meet the entire computerisation cost of all one-branch UCBs and train the directors of UCBs listed by the state government at RBI's cost on corporate governance. Mr Modi rang me up and said that the document is a proper MoU now, but he will not sign the document. His reasoning was that all sick UCBs in Gujarat were controlled by Congress leaders, and when the task force meets the apparent decision will be to wind up these banks. Congress will then say, 'Modi colluded with RBI and closed our banks. I can face such criticism, but why should I make a great institution like RBI face such a criticism?' Thus our first attempt came to a nought. Andhra Pradesh: When we met and I started explaining the scheme, Mr Y.S.R. Reddy stopped me and said that he does not want to understand it. He pointed to his secretary (cooperatives) and told me that he has studied the scheme in detail and has told him that it is in the interest of the state. 'We are signing the MoU,' he declared. He continued, 'We have called a couple of journalists, they are waiting outside, explain to them the scheme, tell them, AP is going to be the first government to agree to sign which will benefit poor people.' Outside I found a huge crowd of around 60 TV channel reporters and print media persons. The scheme details were already circulated, they had only one question to ask, 'When are you signing the MoU?' Without talking to the governor I never wanted to commit to a date. I then received a chit from inside stating, 'We are signing in fifteen days, I will talk to the governor if necessary.' I found myself announcing that we are signing the MoU in fifteen days. By the time I reached the airport CNBC was announcing that the AP

government was signing the MoU with RBI. Within five minutes I get a call from the governor sternly inquiring, 'Who permitted you to sign MoU in fifteen days?' Then he burst into a laugh and congratulated me! When I reached home in Mumbai there was a message that the Gujarat CM wanted to talk to me. Mr Modi came on the line and said, 'You came to me first, I made valuable modifications to your scheme and you are now signing with AP Govt? Please come and sign with us first.' Finally, he agreed that the MoU would be signed with Gujarat immediately after Andhra Pradesh.

6. The problems with the targeted RNBC were manifold on the basis of available evidence and market intelligence. First, the deposits were growing too fast for comfort. Second, the sources of deposits and identity of depositors were virtually impossible to gather. Third, access to records became impossible because the RNBC was not employing agents on its rolls to collect and refund the deposits. The deposits were collected by employees of a different legal entity. There was reluctance on the part of inspecting officers in the RBI to take up in-depth inspection of records. Fourth, it was having several business interests and the linkages across financial and non-financial sectors, including media and airlines, became virtually impossible to fathom. Finally, it always held out that they have thousands of employees on their rolls (though the actual employment of agents was by a separate legal entity) and that any precipitative action would create large-scale unemployment and disaffection. In view of these circumstances, it was concluded that a continuous dialogue and an increasing pressure should be put on it to somehow stop the business. It repeatedly gave promises to comply with the regulatory advice of RBI, but was less than adequate in fulfilling its promises. During forensic audit, large-scale irregularities were observed in the few instances that were pursued by forensic audit. After a period of almost four years of dialogue to ensure that it complied with RBI guidelines, the bank decided to move decisively in the matter and prohibit it from taking fresh deposits. The RBI filed petitions in different high courts to ensure that a hearing was given to the RBI before passing any interim order, especially a stay. It went to Lucknow High Court where a stay was promptly given despite RBI's pleading. RBI went on appeal and the Supreme Court passed an order which showed an inclination to agree with the contentions of the RBI, but preferred in its operative order, to refer the matter back to the bank for considering the contentions and passing necessary orders. After a war of nerves, an agreed solution was found mainly because of the inclinations expressed by Supreme Court. The agreed solution gave time the entity to refund the deposits to the depositors and thus exit the deposit taking business.

7. The finance minister wanted to announce the intention of the governme

to develop Mumbai as a regional financial centre, if not an international financial centre. I explained that the suggestion was impractical. But he informed me that there were political compulsions to make an announcement. He, therefore, wanted to appoint a committee and explore the possibility. A committee under the chairmanship of Percy Mistry was appointed to give a direction to making Mumbai a regional financial centre. It submitted a report with wide-ranging recommendations. A high-level committee on financial sector reform under the chairmanship of Raghuram G. Rajan was appointed by the Planning Commission through a notification in August 2007. We had no occasion to discuss this subject. The committee, set up by the Planning Commission with one of its advisors as the convenor, did not have representation from the Ministry of Finance or the Reserve Bank of India in its membership. The meetings of the committee were hosted by ICICI Bank in Mumbai. A draft report was put in public domain in 2008. However, the final report titled 'A hundred small steps' was submitted on 12 September 2008, a few days after I demitted office.

23. FINANCE AND THE COMMON PERSON

1. Buyers of vegetables ensure that the vegetables are weighed carefully; they look at its quality, feel their texture with palms, and also bargain. Why is it that people do not spend as much time and energy when they deposit thousands of rupees in banks or when they buy insurance? Obviously, they are putting their trust in financial intermediary, either willingly or out of helplessness. Trust is a universal value, but trust is critical in finance. In finance, there is no exchange of goods and services which one can feel instantly. There is only exchanging of money which will give the claim for goods and services in future. If one buys insurance now, he will get money in future, under some conditions. You put a bank deposit now, and you get back the money with interest sometime in future. But, there is nothing tangible like feeling a vegetable. Exchange of money and financial instruments involves movement of claims. Claims over each other from present to future, from one place to another and from one type of risk to another over space or time or risks. This makes the dealings in financial sector, far less tangible than goods and services. When, as common persons, we deal with a financial institution like a bank or an insurance company, we have to give lot of information about us, and in the process, the banker or the insurance company knows a lot about the customer; but the customer has very little information about the institutions. When one buys health insurance, the insurance company knows a lot about the buyer's health condition, but he knows very little about the financial health of the insurance company except

that it has been licensed by the regulator, and may be a little more from friends! Most of the financial intermediaries are limited liability entities. The liability of owners or shareholders is limited to the capital they put in. They gain when there is profit, but when they lose, they can declare insolvency. Therefore, there is always a temptation on the part of the owners or the managers of financial companies to leverage excessively and take excessive risks.

2. General provisions are funds set aside by a company to pay for anticipated future losses. For banks, a general provision is considered to be supplementary capital.
3. Risk-weighted asset (also referred to as RWA) is a bank's assets or off-balance-sheet exposures, weighted according to risk. This is used in determining the capital requirement or Capital Adequacy Ratio (CAR) for a financial institution.
4. In 2005, the policy statement referred to the legitimate concerns with regard to the banking practices that tend to exclude rather than attract certain sections of population, in particular pensioners, self-employed and those employed in unorganised sector. Against this background the statement said that the RBI will encourage banks to cater to the banking needs of the community, including the underprivileged. I added that the nature, scope and cost of services will be monitored to assess whether there is any denial, implicit or explicit, of basic banking services to the common person. We urged the banks to review their existing practices to align them with the objective of financial inclusion.
5. In the policy statement in October 2005, we referred to financial inclusion. Specifically, I said: 'With a view to achieving greater financial inclusion all banks need to make available a basic banking "no frills" account either with "nil" or very low minimum balances as well as charges that would make such accounts accessible to vast sections of population. All banks are urged to give wide publicity to the facility of such a "no frills" account so as to ensure greater financial inclusion.'

24. TEAMS AT WORK

1. The longest hours I spent in a day used to be with my executive assistants, mainly with A.K. Misra, who worked with me for almost four years, Sandip Ghosh and Damodaran. They were always with me, to assist, to guide, to admonish and to provide solace when in tension. Dr Prasad, who was with me in a similar position when I was deputy governor, set high standards for the job.
2. Special Drawing Rights (SDR) is the unit of account for the IMF, and it is not a currency by itself. The value of the SDR is based on a basket of international currencies, reviewed by the IMF every five years. The

weight assigned to each currency is based on the prominence in terms of international trade and national foreign exchange reserves. From 1 October 2016, the renminbi (Chinese yuan) was added to the basket with a weight of 10.92 per cent.

3. Chang Mai Initiative is a multilateral currency swap arrangement among the ten members of the Association of South East Asian Countries. It began with a series of bilateral swap arrangements after ASEAN plus three met in May 2000. In our case, we were not part of the initiative, and we could succeed in a bilateral swap with Japan.
4. The board of the RBI was filled with some of the icons of India. Dr Ashok Ganguly, who had been a director in Lever Brothers and British Airways, expressed that the professionalism of the RBI in enabling the board to perform its functions was, undoubtedly, the best he had come across. That was no small compliment about the functioning of our board. N.R. Narayana Murthy's contribution to making the Payment System of India reach global standards is perhaps not well known. Professor Vaidyanathan and Shashi Rajagopalan, representing agricultural economics and non-governmental organisations, respectively, kept all of us on our toes. Shashi Rajagopalan's sense of right and wrong was matched only by her selflessness and outspokenness. Mr Malegam, a distinguished chartered accountant, was virtually a full-time advisor to the RBI on all issues that mattered. Suresh Neotia had a benign presence in the board, whose support I could always count on.
5. The important legislative actions during the period were:
   - Reserve Bank of India Amendment Act 2006 giving additional powers to the RBI for dealing with and regulating agencies dealing in specified derivatives, determine policy and issue directions in respect of money market participants, making special provisions for lending or borrowing of securities, and enabling RBI to specify any percentage of CRR, etc.
   - The Government Securities Act 2006 replaced the Public Debt Act 1944, enabling inter alia the creation of pledge, hypothecation and lien in respect of government securities, conferring on the RBI the power to inspect as also issue directions, and making electronic records admissible in evidence, among other things.
   - Banking Regulation Act 1949 was amended by Ordinance 2007, thereafter replaced by the Banking Regulation (Amendment) Act, 2007, giving flexibility to the RBI with regard to prescribing form and manner of maintenance of SLR, and requiring laying of notification of exemptions before Parliament in case of banking companies located in SEZ.
   - Payment and Settlement Systems Act 2007.
   - Prevention of Money Laundering (Amendment) Act, 2005 for

amending the Act for requiring specific authorisation for investigation by a police officer, and omitting provision that made every offence punishable under the Act as cognisable.

- Credit Information Companies (Regulation) Act 2005.
- Warehousing Corporation (Amendment) Act 2005.

6. I learnt the truth from his wife after Leeladhar and I retired. Apparently, before meeting me for the second time, Leeladhar discussed with his wife and they agreed that he would convey his continued unwillingness to accept the offer due to personal difficulties. He was happy with the status and perquisites available for the chairman of a bank. Leeladhar did not have the heart to say no when he met me since I welcomed him before he could say no.

25. A GENTLEMAN AND A STATESMAN

1. At the time, I was executive director, International Monetary Fund.
2. A committee was appointed under the chairmanship of M. Narasimham, former governor, RBI, to recommend the path of reforms in the financial sector, which gave its recommendations in April 1991. The recommendations provided the basic framework for the reform of the financial sector. Another committee was appointed by P. Chidambaram, finance minister in the United Front government, in December 1997 to recommend the measures specifically for reform of the banking sector. This committee was also headed by Narasimham. It gave detailed recommendations in April 1998. By then, Yashwant Sinha from the BJP was the finance minister. Political developments did not make any difference to the acceptability of the recommendations in principle.

   The state of implementation of the Narasimham Committee recommendations as of 2003, two decades after they were submitted, gave me an understanding of the political economy of reforms in the financial sector. The Narasimham report of 1998 took cognisance of the fact that our external sector was being opened up with adoption of current account convertibility, and, more important, planned capital account convertibility. It recognised the link between a sound banking system and an open but benign capital account. Among the steps suggested was merger of strong banks. This has not been acted upon by the government. Another recommendation of the committee related to the narrow banking concept, whereby weak banks would be allowed to concentrate on risk-free assets. This has not been implemented either. The committee also recommended the dilution of government ownership in public sector banks from 51 to 33 per cent. While an announcement was made in the budget by Sinha in this direction, there has been no progress. Capital adequacy ratio (ratio of equity to total assets) for Indian banks was recommended at 9 per cent. The RBI achieved it and has been following international standards as they evolve. Other recommendations relating to liquidity adjustment and money markets were also acted upon by the RBI when I was deputy governor and further refined when I joined as governor in September 2003.

3. In the speech, I said, 'It is in this overall scenario, the policy relating to the financial services, and in particular banking, must be considered. It is interesting to note that WTO negotiations on financial services have been cautious and the commitments of many larger economies in the banking sector are rather particularly limited. In other words, in the context of issue of national ownership of financial intermediaries, banks appear to have a unique place in public policy. There are several noteworthy features of ownership and control of banks in all major economies – irrespective of whether they are developed or emerging.'
4. I concluded: 'In conclusion, I would like to emphasise the role of institutions and incentives in ensuring globalisation that benefits all. The global giants in banking all over the world are manned by Indians, educated and trained in India. The best of technology for the most sophisticated banks in the world is provided by Indian companies and by Indians in foreign companies. Yet, banks in India do not as yet appear to be world class, though I have no doubt that our banks could well be on the anvil of being reckoned to be on par with international banks. My submission is that, to reach global standards, and hopefully surpass them, we need to focus on legal, institutional and transactions aspects; and the RBI's measures detailed today try to make a small beginning in addressing some of these issues.'
5. I hinted that given time and good policy, our banks could be world class. Without making a direct reference to the government's decision, I said, 'As regards the legal framework, the Reserve Bank is not very comfortable with lack of clear statutory provision regarding takeover of management of banks.'
6. In December 2003, HSBC tried and succeeded in acquiring significant shareholding in UTI Bank. At that time we were working on improving the guidelines on the takeover of banks. There was lack of clarity on whether HSBC was making only financial investments. We made sure, by insisting on detail and imposing conditions that there was no circumvention. At that time the media did not expect us to succeed. For example, one report said, 'All the same, it might not stop HSBC in its tracks from taking over the UTI Bank. What has happened is indeed a palace coup. The praetorian guards were either asleep or disarmed.' http://www.thehindubusinessline.com/2003/12/18/stories/2003121800010800.htm
7. I sent a formal proposal to the government to approve the innovative

Market Stabilisation Scheme (MSS). The proposal was, no doubt, based on the report of a committee set up in the Reserve Bank, put in the public domain, and then considered in detail in consultation with the government.

8. This incident is described in a book by Raghav Bahl: 'The matter was referred to the RBI, who simply laughed it back at the chairman. "Can't you read the new guidelines? This is not required to come to us anymore." The chairman turned scarlet when I met him with the RBI's order.' Raghav Bahl, *Super Power? The Amazing Race between China's Hare and India's Tortoise*, Penguin Books India, 2010, pp. xxvii-xxviii.
9. My interest in liberalising outflows for investments by our corporates originated in 1993, when I was additional secretary, commerce, presiding over a committee to approve such investments. My argument was that Indian corporates lacked size due to historical controls. They had no domain expertise globally since we did not encourage export-orientation for several years. So, I felt that they could get synergies through acquisitions. I had proposed both liberalisation and shifting of the work to the RBI. The proposal was finally approved and a new regime came into existence in 1996. The preamble to the circular narrates the logic for such liberalisation.
10. 14. (C) The ambassador pointed out that Secretary Snow is coming to New Delhi in November to address these issues. He noted that one of the greatest needs in India is the further liberalization of the financial market, and the USG is confused about the division of labor, as there seems to be a contradiction between the policies of the Finance Minister and the Reserve Bank. The Bank is very conservative and this is the biggest impediment to economic progress. Snow will need guidance on how and where to push. 15. (C) Singh responded that this was the first he had heard of these problems. The Reserve Bank should not be making economic policy, he opined, and should restrict its activities to managing the currency. The finance ministry may be using the Bank to justify its failure to deliver. Reserve Bank Governor Dr Reddy meets with him often, and he would discuss these issues with him. This problem stems from the UPA's failure to identify who runs the financial portfolio. The Communists remain the greatest obstacle and will continue to defeat the government on essentials. [Extracted from: 43447, 10/24/2005 10:56, 05NEWDELHI8231, Embassy New Delhi, CONFIDENTIAL, 05NEWDELHI2949, 'This record is a partial extract of the original cable. The full text of the original cable is not available.', 'C O N F I D E N T I A L SECTION 01 OF 05 NEW DELHI 008231 SIPDIS E.O. 12958: DECL: 10/21/2015 TAGS: PREL, ECON, PGOV, PINR, IN, PK, IR, External Political Relations SUBJECT: JASWANT SINGH BELIEVES THE UPA IS INCAPABLE OF MANAGING THE INDO/US RELATIONSHIP REF: NEW DELHI 2949

26. WORKING WITH CHIDAMBARAM

1. I explained the background to the decisions taken on banning overseas corporate bodies (OCBs). He could understand the background, but did not endorse or demur. I added my concern at the inaction on banning participatory notes. I struggled during my tenure to get the ban imposed on participatory notes. I did not succeed.

   In one meeting, Chidambaram told me that his cabinet colleagues had concerns about the previous government's decision to liberalise the investment regime so Indian corporates could make acquisitions abroad. Why were we allowing the export of capital when we were seeking capital inflows to meet our needs, they wanted to know. They felt that such flows should in any case be permitted in sectors of specific relevance to us. I explained that capital flows cannot be only one way, our corporates should have freedom in financial flows and that control or prioritisations would end up being used to favour or disfavour some.

   He was supportive of freedom for our corporates to expand overseas. I recalled that when he was commerce minister, and I was his additional secretary, I had recommended the Chinese model of attracting foreign direct investments to set up factories in our country. His response was, 'I do not want India to be a nation of employees only. We are also a nation of entrepreneurs.' I was, therefore, not surprised when he did not succumb to pressures within his government to reregulate overseas investments by our corporates.

   When it came to the question of the Market Stabilisation Scheme (MSS), Chidambaram had some discomfort. It was understandable. The MSS imposed fiscal burden on the government. I assured him that the limits to MSS bonds are set by the government only; and hence he has the powers to virtually restrict the scheme without formally abolishing it. He quipped, 'If it is such a good scheme, why did you not do it earlier?' It was in half jest, since he knew the rationale for the timing. I suspect that he was not comfortable but could not deny the logic and take responsibility for the reversal of such an important policy. This scheme proved to be of lasting value to our management of the economy. On the enhanced role assigned to the Reserve Bank of India in regard to external commercial borrowings, he had no difficulty, and was in fact appreciative of transparency that we introduced on the work being transferred to us.
2. In the speech, I pointed out: 'It will be useful to narrate the pros and cons of licensing foreign banks in the emerging economies by drawing liberally from two recent publications. The policy-makers in emerging countries are fully aware of both the benefits and risks arising out of the presence of foreign banks and indeed foreign capital in banks, which leads them to impose a variety of forms of restrictions depending on

the circumstances of each country. The extent of foreign investment, the nature of such investment, the appropriate form of presence and the profile of actual players in the banking sector are usually prescribed by the supervisors taking into account the multiple challenges faced in a given country context including the extent of financial integration sought to be achieved. In brief, each country picks up an appropriate package that is necessitated by the circumstances, which ensures the presence of foreign investors that fully satisfy the fit and proper criteria, and that the presence of foreign banks is a part of the planned strategy for rebalancing efficiency and stability in the financial system.'

3. Chidambaram discussed with me the potential candidates for the position of secretary, Economic Affairs, soon after he joined. He was keen to have a good economist as secretary, perhaps keeping the precedents of Manmohan Singh, Jalan and Montek in view. My response was, 'Sir, you must have a good administrator with finance background. Take a good IAS officer. You have a lot of expertise in economic policy at the helm. You have the PM, deputy chairman and chairman of the Economic Advisory Council, all economists. You are also very knowledgeable. You need an efficient administrator who can get things done.' I could not convince him. That was how Rakesh Mohan was appointed as secretary, Economic Affairs.
4. 'Not so fast, Indian regulator tells banks.' Foreign institutions feel the climate may be turning hostile, Khozem Merchant reports. *Financial Times*, 1 September 2004.
5. As well as public sector Development Financial Institutions (DFIs).
6. This was introduced by the V.P. Singh government, in an apparent attempt to de-politicise the process.
7. These would be voluntary, and not legally binding on the government.
8. We agreed that there was need for greater coordination on public debt management between the RBI and the ministry. Chidambaram and I worked to create institutional arrangements for coordination.
9. In the case of opening up of repo markets to corporate bonds, the RBI was opposed as we felt the markets were not yet developed enough. Chidambaram was very keen. In our discussions, there was some tension but we agreed to disagree about the change, and there was a stalemate of sorts.
10. We were in agreement in most cases. One of the exceptions was SBI. The SBI had, by that time, expanded operations greatly. It needed recapitalisation. We did not feel the time was right for shedding of the RBI's ownership of SBI. But Chidambaram felt that, as part of the reform process, it had to be done. Though I was initially reluctant, once we decided to go ahead, I gave full support to the government. When the government needed money to recapitalise the SBI, the RBI released some funds from profits to facilitate the transaction.

11. In fact, the minister constituted a committee under the chairmanship of Rangarajan to recommend measures for financial inclusion following up on the initiatives taken by us in this regard.
12. Chidambaram took personal interest in the revival of the cooperative credit system, and we worked together in pushing through the work of the Vaidyanathan Committee and implementing it, though the final outcomes did not meet our expectations. I realised that Chidambaram himself was helpless because he could not enforce the conditions for political economy considerations.
13. The minister fully endorsed the efforts to reorganise regional rural banks by merging multiple banks sponsored by a public sector bank in a state. Capital was infused, and their scope of operations expanded. Initially, Chidambaram was not enthusiastic. He knew it would have to be done, but he felt efforts would be futile as the issue was highly politicised. Yet I felt we should do it and a budget provision was made.
14. Chidambaram had made a budget commitment to double the flow of credit to agriculture in two years. The RBI was happy to oblige. He also took special interest in the flow of credit to small industry and infrastructure. The RBI had a tradition of supporting such sectoral credit flow and hence continued to be an instrument of administering the priority sector. There were pressures from several ministries to expand the scope of such priority sector lending while bankers supported it, but with the overall ceiling. But that would dilute the focus of fund flow to more deserving sectors. This was an area where Chidambaram had to resist pressures and we were on the same side. He was also supportive of the phasing out of refinancing by the Reserve Bank, though there were pressures to the contrary.
15. I wanted the power to regulate all NBFCs retained with RBI, but assured him that we would, in reality, restrict regulation only to large companies. Similarly, I requested him to disregard proposals already under contemplation for amendments in the Reserve Bank of India Act and Banking Regulation Act since we were intending to focus on a few, select and critical changes needed to strengthen and clarify the regulatory roles of the RBI. This was accepted and alternative proposals made by the RBI processed by the government. Barring a couple of minor misunderstandings, there was total coordination and, indeed, agreement between us on all legislative changes undertaken.
16. We had a prime minister who had been governor of the RBI, and was also finance minister. In all matters relating to economic policy, he consulted Rangarajan, who was himself a governor before, and Montek Ahluwalia, who had also been on the board of the RBI for several years as finance secretary. All three of them were part of the Planning Commission at some stage or the other and had the benefit of significant insights into

the working of the economy and political economy. Chidambaram used to seek the guidance of the prime minister on important matters relating to the RBI, and I accompanied the minister for his meetings, when required. Rangarajan and Montek, also of the rank of Union cabinet ministers, were sometimes called in by the prime minister to join our discussions. Generally, no one else was present, and no record was kept since they were informal consultations. The finance minister commanded full confidence and unstinted support of the prime minister; and in return, the finance minister was very loyal to the prime minister.

17. This comment was made during an annual Fund-Bank meeting in Singapore. In all the visits, the ambassador or high commissioner used to give receptions, and I was always a silent participant, with this one exception. The minister gave an excellent after-dinner speech, and when I was asked to supplement, I excused myself. The president of the CII insisted that they would like to hear both the minister and governor speak about the Indian economy since they got conflicting signals from the RBI and the government on the policies. To that, I responded by saying that the honourable minister would clarify on my behalf also. That is when he made his comment – which was appreciated by the audience.

    I was attending the meetings of select governors of the Bank for International Settlements regularly. Once he enquired about the content of the meetings. I explained to him that in the main meeting, we exchange views and no formal positions were taken nor minutes kept. I said that I take these into account in confidentially assessing global developments for purposes of our policies. He asked, 'What exactly do you do when you meet there in Basel periodically?' I said, 'Sir, we gather to worry about what we should be worrying about. That helps my thinking.' He smiled. He did not ask for anything further, though he could legitimately demand or seek any report on the proceedings. However, since I was briefing the board of RBI about all such deliberations, and secretary, Economic Affairs, was a member of the board, the minister was assured that I was not holding back anything in particular.

    I enjoyed participation in all the multilateral gatherings with Chidambaram. They provided an opportunity to exchange views on diverse subjects, in an informal setting. He would often call in the morning to enquire about my well-being. On occasions when he did not have a formal meeting over breakfast, he would walk over to my room so that the two of us could go together to chat over breakfast. From the moment the formal meetings commenced, I kept a low profile; whatever I wanted to say was conveyed either through the minister or as authorised by him.

18. The governor and the finance minister have to participate jointly in several multilateral settings. On the sidelines of these meetings, some bilateral

meetings are also held with ministers of other countries. Meetings with representatives of industry and commerce are also arranged by the Indian embassy. Unlike Jaswant Singh, who deputed me to attend IMF, IMFC, G20 and G24 meetings on his behalf, Chidambaram did not like to miss these meetings and he enjoyed interactions with others, while they in turn admired him.

19. His speeches had to be vetted by me before his final approval, though he himself contributed to the draft initially. I did not attend bilateral meetings or other meetings unless the minister wanted my presence for assisting him on a specific item on the agenda.

27. CREATIVE TENSIONS

1. At the height of controversy, Dr I.G. Patel, former governor of the RBI and former director, LSE, commented, 'The proposal to use foreign exchange reserves to accelerate infrastructure development has received much public attention in India recently. Anyone who knows anything knows that the reference to foreign exchange reserves in this connection is only a red herring. It is to draw attention away from the real purpose: which is to indulge in greater deficit financing and even to monetise a part of the deficit in violation of solemn undertakings given to Parliament. If you say so openly, you will be shot down in no time. But if you bring in foreign exchange reserves which are useless and earn nothing and suggest using them for worthwhile purposes, you may hoodwink some people and get by.' (I.G. Patel, *Of Economics, Policy and Development: An Intellectual Journey*, Oxford University Press, 2012, p. 92).
2. The dissent note summed up our institutional position. 'The Reserve Bank's stance has been that the issue of Participatory Notes should not be permitted. In this context we would like to point out that the main concerns regarding the issue of PNs are that the nature of the beneficial ownership or the identity of the investor will not be known, unlike in the case of FIIs registered with a financial regulator. Trading of these PNs will lead to multi-layering, which will make it difficult to identify the ultimate holder of PNs. Both conceptually and in practice, restrictions on suspicious flows enhance the reputation of markets and lead to healthy flows. We, therefore, reiterate that the issuance of Participatory Notes should not be permitted.' (Extracted from the Report of the Expert Group on Encouraging FII Flows and Checking the Vulnerability of Capital Markets to Speculative Flows, p. 59).
3. Mutual support between minister and governor is not uncommon. On this Dr I.G. Patel commented, '...politicians are often required to square circles, which forces them to embrace dubious ideas. How does the governor go about his business in such situations?...' The governor has

to have enough tact and guile to have his say without putting him at the centre of political controversies.' (I.G. Patel, *Of Economics, Policy and Development: An Intellectual Journey*, Oxford University Press, 2012, p. 92).

28. WE PLAN – GOD LAUGHS

1. The global financial crisis or global economic crisis began in July 2007 with the credit crunch in the US. This resulted in the Federal Reserve Bank injecting a large amount of capital into the financial market. By September, the situation worsened. The collapse of Lehman Brothers on 14 September 2008, due to the collapse of stock markets, marked the beginning of policy stimulus and the acute phase of the global crisis. I retired on 5 September 2008.
2. On 19 December 2008, the *New York Times* carried a column by Joe Nocera titled 'How India Avoided a Crisis'. He wrote that bankers were furious with me when I raised interest rates and risk weights, but that after the crisis the view was: 'He saved us'. On 22 December 2008, about dinner time, I was told about what Professor Joseph Stiglitz had said on CNBC TV-18: 'Had the US a governor like Reddy, America would not have been in such a mess.' This statement of Stiglitz made many in India take notice of me positively. Stephen Roach, chief economist, Morgan Stanley, said on 9 November 2009: 'The RBI, Dr Reddy, that is one of the great stories of India. They were fiercely independent and withstood the political pressure to have a more accommodative policy. India has benefitted tremendously from the wisdom and courage of the RBI.' In another piece, he said that only two central bankers sensed the dangers of asset bubbles, namely, Trichet and Reddy, but Reddy had 'the courage to act'. Robert Kuttner wrote a piece in Huffpost Business, titled 'Ask Dr Reddy', on 11 June 2010. He had met me at a UN conference in 2008, just as the financial meltdown was getting critical, and I shared my fears with him. His message in the piece was that I, along with Dr Koo from Japan, and Lord Adair Turner of the UK, was one of the three stars that the US could learn from about regulating the financial sector.

   The year 2009 turned out to be an year of awards from the media, industry associations and cultural organisations. These included: CNBC TV-18, *Economic Times*, *Business Standard* and *Indian Express*. The hesitation that I had in accepting such awards when I was holding public office disappeared. The culmination of awards came soon after the calendar year 2009 ended. On 25 January 2010, early in the morning, the home secretary, Government of India, called me and obtained my consent to the award of Padma Vibhushan by the President of India. I enquired as to who proposed my name for the award. He said, 'Sir, I can tell you this. When your name came up before the committee, every one of us felt honoured to agree.' My curiosity led me to ask Dr Rangarajan, and his reply was: 'Not me; I did not think of it. Manmohan must have suggested your name.'

3. Report of the Commission of Experts of the President of the United Nations General Assembly on Reforms of the International Monetary and Financial System, 21 September 2009. http://www.un.org/ga/econcrisissummit/docs/FinalReport_CoE.pdf
4. IEO - Advisory Group for the Evaluation of the IMF's Performance in the Run-Up to the Crisis. http://www.ieo-imf.org/ieo/files/completedevaluations/01102011Crisis_BP1_Summary_of_Views.pdf. Also, I was a member of the High Level Advisory Panel on the evaluation by the Independent Evaluation Office of 'The IMF and the Crisis in Greece, Ireland and Portugal'. The Panel found that 'Europe was treated differently' – an indictment of governance in the IMF. IEO Evaluation of the IMF and the Crises in Greece, Ireland, and Portugal. http://www.ieo-imf.org/ieo/pages/CompletedEvaluation267.aspx
5. *In the Wake of the Crisis: Leading Economists Reassess Economic Policy*, edited by Olivier Blanchard, David Romer, Michael Spence, and Joseph Stiglitz, published by The MIT Press, Cambridge, Masschusetts, London, England, 2012.
6. *Reform of the International Monetary System – The Palais Royal Initiative*, edited by Jack T. Boorman and Andre Icard, SAGE Publications India Pvt. Ltd., 2011. https://ideas.repec.org/b/emf/booksf/imfreform.html
7. 'The G20 and recovery and beyond', J-P Fitoussi, J. Stiglitz and the Paris Group. http://www.parisschoolofeconomics.eu/en/news/march-2011-the-g20-and-recovery-and-beyond/
8. 'Evolving Economics and Financial System in India, Towards a New Global Financial Architecture: Some Issues and Approaches'. https://www.ineteconomics.org/research/experts/yvreddy
9. *Financial and Fiscal Policies* (co-authored), published by Oxford University Press, in 2014. *Economic Policies and India's Reform Agenda: New Thinking*, published by Orient BlackSwan, in 2013. *Of Economics, Policy and Development – An Intellectual Journey* by I.G. Patel (co-edited), published by Oxford University Press, in 2012. *Global Crisis, Recession and Uneven Recovery*, published by Orient BlackSwan, in 2010. *India and the Global Financial Crisis – Managing Money and Finance*, published by Orient BlackSwan, in 2009.
10. The Per Jaccobson Lecture was titled 'Society, Economic Policies and the Financial Sector' and delivered at the Central Bank Governors' Conference, Bank for International Settlements, Basel, Geneva, in 2012. http://www.bis.org/events/agm2012/sp120624.htm

29. GAME CHANGER

1. Arvind Panagariya (2015): 'The Revolution Begins: With Finance Commission Recommendations, Centre-state Relations Set to Undergo Dramatic Change', http://blogs.timesofindia.indiatimes.com/toi-edit-page/the-revolution-begins-with-finance-commission-recommendations-centre-state-relations-set-to-undergo-dramatic-change/, 25 February, New Delhi. Arvind Subramanian (2015): Ideas for India: Charting a course for the Indian economy, http://www.theigc.org/blog/ideas-for-india-charting-a-course-for-the-indian-economy/ V. Bhaskar, The Fourteenth Finance Commission is to be commended for bringing states to the forefront of the development paradigm. See more at: http://www.epw.in/journal/2015/21/fourteenth-finance-commission/stance-devolution-and-grants.html#sthash.bVsZQPRI.dpuf
2. The term of the commission was extended by two months beyond 31 October 2014 till December 2014, to ensure that our award included consideration of the fact of the bifurcation of united Andhra Pradesh into Telangana and Andhra Pradesh, and their separate memoranda. This created some complications in our work. We had a meeting with Andhra Pradesh in Hyderabad in mid-September 2013. But the state was bifurcated with effect from 2 June 2014. In this context, an additional term of reference was added to the commission. As soon as the additional term of reference was received by us, we examined the obligations cast upon the finance Commission and concluded that the additional reference did not envisage anything more than ensuring that the Fourteenth Finance Commission recognised the bifurcation of Andhra Pradesh, and made suitable recommendations. We held meetings with both the states in the month of September 2014. We worked vigorously on the complex task of reworking the shares of Union and of states. We were keen to make available our report by the time the budget exercises of the Union and states for 2015–16 commenced.
3. The dissent note by Professor Sen itself draws attention to some of the issues in the transition to the rebalancing that the commission proposed. The basic point made by Professor Sen was that 'there was reluctance on the part of the chairman and other members to analyse the transition path from the present situation to that likely after our award.' He, therefore, made specific recommendations in regard to the transition path with some suggested grants-in-aid to the states. The transition path, as suggested by Professor Sen, was that 'the share of tax devolution be set at 38 per cent of the divisible pool in the first year of the award period and maintained at that level unless there is an agreement in the new institutional mechanism to revert to the 42 per cent share of tax devolution as in recommendation No.1 of the main report.'

His suggestion had the potential for creating avoidable uncertainties in regard to tax devolution during the award period. It also meant that the main recommendation of the Finance Commission would be subject to consideration, oversight and approval by another envisaged body. The note of dissent added that 'the space available to continue existing plan grants needs to be widened, at least in the first year of the award period.'

A NOTE ON THE SOURCES FOR THE QUOTES ON THE BACK COVER

- Raghuram G. Rajan, 'The Philosophy of Dr Reddy', *Financial Express*, 28 April 2013
- Joseph Stiglitz, 'Nobel laureate lauds former RBI governor Y.V. Reddy', NDTV interview, 22 December 2008
- P. Chidambaram, 'Reddy and Chidambaram – Embrace of the Gladiators', *Hindu Business Line*, 27 January 2011
- Arvind Panagariya, 'India's Financial Secret Weapon', *Foreign Policy*, January 2009
- Bimal Jalan, 'Reddy Reckoner', *Business Standard*, 30 July 2005
- Joe Nocera, 'How India Avoided a Crisis', *New York Times*, 19 December 2008
- Karina Robinson, 'Guru with the Keys to the Kingdom', *The Banker*, July 2006

INDEX